MOTHERS AND OTHERS

MOTHERS AND OTHERS
THE ROLE OF PARENTHOOD IN POLITICS

Edited by Melanee Thomas
and Amanda Bittner

UBCPress · Vancouver · Toronto

© UBC Press 2017

All rights reserved. No part of this publication may be reproduced, stored in a retrieval system, or transmitted, in any form or by any means, without prior written permission of the publisher, or, in Canada, in the case of photocopying or other reprographic copying, a licence from Access Copyright, www.accesscopyright.ca.

26 25 24 23 22 21 20 19 18 17   5 4 3 2 1

Printed in Canada on FSC-certified ancient-forest-free paper
(100% post-consumer recycled) that is processed chlorine- and acid-free.

Library and Archives Canada Cataloguing in Publication

Mothers and others: the role of parenthood in politics / edited by Melanee Thomas and Amanda Bittner.

Includes bibliographical references and index.
Issued in print and electronic formats.
ISBN 978-0-7748-3458-2 (hardcover). – ISBN 0-7748-3459-9 (pbk).
ISBN 978-0-7748-3460-5 (PDF). – ISBN 978-0-7748-3461-2 (EPUB).
ISBN 978-0-7748-3462-9 (Kindle)

1. Political sociology. 2. Parents – Political activity. 3. Mothers – Political activity. 4. Women – Political activity. 5. Fathers – Political activity. 6. Press and politics. 7. Political culture. 8. Parenthood – Political aspects. 9. Motherhood – Political aspects. 10. Fatherhood – Political aspects. I. Thomas, Melanee Lynn, editor II. Bittner, Amanda, editor

JA76.M675 2017   306.2   C2017-902733-6
                                        C2017-902734-4

Canadä

UBC Press gratefully acknowledges the financial support for our publishing program of the Government of Canada (through the Canada Book Fund), the Canada Council for the Arts, and the British Columbia Arts Council.

This book has been published with the help of a grant from the Canadian Federation for the Humanities and Social Sciences, through the Awards to Scholarly Publications Program, using funds provided by the Social Sciences and Humanities Research Council of Canada.

UBC Press
The University of British Columbia
2029 West Mall
Vancouver, BC V6T 1Z2
www.ubcpress.ca

To all of the academic moms out there, especially our senior colleagues who have played such a crucial mentorship role. Watching you juggle children and successful academic careers has been inspirational. Motherhood and work in general are a tricky combination, and we are so grateful to have such incredible role models.

Thank you.

Contents

Figures and Tables / ix

Acknowledgments / xiii

Introduction

1 The "Mommy Problem"? Gender, Parental Status, and Politics / 3
MELANEE THOMAS AND AMANDA BITTNER

Part 1 Parental Status and Political Careers

2 The (M)otherhood Trap: Reconsidering Sex, Gender, and Legislative Recruitment / 25
ROSIE CAMPBELL AND SARAH CHILDS

3 Lactating Mothers in Parliament: Beyond Accommodation / 46
BARBARA ARNEIL

4 Motherhood and Politics in Latin America: Continuity and Change / 64
SUSAN FRANCESCHET, JENNIFER M. PISCOPO, AND GWYNN THOMAS

5 "Society Is Balanced, So Local Boards Should Be Balanced Too": Gatekeeper Attitudes toward the Gender Balance Law in Iowa / 87
REBECCA J. HANNAGAN AND CHRISTOPHER W. LARIMER

6 Conservative Mothers in Politics: Pushing and Reinforcing Ideological Boundaries / 111
   RONNEE SCHREIBER

Part 2 Communications and Campaign Strategy

7 Private Mom versus Political Dad? Communications of Parental Status in the 41st Canadian Parliament / 135
   MELANEE THOMAS AND LISA LAMBERT

8 Mothers and the Media on the Campaign Trail / 155
   MELISSA K. MILLER

9 Identity and Activism in an Era of Politicized Motherhood / 178
   CARRIE A. LANGNER, JILL S. GREENLEE, AND GRACE DEASON

Part 3 Parenthood and Opinion, Participation and Behaviour

10 The Parent Gap in Political Attitudes: Mothers versus Others / 201
    ELIZABETH GOODYEAR-GRANT AND AMANDA BITTNER

11 Context, Motherhood, and the Gender Gap in Political Knowledge / 226
    JANINE GILES

12 Attitudes toward Work, Motherhood, and Parental Leave in Canada, the United States, and the United Kingdom / 247
    ALLISON HARELL, STUART SOROKA, SHANTO IYENGAR, AND VALÉRIE LAPOINTE

13 Motherhood's Role in Shaping Political and Civic Participation / 268
    BRENDA O'NEILL AND ELISABETH GIDENGIL

14 Toying Around with the Future: Sustainability within Families / 288
    MICHELE MICHELETTI AND DIETLIND STOLLE

Conclusion

15 Gender, Parenthood, and Politics: What Do We Still Need to Know? / 313
    AMANDA BITTNER AND MELANEE THOMAS

Contributors / 339

Index / 343

Figures and Tables

Figures

2.1 MPs' average number of children by sex / 29
9.1 Theoretical model of Politicized Motherhood, politicized parent identity, and activism / 179
10.1 Selected gendered parent gaps / 213
10.2 Right-wing ideology and the parent gap on crime and security / 217
12.1 Traditional gender role ideology, gender typicality of leave takers, and support for parental leave, all countries / 260
12.2 Traditional gender role ideology, gender typicality of leave takers, and support for parental leave, by country / 261
15.1 Proportion of mothers working in paid employment, OECD countries / 317
15.2 Proportion of children living in single- and two-parent households, OECD countries / 318
15.3 Public spending on family benefits in cash, services, and tax measures, OECD countries, 2011 / 321
15.4 Public spending on childcare and pre-primary education, OECD countries / 322
15.5 Flexibility in work-time arrangements, OECD countries, 2010 / 323

15.6 Paid leave reserved for fathers, OECD countries, 2014 / 325

15.7 Comparing women and men, parents and non-parents (pooled data from WVS, 1981–2014) / 329

Tables

5.1 Demographics by board type / 96

5.2 Preferences for gender balance legislation by board type and gender (mean response) / 98

5.3 Preferences for gender balance legislation by board type, gender, and ideology / 100

7.1 MPs' parental status by party and gender in the 41st Canadian Parliament / 144

8.1 Parental status mentions during the Democratic primary, 2008 / 163

8.2 Parental status mentions during the general election, 2008 / 165

8.3 Predicting attitudes toward Clinton and Palin using respondent and press coverage characteristics, 2008 / 170

10.1 Impacts of parenthood on three issue dimensions / 210

10.2 Gendered parent gaps on three issue dimensions / 212

10.3 Testing interest- and socialization-based accounts of parent gaps / 216

10.4 Testing interest- and socialization-based accounts of gendered parent gaps / 219

11.1 Summary statistics of riding-level factors, 2006 Canadian Census / 236

11.2 Effects of postsecondary education rates and employment rates at riding level / 237

11.3 Contextual interactions with women's parental status / 238

11.4 Gender gap in knowledge of party leaders / 239

12.1 Traditional gender role ideology in Canada, the United Kingdom, and the United States / 254

12.2 Determinants of traditional gender role ideology in Canada, the United Kingdom, and the United States / 255

12.3 Support for parental leave by gender ideology and gender typicality of leave takers in Canada, the United Kingdom, and the United States / 258

13.1   Motherhood and political and civic activities / 274
13.2   Ages of children and political and civic activities / 275
13.B1 Motherhood and political and civic activities / 282
13.B2 Impact of motherhood on women's political and civic activities / 283
13.B3 Motherhood, marital status, and women's political and civic activities / 284
13.B4 Motherhood, labour force participation, and women's political and civic activities / 285
14.1   Parents and sustainable toy shopping, 2013 / 295
14.2   Sustainable shopping between parents and non-parents / 299
14.3   Correlates of sustainable toy shopping among parents / 303
15.1   Time spent performing care duties, adults aged 18 and over, OECD countries / 319
15.2   Average attitudes toward women, engagement, and family across waves of the WVS / 328
15.3   Average attitudes toward women, engagement, and family, OECD countries / 331

Acknowledgments

The puzzle that underlies this project owes a lot to Lisa Lambert and Janine Giles, two University of Calgary doctoral students. In 2011, Lisa sent us an article about mothers in politics and said that "there needs to be a book written and titled ... *Mothers and Others*. I believe that the difference between mothers and non-mothers (in politics, earnings, etc.) is at least as big as the gap between men and women and may actually account for the gender gap." Lisa, a politically astute mother of two, got us thinking about this important question regarding parenthood and politics. At the time, the rest of us were childless, but we were all interested in gender and politics even though we knew little about parenthood and politics. We loved the idea of "mothers and others," so the four of us began planning excitedly. There's nothing like a snappy title to get one motivated and excited about a new project.

Our planning led to a workshop entitled Mothers and Others in Banff, Alberta, in the fall of 2012, an event that could not have occurred without the incredible planning and on-the-ground efforts of both Lisa and Janine. At that point, Amanda Bittner had just welcomed her first child, and an unanticipated consequence of new motherhood was that she found herself unable to attend (it never dawned on her while pregnant that a baby might impede her ability to do parts of her job). The event was nonetheless a huge success. Over two days, papers were presented by Barbara Arneil, Sylvia Bashevkin, Rosie Campbell, Sarah Childs, Grace Deason, Jackie Filla, Susan

Franceschet, Elisabeth Gidengil, Janine Giles, Jill Greenlee, Rebecca Hannagan, Allison Harell, Samara Klar, Isabelle Kurschner, Lisa Lambert, Carrie Langner, Valerie Lapointe, Christopher Larimer, Heather Madonia, Brenda O'Neill, Jennifer Piscopo, Stuart Soroka, Gwynn Thomas, and Melanee Thomas. We were also lucky enough to hear from sitting politicians, including Danielle Smith (then leader of the official opposition of Alberta), Karen Sorenson (mayor of Banff), Florence Christophers (councillor, Town of Okotoks), Anne Wilson (NDP candidate), and Danielle Chartiers (MLA for Saskatoon-Riversdale, Province of Saskatchewan).

We are so grateful for the contributions of our participants: we had two incredible days of engaged and lively discussion about the role of parenthood in politics and the implications of the gendered dynamics of parenthood. Our excitement was only increased by the opportunity to talk about mothers and others with a group of interested and brilliant scholars and politicians, and we knew that we had the potential for an exciting book on our hands.

We want to thank all of our contributors for helping this book to come together. It has been wonderful working with you all, and we greatly appreciate your professionalism, enthusiasm, and accommodation of our various editorial demands.

We would also like to thank our respective departments for their support throughout this process. Melanee Thomas thanks the Department of Political Science at the University of Calgary, and Amanda Bittner thanks the Department of Political Science at Memorial University.

The publication of this volume occurred because of considerable financial support that we received throughout the project, and we are grateful to all of the organizations and individuals that helped us along the way. We received funding from the Social Sciences and Humanities Research Council of Canada in the form of a workshop grant, as well as from Memorial University, the University of Calgary, the Canadian Opinion Research Archive, and the Sheldon Chumir Foundation for Ethics in Leadership.

We want to thank Emily Andrew at UBC Press for her enthusiasm for this project and for helping us to move it from an idea on a sheet of paper to a published book. Amanda has worked with Emily on more than one project now, and it has been a real privilege. This was Melanee's first project with UBC Press, and Emily's enthusiasm and guidance made the process a breeze. This book could not have come together without the excellent research assistance of Josh Smee (who was essential for the backgrpund work on Chapter 15) and Shannon Fraser, who used her eagle eyes at the end to improve the book and create the index. We would also like to thank Randy Schmidt for enthusiastically accepting us among his authors once Emily left UBC Press. It has been a pleasure working with such a professional team at UBC Press, and we could not have done this without them. We would also like to acknowledge the excellent comments and suggestions from our anonymous reviewers and the Editorial Board at UBC Press, who were incredibly enthusiastic about the project but also made careful and thoughtful suggestions about how to improve it.

Finally, we would like to thank all of the mothers who have worked and continue to work in politics. Your job is far from easy and frequently thankless. Your ability to wear many hats at once in the service of others (be they constituents or children) is remarkable and inspiring. We hope that by highlighting the role of motherhood in politics we can facilitate further conversations about the important role of care in our society and the need both to accommodate caregiving and to set up institutions wholly in support of society's care needs.

INTRODUCTION

1

The "Mommy Problem"?
Gender, Parental Status, and Politics

MELANEE THOMAS and AMANDA BITTNER

It seems like a classic case of "damned if you do, damned if you don't." When women in politics are mothers, reporters and opponents question them about their competence in both their private lives and their public lives. For example, when Attorney General of Illinois Lisa Madigan was rumoured to be running for governor in 2014, she was asked three times in a single interview if she could simultaneously raise her children and be an elected official. First she was asked "whether she could serve as governor and still raise her kids the way she wants to"; then she was "pressed further on whether she could simultaneously hold both jobs – governor and mom" – and when she noted that, as attorney general, she already balanced both jobs she was "reminded that being governor is a lot more demanding than attorney general" (McKinney 2012). She ultimately chose not to run for governor and instead sought re-election as attorney general (Pearson, Long, and Garcia 2013). It is difficult if not impossible to find a case in which a father was comparably harangued about his ability to balance his (potential) elected position and his parental status.

Yet, when political women don't have children, they face attacks and questions about their ability to understand or care about key policy domains. Members of both the opposition and her own party characterized Julia Gillard, then prime minister of Australia, as being unable to feel empathy because she chose not to have children (Kelly 2011). Similarly, a staffer from an opposing political party attacked Danielle Smith, a candidate for public office and the potential premier of Alberta, by questioning her sincerity on child and family issues because Smith didn't have "children of her own." In response, Smith released a candid statement about her struggles with infertility (Strapagiel 2012). Again, it's difficult if not impossible to find cases in which men have been likewise attacked for not having children. We are aware of no man who has made a public declaration of his virility or fertility to respond to such a personal attack.

For women in politics, this "damned if you do, damned if you don't" setup gives rise to difficult questions about strategy and practice. For students and scholars of gender and politics, it suggests that we must ask how career politicians, voters, and the media navigate the interaction among gender, parental status, and politics.

Although this literature has yet to be well developed, academic research on politics and motherhood suggests that, to be successful politicians, women must "do politics" as men by downloading family responsibilities onto someone else or eliminating them altogether (McKay 2011; van Zoonen 1998, 2006). The implication is that, unless women can remove or at least minimize family obligations, or the *anticipation* of future family obligations, a career in politics is not an option for them. The same is not perceived to be true for men; instead, they can have families and seek elected office at the same time because it is presumed that someone else is at home to parent the children. However, experimental research shows that female politicians with children are viewed more favourably than female politicians without children. In contrast, male politicians without children are viewed more favourably than male politicians with children (Stalsburg 2010). Why, then, does conventional wisdom state that politics and motherhood – real or anticipated – do not mix? What are the implications of this view for policy outcomes? For broadly held political attitudes? For political careers and campaign strategies? A systematic analysis of how actual mothering roles affect political behaviour, ambition, attitudes, and careers is required. We don't actually know much about the relationship between parenthood and politics.

Unfortunately, conjecture dominates assumptions about gender, parental status, and politics, as evidenced by the experiences of Madigan, Gillard, and Smith described above. Research on political representation has yet to evaluate systematically whether being a parent influences who is elected, how those elected perform their legislative roles, and how they are perceived and evaluated by the public. Similarly, parental status is certainly presumed to change women's and men's political attitudes and behaviour – as shown by prolific media coverage of "soccer moms," "hockey moms," and "NASCAR dads" during election campaigns (Carroll 1999; Elder and Greene 2007). Yet, though research on public opinion and political participation confirms the existence of several gender gaps in political attitudes, values, and actions between women and men, it has not yet fully addressed whether parental status informs or changes these gaps.

This book seeks to fill a substantial gap in the existing literature on gender and politics. We bring together scholars of political careers, party organizations, political behaviour and representation, and public policy to discuss the role of parental status in political life. Although the role of motherhood is specifically cited in the academic literature and the popular press as a barrier to women's political careers, empirical evidence suggests that the relationships among gender, parental status, and politics are complex and warrants further investigation. Yet to date this topic has not received much examination.

Our intellectual starting point is that being a parent is a gendered political identity that can influence *how, why,* and *to what extent* women (and men) engage with politics. The notion that parenthood – that is, caring for and raising dependent children – is a gendered political identity, we think, isn't controversial. Women and men are affected differently by parenthood, and society perceives mothers and fathers differently, for a number of complex and interrelated reasons. At times, the constituent parts interact: woman and parent (mother), man and parent (father); at other times, patterns might hold for all parents regardless of gender. Importantly, we do not actually know much about the interaction of parenthood and politics, regardless of whether we specifically discuss mothers or fathers. Much of this book focuses on motherhood, though fatherhood is also assessed by a number of the contributors.

Scholars of gender and politics have examined *how, why,* and *to what extent* women and men engage with politics, providing important insights. It is important to extend this research further, to incorporate *parenthood* into our assessment of these three questions. These questions are citizen focused rather than state or policy focused or something else, and the chapters in this book, in their attempts to answer these questions, are also necessarily citizen focused. We do not assess, for example, public policy making on parental leave, childcare, reproduction, and the like. This book looks at three main areas of citizen engagement with the political system to assess the role of parenthood: political careers; citizens, media, and party/candidate strategic communications; and public opinion and political participation. We do not claim to cover exhaustively all aspects of politics related to parenthood. We simply aim to take part in a conversation in which parenthood is incorporated as an explanatory variable, influencing the nature of political engagement.

Parental Status and Political Careers
Angela Merkel (Germany), Julia Gillard (Australia), Condoleezza Rice (United States), Helen Clark (New Zealand), and Kim Campbell (Canada) all have two things in common. First, each holds or has held a high executive position in government. Second, each is childless. Studies demonstrate that women legislators are more likely to be single and childless than they are to be mothers, while male politicians are predominantly family men (van Zoonen 1998, 2006). But other women, such as Indira Gandhi (India), Margaret Thatcher (United Kingdom), Erna Solberg (Norway), and Michelle Bachelet (Chile) have been successful political executives *and* mothers. That some women in politics are mothers while others are not is indicative that there is no "one size fits all" rule about motherhood and politics and suggests that more research is necessary to understand the relationships between political women's careers and key aspects of their private lives, such as their children.

We suspect that gender stereotypes constitute one explanation of the presumption that motherhood specifically is incompatible with a political career. Much of the literature on women candidates suggests that stereotypical views of women's roles and abilities can damage their political careers, especially when the office that they seek is high powered and masculinized, such as a presidency (Murray 2010). Common gender stereotypes present women as warm, gentle, and kind, while men are seen to be aggressive, assertive, and decisive (Huddy and Capelos 2002; Huddy and Terkildsen 1993). Masculine stereotypes are more desirable for politics and elected office than feminine stereotypes, especially at the highest levels (Huddy and Terkildsen 1993). Other gender stereotypes present women as honest, trustworthy, and full of integrity (Fridkin Kahn 1994; Huddy and Capelos 2002). These tropes can be used to women's advantage in some (but not all) contexts, such as when issues of compassion or care are the most important for an electorate or when scandal leads voters to prefer candidates perceived to be more honest than the status quo (Bruckmüller and Branscombe 2010; Carlin and

Winfrey 2009). This advantage rests on voter knowledge; in low-information contexts, voters are more likely to fall back on gender role attitudes and stereotypes (Alexander and Andersen 1993; also see Cutler 2002).

As a subset of women, mothers are stereotyped both positively as being caring, understanding, and virtuous (Kanter 1977) and negatively as being those who scold and punish (Carlin and Winfrey 2009). Although these stereotypes can be deployed to a candidate's or politician's advantage, they can also cue that mothers have responsibilities in the private sphere, undermining their perceived leadership in the public sphere (Carlin and Winfrey 2009; Kanter 1977).

Although these stereotypes might seem to be straightforward, their effects in politics are not. Research suggests that women in politics are also stereotyped as a specific subset of women. Notably, female politicians are stereotyped as having considerably lower levels of integrity and empathy than women in general as well as lower levels of leadership ability and competence than male politicians (Schneider and Bos 2013). Furthermore, women professionals are more likely to be stereotyped as competent and capable leaders than women in politics, leading scholars to conclude that "female politicians seem to be 'losing' on male stereotypical qualities while also not having any advantage on qualities typical of women" (Schneider and Bos 2013, 17). What does this mean for mothers who seek political careers? It is not immediately clear that there is sufficient justification to assume that stereotypes about women in general or subsets of women – politicians and mothers – will map easily onto each other. One might expect that these stereotypes cut a number of ways, some positively and others negatively, so further investigation is needed.

Stereotypes comprise only some of the challenges facing mothers with political careers. Another is the double day, especially the difficulties of navigating childcare. Time-use studies suggest that many women, but not many men, put in a double day of paid work outside the home and unpaid work inside it. Burns, Schlozman, and Verba (2001) found that the household division of labour in 1990 was similar to that of the 1950s. More recent time-use surveys indicate that, though married men perform more housework now than in 1965, women continue to spend far more time on household chores than men, even when they are working comparable hours outside the home (Eagly and Carli 2007; see also Hook 2006; Lowndes 2004; Ravanera, Rajulton, and Burch 2002; Ravanera, Rajulton, and Turcotte 2003). The same studies also show that "mothers provide more childcare [now] than in earlier generations," such that "employed mothers in 2000 spent as much time interacting with their children as mothers without jobs did in 1975" (Eagly and Carli 2007, 52, 54).

In politics, the difficulties caused by gendered time use with respect to children and the double day were shown in sharp relief by Anne Marie Slaughter as she left her post as the first female director of policy planning at the State Department. She suggested that rigid political schedules prevented her from being "both the parent and [the] professional I wanted to be" (Slaughter 2012, 1). Importantly, this was not the case in her demanding academic career prior to politics, nor does it appear to be the case for many men or at least for as many men as women. This suggests that the rigid political schedule conflicts with gendered expectations and experiences of parenting.

In this book, we probe what this means for women who have, or want to have, political careers, and many of the chapters here begin by asking different types of questions. If women choose to have children as well as political careers, what supports are there to help balance this particular kind of work and family life? Are these supports comparable to those of other workplaces in the private or public sector? Are political contexts such as legislatures able to facilitate mothers in politics? If so, how? If not, which specific barriers are in place, and how might they be removed? Are women in politics less likely to be mothers? If yes, is it because it is too difficult to balance a political career with the double day or modern expectations of the hours that mothers must dedicate to childcare? Or are political parties and elites less likely to recruit women with children to political careers because of the stereotypes outlined above? How and why is this different for fathers? Are men in politics able to download their parental responsibilities onto others in ways that women cannot or choose not to? Or do they face comparable difficulties balancing political work and family life?

The chapters in this book assess many of these questions in different political contexts. In Chapter 2, Rosie Campbell and Sarah Childs, for example, assess legislative careers and recruitment in Britain to understand better how parties target and treat mothers (if at all). They ask how the mother politician and representations of motherhood play out in UK politics, and they assess how motherhood – and gender – can best be integrated into the legislature. They argue that incorporating an ethic of care into political institutions is likely to be most effective for both women and parents.

Barbara Arneil assesses in Chapter 3 tangible challenges faced by legislators who are or will become mothers with infants while in office. In particular, she asks about the effects of being elected for only a four- to five-year window on availability of and willingness to take maternity leave. She also asks about the impact of working in a "formal and ritual-laden chamber" as well as the lack of control over the daily schedule (division bells, unpredictable vote times) compared with a more informal workplace for lactating women and on breastfeeding generally. Arneil also notes the pressure on legislators to be public role models and advocates for "breast is best," a pressure that many mothers find difficult (even when not in the public eye), and she wonders what impact that might have on legislators' strategies for balancing motherhood with legislative careers. To answer these questions, Arneil assesses recent experiences in Canada, Australia, and Britain, and she finds that female MPs face particular challenges because of the nature of parliamentary careers, arguing that it is only with a combination of mother-friendly policies instituted in legislatures that mothers can really balance these competing pressures.

In Chapter 4, Susan Franceschet, Jennifer Piscopo, and Gwynn Thomas turn our attention to a different part of the world, asking questions particularly important in the Latin American context. They ask how maternalism shapes Latin American politics today. In particular, they wonder whether (as has been the case in the past) female politicians are seen to be caretakers of nationwide "families"; whether motherhood structures legislative behaviour when they are in office and their access to politics more generally; and whether policies designed to increase participation and equality continue to be shaped by maternalism. They find that the gendered division of labour continues to shape women's political opportunities and that society continues to apply gendered norms of caretaking and social issues to the understanding of women's politics. The authors also find that democracy has strengthened discussions of women's rights and equality, thus expanding opportunities for women's political engagement and involvement.

For some time, scholars have assumed that local municipal politics are more female friendly and perhaps more family friendly than state-level or national-level legislative careers. Rebecca Hannagan and Christopher Larimer assess in Chapter 5 the impact of gender quotas on local boards and committees in Iowa. They ask whether more and younger women are involved in local politics and whether their involvement indicates a perception that local politics facilitates greater balance between family and work responsibilities or whether there is something entirely different about local politics that attracts younger women. They find that recent legislation is indeed supportive of young families (including mothers) since it facilitates increased participation of women in local politics.

Ronnee Schreiber shifts the focus yet again in Chapter 6, in which she looks at the constructions of motherhood by leaders of national conservative organizations representing women's interests. The focus on conservative women is interesting because they have had dual pressures placed on them, including both promoting traditional gender roles and encouraging women's political participation. Specifically, Schreiber asks how these women characterize motherhood and articulate their views of it in relation to their professional goals and those of other political women; she essentially seeks to understand how they see and deal with the "juggle" of personal and professional responsibilities. Through in-depth interviews with these leaders, she finds that their perspectives are varied but that the women are unified in seeing the mommy struggle or work-life balance in private terms. That is, they do not see a role for the state in "helping" them to manage their personal and professional lives, but they recognize as essential the roles of their husbands (and extended families) in supporting their careers.

The chapters in this section fit closely with one another, questioning the nature of the political career, the stereotypes about motherhood/parenthood, and the practical challenges that parents face in political careers. In many ways, they raise more questions than answers, pointing to the need to continue this avenue of research in the future.

Communications and Campaign Strategy

Another important set of questions arises once women are in politics, either as candidates or as elected officials. How does parental status influence their strategic actions, communications, and interactions with constituents and the media? Are these considerations driven by an awareness of gender-based stereotypes or broadly held views about mothers or by other factors, such as party affiliation and ideology? And how, why, and to what extent do the media frame and respond and contribute to the relationships among gender, parental status, and politics?

It is safe to assume that women in politics (just like men) are rational actors (Dolan 2005, 42), which suggests that their motivations for seeking public office are multifaceted and contain many factors outside their gender identity. This suggests that, though gender-based factors might spark some women's interest in politics, that interest could be sparked by many other factors. Furthermore, because women are rational actors, they are probably aware of the stereotypes about them and evaluate when, how, and why to take them into account when presenting themselves to the public through their communications. This would lead us to expect that female politicians' communications and media interactions might be different from men's but in specific, strategic, and subtle ways.

Research confirms that this is the case: few differences emerge in women's and men's campaign websites that cannot be explained by other factors, such as party affiliation, confounding stereotypical expectations that women and men will emphasize different issues in their campaigns. Slight variations might appear when women run against other women rather than men, indicating that emphasizing certain issues in campaign communications might be "strategic behaviour on the part of these women to simultaneously counter and benefit from gender-based stereotypes voters may hold about them" (Dolan 2005, 37). Although women and men in politics present themselves in similar ways, their motivations to do so might be different, especially in relation to their parental status.

Even the most careful communications strategy cannot entirely control how the media cover, frame, and analyze women in politics. Research shows that the media might simply not give women in politics as much coverage as men in politics (Heldman, Carroll, and Olson 2005); although this trend appears to be diminishing over time for candidates for executive office (Miller, Peake, and Boulton 2010; Trimble 2007), it might still hold for other levels of government and politics. Studies also show that the media tend to focus on women politicians' personal characteristics, appearances, and private lives but on men's skills and abilities (Miller, Peake, and Boulton 2010; Trimble 2007; Trimble et al. 2013). In some contexts, coverage of women politicians' private lives is explicitly about their children (van Zoonen 2006), while in others children are ignored in favour of marital status and sexuality (Trimble et al. 2013).

Like the stereotypes outlined above, communication strategies and coverage can cut a number of ways, and it is not entirely clear when and why the cut is positive for some women in politics but negative for others. Part of the explanation might rest with a female politician's ability to present herself plausibly as a "good" or traditional mother. For example, Sarah Palin is a self-described "hockey mom" and has been framed by the media as a traditional mother. As a result, after she gave birth while in office as governor of Alaska, the overall tone of the coverage was positive and sympathetic, especially after the child was diagnosed with Down's syndrome (Loke, Harp, and Bachmann 2011). In contrast, another governor who gave birth while in office – Jane Swift of Massachusetts in 2001 – was vilified as a mother while her competence as a politician was questioned. Media reports consistently challenged how she would balance work and family, even though her husband was staying at home with the children. Importantly, the media presented her husband as a man who couldn't possibly be happy but who also couldn't possibly care for their children as well as Swift herself (Loke, Harp, and Bachmann 2011). Palin and Swift are similar enough on policy and party grounds – both are Republicans who oppose equal marriage – suggesting that the differences in their media coverage rest with other factors. Because there was no question that Palin would be her child's primary caregiver, she did not disrupt the dominant narrative of white, heterosexual, middle-class families in the United States. Swift, as the breadwinner with a stay-at-home husband, did disrupt that narrative and apparently was punished for doing so.

Three chapters in this section examine the issue of women and motherhood in the media more extensively. Melanee Thomas and Lisa Lambert open the section by looking in Chapter 7 at the actions of politicians, focusing on the political communication strategies of members of Parliament in Canada. They ask to what extent (and why) legislators choose to present their families and discuss their parental status in their official communiqués (both online and in their constituencies through the mail). Their research suggests that the decisions of MPs appear to be conditioned by gender, party affiliation, and province. Interestingly, Thomas and Lambert also find that some women choose not to integrate their parental status into their campaigns out of security concerns, a consideration not echoed by their male peers.

In Chapter 8, Melissa Miller shifts the focus and looks at press coverage of female political candidates, zooming in on the campaigns of two high-profile "political mothers," Hillary Clinton and Sarah Palin, in their respective 2008 runs for executive office. Miller asks whether traditional stereotypes continue to plague women's (and mothers') media coverage and whether motherhood actually benefits female candidates. The comparison of Clinton with Palin is particularly useful in that Clinton downplayed her role as a mother, while Palin celebrated and drew attention to motherhood in her campaign. Miller finds that voter stereotyping of women on the campaign trail seems to be on the decline and that voters might perceive feminine traits (and motherhood) in a particularly positive light. Both Miller and Thomas and Lambert highlight the strategic choices made by mothers on the campaign trail and in office, since either downplaying or promoting their parental status can benefit them in different situations.

Carrie Langner, Jill Greenlee, and Grace Deason take our focus to a new domain in Chapter 9 as they assess the extent to which parenthood has become politicized in recent years and whether or not this increased politicization (for both women and men) has affected the political engagements and activities of mothers and fathers. They argue that the Internet and social media have played major roles in politicizing motherhood (and, increasingly, fatherhood), and as a result parents have become more vocal. This fascinating chapter straddles the topics of media and individual behaviour and provides a good segue into the next section, which looks more closely at the impact of parenthood on the opinions, attitudes, and actions of "regular" citizens.

Parenthood and Opinion, Participation and Behaviour

We know a great deal about the effect of gender on public opinion and political participation. Women vote at comparable, or even slightly higher, rates to men in most post-industrial democracies (Beckwith 1986; Campbell 2006; Gidengil et al. 2004; Welch 1977). In some contexts, women are as likely as men to participate in protest activities (Gidengil et al. 2004), and women are considerably more likely than men to engage in political and ethical consumerism (Childs 2004; Stolle and Micheletti 2013). However, men are considerably more likely than women to participate in more conventional political activities, such as working on political campaigns, donating to campaigns or causes, joining political organizations or parties, contacting government officials, and running for elected office (Burns, Schlozman, and Verba 2001; Childs 2004; Gidengil et al. 2004; Inglehart and Norris 2000; Young and Cross 2003).

Similarly, we know that women and men have different partisan preferences. Women are more likely than men to support left-leaning parties in a number of established democracies (Carroll 1988; Gidengil et al. 2003, 2005; Inglehart and Norris 2000). In some cases, notably the United States, this gender gap in vote choice is driven by men's shift to the right (Kaufmann and Petrocik 1999; Wirls 1986). Considerable gender gaps exist in policy preferences as well: women are more likely than men to support social programs and the welfare state (Schlesinger and Heldman 2001) and to use their concerns about these programs to evaluate economic issues (Gidengil 1995). Women are also less likely than men to support war and military intervention (Brooks and Valentino 2011; Conover and Sapiro 1993; Togeby 1994) and some forms of supranational integration, such as the European Union (Nelsen and Guth 2000). Women are more likely than men to support liberal policies on civil rights with respect to race (Hutchings et al. 2004) and sexual orientation (Herek 2002).

It is also well established that women are less psychologically engaged with politics than men. Women report lower levels of political interest (Bennett and Bennett 1989), subjective political competence (Bennett 1997; Thomas 2012), and political ambition (Fox and Lawless 2011) than men. Men consistently score higher than women on political knowledge measures (Stolle and Gidengil 2010), in part because men are more likely than women to guess (Mondak and Anderson 2004). The stereotypes discussed above also play roles in this knowledge gap, for women cued with a negative stereotype about women in politics tend to perform more poorly on political knowledge tests (McGlone et al. 2006; Thomas, Harell, and Gosselin 2013). Importantly, the gender gap in political knowledge disappears when knowledge about government programs and services is evaluated rather than just the names of cabinet ministers and political executives (Stolle and Gidengil 2010).

Although we know less about the effects of parental status on political attitudes and behaviour, analyses of parental status and politics are often gendered. If pundits or party activities are any guide, parental status should have a considerable effect on individuals' political behaviour, preferences, and participation. In the 2004 American presidential election, for example, candidates courted "NASCAR dads" and "security moms." The latter trope presents mothers as a bloc hawkishly concerned about security and defence, presumably open to the Republicans' tough talk on these issues. Similarly, NASCAR dads are presented as low- to middle-income white fathers in suburban and rural areas; although the Democrats' economic policies should be attractive to such fathers, the social conservatism of the Republican Party often wins them over (Elder and Greene 2007). The appeal of both tropes for pundits is apparent, but neither security moms nor NASCAR dads appear as a voting bloc in American politics. Instead, Elder and Greene (2007) find differences between mothers and women without children on social welfare issues but few differences between fathers and men without children. These findings suggest that parental status is related to political attitudes and behaviour for women in ways that might not be the same for men (Elder and Greene 2007).

Taken together, research findings suggest that, like gender, parental status is but one identity that can affect political behaviour, public opinion, and policy preference. These identities can create conflicting policy choices and behaviour options. Sorting through the conflicts might depend on how an identity is cued. One experimental study (Klar 2013) cued parental and partisan identity by naming the identity, cuing it in terms of efficacy (i.e., the group is empowered, and the government listens to it), and then cuing it in terms of threat. The results show that identities cued with equal strength tend to cancel each other. However, threatened identities outweigh other cued identities, giving the threatened identities the most influence on policy preferences (Klar 2013).

We suspect that gender and parental status are but two of several, potentially conflicting, identities that influence political attitudes and behaviour. Research on the combined effects of gender and other politicized identities, such as race, suggests that behaviour and attitudes that underpin "average" or "typical" gender gaps are exhibited only by specific subgroups of women. For example, the gender gap in presidential vote choice in the United States is a predominantly white phenomenon (Lien 1998). Similarly, though women perform as well as men on political knowledge tests about government programs and services, some women who need them the most – low-income, immigrant, and older women – know the least about them (Stolle and Gidengil 2010). When these results are taken together with Elder and Greene's (2007) conclusion that parental status affects women's political attitudes and behaviour differently than men's, the implication is that the relationships among gender, parental status, and politics are complex.

The final set of chapters in this book not only increases our understanding of the role of parental status in political participation and attitudes but also demonstrates the complexities of these competing identities. In Chapter 10, Elizabeth Goodyear-Grant and Amanda Bittner assess Canadian attitudes on three issue dimensions – cultural activities, social welfare, and crime and security – to determine whether there are consistent parental gaps. They find that parents tend to be more conservative on issues related to both culture and crime and security but that there are few gender-based parent gaps. That is, mothers and fathers do not differ much from one another, though they do differ from non-parents fairly consistently. Why these differences occur is much less clear, and their research points to the need for further investigation.

Janine Giles looks at political knowledge in Chapter 11 to assess whether parental status has a role in the acquisition of political information. She focuses on aggregate patterns at the local level to determine whether gender gaps in knowledge remain in "gender progressive" contexts. In particular, she asks whether the socio-economic context (including parenthood) has an impact on the level of political knowledge. She finds that this context does indeed influence women's levels of knowledge but that parenthood has little impact.

In Chapter 12, Allison Harell, Stuart Soroka, Shanto Iyengar, and Valérie Lapointe focus on attitudes toward public policy as they assess the extent to which traditional ideologies about gender roles influence voters' perceptions of parental leave policies. Assessing attitudes from surveys in Canada, Britain, and the United States, they find that those supporting traditional gender roles are less likely to support generous terms of parental leave and that these individuals are also more likely to penalize "non-traditional" leave seekers (e.g., fathers and single mothers). Their chapter points to the important links between basic values and state support for family policies.

Brenda O'Neill and Elisabeth Gidengil turn our attention in Chapter 13 to political participation, focusing on parental gaps among women because of the gendered impact of parental status. They ask two main questions. First, does motherhood affect women's civic and political participation? Second, if it does affect such participation, to what extent is this effect mediated by the age of children at home? They find that the mere presence of children in the home is not enough to decrease women's political participation (except among single parents) but that the ages of children are important: women with children aged five to 12 are more likely than other women to participate in some activities. Apparently, having school-aged children *increases* women's likelihood of doing volunteer work and signing petitions.

Michele Micheletti and Dietlind Stolle assess still another piece of the puzzle in Chapter 14, also focusing on the increased political activity of parents. They assess whether children help to mobilize their parents by examining political consumerism in Sweden. They find that parents of older children are more aware of environmental sustainability issues in relation to food and toys and that there is a gendered parent gap in awareness and concern: mothers are more concerned than fathers about these issues. Taken together, all of these chapters point to the complex relationships among gender, parenthood, and citizen engagement. Parenthood can influence and mobilize parents in some circumstances, and the effect is not always equal for mothers and fathers.

Understanding the Impact of Motherhood on Politics

This book uses the questions outlined above – how, why, and to what extent parental status affects how citizens engage with politics – to examine the three domains of political careers, media and campaign strategy, and participation and behaviour. Each chapter highlights the existing knowledge about gender, parental status, and politics as it relates to the topic before presenting new research on the extent to which (gendered) parental status matters.

The volume touches on a number of pertinent issues and controversies related to gender and politics. The chapters look at the role of parenthood in different contexts and from different angles, using different research methodologies and data sets, to bring together cutting-edge insights into contemporary issues in gender and politics. By combining analyses that use data from a variety of sources (including opinion surveys, government-collected national statistics, party- and candidate-produced flyers, websites, and other mailouts, national media reports, and qualitative interviews with candidates and other political activists), this book sheds light on the impact of motherhood on politics in a way that has not been done to date.

Although there is a rich literature on gender and politics, and a rich literature on the impact of motherhood in a number of other disciplines (e.g., sociology, labour studies, and health, to name a few), there is little work to date on the role of motherhood (or parenthood) in politics. This book attempts to push that dialogue forward, furthering our knowledge while also raising more questions in the process and pointing to issues that we still don't really understand.

Our concluding chapter re-evaluates the questions presented and the contributions made by our authors, and it assesses newly collected comparative data that will help us to understand what we might expect in politics in the future from both parents and non-parents. One thing that comes through clearly in our conclusion is that most states agree that paid work and private care responsibilities (i.e., parenting) must be balanced with one another and that the state has a large role to play in that balance. We find it striking that the same is not said about political careers. We contend that important discussions are required in most democratic states about the roles of parents, and mothers in particular, in politics. We also propose a research agenda to further evaluate the roles of gender and parental status in politics.

References

Alexander, Deborah, and Kristi Andersen. 1993. "Gender as a Factor in the Attribution of Leadership Traits." *Political Research Quarterly* 46 (3): 527–45. http://dx.doi.org/10.1177/106591299304600305.

Beckwith, Karen. 1986. *American Women and Political Participation: The Impacts of Work, Generation, and Feminism.* New York: Greenwood Press.

Bennett, Linda L.M., and Stephen Earl Bennett. 1989. "Enduring Gender Differences in Political Interest: The Impact of Socialization and Political Dispositions." *American Politics Quarterly* 17 (1): 105–22.

Bennett, Stephen Earl. 1997. "Knowledge of Politics and Sense of Subjective Political Competence: The Ambiguous Connection." *American Politics Research* 25 (2): 230–40. http://dx.doi.org/10.1177/1532673X9702500205.

Brooks, Deborah Jordan, and Benjamin A. Valentino. 2011. "A War of One's Own: Understanding the Gender Gap in Support for War." *Public Opinion Quarterly* 75 (2): 270–86. http://dx.doi.org/10.1093/poq/nfr005.

Bruckmüller, Susanne, and Nyla R. Branscombe. 2010. "The Glass Cliff: When and Why Women Are Selected as Leaders in Crisis Contexts." *British Journal of Social Psychology* 49 (3): 433–51. http://dx.doi.org/10.1348/014466609X466594.

Burns, Nancy, Kay Lehman Schlozman, and Sidney Verba. 2001. *The Private Roots of Public Action*. Cambridge, MA: Harvard University Press.

Campbell, Rosie. 2006. *Gender and the Vote in Britain*. Colchester, UK: ECPR Press.

Carlin, Diana B., and Kelly L. Winfrey. 2009. "Have You Come a Long Way, Baby? Hillary Clinton, Sarah Palin, and Sexism in 2008 Campaign Coverage." *Communication Studies* 60 (4): 326–43. http://dx.doi.org/10.1080/10510970903109904.

Carroll, Susan J. 1988. "Women's Autonomy and the Gender Gap: 1980 and 1982." In *The Politics of the Gender Gap: The Social Construction of Political Influence*, edited by Carol A. Mueller. Newbury Park, CA: Sage Publications, 236–57.

–. 1999. "The Disempowerment of the Gender Gap: Soccer Moms and the 1996 Elections." *PS: Political Science and Politics* 32 (1): 7–12. http://dx.doi.org/10.1017/S1049096500048721.

Childs, Sarah. 2004. "A British Gender Gap? Gender and Political Participation." *Political Quarterly* 75 (4): 422–24. http://dx.doi.org/10.1111/j.1467-923X.2004.00646.x.

Conover, Pamela Johnston, and Virginia Sapiro. 1993. "Gender, Feminist Consciousness, and War." *American Journal of Political Science* 37 (4): 1079–99. http://dx.doi.org/10.2307/2111544.

Cutler, Fred. 2002. "The Simplest Shortcut of All: Sociodemographic Characteristics and Electoral Choice." *Journal of Politics* 64 (2): 466–90. http://dx.doi.org/10.1111/1468-2508.00135.

Dolan, Kathleen. 2005. "Do Women Candidates Play to Gender Stereotypes? Do Men Candidates Play to Women? Candidate Sex and Issue Priorities on Campaign Websites." *Political Research Quarterly* 58 (1): 31–44. http://dx.doi.org/10.1177/106591290505800103.

Eagly, Alice H., and Linda L. Carli. 2007. *Through the Labyrinth: The Truth about How Women Become Leaders*. Boston: Harvard Business School Press.

Elder, Laurel, and Steven Greene. 2007. "The Myth of 'Security Moms' and 'NASCAR Dads'? Parenthood, Political Stereotypes, and the 2004 Election." *Social Science Quarterly* 88 (1): 1–19. http://dx.doi.org/10.1111/j.1540-6237.2007.00443.x.

Fox, Richard, and Jennifer L. Lawless. 2011. "Gendered Perceptions and Political Candidacies: A Central Barrier to Women's Equality in Electoral Politics." *American Journal of Political Science* 55 (1): 59–73. http://dx.doi.org/10.1111/j.1540-5907.2010.00484.x.

Fridkin Kahn, Kim. 1994. "Does Gender Make a Difference? An Experimental Examination of Sex Stereotypes and Press Patterns in Statewide Campaigns." *American Journal of Political Science* 38 (1): 162–95. http://dx.doi.org/10.2307/2111340.

Gidengil, Elisabeth. 1995. "Economic Man – Social Woman? The Case of the Gender Gap in Support for the Canada–United States Free Trade Agreement." *Comparative Political Studies* 28 (3): 384–408. http://dx.doi.org/10.1177/0010414095028003003.

Gidengil, Elisabeth, André Blais, Neil Nevitte, and Richard Nadeau. 2003. "Women to the Left? Gender Differences in Political Beliefs and Policy Preferences." In *Gender and Electoral Representation in Canada*, edited by Manon Tremblay and Linda Trimble, 140–59. Don Mills, ON: Oxford University Press.

–. 2004. *Citizens*. Vancouver: UBC Press.

Gidengil, Elisabeth, Matthew Hennigar, André Blais, Neil Nevitte, and Richard Nadeau. 2005. "Explaining the Gender Gap in Support for the New Right: The Case of Canada." *Comparative Political Studies* 38 (10): 1171–95. http://dx.doi.org/10.1177/0010414005279320.

Heldman, Caroline, Susan J. Carroll, and Stephanie Olson. 2005. "She Brought Only a Skirt: Print Media Coverage of Elizabeth Dole's Bid for the Republican Presidential Nomination." *Political Communication* 22 (3): 315–35.

Herek, Gregory. 2002. "Heterosexuals' Attitudes toward Bisexual Men and Women in the United States." *Journal of Sex Research* 39 (4): 264–74. http://dx.doi.org/10.1080/00224490209552150.

Hook, Jennifer L. 2006. "Men's Unpaid Work in 20 Countries, 1965–2003." *American Sociological Review* 71 (4): 639–60. http://dx.doi.org/10.1177/000312240607100406.

Huddy, Leonie, and Theresa Capelos. 2002. "Gender Stereotyping and Candidate Evaluation: Good News and Bad News for Women Politicians." In *The Social Psychology of Politics: Research, Policy, Theory, Practice*, edited by Ottati Victor et al., 29–53. New York: Kluwer Academic.

Huddy, Leonie, and Nayda Terkildsen. 1993. "Gender Stereotypes and the Perception of Male and Female Candidates." *American Journal of Political Science* 37 (1): 119–47. http://dx.doi.org/10.2307/2111526.

Hutchings, Vincent L., Nicholas A. Valention, Tasha S. Philpot, and Ismail K. White. 2004. "The Compassion Strategy: Race and the Gender Gap in Campaign 2000." *Public Opinion Quarterly* 68 (4): 512–41.

Inglehart, Ronald, and Pippa Norris. 2000. "The Developmental Theory of the Gender Gap: Women's and Men's Voting Behavior in Global Perspective." *International Political Science Review* 21 (4): 441–63. http://dx.doi.org/10.1177/0192512100214007.

Kanter, Rosabeth Moss. 1977. *Men and Women of the Corporation*. New York: Basic Books.

Kaufmann, Karen M., and John R. Petrocik. 1999. "The Changing Politics of American Men: Understanding the Sources of the Gender Gap." *American Journal of Political Science* 43 (3): 864–87. http://dx.doi.org/10.2307/2991838.

Kelly, Joe. 2011. "Mark Latham Says Julia Gillard Has No Empathy Because She's Childless." *Australian*, April 4, 2011. http://www.theaustralian.com.au/national-affairs/mark-latham-says-julia-gillard-has-no-empathy-because-shes-childless/story-fn59niix-1226033174177.

Klar, Samara. 2013. "The Influence of Competing Identity Primes on Political Preferences." *Journal of Politics* 75 (4): 1108–24. http://dx.doi.org/10.1017/S0022381613000698.

Lien, Pei-Te. 1998. "Does the Gender Gap in Political Attitudes and Behavior Vary across Racial Groups?" *Political Research Quarterly* 51 (4): 869–94. http://dx.doi.org/10.1177/106591299805100402.

Loke, Jaime, Dustin Harp, and Ingrid Bachmann. 2011. "Mothering and Governing: How News Articulated Gender Roles in the Cases of Governors Jane Swift and Sarah Palin." *Journalism Studies* 12 (2): 205–20. http://dx.doi.org/10.1080/1461670X.2010.488418.

Lowndes, Vivien. 2004. "Getting On or Getting By? Women, Social Capital, and Political Participation." *British Journal of Politics and International Relations* 6 (1): 45–64. http://dx.doi.org/10.1111/j.1467-856X.2004.00126.x.

McGlone, Matthew S., Joshua Aronson, and Diane Kobrynowicz. 2006. "Stereotype Threat and the Gender Gap in Political Knowledge." *Psychology of Women Quarterly* 30 (4): 392–98. http://dx.doi.org/10.1111/j.1471-6402.2006.00314.x.

McKay, Joanna. 2011. "'Having It All?' Women MPs and Motherhood in Germany and the UK." *Parliamentary Affairs* 64 (4): 714–36. http://dx.doi.org/10.1093/pa/gsr001.

McKinney, Dave. 2012. "Lisa Madigan Refuses to Tip Hand on Governor's Race." *Chicago Sun-Times*, September 4, 2012. http://www.suntimes.com/news/elections/14938617-505/lisa-madigan-refuses-to-tip-hand-on-governors-race.html.

Miller, Melissa K., Jeffrey S. Peake, and Brittany Anne Boulton. 2010. "Testing the *Saturday Night Live* Hypothesis: Fairness and Bias in Newspaper Coverage of Hillary Clinton's Presidential Campaign." *Politics and Gender* 6 (2): 169–98. http://dx.doi.org/10.1017/S1743923X10000036.

Mondak, Jeffrey J., and Mary R. Anderson. 2004. "The Knowledge Gap: A Reexamination of Gender-Based Differences in Political Knowledge." *Journal of Politics* 66 (2): 492–512. http://dx.doi.org/10.1111/j.1468-2508.2004.00161.x.

Murray, Rainbow. 2010. "Introduction and Framework." In *Cracking the Highest Glass Ceiling: A Global Comparison of Women's Campaigns for Executive Office*, edited by Rainbow Murray, 3–28. Thousand Oaks, CA: Praeger Publishing.

Nelsen, Brent F., and James L. Guth. 2000. "Exploring the Gender Gap: Women, Men, and Public Attitudes toward European Integration." *European Union Politics* 1 (3): 267–91. http://dx.doi.org/10.1177/1465116500001003001.

Pearson, Rick, Ray Long, and Monique Garcia. 2013. "Lisa Madigan Takes Pass on Governor's Race." *Chicago Tribune,* July 15, 2013. http://articles.chicagotribune.com/2013-07-15/news/chi-lisa-madigan-illinois-attorney-general-reelection_1_speaker-madigan-governor-quinn-campaign.

Ravanera, Zenaida, Fernando Rajulton, and Thomas K. Burch. 2002. "Effects of Community and Family Characteristics on Early Life Transitions of Canadian Youth." Paper presented at the Population Association of America conference, Atlanta.

Ravanera, Zenaida, Fernando Rajulton, and Pierre Turcotte. 2003. "Youth Integration and Social Capital: An Analysis of the Canadian General Social Surveys on Time Use." *Youth and Society* 35 (2): 158–82. http://dx.doi.org/10.1177/0044118X03255030.

Schlesinger, Mark, and Caroline Heldman. 2001. "Gender Gap or Gender Gaps? New Perspectives on Support for Government Action and Policies." *Journal of Politics* 63 (1): 59–92. http://dx.doi.org/10.1111/0022-3816.00059.

Schneider, Monica C., and Angela L. Bos. 2013. "Measuring Stereotypes of Female Politicians." *Political Psychology* 35 (2): 245–66. http://dx.doi.org/10.1111/pops.12040.

Slaughter, Anne-Marie. 2012. "Why Women Still Can't Have It All." *Atlantic,* July–August, n. pag. http://www.theatlantic.com/magazine/archive/2012/07/why-women-still-cant-have-it-all/309020/?single_page=true.

Stalsburg, Brittany L. 2010. "Voting for Mom: The Political Consequences of Being a Parent for Male and Female Candidates." *Politics and Gender* 6 (3): 373–404. http://dx.doi.org/10.1017/S1743923X10000309.

Stolle, Dietlind, and Elisabeth Gidengil. 2010. "What Do Women Really Know? A Gendered Analysis of Varieties of Political Knowledge." *PS: Political Science and Politics* 8 (1): 93–109.

Stolle, Dietlind, and Michele Micheletti. 2013. *Political Consumerism: Global Responsibility in Action.* Cambridge: Cambridge University Press. http://dx.doi.org/10.1017/CBO9780511844553.

Strapagiel, Lauren. 2012. "Alberta Election 2012: PC Staffer Resigns after Tweet Questions Wildrose Leader Danielle Smith's Lack of Children." *Huffington Post Canada,* March 31, 2012. http://www.huffingtonpost.ca/2012/03/31/pc-staffer-resigns-danielle-smith-wildrose-tweet_n_1393807.html.

Thomas, Melanee. 2012. "The Complexity Conundrum: Why Hasn't the Gender Gap in Subjective Political Competence Closed?" *Canadian Journal of Political Science* 45 (2): 337–58. http://dx.doi.org/10.1017/S0008423912000352.

Thomas, Melanee, Allison Harell, and Tania Gosselin. 2013. "Cuing the Gap: Gender and Psychological Orientations to Politics." Paper presented at the Gender and Political Psychology Workshop, Naperville, IL, August 26, 2013.

Togeby, Lise. 1994. "The Gender Gap in Foreign Policy Attitudes." *Journal of Peace Research* 31 (4): 375–92. http://dx.doi.org/10.1177/0022343394031004002.

Trimble, Linda. 2007. "Gender, Political Leadership, and Media Visibility: *Globe and Mail* Coverage of Conservative Party of Canada Leadership Contests."

Canadian Journal of Political Science 40 (4): 969–93. http://dx.doi.org/10.1017/S0008423907071120.

Trimble, Linda, Angelina Wagner, Shannon Sampert, Daisy Raphael, and Bailey Gerrits. 2013. "Is It Personal? Gendered Mediation in Newspaper Coverage of Canadian National Party Leadership Contests, 1975–2012." *International Journal of Press/Politics* 18 (4): 462–81. http://dx.doi.org/10.1177/1940161213495455.

van Zoonen, Liesbet. 1998. "'Finally, I Have My Mother Back': Politicians and Their Families in Popular Culture." *International Journal of Press/Politics* 3 (1): 48–64. http://dx.doi.org/10.1177/1081180X98003001005.

–. 2006. "The Personal, the Political, and the Popular: A Woman's Guide to Celebrity Politics." *European Journal of Cultural Studies* 9 (3): 287–301. http://dx.doi.org/10.1177/1367549406066074.

Welch, Susan. 1977. "Women as Political Animals? A Test of Some Explanations for Male-Female Political Participation Differences." *American Journal of Political Science* 21 (4): 711–30. http://dx.doi.org/10.2307/2110733.

Wirls, Daniel. 1986. "Reinterpreting the Gender Gap." *Public Opinion Quarterly* 50 (3): 316–30. http://dx.doi.org/10.1086/268986.

Young, Lisa, and William Cross. 2003. "Women's Involvement in Canadian Political Parties." In *Women and Electoral Politics in Canada*, edited by Manon Tremblay and Linda Trimble, 92–109. Don Mills, ON: Oxford University Press.

PART 1
PARENTAL STATUS AND POLITICAL CAREERS

2

The (M)otherhood Trap

Reconsidering Sex, Gender, and Legislative Recruitment

ROSIE CAMPBELL and SARAH CHILDS

In almost all lower legislative houses across the globe, women are numerically underrepresented relative to their presence in the population. For feminist scholars and activists, this is considered an unnatural state of affairs and both a site and a sign of injustice; supporters of democracy – those who believe in the concept of political equality – should also be troubled by this sexual inequality. The case for women's political presence frequently made by feminist theorists and activists identifies symbolic and substantive reasons, in addition to justice and political equality arguments, for women's equal descriptive representation (Dovi 2007; Mansbridge 1999; Phillips 1995). The assumption, often explicitly qualified, is that the presence of women will lead to "better" representation for women.

If the principle of women's political presence merely demands the presence of biological women, feminist scholarship and activism draw attention to the heterogeneity of women, hence the attention to *which* women are present. Differences of class and race are most emphasized, though sexuality, disability, and age have been part of the Anglo-American debate (Childs and Lovenduski 2012; Mateo Diaz 2005).[1] In different contexts, of course, other identities, such as caste or rural background, can also be identified. Motherhood has hitherto rarely been presented in the feminist literature as a politically salient difference among women that warrants descriptive representation in and of itself. Fiona Mackay (2001) and the late Joanna McKay (2011) are rare exceptions, and we return to these sources later. But how is it that feminists have mostly "missed" the question of the political presence of the mother? Some of the explanation lies precisely in the focus on demand side factors – attention has been less on who the women are in the supply pool (those who will benefit from quotas, as Mackay [2001, 72] writes) and more on what happens to these women when negotiating the processes of legislative recruitment. It also reflects the cultural saturation of the sexual division of labour within Western societies. It is still too easily accepted that women compared with men will have less interest and reduced participation in electoral politics (Mackay 2001, 64) because their continuing and unequal responsibility for child and other care, as well as wider activities in the home, inhibit their presence in the supply pool for politics (Childs 2008; Kenny 2011; Lawless and Fox 2005). As scholars of electoral politics, we are not surprised by and consequently have not given sufficient attention to or been critical of situations in which women talk of delaying entry into formal politics until their children are teenagers or have left home or who talk of their childlessness as a positive status for political participation.

To take the descriptive representation of the mother and the "case" for her political presence more seriously, we revisit accounts of women's political recruitment to see if we can "find" the mother, either explicitly addressed or, as we suspect, lurking in the shadows. We then examine how the mother politician and representations of mothers play out in UK politics. Then we turn to evaluating the case for the political presence of the mother. In so doing, we find ourselves mostly in sympathy with Fiona Mackay's 2001 *Love and Politics: Women Politicians and the Ethics of Care*, in which Mackay argues that including women fully in politics requires that we adjust political institutions to incorporate ethics of care. This approach reminds us that women and men can both be parents and have careers and that any elision of women, motherhood, parenthood, and careers should be illuminated and resisted.

Descriptively Representing the (M)other and the Conflation of Women/Mothers

The story of women's descriptive representation in politics used to be relatively straightforward, pointing to the importance of particular cultural, socio-economic, and political factors. Broadly speaking, higher numbers of women legislators were found in countries that were egalitarian and secular and had experienced women's enfranchisement early. More female MPs were found where women participated in the public sphere more generally, and in the pipeline professions more specifically, and where the society was broadly social democratic. Higher representation was also frequently related to proportional systems of election (with higher district and party magnitude), in which left parties were dominant and women were present in higher levels in political parties. Centralized party selection gender quotas and where the female vote was salient were also positive indicators of women's representation. Over the past decade or so, this story has become more complicated, with multiple paths identified to both high and low levels of women's representation around the world (Dahlerup and Freidenvall 2005; Krook 2010; Paxton and Hughes 2008). International actors and gender quotas are now widely recognized as playing particularly key roles. Thus, the focus is now on the structural features of political institutions rather than on women's wider societal place and activities (Krook 2009, 2010; Paxton, Kunovich, and Hughes 2007).

Norris and Lovenduski's (1995) supply-and-demand model of political recruitment, which has had worldwide reach, remains a key framework for understanding women's representation. It incorporates appreciation of gendered norms and gender relations (Krook 2009, 2010; Kenny 2009, 27), and it recognizes the need to "move beyond the formal process" of selection to analyze the "attitudes, values and priorities of party selectors" (Norris and Lovenduski 1995, 9). Their model also helps us to understand better the descriptive representation of mothers: assumptions about mothers with young children lacking time might well be held by the selectorate (107). Further, when discussing the interaction of marital status, children, and gender, attention is drawn to the fact that marital status might be considered disadvantageous for married women yet advantageous for married men (116), though they find no direct evidence of selectorate discrimination on these grounds (122).

Turning to candidate resources, the negative impact of the gendered division of labour on women and sometimes explicitly mothers plays out in the United Kingdom, not least with respect to finances, especially for working-class candidates (Norris and Lovenduski 1995, Chapter 8). And, on the supply side, access to flexible time (156) and childcare, especially during the month-long formal campaign, is explicitly highlighted (157–58). Children and marital status are found to be particularly negative characteristics for women's participation as candidates in the UK Conservative Party (164). Scholars of gender and politics might then want to think more carefully about how the presence of children affects candidates' chances of selection. Perhaps those who have the means to delegate care for their children (either paid for or given freely by another/others) might find their parental status a positive resource that they can utilize to claim a connection with the "real world"; individuals who benefit from their parental status in this way are likely men more often than women. Parents who struggle to negotiate care or are judged as "carers" by selectorates might find that their parental status negatively affects their chances of selection, and this group will likely contain more women than men. Thus, in welfare states where caring work remains a private function, it is a mistake to treat parenthood as a demographic characteristic that has the same resource implications for women and men (Lewis 1992). In terms of candidate motivation, Norris and Lovenduski (1995, 170–71) found sex to be a predictor of lower levels of candidacy: women thought that they lacked experience, felt unqualified for the job, and were more likely than men to give "slightly higher priority" to their families.

Research Design: The Experience of the (M)other MP in the UK Parliament

According to McKay (2011, 727), the mother in UK politics faces additional burdens: a parliamentary timetable and hours incompatible with *"women MPs with carer responsibilities"* (emphasis added); no maternity leave provision and breastfeeding not yet normalized; a 24/7 work model premised on "out of hours" networking; the necessity of "military planning" and supportive partners or brought-in care; and the burden of representing constituencies some distance from London. "Maternal guilt" is also identified. On the basis of her data, McKay is confident that mothers are less likely to seek selection for Parliament.

In this chapter, we explore how we might incorporate the mother – and indeed the carer – into discussions of representation. We undertook new quantitative data collection and then reanalyzed extant interview data with UK MPs. Until now, there has been no reliable data on the parental status of British MPs. To rectify this gap, we conducted a six-question survey of all British MPs in the spring of 2013. The speaker of the UK House of Commons and the Commons Diversity and Inclusion Unit supported the survey.[2] The number of survey questions was kept to a minimum to encourage MPs to participate, and the survey was advertised in *Commons View* magazine, circulated to parliamentary staff. The six survey items were party, biological sex, number of children, children's dates of birth, MP's date of birth, and year of entry into the House. In total, 210 completed surveys were returned, a healthy response rate of 32 percent. The data set was then "topped up" through public sources such as the parliamentary record

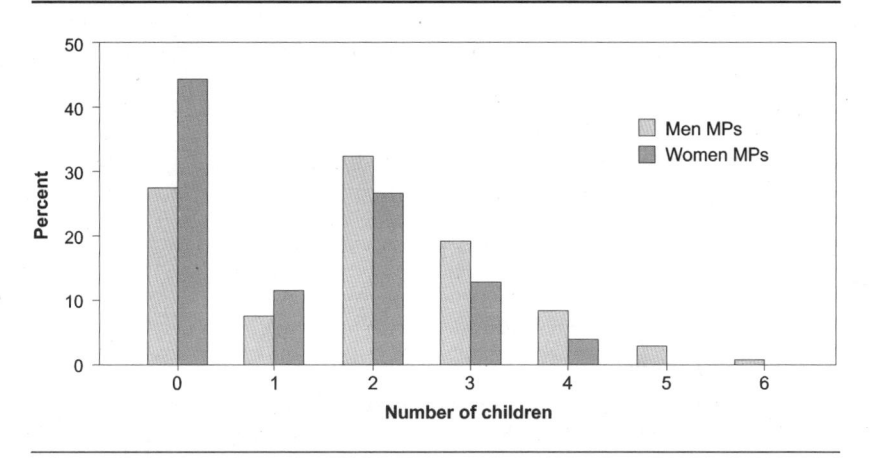

FIGURE 2.1
MPs' average number of children by gender

website and personal webpages. This created a complete data set of 647 MPs for many of our survey items, with the exception of the dates of birth of MPs' oldest children (children's birth dates are rarely recorded in the public domain).

The results demonstrate a staggering difference in the parental status of British men and women MPs. The most striking finding is that some 45 percent of women MPs compared with only 28 percent of men MPs have no children (Figure 2.1). When MPs do have children, on average men MPs have 1.9 children compared with 1.2 for women MPs. There is also a sex difference in the ages of MPs' children: the average age of an MP's eldest child when the MP first entered Parliament is 12 years old for men and 16 years old for women. Compared with the national population, the Office of National Statistics (ONS) found that 20 percent of women born in 1966 remained childless by the age of 45. In our study of MPs, 45 percent of women had no children, more than twice the average among women born in 1966. Furthermore, in 2012, among higher managerial and professional parents, women had 1.65 children on average and men had 1.76 (classified by their own current or most recent job, 2012 ONS Labour Force Survey).

We have, for the first time, clear evidence of a substantial difference in the parental status of UK MPs. Women MPs are much more likely to be childless than men MPs; when they do have children, they have significantly fewer of them; and they enter Parliament when, on average, their children are four years older than those of men MPs. Furthermore, women MPs also have smaller completed family sizes than other professional women. All of this suggests that mothers – not just women – are significantly under-represented. To investigate this further, we turn to qualitative interview data, first from Labour women MPs (gathered in 1997, 2000s, and 2009), to "seek out" the mother in the accounts that these representatives give of political recruitment processes in UK party politics and of working in Parliament (Childs 2004, 2008; Childs and Webb 2012).[3]

New Labour's Women MPs

1997 Data: Supply and Demand
When talking about women's descriptive representation in general terms, Labour's new women MPs emphasized supply explanations to a greater extent than demand (Childs 2004). There was acknowledgment of the difficulties of combining domestic and familial responsibilities. As one put it, "if you've got children, you can't do the things you need to do in the party [to] get to the point of standing for Parliament." When talking about *their own* participation in politics, five women MPs spoke of familial responsibilities more than any other factor as obstacles to their participation. In addition, 12 cited a lack of familial responsibilities as a *resource* that enabled their participation, again the most cited resource. These women MPs either did not carry familial responsibilities or benefited from supportive partners who had equal or primary familial responsibilities. In these findings, then, a differentiation was drawn by women MPs between themselves and "other" women, the latter thought either to lack the supply side resources of women MPs or to experience supply-side obstacles that women MPs did not claim to face.[4]

2000s: All about the Hours
Having been in Parliament for three years, reinterviewed Labour women MPs were clearly unhappy with the "ridiculous"[5] and ineffective/inefficient[6] parliamentary hours, with the 24/7 nature of the job, and with having two places of working and living.[7] It was not only Labour women MPs who were keen on parliamentary reform,[8] but many of them were more vocal about it.[9] Men MPs were more likely to resist change,[10] though there was also some criticism of "establishment" women defenders of the status quo.[11] Employing one's partner/husband as part of the parliamentary or constituency team or

his giving up his job was one means of reconciling work/life and Parliament/constituency,[12] just as men MPs have "wives"[13] "back" in the constituencies looking after their homes.[14] Two women MPs[15] (one with children, the other without children) thought that their relationships with their partners were better for them having moved to the constituencies; at Westminster, the partner felt like a "spare part," and they did not "have a life together while Parliament [wa]s sitting." Another MP agreed that the "other halves feel like strangers" when they go to Parliament,[16] and a third found the House lonely in contrast to her full family life.[17] Two MPs were explicit that ministerial ambitions would need to wait or were not in the cards,[18] another talked of having waited until her kids had grown up before entering full-time politics,[19] and yet another, "looking back," was glad not to have been elected in 1992, as their children would have been younger at that time.[20]

2009 Data: Reflecting on the End of an Era
The 2009 reinterviews with Labour women MPs were undertaken against the backdrop of a parliamentary expenses scandal,[21] which left some of the interviewees despondent about representations of themselves and their colleagues. A number of them focused on restrictive accommodation and travelling allowances for MPs under the new expenses regime.

"*We still don't have maternity leave.*"[22] MPs are self-employed and as such are not covered by statutory maternity leave and pay provisions. Arrangements are ad hoc and subject to parliamentary considerations, not least by the whips.[23] Despite one woman MP suggesting a "real shift" in the acceptance of "moms and dads"[24] – and breastfeeding rooms have been established though "hidden away"[25] (for more discussion on this topic, see Arneil, this volume) – another MP recounted voting in Parliament one day, giving birth the next, and replying to constituents the day after,[26] and she told of one of her colleagues being back in Parliament on whipped business 10 days after giving birth. In her view, a third person could cover much of this work, if not the voting, and she claimed that there is no ministerial protocol to cover a minister's childbearing.

"*We work here, and then we work in the constituency.*"[27] The next question for the MP mother[28] is where to live. This preoccupied a number of the women MPs, who, given preferences among party selectorates for localism, might not have much choice in the matter (Childs and Cowley 2011). The choice to reside in London or in the constituency appeared to reflect the ages of children, though the "n" of MPs with children is low here. Young children are more easily accommodated in London. Having secondary school–aged children at the time of election appeared to be associated with moving the family home into, or near, the constituency.[29] For the MP with a working partner who expected the MP to co-parent, living in London was also thought to be the only workable solution.[30]

The assumption that MPs' families should be based in the constituencies is also linked by women MPs to the supply of women seeking parliamentary candidacy: accommodation schemes underpinned by the assumption that male MPs live a single life in London would lead to women (and some young men) deciding against a parliamentary life when "you cannot have contact with your family" and if the expectation is that "family life will cease."[31] Just one MP suggested that women were emotionally predisposed to be more reluctant to leave their school-aged children. This MP also held that many women would not even find themselves in the supply pool since, when children are very young, women are often "pretty well single parents," "so it never crossed your radar screen to think of being an MP."

There was no sympathy for the model of the MP "*pied à terre.*"[32] Indeed, a return to the era of the male/father MP having his London flat, with his wife and children remaining in the constituency, was much criticized, for it engenders family breakdown and divorce,[33] and accommodations could be in less costly and less safe parts of London.[34] According to one MP, the whole debate about the expenses scandal had been conducted in the terms of "wives":

> There's a default position that MPs are men ... There's been some kind of aberration over the last 12 years that's coming to an end, that somehow we need to get back to where we were, with these MPs being men.[35]
>
> I think most mums would go, well, so where are my kids going to come? ... It might put them off. They might think to themselves, actually, everything I worried about, about being able to combine this with family life, is being reinforced by what they're doing.[36]

For one of her colleagues, the impact could only be negative for women's descriptive representation and for the descriptive representation of those with family responsibilities: "I can see a situation in 10 years on, where there's some kind of enquiry why there are fewer women in Parliament, and fewer people with family responsibilities."[37]

New rules about overnight accommodation and the issue of outer London/nearby constituencies, together with concerns about the payment of family travel between Parliament and the constituencies, also generated critical views: first, of commuting, noting that it would be bearable if normal business hours were kept but not doable given that the House rises late in the evening, with concerns about women's safety late at night;[38] second, of the need to cover the cost of family travel. For an MP on a single income, the cost was thought to be prohibitive.[39]

The next question for the mother MP was childcare.[40] Discussing domestic relations, a number of MPs revealed that their husbands had given up their careers to enable their wives to pursue parliamentary careers and had become the primary caregivers of the children, even if, as one MP maintained, "there wasn't a day" when she wasn't involved in their care.[41] The issue – widely articulated at the time of the interviews – of whether MPs should be able to employ members of their families was raised.[42] The importance of working with husbands and partners, and more generally of the supportive male partner, was strongly articulated.[43] As in other "small businesses," their employment made sense to the women who did so. For one, until her husband became her employee, they "never saw each other," "never talked to each other," and were growing apart.[44]

Seeking a House "more like a normal job of work."[45] The issue of parliamentary hours, and the accompanying parliamentary and constituency workload, dominated much of the discussion of the challenges that MPs had faced since 1997. This was articulated as both an individual issue and a gendered concern, something that new women MPs had failed to change sufficiently (Childs 2008).[46] The MPs' workload was all-consuming, relentless,[47] and physically and mentally exhausting.[48] Family life had become a challenge;[49] arrangements had frequently got "buggered up,"[50] and family life had been "thrown out of the window."[51] Conversely, one MP[52] admitted that she had been able to "use up a considerable amount" of her time precisely because she did not have family responsibilities, except for a "short period" of caring for her parents. One London-based MP whose constituency was outside London, while "more or less" able to take her children to school, only saw them at dinner on Saturday evening, on Sunday afternoon, and when travelling back to London on Sunday evening.[53] On top of that, she was "frazzled" because of the hours and had to "put in a real effort to be nice to them when you do see them"; otherwise, they would "have this idea that their mother was a person who appeared every so often and shrieked her head off at them and then disappeared again." She continued: "And I personally regret that, and I think if I'd known it was going to be like that I'm not sure if I'd [have] taken the job."

It is often said that geography divides MPs – male and female – between those who advocate nine to five and those who advocate a shorter, concentrated parliamentary week with longer hours.[54] Even among those who would not personally benefit, a good number of Labour's 1997 intake of women favoured a "core hours" reform,[55] enabling MPs to decide how to complete their work outside those hours.[56] Business hours would not only be better for women and others with London family lives/caregiving responsibilities but also constitute a good reform:[57] they would turn the House into a more normal place of work; end the uncertainty about when one needed to be present in the House (i.e., provide MPs with greater autonomy);[58] prevent MPs from being "trapped" in the building and having to eat there;[59] enable MPs to get to bed at a "decent hour";[60] help to prevent marital discord/breakdown[61] (one MP lamented that she didn't "get to sleep with [her] husband very often"[62]); reduce patronage powers of the whips to permit absence from a vote[63] (one MP said that she was refused an absence to visit a dying parent and that a colleague could not attend her wedding anniversary dinner[64]); and dilute the macho, workaholic, gentlemen's club, and late-night culture,[65] which one MP illustrated by citing the defence of MP Chris Mullins: "He didn't want the earlier hours because he wanted to assure his wife he wasn't walking the streets of London."[66] And all of this, at least according to one MP, is exacerbated by ministerial responsibilities. She talked of the "sheer brutality" of what happened to family life – an impact that ultimately made her wonder if, having the time again, she would have waited until her children had left home or at least if she would have thought more seriously about whether she wanted "to do it or not." She too noted the role of patronage in protecting some MPs.[67]

"*What kind of women are you pitching for?*"[68] One MP who compared the benefits and costs of being an MP with those of comparably educated and experienced professional women concluded that the other women "probably had a better deal."[69] A colleague speaking in the context of the cost of travelling with her family to and from the constituency on a single MP's income stated that, "if you're trying to work out what to do with your life, and you've got a family, and you're in a position to make some choices, you've got to be clear that you can manage it all."[70] Another talked of spending much of her salary paying for the care of one of her parents – something that would not have been possible without a partner.[71] Another MP added that, if an MP was "stinking rich," the

> whole lot of issues women face will just disappear, because you can afford the childcare, you can perhaps afford two better homes, and you can afford all the things that otherwise make it quite difficult. Hence, if you want women who would otherwise be lawyers, head teachers, deputy–head teachers, ... run a business, ... capable women, ... they've got to see a way to make it work sensible [sic] for themselves and their families ... They can pick their careers, and we've got to make it that some of them will pick politics.[72]

We must, as another put it, be "careful not to end up with ... the very young people for whom their lives are very flexible ... or [the] very old ... My family is grown up, I've got enough money that it doesn't really matter."[73] In such a scenario, Parliament would lose those in the "middle." The professional politician would dominate the House.[74]

Conservative MPs, Male and Female
Interviews with Conservative women and men MPs, and Conservative women ex-MPs now in the Upper Chamber, permit us to compare attitudes by sex and to explore differences that might well be explained by party affiliation. The first observation is the extent to which issues of motherhood, and indeed gender, are evident in responses to interview questions related to women's descriptive representation in the Conservative Party. Here is one illustration:

> When I was first an MP, I didn't really understand all this stuff. And I said, "I can do exactly the same as men can do, I can work all the long hours, I can stay up all night and in an all-night debate." ... I was a perfectly healthy young woman with no children and a husband who could look after himself and was okay. But once you have a child then you're not free to stay up all night and do all-night debates, etc. ... Because men expect women to do things the way men do, they say, oh, she's not very good. She didn't come to this meeting, or she didn't go to that, or she's never damn well in at half past eight in the morning. Well, I'm never in at half past eight in the morning because I'm taking my child to school at

half past eight in the morning, so I don't sit around the tea room having breakfast when they have their little chats ... And, if you don't conform, then you're seen as not being up to the job, and I think that is holding women back.

The team of which I'm a member had an away day ... Now, if you're a well-organized woman with a child, of course you can stay away overnight, but they organized this five days before the party conference. I was taking three days away from my child in the following week for the party conference ... I don't ever want to leave my child for more than three nights. It is also totally unreasonable to drive for three and a half hours and back three and a half hours to meet the same people you could meet in London by walking across the road ... But they simply couldn't see it, they couldn't see it ... And I know that the implication there was "not committed." ... It excluded me from doing the job that I want to do and want to do well because I have a child to look after ... It's when unreasonable demands are made on you for the sake of the way the old boys' network does it. Well, let's go down to the country, chaps, because it'll be awfully nice, and we might get a shoot while we're there ... They have no idea that they were discriminating against me in a big way because I'm a mother ... I tried [to articulate my concerns to them], but I know it was totally falling on deaf ears. They made up their minds that, because I'm a woman and because I'm a mother, well, I'm not really so committed.[75]

Women's underrepresentation as Conservative MPs and ex-MPs is located in both supply-side and demand-side explanations. There was admission of selectorate discrimination by both male and female Conservative MPs,[76] with women selectors being particularly identified.[77] In regard to supply, and like some Labour women, the importance of supportive male partners/husbands was identified by Conservative women, though not by Conservative men.[78] One talked about her "absolutely brilliant" husband.[79] Another asked "how many women in this world who've got husbands who will not mind their wives being an MP?"[80] Yet another considered that husbands will dislike their wives if they undertake such an "all-consuming" and "high-profile job."[81] A colleague feared that even the supportive husband ultimately gives "up in the end."[82] What if one's husband does not agree to move to the constituency, asked another.

The main problem for women's descriptive representation was thought to be mothering.[83] For two men, this was biological, the "natural order of things,"[84] since "men don't get pregnant."[85] A female colleague observed that "not everybody [read women] wants somebody else bringing up your children" (see also Schreiber, this volume).[86] And motherhood (read care by the mother) "coincides" with earning a living and spending time "demonstrating your commitment" in politics.[87] Women, according to one man, "have more sense ... You've got to be pretty darned determined and possibly ... dotty to want to sacrifice all that to come into this bear garden"[88] – with politics accepted as being aggressive, confrontational, and unfeminized by male and female MPs.[89] The latter are said to suffer from maternal guilt, whereas the former are said not to experience paternal guilt.[90] They are, rather, "a little more single-minded," realizing only after the 7 p.m. vote that "they wanted to have some supper," so they might as well go home.[91]

Tension between Parliament and the constituency was again recognized. One MP recounted how, having agreed in her selection to school her children in the constituency, she later moved them to London for a better family life;[92] another recognized that a partner has to agree where the family will live;[93] and a male MP admitted that he'd spent two years away from his family once elected since he'd promised his constituency that he'd move there.[94] Two MPs, male and female, questioned the adequacy of the MP salary. Turning to MPs' workload, one female ex-MP thought that it was much better now – MPs have "more money" and "more time off."[95] Two sitting women MPs claimed that the whips were favourably disposed to requests for time off for school plays and so on,[96] though one female colleague argued that only half the party would engage in such gendered terms.[97] The all-consuming lifestyle and parliamentary hours were identified by Conservative women MPs, like New Labour women MPs, as problematic, especially for young women[98] and women with "obligations to a family."[99] But there was also a sense that Labour women MPs' critique of parliamentary hours was both mistaken and political. A Conservative female ex-MP found their militancy – "I'll work till six, and then I'm off" – unattractive;[100] a male colleague resented those whom he considered "whingers" engaged in a "crusade for womanhood," contending that the earlier committee starting times meant that MPs were unable to take their children to school – they had been "cutting off their noses" to spite their faces.[101]

The apparent solution to women's descriptive representation was said to be the recruitment of older women.[102] This was the experience of three of the interviewed women MPs.[103] Another identified herself as a non-mother.[104]

Such women, in the words of one male MP, are "full of experience" and "now have the time," and they might well benefit from a husband who is thinking of retiring; they will be less "torn."[105] One woman MP perceived that older women are less threatening since they do not make men "edgy."[106] Note that in these discussions, and though there might be recognition of the difficulty of reconciling younger women's lives with Parliament,[107] the solution is for women to wait to participate rather than to reform politics – *the problem is with women and not the party or the House*. Indeed, when one serving woman MP stated that she was not interested in a ministerial position until her children were older, she agreed that women's later entry into Parliament might turn out effectively to leave government to young men.[108]

Problematizing the "(M)other" Frame

The mother clearly has it harder than the non-mother (or men, whether single or fathers) in politics, whether we look at the hard data of their descriptive representation or the reflections of women and men MPs. It would indeed be easy to place the mother in one category and the non-mother in another category requiring political presence. We argue that such a contrast would be mistaken. For one thing, the female non-mother, who lacks direct experience of childbearing, might nonetheless share the experiences of the mother because of society's inability to distinguish between the mother woman and the non-mother woman. In the world of paid work, such reasoning underpins the reluctance to employ a woman of childbearing age in case she becomes pregnant. The same might well be true of politics, with party selectorates judging the non-mother woman as if at some point she will become a mother. On the supply side, the non-mother might not be so disadvantaged, at least not on first appearance. She can be said to be in a position to acquire the necessary supply-side resources of the man (single or father) (e.g., time, political experience, sufficient income), though we might want to temper such optimism given the dimensions of the gendered division of labour premised not on motherhood but on femaleness as well as the additional resources premised on maleness (e.g., networks, presumed leadership characteristics). There is also the risk of dividing women so that the political representation of one group of women becomes a zero-sum game between the recruitment of non-mother women and mothers, though this might be resolved by additional quota, mixed quota, or reserved seats. There is, in any case, an additional concern: If the case for the political presence of women is liable to accusations of essentialism, then how much more true is this for the presence of mothers?[109]

Our biggest concern about making the case for the political presence of mothers *qua* mothers, however, is what it says, or more precisely what it does not say, about fathers, parenthood, and care more generally. Here we find our ideas in agreement with Mackay's *Love and Politics*, published more than a decade ago but in our view underused in subsequent research (our own included). Mackay (2001, 64) makes the important point that women's caregiving responsibilities are not simply a supply-side factor that explains away women's underrepresentation in politics; rather, they are "inextricably linked to men's resistance as political players, as social actors and as partners," and the refusal to recognize care is complicit with construction of the political actor as "unencumbered" and with the design of political institutions (120). Mackay puts this more baldly: "Women and their 'baggage', that is their children, their elderly parents, their homes and their relationships are problematized – rather than the dominant values and existing care blind structures which serve to exclude" (73).

Mackay (2001, 74, 146) is also clear about the risks of assuming that only women have caregiving responsibilities, not wishing to reinforce the idea that male politicians do not have them. Indeed, the fact that men's caregiving needs and responsibilities are met by others is constitutive of their privileged position as unencumbered even as they are blind to this position, "consuming and benefiting from large amounts of care whilst also celebrating their self-sufficiency and denigrating those who carry out care work" (165). Is this not why women are criticized for asking for "special favours" (69)?

Politics as currently set up clearly assume that the representative has no caregiving to do. This is why mothers, and to a lesser extent many women, find participating in politics beyond them. Yet, by adopting the motherhood frame, there is the risk of reconstituting mothers and women politicians (for the non-mother cannot escape the charge) as the only individuals with caregiving responsibilities. This hides childcare work, for the mother has to act like the non-mother to succeed in politics, by outsourcing the care to a partner, paying for the care, or adding it to her already considerable representative responsibilities and thereby jeopardizing the quality of both her representation and her caregiving. The association of the mother representative with care also hides the caregiving of other women representatives who might not be mothers but who still have domestic and other caregiving responsibilities – most likely of elderly parents and partners – as well as men who wish to provide care and participate in politics and thus be similarly excluded from formal politics as currently organized. And it does all this without challenging the "male-politician-norm," leaving the woman as the "female-politician-pretender" (Childs 2004).

Now, a case could be made for the political presence of caregivers as a group, including mothers, fathers, and those caring for other dependants. Again, we hesitate to advocate this approach. And it is here that we take issue with part of Mackay's (2001, 89, 118) analysis. Mackay draws stronger links between descriptive and substantive representation and care, suggesting that women's experiences of care "might give rise to political competencies or political values" (4) and that they constitute grounds for their political presence and bases of their substantive representation. In our view, rather than seeing caregiving as that which only some individuals engage in – something that one group possesses and that therefore requires representation, descriptive and substantive – it is better to see it as an activity rather than a possession. Put crudely, caregiving is a necessary human and societal function, and politics should be restructured to accommodate it fully, making it compatible with representative politics.

Conclusion: Reconfiguring UK Political Life

The 2008–10 UK Speaker's Conference on Parliamentary Representation made some recommendations to reform politics that are useful here since they bear directly on the issue of caregiving:

- establish a formal code of campaigning conduct disallowing reference to family background;
- [reform the] ways in which the House operates;
- parties will draw up maternity, paternity, and caregiving leave provisions;
- establish a crèche (since achieved);
- provide part of MPs' pay as childcare vouchers (since achieved);
- review parliamentary sitting hours (some reforms approved in the summer of 2012);
- draw up and review guidelines to clarify circumstances when a child under one can accompany an MP parent within restricted areas of the House; and
- end strident, hostile, and intrusive reporting of politicians' private lives.

An additional recommendation – the routine publication by parties of candidate diversity data – did not include parenthood as a specific category. A significant additional structural reform, not included in the Speaker's Conference report, would be to permit job sharing for MPs (Campbell and

Childs 2013).[110] Even if there are legal issues that need to be resolved – not least to enable "the representative" to refer to more than a single individual – we see no reason why the job of an MP cannot be shared by two individuals.

In this chapter, we have explored the political representation of the (m)other in the UK Parliament. Mothers are currently underrepresented among MPs. Our data for the 2010 Parliament show that fewer female MPs are mothers compared with male MPs who are fathers and that the mothers present have fewer and older children relative to the fathers present. As shown in the chapters that follow, this pattern is replicated internationally. The interview data illustrate the difficulties of combining parliamentary life with caregiving responsibilities, which disproportionately affect women. Nevertheless, to argue for the political presence of mothers *qua* mothers is too risky, in our view, in regard to both essentialism and the representation of caregiving as a particularly female responsibility. The adoption of gender quotas to enhance women's political presence is a strategy that we advocate, but on their own such quotas will, at best, deliver into Parliament candidates who can successfully participate in its current setup – in other words, those who do not undertake caregiving duties. To incorporate the mother fully into politics demands a reconfiguration of political life to accommodate caregiving. If we wish to challenge the elision of woman, mother, and parent, then politics has to be reconfigured to incorporate the human as a caring being rather than *homo economicus*.

Notes

1. That said, this pattern of female representatives rarely sharing the social backgrounds of women in the electorate also holds for men but is less frequently problematized (Childs and Lovenduski 2012).
2. We would particularly like to thank Anne Foster. Bristol and Birkbeck funded the survey postage.
3. Funded by the Leverhulme Trust and ESRC (Economic and Social Research Council).
4. Interestingly, too, the MPs highlighted party demand in accounting for *their own* selections, tempering their earlier emphasis on supply-side explanations in general.
5. Interview 3.
6. Interviews 18 and 15.
7. Interviews 9, 8, 14, 2, 27, 16, 4, and 25. One MP (interview 4) made it clear that having taken more than a decade to get elected she was not about "to say sorry, I don't like it, I want to go home."
8. Interviews 16 and 5.
9. Interviews 3, 13, 25, 22, and 9.
10. Interviews 27 and 9.

11 Interviews 5 and 9. Naming Betty Boothroyd and Gwyneth Dunwoody.
12 Interviews 8, 13, 7, and 15.
13 Interview 22.
14 Interview 25.
15 Unnumbered interview for anonymity.
16 Interview 16.
17 Unnumbered interview for anonymity. If the partner was "fully consumed" in politics, then she could not see how a relationship would work.
18 Unnumbered interview for anonymity.
19 Unnumbered interview for anonymity.
20 Unnumbered interview for anonymity.
21 The 2009 British expenses scandal resulted from the *Daily Telegraph*'s freedom of information requests to obtain MPs' expense claims. A large number of MPs were sacked or stood down as a result of the revelations. In only a small number of cases had MPs broken the law, most having remained within the letter, if not the spirit, of the regulations. The scandal provoked a huge public response and resulted in the creation of a new expenses regime.
22 Interview 22.
23 Whips are MPs and peers appointed to organize their party's contribution to parliamentary business (see http://www.parliament.uk/about/mps-and-lords/principal/whips/).
24 Interview 22.
25 Interview 25.
26 Interview 7.
27 Interview 20.
28 This would also be true for a caregiving father MP.
29 Unnumbered interview here for anonymity.
30 Interview 2; the example given is of a male MP.
31 Interview 2; see also interview 14.
32 Interviews 8, 11, 30, 31, and 32.
33 Interviews 2 and 13.
34 Interview 12.
35 Interview 11; see also interview 30.
36 Interview 32.
37 Interview 12.
38 Interviews 2, 11, and 31.
39 Interview 20.
40 Again, this would also impact the caregiving father.
41 Interview 7.
42 One MP suggested that rich Conservative Party male MPs could simply stop paying their wives (interview 22).
43 Interviews 13, 15, 22, and 25 in regard to the care of her mother.
44 Interview 2.
45 Interview 2.

46 Interviews 3, 14, 30, and 32. One MP argued that Harriet Harman (the longest-serving woman MP in the House of Commons and an ex-cabinet minister) could have done more, but the "dead hand of the establishment has got hold of her in some way" (interview 14). Another mentioned that those who liked the culture of long hours but were leaving Parliament voted to overturn the New Labour reforms, and yet another thought that those who had pushed for reforms either saw their children grow up or had their partners give up work to care for them (interview 30).
47 Interviews 3, 11, and 15.
48 Interviews 25, 4, 7, 8, 23, 31, and 33.
49 Interview 13.
50 Interview 14.
51 Interview 23.
52 Interview 15.
53 Unnumbered interview for anonymity.
54 Interviews 26, 13, 20, 22, and 31.
55 Interviews 26, 30, 3, 4, 25, and 32. Two interviewees (25 and 15) also made this point in 2000.
56 And, for ministers, red-box-free evenings (interview 4).
57 Interviews 15 and 25.
58 Interviews 15 and 20.
59 Interview 25.
60 Interviews 4, 7, 25, and 32.
61 Interview 26.
62 Interview 7.
63 Interviews 30 and 13.
64 Unnumbered interview for anonymity. Apparently, because other MPs had already been permitted to attend a football match on both occasions, the woman MP had to be present.
65 Interviews 4 and 25.
66 Interview 7. One MP contended that reform should have been framed not as a women's issue but as an issue of the workload and role of an MP (interview 31).
67 Unnumbered interview for anonymity.
68 Interview 20.
69 Interview 2.
70 Unnumbered interview for anonymity.
71 Unnumbered interview for anonymity.
72 Interview 20; this was a sentiment shared almost in the same words by interviewee 22.
73 Interview 32.
74 Interview 33.
75 Interview G.
76 Interviews C, H, K, Q, and T.
77 Interviews U, I, and D.
78 Interviews A, B, D, E, and O.

79 Interview A.
80 Interview O.
81 Interview D; see also interview O.
82 Interview E.
83 Ibid.
84 Interview H.
85 Interview I.
86 Interview B.
87 Interview V.
88 Interview I.
89 Interviews K, E, and O.
90 Interview D.
91 Ibid.
92 Unlettered interview for anonymity.
93 Interview B.
94 Unlettered interview for anonymity.
95 Interview E.
96 Interviews C and D.
97 Interview O.
98 Interviews F and K.
99 Interview K.
100 Interview V.
101 Interview U.
102 Interviews V, P, and K.
103 Unlettered interview for anonymity.
104 Unlettered interview for anonymity.
105 Interview K.
106 Interview C.
107 Interviews K and P.
108 Unlettered interview for anonymity.
109 In both accounts, essentialism might be refuted on the ground of gender and not biology.
110 We see no prima facie reason why ministerial positions cannot similarly be job-shared.

References

Campbell, Rosie, and Sarah Childs. 2013. "Job Share for MPs." http://www.huffingtonpost.co.uk/dr-rosie-campbell/parliament-job-shares-mps_b_2740931.html.

Childs, Sarah. 2004. *New Labour's Women MPs: Women Representing Women*. London: Routledge.

–. 2008. *Women and British Party Politics: Descriptive, Substantive, and Symbolic Representation*. London: Routledge.

Childs, Sarah, and Philip Cowley. 2011. "The Politics of Local Presence: Is There a Case for Descriptive Representation?" *Political Studies* 59 (1): 1–19. http://dx.doi.org/10.1111/j.1467-9248.2010.00846.x.

Childs, Sarah, and Joni Lovenduski. 2012. "Political Representation." In *The Oxford Handbook of Gender and Politics*, edited by Georgina Waylen, Karen Celis, Johanna Kantola, and Laurel Weldon, 489–513. Oxford: Oxford University Press.

Childs, Sarah, and Paul Webb. 2012. *Sex, Gender, and the Conservative Party*. London: Palgrave Macmillan. http://dx.doi.org/10.1057/9780230354227.

Dahlerup, Drude, and Lenita Freidenvall. 2005. "Quotas as a 'Fast Track' to Equal Representation for Women: Why Scandinavia Is No Longer the Model." *International Feminist Journal of Politics* 7 (1): 26–48. http://dx.doi.org/10.1080/14616740420003246 73.

Dovi, Suzanne. 2007. "Theorizing Women's Representation in the United States." *Politics and Gender* 3 (3): 297–319. http://dx.doi.org/10.1017/S1743923X07000281.

Kenny, Meryl. 2009. "Gendering Institutions: The Political Recruitment of Women in Post Devolution Scotland." In *Politics*, Edinburgh Research Archive. https://www.era.lib.ed.ac.uk/handle/1842/4044.

—. 2011. "Gender and Institutions of Political Recruitment." In *Gender and Political Institutions*, edited by Mona Krook and Fiona Mackay, 21–41. Basingstoke, UK: Palgrave Macmillan.

Krook, Mona. 2009. *Quotas for Women in Politics*. New York: Oxford University Press. http://dx.doi.org/10.1093/acprof:oso/9780195375671.001.0001.

—. 2010. "Women's Representation in Parliament: A Qualitative Comparative Analysis." *Political Studies* 58 (6): 886–908.

Lawless, Jennifer, and Richard Fox. 2005. *It Takes a Candidate: Why Women Don't Run for Office*. Cambridge: Cambridge University Press. http://dx.doi.org/10.1017/CBO9780511790898.

Lewis, Jane. 1992. "Gender and the Development of Welfare Regimes." *Journal of European Social Policy* 2 (3): 159–73. http://dx.doi.org/10.1177/095892879200200301.

Mackay, Fiona. 2001. *Love and Politics: Women Politicians and the Ethics of Care*. London: Continuum International Publishing Group.

Mansbridge, Jane. 1999. "Should Blacks Represent Blacks and Women Represent Women? A Contingent 'Yes.'" *Journal of Politics* 61 (3): 628–57. http://dx.doi.org/10.2307/2647821.

Mateo Diaz, Mercedes. 2005. *Representing Women? Female Legislators in West European Parliaments*. Colchester, UK: ECPR Press.

McKay, Joanna. 2011. "Having It All? Women MPs and Motherhood in Germany and the UK." *Parliamentary Affairs* 64 (4): 714–36. http://dx.doi.org/10.1093/pa/gsr001.

Norris, Pippa, and Joni Lovenduski. 1995. *Political Recruitment*. Cambridge: Cambridge University Press.

Paxton, Pamela, and Melanie Hughes. 2008. "Continuous Change, Episodes, and Critical Periods." *Politics and Gender* 4 (2): 233–64.

Paxton, Pamela, Sheri Kunovich, and Melanie Hughes. 2007. "Gender in Politics." *Annual Review of Sociology* 33 (1): 263–84. http://dx.doi.org/10.1146/annurev.soc.33.040406.131651.

Phillips, Anne. 1995. *The Politics of Presence*. Oxford: Oxford University Press.

3

Lactating Mothers in Parliament
Beyond Accommodation

BARBARA ARNEIL

Although there are many kinds of activities that either mothers or fathers can engage in while raising their children, only women, as it stands today, are capable of breastfeeding their babies. For lactating women who are also MPs, the problem of reconciling their professional responsibilities as elected representatives while providing the best start for their children, according to most health-care providers, is unique to them *as mothers*. Breastfeeding as an activity occurring multiple times every day but not yet welcomed in the formal institutions of Parliament illustrates the barriers faced by a specific kind of embodied and gendered parent: namely, the lactating mother. This chapter builds upon the previous chapter, which outlined the lack of mothers in elected politics, by focusing squarely on mothers as politicians and the degree to which formal political institutions accommodate their bodily needs and those of their children in ways that respect how mothers approach the issue.

Breastfeeding and paid work in more general terms can be seen as a contradiction. A large literature shows that reconciling the two is exceptionally challenging, both because broad societal norms create barriers and because, unlike the "public"/scheduled act of paid work, breastfeeding is a "private" activity that cannot easily be scheduled in a predictable way. It is particularly difficult for members of Parliament to reconcile the need to serve their constituents with the need as mothers to care for their infants, for they face several additional barriers, including (1) being elected for a four- to five-year window so that, even if maternity leave is available, MPs think that they should not take it; (2) a formal and ritual-laden "chamber" that creates a more hostile environment for breastfeeding than an informal workplace; (3) division bells and unpredictable times for votes that create particular kinds of conflicts for lactating MPs; and (4) pressure to be role models as public figures for "breast is best."

Building upon this analysis of both general and specific barriers to breastfeeding, I conclude that two things are required if Parliament is to be fully inclusive of lactating mothers. First, a full range of policies is needed to support a diversity of mothers and infants rather than the current reality of piecemeal and/or incomplete supports, including, as will be discussed, daycare facilities, rooms for breastfeeding near the chamber, "pumping" rooms and refrigerators/storage facilities, proxy votes, substitutes for women absent from Parliament, and maternity leave policies. All of these policies must be undergirded by a shift in the culture of Parliament to accept two basic principles: a mother is the best judge of her child's interests, rather than the speaker or other politicians, and there is a fundamental right to breastfeed whenever necessary, including in the Legislative Assembly.

Second, as important as these specific provisions are along with the principles of accommodation underpinning them, ultimately what needs to be challenged and changed are three basic societal norms that continue to create fundamental cultural barriers to breastfeeding: (1) the singular construction of the female breast as sexual; (2) the stringent application of a public/private divide, including attempts to "unencumber" the woman of her "private" role in reproduction while she is in the public sphere of work; and (3) notions of what efficiency and decorum require in the workplace, which in the case of Parliament become the arcane "strangers" rule invoked in all three countries under study (Canada, Australia, and Britain) to justify the ejection of nursing infants from Parliament.

I use case studies from these three countries of female politicians facing official censure for breastfeeding in Parliament since 2000. In each country, Parliament eventually introduced partial or piecemeal policies that failed to address the diversity of women's needs while leaving untouched the norms that led to their exclusion in the first place and continue to exclude the lactating mother from the normal business of the chamber. If the two dimensions of the problem as described above are not addressed – that is, the need for a diverse and encompassing set of policies and a challenge to society's deeper gendered norms around breastfeeding at work – then parliaments will continue to create barriers to women of childbearing age who wish to enter politics and to place inequitable burdens on those already in politics who wish to breastfeed their infants.

Breastfeeding in the House: Three Case Studies

Britain

In April 2000, Julia Drown, the former MP for Swindon, England, asked for clarification from Speaker of the House Betty Boothroyd about whether she could breastfeed her baby during a sitting of a standing committee. The speaker issued a letter stating that the member could not breastfeed on the grounds that "bringing refreshment" into a committee room was not allowed and that "strangers" (anybody other than the committee members and parliamentary officers) were forbidden from being in the House or committees. Within a month, Drown, accompanied by Tessa Jowell (minister for women) and Margaret Hodge (minister for employment and employment opportunities), along with two MPs representing the Conservative and Liberal Democratic Parties, met with the speaker to discuss the issue further (Sear, Miller, and Lourie 2003, 2).

After this meeting, the speaker reiterated her ruling that neither breast- nor bottle-feeding would be allowed in the House or committees. Likely realizing that the original reasoning based upon the strangers rule in Parliament and a prohibition against refreshments in a committee room would sound ridiculous and archaic to the British public, including working mothers, the speaker came up with other reasons that would likely have broader appeal: workplace efficiency and the best interests of the child. "I do not believe that the feeding of babies ... is conducive to the efficient conduct of public business," the speaker claimed. "Nor do I think that the necessary calm environment in which to feed babies can be provided in such circumstances" (quoted in Sear et al. 2003, 2). She concluded that members should use either the ladies' lounge or their private offices to feed infants. Within a week, Julie Morgan, MP for Cardiff North at the time, tabled a motion in the House that breastfeeding should be allowed in standing and select committees, but the speaker held firm (Sear et al. 2003, 2.).

The following year a new speaker, Michael Martin, indicated that he was looking for a compromise solution to the issue. Three motions were then tabled in December 2001. The first, Morgan's motion, supported by 74 MPs, reasserted the right of women to breastfeed in chamber and committee, arguing that "mothers are the best judges of where to feed their babies and that no honourable Members should be prevented from taking part in

Commons business." The second, supported by 75 MPs, deplored "plans to allow breastfeeding in the Chamber" and called for "improved facilities ... to enable breastfeeding to take place in comfort and privacy" (United Kingdom 2001a). The third supported the status quo, arguing that breastfeeding in the House or committees "is neither in the interests of the children themselves, nor the proper conduct of the business of Parliament" (United Kingdom 2001b). By 2002, in response to all three motions, the Commons Administration Committee recommended that the ban on breastfeeding be overturned (Markham 2001; Sear et al. 2003, 3–5). The speaker was expected to implement the recommendations. However, he ultimately ruled that the ban would continue but that additional facilities to allow breastfeeding in private be created in the Parliament buildings (Sear et al. 2003, 3–5; see also Campbell and Childs, this volume).

In 2011, a new member of the House of Lords, Baroness Byrony Worthington, created, according to the right-wing newspaper the *Telegraph* (Kite 2011), "something of a revolution" as the "first Member of the Lords to breastfeed in its precincts" and because she "secured a visitor's pass for her babysitter." When asked if breastfeeding would be allowed in the chamber, the speaker of the House of Lords, Lord Strathclyde, said "I am sure that if there was a request for us to look into this then the relevant committee would examine it with great care and sensitivity." But when the baroness mistakenly assumed that she could bring her baby into the lobby for a vote, she was prevented from entering because of the stranger rule. "I tried to go through the division lobby with him once and the clerks were so nice, they said 'You could always change the law, my lady.'" And though she claimed that "it's all been very positive," she added that "there are no changing facilities and things like that but we manage and I'm sure there will be one day." At the end of the day, she was left to breastfeed her infant in her private office "or in one of the toilets where there is a nice chaise-longue." Despite headlines in the newspapers about a "revolution" in the House of Lords, what happened was in fact a reiteration of the continuing policy to ban lactating mothers and their infants from both the House and committees. This rule remains in place.

Australia

In February 2003, in the Legislative Assembly of Victoria, Australia, newly elected Kirsty Marshall began breastfeeding her baby in the Lower House chamber just before Question Period was to begin. She was asked to leave by the sergeant-at-arms, who cited Standing Order 30, which prohibited "strangers" from being on the floor of the House while it was in session. The reasoning followed that of Betty Boothroyd in the United Kingdom: since the baby was not an elected member of the Legislative Assembly and thus a stranger, he must leave (and his mother with him) (Maddigan 2003). When asked by reporters about her decision to breastfeed in the chamber, she said "I didn't come here to make a statement or to break the rules" (Marshall et al. 2003). Moreover, she made it clear that as an elected member it was her duty to attend, and thus she had refused maternity leave: "It's really important for me that my job, as a Parliamentarian, is the most important thing that I'm here [sic]. I could have taken, you know, six weeks off and relaxed and been at home, but I wanted to be here so much and as long as everything is working well and in balance, I'll continue to do so" (Marshall et al. 2003).

Judy Maddigan, speaker of the legislature at the time, wanted to make it less of a "blokey place" (Marshall et al. 2003) and asked the Procedure Committee to review the standing orders on strangers, specifically to decide whether an exception could be made for nursing mothers (Maddigan 2003, 2). This request produced strong public reactions on both sides, with opinion running strongly against the idea that babies should be allowed in the legislature for the purpose of breastfeeding. A phone poll in a daily newspaper recorded 11,800 callers opposed to breastfeeding in the House and only 2,800 who supported it, and, "by the third day of the saga, the Member's capacity as both mother and Member of Parliament w[as] being questioned in the media" (Maddigan 2003, 4).

When the issue was referred to a committee, the recommendation was to permit breastfeeding in the chamber to highlight the benefits of breastfeeding and to make the legislature more inclusive for women, but it would be allowed at the discretion of the speaker (Maddigan 2003, 5–6). Ultimately, unlike the speaker in the United Kingdom who rejected the recommendations and upheld the ban on breastfeeding in the House and committees, the speaker of the Legislative Assembly of Victoria supported the recommendation to allow women to breastfeed in the House, and the ruling was implemented in May 2003. The issue resonated through other state legislatures and the national Parliament in Australia because, in the process of coming up with its own recommendations, the Victoria legislature canvassed other legislative bodies about their policies on nursing mothers (Maddigan 2003, 4–5).

Whereas the Victoria legislature sought to reconcile working as an MP, including being present in the House for votes or Question Period, with the right to breastfeed in public, specifically in the chamber, several other legislatures separated breastfeeding from the chamber, to be done only in private, or provisions were made to ensure that, should there be a vote, pairing the MP with a member of the opposing party, votes would cancel each other. In other words, keeping (at least) two MPs from voting was deemed to be a "more appropriate direction to take" than facilitating an MP's work by allowing breastfeeding in the legislature (Maddigan 2003, 5). The rationale was that having women breastfeed in private "alleviat[es] the stress on both mother and infant in the Chamber" (Maddigan 2003, 5). The informal "pairing" policy not only prevents MPs from having their votes recorded in the House but also assumes that breastfeeding can only be done in private, in the best interests of both child and mother, even if the MP prefers to be present for the vote and believes that breastfeeding in the House is fine for her infant. The question raised here is whether the mother or the speaker is a better judge of what causes stress for the infant.

This imposed division between private breastfeeding and public chamber was taken further by Robert Doyle, then the Liberal leader of the opposition in Victoria. When asked by the media whether Marshall should be breastfeeding in the chamber, he said that it might be best if she were to absent herself from the chamber altogether and take leave, since in his view doing so would be in the best interests of her child:

> I have no objection to people breastfeeding in their workplace ... I'm not sure that I would want them breastfed during question time, it's not exactly the most relaxing and comfortable of circumstances. So I think the real decision should be what is best for the baby, ... and if that means that we have to allow Kirsty Marshall to be absent, then we're not going to complain about that, I mean we can be reasonable about it; it's a matter of doing what's best for the baby. (Marshall et al. 2003)

It is striking here that Doyle and the speakers of other Australian legislatures assume that they can better assess "what's best for the baby" than the mother herself and that this assessment ought to trump both the mother's opinion and, in this case, Marshall's sense of obligation to be present as an elected member of the legislature.

Shortly after the Marshall decision came down in the Victoria legislature, the Senate and House of Representatives of Australia re-examined their policies on breastfeeding in their respective chambers. The Senate ultimately recommended an exception to the stranger rule that "access to the Chamber floor be allowed in respect of a senator breastfeeding an infant" (Australia

2009). In contrast, the House of Representatives Standing Committee on Procedure framed its analysis through a resolution from all party whips recommending the use of proxy voters (Australia 2007, 4), assuming (again) that breastfeeding is a wholly private activity and that nursing mothers in elected office must have somebody else (a proxy) to represent them in public.[1]

Overall, the Australian cases show that, though the Victoria legislature and the Senate of Australia sought to reconcile lactation with work by allowing women to breastfeed in the chamber, the other state legislatures and the House of Representatives developed policies rooted in the firm separation of parliamentarian and mother into different physical spaces. Furthermore, they justified this separation for breastfeeding members by assuming that they knew better than the mother herself the best interests of her baby. There is no recognition in these policies that, while some women prefer to breastfeed in private and some infants might feed better in a quiet environment, other mothers prefer to be in the House and breastfeed in public, and their infants might care little about what is going on around them.

Canada

In February 2011, a vote was called as Sana Hassainia, an NDP MP, just finished breastfeeding her son in the lobby of the House of Commons. When she could not find her husband, she took the baby into the House. A page asked Hassainia to leave on instructions from the speaker since her baby was a "stranger" and thus forbidden from being in the House. The speaker later said that there had been a misunderstanding, that he had not asked the page to ask her to leave, only that he had asked for those around her, who had been taking pictures, to come to order (Smith 2012). Although there was nothing in the rules about the presence of babies in the House, the speaker was nonetheless quoted as saying that "MPs should try to arrange childcare as best they can" but that, "*in cases of emergency,* babies are allowed" (Hampson 2012; emphasis added). Thus, breastfeeding infants can be present in the House but only in cases of *emergency.* Again, the default assumption is that breastfeeding in public and at work is an extraordinary occurrence and under normal conditions should occur elsewhere.

The public response to Hassainia was hostile. Over 1,000 comments were left on the CBC website in response to a report on the story, with the majority saying, "in the real world, working mothers send their children to daycare," "at $157,000 a year, get a babysitter," "some places are not for children," and so on. Moreover, the ratio of agrees to disagrees for these negative comments ran about 4:1, suggesting that citizens, or at least those who take the time to leave comments, are generally opposed to breastfeeding in the House and have little sympathy for conflicts faced by MPs (CBC News 2012). The oft-repeated suggestion in these comments that Hassainia should stop complaining and hire a babysitter or get daycare misses the central problem that the infant needed not just to be cared for but also to be *breastfed*. This only the mother can do, though bottle-feeding previously pumped breast milk would be possible by somebody else.

Although most working Canadian women can breastfeed their children by taking maternity leave, this option is not available to Canadian MPs. Hassainia did take *unpaid* leave for two months, but her baby still needed to be fed on her return to Parliament. Thus, when she was asked by the media about maternity leave, she responded like Marshall in Australia: "Even if I had the opportunity to take maternity leave, I wouldn't have taken it, because I felt I should be back at work as soon as possible representing my constituents" (quoted in Hampson 2012). In other words, Hassainia took her baby into the House out of an immediate sense of necessity, both as a parent and as an elected representative.

※

Overall, these three mothers were simply trying to serve two sets of responsibilities simultaneously. In so doing, they faced a barrage of media scrutiny of their decisions and questions about their fitness as both mothers and elected politicians. Structural impediments were not held responsible for the conflicts that these women MPs faced; instead, their "choices" and behaviours were characterized as problematic.

These three cases of elected MPs facing censure for breastfeeding in the chamber or committees began with the decision to forbid breastfeeding, but they ultimately led to three different rulings. In all three cases, breastfeeding was initially viewed as irreconcilable with the arcane rules of parliamentary governance, because babies nursing at their mothers' breasts were deemed to be "strangers" in the House. It is deeply ironic that an infant nursing on his or her mother's breast would be deemed a stranger, for one would be hard pressed to find two human beings more intimately involved with each other – the very opposite of strangers. It is also problematic to apply this rule to nursing babies because expulsion of the stranger from the floor of the chamber necessarily requires expulsion of the MP too. Indeed, to ban the baby is to ban the mother. The effect is also to ban nursing mothers from work as elected MPs. In the United Kingdom, breastfeeding was also forbidden because "refreshments" were not allowed in the House or committees. This argument is nearly as odd as the stranger rule, for it puts breast milk in the category of a beverage that might be consumed by someone elected to serve in the chamber or on a committee. Not only is this bizarre, given that the breast milk was intended for the infant in each case, but also it fails to reflect the reality of breastfeeding (i.e., nourishment that infants receive for the first months of their lives).

Despite these similarities, the ultimate ruling in each case was different. In the United Kingdom, there is a complete prohibition of breastfeeding in both Houses of Parliament, coupled with maternity leave and increased facilities for breastfeeding. In Canada, breastfeeding in the House of Commons is allowed only in cases of "emergency," and no maternity leave is offered, nor are additional facilities provided. A general right for MPs to breastfeed exists in Australia alone, where it is restricted to the Victoria legislature and the Senate of Australia at the discretion of the speaker, with women often being encouraged to breastfeed in private with the introduction of proxy or twinned votes. Breastfeeding remains forbidden in other state legislatures and the House of Representatives. The reasons given for forbidding breastfeeding in the cases described above were efficiency/decorum of the chamber and/or what was deemed to be in the best interests of the child. To understand these decisions with respect to MPs breastfeeding at work, especially when the same governments trumpet the idea that "breast is best," we need to examine general norms in society about breastfeeding at work and specific norms in Parliament itself.[2]

General Barriers to Breastfeeding at Work

If we step back from Parliament and examine the larger debate over breastfeeding in public and specifically in the workplace, there is a central and profound contradiction between governments that promote breastfeeding as an unadulterated good that all mothers should view as their first responsibility (even if it is to be done in public) and the numerous barriers and prohibitions to breastfeeding at work. If one takes seriously two realities – (1) some mothers cannot or think that they should not take maternity leave but want their babies to have the benefits of breast milk and (2) nursing babies do not follow a regular schedule, making breastfeeding unpredictable – then it is inevitable that some women will have to breastfeed their infants at work or need to pump their breast milk and have others feed their babies instead. Yet barriers remain to breastfeeding at work, including sexualized norms about the female breast, the public/private divide, the self-contained worker, and the best interests of the child. Each of these norms will be considered in turn.

Breastfeeding in public, including at work, involves a *non-sexual* "display" of women's breasts. This construction appears to be more unsettling to society than the more ubiquitous *sexual* display of women's breasts. Indeed, when breasts are used for non-sexual purposes, they present a direct challenge to the dominant heterosexual male gaze that constitutes them as having a singular, and highly sexualized, meaning. Thus, "social views of the breast as a primarily sexual object" lead directly to "breastfeeding [being viewed] as a suspect activity" (Rodriguez-Garcia and Frazier 1995, 111).

This sexualized norm of women's breasts is key to understanding opposition in Canada to breastfeeding in the workplace (Arneil 2000). Further evidence of this norm is found in the United States, where legislation was required by 29 states to exempt breastfeeding from *indecency laws* (NCSL 2014). But perhaps the strongest response to this norm comes from Britain. There a 2005 European Union film designed to increase voter turnout for parliamentary elections included a glimpse of a breastfeeding woman's nipple, leading the British Cinema Advertising Association to demand that the filmmaker cut the image because it was "too overtly sexual" (Barkham 2004). Alistair Gammell, who produced the film, argued that breastfeeding is "a natural act, not a sexual one," and Julia Drown, the MP banned from breastfeeding in Parliament, called it "a strange decision. If the British are offended by bosoms, why do we have millions thrust in our faces every day by the tabloids?" (quoted in Barkham 2004). It is richly ironic that the clearly sexualized image of the topless page 3 girl is not banned from publication (still online, though excluded, as of January 2015, from the print version of the *Sun*), but a nipple used for breastfeeding in an EU-sponsored film is.

Breastfeeding is also controversial in the workplace because it challenges a fundamental divide between public and private spheres in relation to women in general and mothers in particular. Breastfeeding at work means that the separate roles of employee and mother happen at the same time and in the same place, since the modern workplace is constructed as a formal space where efficiency and decorum reign. Thus, the most common tendency is to insist that it become a fully *private* activity that, to maintain efficiency and order, must be separated physically from the workplace.

In addition, breastfeeding at work is difficult because it violates the norm of the self-contained modern worker fully in control of her time and body. As Mikhail Bakhtin (1993) famously argued in his notion of the grotesque body, capitalist society insists on a body at work that simply does not exceed its limits. Thus, a lactating mother subject to unpredictable natural forces (the letdown of her milk) and not fully in control of her body or time is an object of repulsion since, as Bakhtin notes, bodily fluid of any kind is considered "disgusting" or a transgression of the civil order and market economy. In the most important Canadian case dealing with breastfeeding and work (*Poirier v. British Columbia*), the woman was asked by her employer (the BC government) to stop breastfeeding at lunchtime seminars because several of her colleagues found it "disgusting" (Cox 1997). In short, a breastfeeding woman violates assumed ideals about the self-contained worker.

The final barrier to breastfeeding at work is found in assumptions about what is in the "best interests of the child." Whereas the previous three norms claim that women should not breastfeed at work because it interferes with the efficiency and decorum of the workplace, this norm rests on the assumption that breastfeeding at work is problematic for the child because no infant can nurse properly in a busy and noisy work environment. The more busy or noisy the workplace, the more likely critics will argue that it is not an appropriate place for babies to nurse. Once again, this view supports the idea that the private home or office or ladies' lounge is a better venue than the chamber or committee for the baby. Not only opponents but also supporters of breastfeeding in public argue that mothers should always create quiet environments in which to breastfeed their infants. Thus, for example, both the BC guidelines for *Breastfeeding Healthy Term Infants* (Perinatal Services BC 2012, 10) and the Royal Children's Hospital Melbourne (2010) guide to breastfeeding encourage women to find a "calm quiet environment," while the La Leche League suggests that mothers "nurse in a quiet, darkened room or a place that is free from distractions" (Brussel 2001, 136, 138).

Of course, for many mothers and infants, peace and quiet do make breastfeeding optimal, and provisions should be made for them to breastfeed in such an environment. But this is not true for all infants. One extreme example is provided by Canadian MP Lysane Blanchette-Lamothe, whose infant continued to nurse quietly in the midst of the 2014 shooting in Canada's Parliament buildings (CTV News 2014). The claim that peace and quiet are in the best interests of *all* children seeks to replace the mother's judgment of what is right for her infant with that of her employer.

Thus, the fundamental contradiction between breastfeeding as a universal good and barriers to engaging in it in public and at work is the result of these four underlying norms. Taken together, they help to explain why breastfeeding was initially banned in all three parliaments as noted above.

Specific Barriers to Female MPs

In addition to these general barriers, MPs face specific barriers that make reconciling breastfeeding with work even more challenging. These latter barriers include the short electoral cycle and maternity leave, the formal nature of Parliament, the call to vote, and the pressure as MPs to be role models.

First, electoral cycles are typically between four and five years, thus making maternity leave problematic for MPs. When the tenure of a woman's job is less defined, taking leave for six months to a year can be a plausible option. Mothers can breastfeed during their leave without coming into conflict with their work. But for MPs taking any leave after being elected by constituents to represent their interests for four years is often seen as untenable, both by constituents and by MPs themselves. This does not mean that maternity leave is not generally available to MPs; indeed, 62 percent of parliaments around the world offer the same maternity leave provisions for parliamentarians as those provided to the general public (Palmieri 2011, 93). Instead, the reality is that, even with a formal leave policy, MPs' sense of responsibility to their constituents created by the electoral cycle makes actually taking leave untenable, especially if the MP plans to seek re-election. This is why both Marshall and Hassainia reported that they would not have taken maternity leave. So breastfeeding infants during their first weeks of life while the mother MPs are at work is a reality for them.

Second, the issue of "efficiency" or appropriate decorum in the workplace is attenuated when the workplace is the House of Commons, House of Lords, Senate, or other Legislative Assembly. These spaces are more formal and laden with ritual than the typical workplace. The first and most important indicator is the "stranger" rule used to justify the censure of female MPs for breastfeeding their babies. Very few workplaces have comparable rules about who can or cannot be present, and even fewer would apply them to a nursing infant. Similarly, the rule that "refreshments" are not to be served in some parliaments points to atypical formality and decorum.

Beyond these specific injunctions is an underlying sense among many parliamentarians that it is simply "not proper" for behaviour such as breastfeeding to occur in the hallowed halls of Parliament. As an Australian parliamentary research paper on "Children in the Parliamentary Chambers" notes, "there is a view that parliament is no ordinary workplace, but rather, a formal place for serious work with the sanctity of a church or a court of law" (Australia 2009). Thus, the division between public and formal and private and natural made above is even stronger when the workplace is the Legislative Assembly.

Third, division bells call for votes on short notice and at unpredictable times, leading to situations in which MPs are required to be in the House without much lead time. This was a key issue for MP Hassainia, who took her baby into the House because "I was not in my office at that moment, and there was an unexpected call to vote" (quoted in Hampson 2012). Thus, in a parliamentary system, the unpredictability of both breastfeeding and voting creates even greater potential for conflicting schedules than in other workplaces.

Fourth, MPs face pressure to be important role models for "breast is best" campaigns. Whereas the first three additional barriers that MPs face are unique to their workplace, this fourth barrier reflects the pressure on them to be models for what is in the public interest. This attenuates the contradiction between being "good" MPs at work and being "good" mothers who breastfeed their babies as per their government's public health campaigns. Without the ability to breastfeed at work, MPs who choose other options, such as bottle feeding, open themselves up to censure for failing to demonstrate publicly that breast is best.

Several MPs have noted that, by failing to allow mother MPs to breastfeed, a golden opportunity has been missed. Karen Gillon, a member of the Scottish Parliament, argues "that the most effective way in which the Parliament could promote the issue of breastfeeding would be by not placing barriers in front of members of the Scottish Parliament ... who choose breastfeeding as the best start for their babies and feed them in the Parliament complex" (Scotland 2000). Similarly, in the British House of Commons, the National Childbirth Trust said that the speaker "had wasted an opportunity to set an example to women about breastfeeding" (BBC 2002). Belinda Phipp, chief executive of the National Childbirth Trust, noted that, "as the Commons is an open and public building, this is a rare and wasted opportunity to set an example to women across the UK that breastfeeding is and should be accepted in public places" (BBC 2002).

While advocates of breastfeeding understandably try to use parliamentarians for their campaigns to open up spaces for women in society generally, their argument that MPs should serve as role models for others increases expectations of mother MPs to breastfeed. Thus, when they opt for bottle feeding, they face criticism for failing to be sufficiently good role models to the public even as they choose whether or not to breastfeed in light of all the barriers described above in society generally and their workplace particularly. Again, women should be able to choose what works best for them and their infants, and provisions must be made to ensure that options are available, including storage facilities, pumping equipment, and areas for bottle-feeding infants.

Conclusion: Including Nursing Mothers in Parliament

Ultimately, two things are necessary to allow lactating mothers to reconcile their responsibilities and desires as both MPs and mothers. First is implementation of a full, rather than a partial, range of policies to support the variety of practices among lactating mothers and their infants. Second is to challenge and overturn the norms underpinning barriers to breastfeeding in society and the chamber, as described above. These two recommendations would allow mother MPs who wish to breastfeed to do so without fear of censure or sanction. Let me summarize each in turn.

The case studies presented earlier in this chapter demonstrate that what is typically missing, but desperately needed when designing a policy on nursing MPs, is recognition that the best interests of the child and the mother will vary. This recognition necessitates a diverse set of policies to make parliaments inclusive of all MPs. These policies might start with according MPs the right to maternity leave. But this cannot be the only policy response, nor should it be forced on mother MPs who want to return to work earlier than their leave allows. If they choose to return to work early, then it must be accepted that mothers who want to breastfeed their babies should be able to do so, even if they are working MPs. Thus, MPs must be given the right to breastfeed in all their work environments. This is especially important because they often opt against taking maternity leave out of a sense of responsibility to their constituents to be present in the House and on committees. Division bells only exacerbate the need for the right to breastfeed, given that MPs must be present in the House on short notice and at unpredictable times. Breastfeeding should be a right in the course of business for MPs, not something allowable only in emergencies (Canada) or forbidden altogether (United Kingdom).

Other MPs might prefer not to breastfeed in public, so in addition to the right to breastfeed in Parliament provision must be made for private rooms, ladies' lounges with comfortable chairs, and properly furnished offices to facilitate breastfeeding. In addition, there should be policies that allow pairing or proxy voting to ensure that the MP's voice is recorded in votes of the House even when the MP needs to feed her baby and does not want to do it in the House. Another set of MPs might prefer to bottle-feed or pump breast milk, so onsite childcare and equipment that will facilitate breast pumping, storing, and heating milk or formula are also required. These policies should not be seen as replacements for the right to breastfeed. Instead, they are designed to support the full diversity of nursing mothers' needs. They also reflect the argument that MPs should be able to make decisions about what is in their infants' best interests without feeling any particular burden to be breastfeeding role models.

On their own, these policies are insufficient to fully afford women MPs breastfeeding rights. Indeed, the main legal principle under which the right of breastfeeding at work has been advanced is "accommodation," which requires employers, including parliaments, to accommodate people who might be "different" in various ways in the workplace. Accommodation assumes "an implicit acceptance that social norms should be determined by more powerful groups in society, with manageable concessions being made to those who are 'different'" (Day and Brodsky 1996, 435). Thus, enacting policy only to accommodate nursing mothers accepts pre-existing gendered norms of both the body and the workplace as valid. These norms are predicated on a male body in control of bodily fluids and a schedule in ways that lactating mothers are not (Blum 1993, 295). Thus, policies predicated only on accommodation tend toward "unencumbering" women of their biological reproduction rather than seeking ways to facilitate it. This is reflected in policies insisting that women breastfeed outside the workplace through mandatory leave or that they separate the private role of breastfeeding from the public role of worker or MP by breastfeeding only in private. The most extreme cases predicated on these norms insist that nursing mothers use pumping rooms instead of breastfeeding, since women are then fully in control of their bodies and schedules (Arneil 2000, 364).

Thus, as important as accommodation might be for enacting the full set of policies described above, it leaves unchallenged the societal norms that created the barriers in the first place. Any victory won with respect to the right to breastfeed at work, including in parliaments and legislatures, is but a first step, and perhaps changes in practice and institutional behaviour can pave the way to deeper changes in the norms of society. The ultimate goal must be "to privilege *our* [women's] access to breastfeeding as a sensuous, non-commodified experience of our bodies" (Blum 1993, 297). As a result, the policies required to reconcile breastfeeding with an MP's work demand immediate action and accommodation, but the longer-term goal of fully inclusive parliaments requires that norms constituting the female breast as singularly sexual, asserting a fundamental public/private divide for working mothers because of either repulsion to lactation or decorum/business of the workplace, or assuming the child's best interests can be better determined by somebody other than the lactating mother must be challenged and replaced.

Notes

1 The committee could not come to any agreement on the proxy issue because of the fear that it would set a dangerous precedent for others, but it did recommend three months of maternity leave and increased childcare in the House (Australia 2007, 9). The proxy vote for breastfeeding mothers was eventually reintroduced in 2008 by the Labour government (Australia 2007, 9); however, in September 2015, the Liberal Party's chief whip, Scott Buchholz, ignored the standing order that ensured a proxy vote for lactating mothers and "advised" MP Kelly O'Dwyer "to express more milk for her newborn baby to avoid her breastfeeding interfering with her duties in the parliamentary chamber" (Bourke 2015).
2 For example, a brochure issued by the Australian government's National Health and Medical Research Council argues that "breastfeeding is best." "Giving Your Baby the Best Start," n.d., https://www.nhmrc.gov.au/_files_nhmrc/publications/attachments/n55e_infant_brochure.pdf. Canada's Public Health Agency website states that breastfeeding gives babies "the best possible start in life." "Breastfeeding and Infant Nutrition," 2010, http://www.phac-aspc.gc.ca/hp-ps/dca-dea/stages-etapes/childhood-enfance_0-2/nutrition/index-eng.php. The United Kingdom's National Health Service website similarly features positive video testimony from breastfeeding mothers and lists several reasons why "breastfeeding is the healthiest way to feed your baby." "Why Breastfeed," 2012, http://www.nhs.uk/Conditions/pregnancy-and-baby/Pages/why-breastfeed.aspx#close.

References

Arneil, Barbara. 2000. "The Politics of the Breast." *Canadian Journal of Women and the Law* 12: 345–70.

Australia. House of Representatives. 2007. *Options for Nursing Mothers* [Standing Committee on Procedure]. Canberra: Parliament of the Commonwealth of Australia.

–. Parliament. 2009. *Children in the Parliamentary Chambers*. Research Paper 9, 2009–10, by Mark Rodrigues. Canberra: Politics and Public Administration Section. http://www.aph.gov.au/About_Parliament/Parliamentary_Departments/Parliamentary_Library/pubs/rp/rp0910/10rp09?print=1#_Toc246394478.

Bakhtin, Mikhail. 1993 [1941]. *Rabelais and His World.* Translated by Hélène Iswolsky. Bloomington: Indiana University Press.

Barkham, Patrick. 2004. "British Censors Ban Nipple in European Election Film." *Guardian*, May 22. http://www.theguardian.com/politics/2004/may/22/uk.advertising/print.

BBC News. 2002. "MPs' Breastfeeding Deal." British Broadcasting Corporation, March 8. http://news.bbc.co.uk/2/hi/uk_news/politics/1860947.stm.

Blum, Linda M. 1993. "Mothers, Babies, and Breastfeeding in Late Capitalist America: The Shifting Contexts of Feminist Theory." *Feminist Studies* 19 (2): 290–311. http://dx.doi.org/10.2307/3178367.

Bourke, Latika. 2015. "Liberal MP and New Mum Kelly O'Dwyer Told to Express More Breast Milk to Avoid Missing Votes in Chamber." *Sydney Morning Herald*, September 17.

Brussel, Carol. 2001. "When a Baby Won't Nurse." *New Beginnings* 18: 136–38. http://www.llli.org/nb/nbjulaug01p136.html.

CBC News. 2012. "MP Says Her Baby Was Kicked Out of House." CBC News, February 8. http://www.cbc.ca/news/politics/story/2012/02/08/mp-baby-house-removed.html.

Cox, Wendy. 1997. "BC Woman Seeks Tribunal Ruling to Breastfeed at Office." *Globe and Mail*, March 18, A8.

CTV News. 2014. "Hidden in Alcove, MP's Nursing Infant Stayed Quiet during Shooting." CTV News, October 23. http://www.ctvnews.ca/canada/hidden-in-alcove-mp-s-nursing-infant-stayed-quiet-during-shooting-chaos-1.2067885.

Day, Shelagh, and Gwen Brodsky. 1996. "The Duty to Accommodate: Who Will Benefit?" *Canadian Bar Review* 75: 433–73.

Hampson, Sarah. 2012. "Baby in the House: Why MP Sana Hassainia Doesn't Plan to Do It Again." *Globe and Mail*, February 20. http://www.theglobeandmail.com/life/relationships/baby-in-the-house-why-mp-sana-hassainia-doesnt-plan-to-do-it-again/article547589/.

Kite, Melissa. 2011. "Breastfeeding Baroness Launches Quiet Modernisation of House of Lords." *Telegraph*, May 22. http://www.telegraph.co.uk/news/politics/8527850/Breastfeeding-baroness-launches-quiet-modernisation-of-House-of-Lords.html.

Maddigan, Judy. 2003. "A (Little) Stranger in the House – Breastfeeding in Australian Parliaments." Paper presented by Judy Maddigan, Speaker of the Legislative Assembly, Victoria, Australia.

Markham, Peter. 2001. "Breastfeeding Ban Lifted in the House." *Daily Mail*, December 3, 21. http://www.dailymail.co.uk/news/article-87454/Breastfeeding-ban-lifted-House.html.

Marshall, Kirsty, Robert Doyle, Prue Goward, and Judy Maddigan. 2003. "Victorian MP and Baby Ejected from House." Interview with Ben Knight. *PM*, ABC Local Radio, February 26. http://www.abc.net.au/pm/stories/s793397.htm.

National Conference of State Legislatures (NCSL). 2014. "Breastfeeding State Laws." http://www.ncsl.org/issues-research/health/breastfeeding-state-laws.aspx.

Palmieri, Sandra. 2011. "Gender-Sensitive Parliaments: A Global Review of Best Practices." Geneva: Inter-Parliamentary Union.

Perinatal Services BC. 2012. *Breastfeeding Healthy Term Infants*. Vancouver: Perinatal Services BC.

Rodriguez-Garcia, R., and Linda Frazier. 1995. "Cultural Paradoxes Relating to Sexuality and Breastfeeding." *Journal of Human Lactation* 11 (2): 111–15. http://dx.doi.org/10.1177/089033449501100215.

Royal Children's Hospital Melbourne. 2010. "Cleft Lip and Palate Infant Feeding." http://www.rch.org.au/kidsinfo/fact_sheets/Cleft_lip_and_palate_infant_feeding/.

Scotland. Parliament. 2000. *Official Report, Plenary, 18 May 2000*. Edinburgh: Parliament of Scotland. http://www.scottish.parliament.uk/parliamentarybusiness/28862.aspx?r=4234&mode=html#iob_27971.

Sear, Chris, Vaughne Miller, and Julie Lourie. 2003. *Breastfeeding in Parliament*. SN/PC/508. London: House of Commons Library.

Smith, Joanna. 2012. "MP and Her Baby Welcome Back in Commons after 'Misunderstanding.'" *Toronto Star*, February 8. http://www.thestar.com/news/canada/2012/02/08/mp_and_her_baby_welcome_back_in_commons_after_misunderstanding.html.

United Kingdom. Parliament. 2001a. *Early Day Motion 520 (EDM-520)*. London: Parliament of the United Kingdom. http://www.parliament.uk/edm/print/2001-02/520.

—. 2001b. *Early Day Motion 522 (EDM-522)*. London: Parliament of the United Kingdom. http://www.parliament.uk/edm/print/2001-02/522.

4

Motherhood and Politics in Latin America
Continuity and Change

SUSAN FRANCESCHET, JENNIFER M. PISCOPO, and GWYNN THOMAS

How does maternalism shape Latin American politics today? In Latin America, the ideology of maternalism – the idealization of women's familial roles and caretaking abilities – historically structured women's access to office. Maternalism celebrates mothering and motherhood, framing all women (whether parents or not) in terms of their ability to nurture and care for others. Existing gender scholarship on Latin America, whether in history, sociology, or political science, has emphasized how maternalism has shaped women's political activism and electoral participation, creating both structural constraints and opportunities for women engaged in politics. The opportunities especially contrast with the limitations that mothers in elected politics have faced in the Westminster parliaments discussed in the previous two chapters. In Latin America, women in earlier decades used maternalism to pursue and justify their political careers, positioning themselves as national caretakers – Elsa Chaney's "super-madres" (1979) – or crusaders for democratization and national well-being – Sonia Alvarez's "militant mothers" (1990). In this chapter, we ask whether such frames and justifications still hold in contemporary Latin America.

Are female politicians still viewed as caretakers of larger national families? Does motherhood continue to structure women's access to politics or their behaviour in office? Does maternalism continue to shape the public policies designed to increase women's political participation and equality? Here we examine how today's politically active women navigate both the symbolic and the material effects of maternalism in their lives. We use the terms "maternalism" and "motherhood" interchangeably throughout the chapter to signal the cultural ideologies that ascribe to women the morally superior qualities of selflessness, nurturing, and caring, which govern how they rear their own children as well as how they serve communities and nations. Although such ideologies are not unique to Latin America, the region's history of civil conflict, authoritarianism, and redemocratization has interacted with maternalism in specific ways.

We argue that the intersection of motherhood and politics in Latin America today shows dimensions of both change and continuity, infusing women's political practice in more complex ways than in earlier periods. Change appears in the ideas that govern how and when women participate in formal politics: Latin American women no longer need to justify entering elected office as an extension of their mothering roles. Although female politicians do view their motivations and policy preferences in gendered terms, these frames are more varied than straightforward maternal appeals to women's "natural" caretaking skills. Continuity, however, appears in the way that motherhood erects structural barriers for female politicians. Ideas about women in public office have changed, but societal expectations that they "should" be mothers and thus caretakers have not shifted as dramatically. Fulfilling these expectations creates structural barriers for women who seek political careers (or any professional careers), and these obstacles are reinforced by public policies that leave this gendered division of labour unquestioned.

To explore the mixing of motherhood and politics, we draw on published research from across the region and on original interviews conducted with legislators in Argentina, Chile, Costa Rica, and Mexico. In the first section, we present the historical evolution of the connections between maternalism and politics in Latin America through the era of democratization that began in the 1980s. In the second section, we focus on how motherhood shapes formal politics today by examining how society positions women, and how women position themselves, as political leaders. Here we emphasize the dimensions of change for maternalism and justifications for women's political careers: democracy has strengthened discourses of women's equality and rights, though society continues to associate women's politics with gendered norms of caretaking and attention to social issues. We also argue that women's political opportunities remain profoundly shaped by the gendered division of labour. The assignment of domestic and childcare responsibility to women remains a powerful cultural norm. We further demonstrate this continuity by showing how public policies reinforce this norm through the assumption that mothers are the primary caretakers in the home. We conclude the chapter by tying these two sections together, noting that, while ideational change has expanded women's opportunities for political activism and electoral politics, women still struggle with structural problems.

Maternalism in Latin America: Then and Now
Definitions of motherhood are socially produced in the intersection of the biological ability to conceive a child and the social expectations around caring for children. Definitions of motherhood, fatherhood, and parenthood are influenced by gender and other powerful social hierarchies, including class, race, and ethnicity. Thus, definitions of motherhood, fatherhood, and family are inherently political sites where both power and privilege are reproduced and contested.

For example, throughout colonial and modern Latin America, familial metaphors helped to legitimate political power. In the colonial era, the political ideology of patriarchalism justified a ruler's power over his subjects by appealing to the seeming naturalness of men's authority over families and of elite men's authority over extended households. In the early 19th century, Latin America's newly independent and liberal states rejected the tenets of patriarchalism that justified the public rule of a distant monarch over adult, propertied men but preserved notions naturalizing men's private patriarchal control over women, children, and other dependants in the household (Dore 2000; Thomas 2011a). As feminist critics have signalled, liberalism's theory of men's political equality was built upon the private inequality of women (Pateman 1988). A hallmark of Latin America in the 19th century and early 20th century was an elite belief that political stability and economic prosperity depended on the strength of upper-class families. This ideology supported the political and social power of elite patriarchs while limiting political participation by all women (and poor, working-class, and Indigenous men) (Dore 2000).

Nonetheless, elite and middle-class women argued for expanded public roles by appealing to "republican motherhood": that is, women's roles as bearers and nurturers of future citizens justified their access to educational and economic opportunities (Lavrín 1995). Consequently, maternalism had a profound impact on the first wave of the women's movement in Latin America. Feminists in the early 20th century turned to women's familial roles to justify legal rights (granting married women control over their children, property, and wages as well as labour protection) and social rights (increasing women's educational opportunities and improving women's maternal health). Suffrage activists argued for women's citizenship by connecting the civic duty of voting to women's roles as wives and mothers (Lavrín 1995).

Yet maternalism did not just provide reformers with a strategic discourse: throughout the 20th century, politically active women also understood their participation through these norms. In Chaney's path-breaking study of women and politics in Chile and Peru in the 1960s, she used the term *supermadre* ("super-mother") to capture how women understood and justified their entry into public office as an extension of their caregiving roles in the family. Summarizing her interviews, Chaney (1979, 5) noted that "the female public official often is forced to legitimize her role as that of a mother in the larger 'house' of the municipality or even the nation, a kind of *supermadre*. The command echelons however are reserved for men." Chaney also found that "women overwhelmingly agreed to a division of labour in the polity that parallels the traditional, unequal roles of men and women in the family. Both men and women believe that women should participate in politics, but in a style that reflects 'the political institution of the divisions of tasks in the family'" (21).

Chaney's work sparked 30 years of research on the relationship between Latin American women's political participation and their maternal roles. This connection was most thoroughly explored in the context of Latin America's pro-democracy movements, which began in the 1970s and 1980s. Authoritarian regimes shut down traditional spaces of political participation, but women were able to enter politics by extending their private caregiving roles into the public. They launched and participated in human rights movements that shamed military governments for destroying families, most famously in the case of the Mothers of the Plaza de Mayo in Argentina. By mobilizing as mothers, women exposed the hypocrisy of a national security ideology that claimed to protect both the nation and the family (Taylor 1997; Thomas 2011a). Maternal justifications also underscored women's involvement in the popular movements dedicated to improving access to basic resources and the feminist movements seeking more radical changes to women's status (Alvarez 1990; Jaquette 1994). Essentially, women used their maternal identities, ostensibly apolitical, to mobilize publicly and make policy demands. This framing of women's leftist activism as an extension of their caregiving roles became known as "militant motherhood" (Alvarez 1990).

However, right-wing and conservative women have also justified political action through maternalist discourses. For instance, drawing on their roles as homemakers, right-wing women in Chile organized the March of the Empty Pots, a large-scale protest against the elected socialist government of Salvador Allende (Baldez 2002; Power 2002). In Nicaragua, women organized against the left-wing Sandinista government during its armed struggle with the right-wing Contras, particularly protesting the Sandinista draft (Bayard de Volo 2001). On both the left and the right, activists used maternalism to emphasize women's political activism as a response to crises brought about by government neglect or failure. This framing consequently implied that the return to normal politics – typically democratic politics – would allow women to return to their apolitical roles as mothers (Franceschet 2005). Yet many of these women did not return to their private roles. Instead, they sought elected positions in the new and emerging democracies.[1]

Nonetheless, the region's fledgling democracies were not immediately welcoming to women who sought public office. The return to electoral politics meant the return of male political actors, who often did not want to share political power with women despite their centrality to the pro-democracy movements. Even by 2000, when all Latin American countries were democratically governed, women comprised only 12.6 percent of the region's lower or unicameral legislatures.[2] By January 2014, however, their representation had climbed to 23 percent, placing the region below the Nordic countries but on par with those of Europe (Htun and Piscopo 2014).

Women's recent electoral gains are largely explained by the adoption of gender quota laws, driven by concerted action by women demanding greater access to elected positions (Htun and Piscopo 2014). Quotas require political parties to nominate a specified percentage of female candidates, typically between 20 and 50 percent. Quotas have been highly successful in some countries: in 2015, women comprised 53 percent of the legislature in Bolivia, 42 percent of the legislatures in Ecuador and Mexico, and more than 30 percent of the legislatures in Costa Rica and Argentina. However, their legislative representation is much lower in countries with poorly designed quotas (e.g., Brazil and Paraguay) or no quotas (e.g., Chile).[3] Gender quotas have largely been adopted using discourses of women's equality. Although supporters sometimes used maternalist arguments to support gender quotas, positioning women as agents of change whose superior morality would make politics less corrupt and more responsive to marginalized constituents (Marx, Borner, and Caminotti 2007), more common were arguments based upon the centrality of gender equality to modernity and thus democracy (Krook 2009; Towns 2010).

Moreover, women have been elected as chief executives in many of the most powerful and developed countries in Latin America, including Chile (Michelle Bachelet, 2006–10 and 2014–18), Argentina (Cristina Fernández de Kirchner, 2007–11 and 2011–15), Costa Rica (Laura Chinchilla, 2010–14), and Brazil (Dilma Rouseff, 2011–15 and 2015–16). In a notable shift, these female presidents did not enter politics to rescue their respective countries, nor do they come from political dynasties or represent traditional, idealized images of motherhood. Fernández de Kirchner followed her husband into the Argentine presidential mansion, but she had developed her own political career as a multi-term senator. Most spectacularly, Bachelet is divorced and has a third child from a long-term relationship outside marriage. Latin America as a region has led the way in electing powerful women presidents, surpassing all other areas of the world.

Democracy in Latin America has thus emphasized gender equality over gender difference, mixing new opportunities with old legacies. On the one hand, motherhood remains culturally important throughout the region, as evidenced by recent public opinion data (Franceschet, Piscopo, and Thomas 2016; Piscopo 2011) and by female activists who protest the harm of neoliberalism to families (Eltantawy 2008). On the other hand, democratic Latin America has improved women's legal status in family law, adopted laws to eradicate gender-based violence, and promoted equality throughout society and the workforce (Htun and Piscopo 2014). The adoption of gender quota laws and women's electoral gains demonstrate that women now seek political careers across government branches.

Changing Ideas about Motherhood and Formal Politics

Given that democratization has involved both continuity and change in the intersection between motherhood and politics, female politicians in Latin America are continually reformulating this relationship. Women in elected office no longer need to frame their public roles in exclusively maternal terms, but gender remains a powerful referent for politically active women in Latin America today (as elsewhere). We find that women in congress, who spend their time proposing, deliberating, and voting on legislative initiatives, draw on gendered (though not necessarily on maternal) experiences in their day-to-day policymaking work and that gender norms still shape which policy issues they represent. Motherhood exerts more direct influence over women who seek and occupy the pinnacle of political power – the presidency – since these female politicians must navigate the public's gendered expectations about women's appropriate behaviour in a much more visible way.

Maternalism and Executive Office
Maternalist ideologies have arguably left their deepest imprint in the presidential mansions of Latin America. The first Latin American woman *elected* to a presidency was Violeta Chamorro. In 1990, following a civil war in Nicaragua, she defeated Daniel Ortega, who represented the socialist Sandinista government. Chamorro claimed that her maternal identity drove her into politics since she was responding to the extraordinary circumstances presented by the ongoing civil war. Her campaign drew on the image of her family, especially her husband, Pedro Joaquín Chamorro, martyred by the brutal Somoza dictatorship overthrown by the Sandinistas. She argued that her identity as a traditional Nicaraguan mother (apolitical, self-abnegating) gave her the skills needed to lead Nicaragua. As a mother, Chamorro argued that she offered Nicaraguans the best hope for peace and political reconciliation; she famously campaigned all in white and drew on the imagery of the Virgin Mary. Thus, her campaign was based upon the symbols of "wife, widow, mother, and virgin" (Kampwirth 1996, 72). In leveraging maternalism to legitimate her presidential bid, her self-presentation constituted a textbook example of the Latin American *supermadre*.

This overt maternalism, however, has been absent from the campaigns of recent female presidents. Michelle Bachelet's 2006 presidential bid is particularly instructive. Bachelet stands out among women executive leaders in terms of her vocal commitment to gender equality and her willingness to confront sexism in Chilean politics (Franceschet and Thomas 2010). As a candidate, she explicitly challenged the masculinist bias in expectations about political leadership. In one television spot, Bachelet argued that "strength knows no gender, and neither does honesty, conviction or ability. I bring a different kind of leadership, with the perspective of someone who looks at things from a different angle. Let us change our mentality; when all is said and done, a woman president is simply a head of government who doesn't wear a tie" (quoted in Thomas 2011b, 76).

Bachelet did invoke motherhood, however, to create a connection with everyday citizens. She argued that her identity as a single mother gave her insight into the everyday lives, concerns, and struggles of Chileans, especially women. Thus, she sought to highlight the political relevance of the everyday caring roles and responsibilities of all Chileans. She balanced her portrayal of her "feminine leadership" with her educational achievements (a medical doctor fluent in five languages) and her past political experience, particularly as minister of defence (Franceschet and Thomas 2010; Thomas 2011b). Josefina Vázquez, in her unsuccessful bid for the Mexican presidency in 2012, similarly drew on expectations about motherhood and politicians. In a well-known interview, she positioned herself as follows: "I am a woman, I am a housewife, I am a government official, I've been twice a government secretary, I've been leader of a parliamentary group, I am an economist ... Every night we [women] return to the kitchen to check the refrigerator and see if everything is ready or what needs to be bought the next day" (quoted in Archibold 2012). Bachelet and Vazquez saw both their maternal identities and their professional expertise as drawing them closer to their constituents.

Yet female candidates' nuanced use of maternalism has not always been reflected in how others – notably the media and the political establishment – respond to their candidacies or their leadership once in office. In Brazil, for example, Dilma Rousseff enjoyed a reputation as an unyielding negotiator and a highly competent technocrat, yet outgoing President Luiz Inácio "Lula" da Silva referred to her as the "mother of Brazil" (quoted in Cruz Pires 2011). In Chile, the media also positioned Bachelet as "the mother of the nation," and some political commentators even speculated that her high approval ratings resulted not from her political or policy successes but from the *cariñocracia* ("caring-ocracy") created by her personal likeability and Chileans' emotional connection to her presidency (Navia 2009). This critique of Bachelet, promoted by political pundits and opposition politicians, exemplified a pattern of attacks claiming that she lacked strong and decisive leadership (Valdés 2010). Notably, Bachelet ended her first presidential term with historically high approval ratings. Critiques of her leadership disappeared in the 2013 presidential contest when Bachelet, again the clear front-runner, defeated the conservative female candidate, Evelyn Matthei.

Although women can clearly win presidencies in Latin America, they must continually balance the cultural importance of maternalism with the masculine construction of the office. In Brazil, Rousseff's first campaign complemented her assertiveness (a culturally masculine trait) with her compassion (a culturally feminine trait): when her grandchild was born during the campaign, strategists used the birth to soften her image and reduce the negative, gendered perceptions of her tough persona.[4] Similarly, Cristina Fernández de Kirchner ran two successful campaigns in Argentina based upon her assertive character and her policy record, which included the deliberate eschewing of women's issues. Yet Fernández also displayed an exaggerated femininity in her personal appearance, with her dress, hairstyles, and vocal inflections evoking the great Argentine icon Evita Perón, who had mastered maternalist politics by positioning all Argentines as the children whom she had never had. Laura Chinchilla, the successful presidential candidate in Costa Rica, also used gendered appeals to moderate the toughness associated with her party's neoliberal economic policies. For instance, she publicly displayed "tears of sorrow" after making campaign stops in impoverished communities.[5] In Peru, presidential candidate Keiko Fujimori highlighted her qualifications by drawing analogies between running countries and running households.[6]

Consequently, women who seek executive office in Latin America face some of the same challenges as their counterparts outside the region (Murray 2010): they confront gender bias in the media, and they must prove that they can take on the tough job of the presidency while remaining essentially feminine. Latin American executives thus publicly display their maternal qualities to demonstrate their credentials and win votes. Although Bachelet most explicitly challenged the implicit masculine criteria of the presidency, no female president or presidential candidate has escaped the gendered dimensions of the office. Irrespective of whether female politicians' demonstrations of femininity are strategic or genuine, the politicians and their advisers clearly recognize the continuing cultural power of appeals to maternalism specifically and traditional gender roles generally. The tight linkage between maternalism and politics found in the ideals of the "supermother" and "militant mother" has weakened, but female executives must still demonstrate their caring and nurturing abilities. Gendered beliefs about the importance of women's roles as mothers and caregivers still influence the broader political context in which women compete for political office (Thomas 2011b; Thomas and Reyes-Housholder 2015).

Gender Norms and Legislative Office

Although national legislators usually receive less media attention than executives, women in congress must also confront tensions among gender norms, maternalism, and political priorities. Like their presidential counterparts, female legislators – also largely drawn from the upper or upper-middle classes – recognize the political power and salience of ideas about gender difference. Interviews with legislators reveal that gender norms influence women's policy preferences and day-to-day legislative work.

For example, many women legislators do not mention classically maternal notions of caregiving but still invoke women's socially minded perspectives. A Chilean deputy said that women have "a perception of politics that is more in service of the population, it has to do with the common good," and compared with men, who are more partisan, women in congress can work more easily with women from other parties.[7] Another said that "women have more contact with the real world, with the situation that happens within the family."[8] Similarly, female legislators in Mexico believed that "women have a unique vision of endurance and suffering ... It is women's overall vision"; moreover, "women are closer to the people and have policies focused on society."[9] For example, an Argentine legislator described her role on the finance committee as follows: "For me, the economy is about society, and I represent society. I am not only concerned with whether the numbers balance or not but about the social implication ... The other men that work on the economy do not have this social vision."[10] Unlike their predecessors, these female politicians were not justifying their political participation or policy influence via their maternal roles, but they were claiming a broader feminine perspective that emerged from their gendered experiences.

These feminine perspectives translate into distinct policy perspectives, with many interviewees reporting that female legislators specialize in social policies generally and gender equality specifically. For instance, a Mexican senator explained that "women have a more sensitive vision on questions related to women, children, the elderly, and other matters of well-being."[11] An Argentine legislative analyst concurred, noting that "male legislators are colder on social themes; they do not think about the social fabric."[12] One Argentine deputy believed that these perspectives were not just supplied "naturally" by gender identity or socialization but expected of female office-holders by their constituents and peers: "Women have a *doble cargo* ['double duty']: they must know every policy area that men know, and they must know women's issues too."[13] Thus, though women might no longer be required to mother the nation, they are still expected to care for the disadvantaged and to champion women's issues, expectations not placed equally on men.

Empirical studies support these comments, with researchers consistently finding that female legislators in Latin America dedicate more time than male legislators to social policies and gender policies (Jones 1997; Piscopo 2014a; Schwindt-Bayer 2010; Taylor-Robinson and Heath 2003). Whether by choice or because of gendered expectations, female legislators hold more seats than male legislators on committees related to women, families, and social issues such as health or education, and fewer seats on political and economic committees (Heath, Schwindt-Bayer, and Taylor-Robinson 2005). Similarly, female legislators are more active than their male colleagues in authoring bills focused on women's rights, issues involving children and families, and social issues (Miguel 2012; Piscopo 2014a). In Argentina, for example, between 1989 and 2007 women introduced 80 percent of all bills to legalize abortion and expand access to contraception, 69 percent of all bills improving women's protection from domestic violence, and 73 percent of all bills addressing sexual harassment in the workplace (Franceschet and Piscopo 2008, 410). The gendered policy concentrations of female legislators in Latin America parallel evidence from other regions, including the global North (Catalano 2009; Celis 2006; Swers 2014) and the global South (Devlin and Elgie 2008; Walsh 2012; Yoon 2011).[14]

Latin American interviewees especially highlighted issues related to women, children, and families as critical to their agendas. A Chilean deputy said that "it has been us women who have been more concerned with themes like family violence, family support payments. Protecting children and addressing violence are precisely the themes that matter to women."[15] Indeed, female legislators in Chile were the initiators and key supporters of current laws on sexual harassment and domestic violence.[16] Similarly, Mexican female legislators have been critical in pushing for quota reforms and other measures that protect women's political rights (Piscopo 2016). Women deputies and senators in Argentina pushed through the nation's landmark bill that made contraception free and universal (Piscopo 2014b).

Although female legislators' policy preferences do support arguments that women's presence is necessary for promoting women's interests, female legislators' concentration in women's issues and social issues has certain drawbacks. Gender equality and social policies continue to be less prestigious and less visible than policies related to the economy or "high politics," reinforcing women's marginalization in politics (Miguel 2012; Schwindt-Bayer 2010). Women legislators in Latin America – like their counterparts elsewhere in the world – must confront the gendered hierarchies within politics that place less value on women and the issues associated with them.

Continuing Challenges: Motherhood and Gendered Labour

The relationship between maternalism and women's political action has been redefined by a new generation of female executives and legislators who have found alternative ways of framing their political participation and expressing their policy preferences. Women can use discourses on gender equality to challenge the limitations of maternalism in politics and policy. Yet changing ideas have not eliminated the structural barriers that motherhood poses for the political careers of women in Latin America and throughout the world. These structural barriers work in two ways. First, the cultural value of motherhood and the gendered division of labour have practical, day-to-day implications: individual female politicians face numerous obstacles balancing the demands of a political career with the expectations about women's appropriate roles and behaviour. Second, cultural values and gender roles are reinscribed at the macrolevel in public policies that continue to reflect maternalist norms and maintain women's greater responsibility for taking care of their families.

Barriers at the Individual Level

As is the case elsewhere, women politicians across Latin America often report great difficulty in reconciling the demands of their roles as both mothers and politicians. Politically active women in Chile routinely blame the enormous challenges of reconciling family life with a political career when explaining women's relative absence from congress (Franceschet 2005). Female legislators in Argentina share this perspective. For example, an Argentine deputy from a right-leaning party described the problem of business hours: her delegation met during the evening, which interfered with her childcare. "I tried to convince them to change the hours of the meetings, and they stopped respecting me ... In the end, I had to tell them that I might not always be there."[17] A socialist deputy also noted that "the rules of the chamber assume that the deputies can engage in politics 24 hours a day; it is a norm set up for men."[18] Another Argentine deputy went further, speculating that her male colleagues prefer to schedule strategy meetings during the evening because they know that many women will not attend them.[19] In this view, men's dominance of politics is assured as long as the sexual division of labour limits women's ability to dedicate the same hours to political work.

Indeed, the double day creates an enormous barrier for female politicians. An Argentine deputy reported that women are "limited by the time they must spend on housework and reproductive work, and these tasks limit the time that women can dedicate to political participation."[20] Her colleague similarly lamented these restrictions: "We've arrived at the ceiling: women still have domestic responsibilities, and this will limit their political possibilities."[21] A Chilean deputy phrased the sentiment similarly: "We [women] are in the public world but with a heavy backpack that says 'domestic work' on our back and that makes our careers go very slowly."[22] Another lamented that "the congress demands so much of women, as if they don't have any other responsibilities; well, the men do not actually have other responsibilities ... They use the task of childcare against women, arguing that it means women cannot participate in the most important discussions."[23] In this, the experiences of women in politics in Latin America echo those of their peers elsewhere, highlighted in Chapters 2 and 3 of this volume.

Biographical data on legislators' backgrounds show the effects of caregiving responsibilities on women's political careers. Scholars find substantial differences in the family lives of female politicians compared with those of male politicians. An early study on Costa Rican legislators found that female politicians were less likely to be married and to have fewer children than male politicians (Saint-Germain 1993), and more recent studies from Argentina, Brazil, Colombia, and Costa Rica confirmed this result (Marx, Borner, and Caminotti 2007; Schwindt-Bayer 2011). Likewise, notable gender differences appear when comparing the biographies of male and female legislators serving in Argentina between 1999 and 2009.[24] For example, women were more likely than men to be divorced, single, or widowed. In the Senate, whereas 85 percent of male senators were married, only 66 percent of female senators were married, and there were twice as many divorced or single female senators.[25] Likewise, male representatives were also more likely to be fathers and to have more children than female representatives.[26] In the House, most women had between one and two children (43 percent), whereas most men had between three and seven children (61 percent). In the Senate, most men and most women had between three and seven children; however, more male senators (66 percent) had large families compared with female senators (53 percent). These results demonstrate that female office-holders reconcile political work and family life by having smaller families, a trend seen in other national contexts, from Great Britain (Campbell and Childs, this volume) to South Africa (Walsh 2012, 127).

Female politicians also face hurdles because their careers violate traditional gendered expectations about appropriate public activities for women and a family's honour. Political meetings reflect men's schedules and are often held in the evenings in restaurants or bars. An Argentine deputy expressed frustration with the reputational costs of attending such meetings.[27] A young female legislator in Argentina also navigated the stereotypes associated with women's public activity: "The minute he [the party boss] placed me on the list, they [other party members] started saying I slept with him. They forgot I spent three years in the neighbourhood organizing for the vote."[28] Frequently, such slurs boomerang back to the female politicians' spouses and families. As a long-time Mexican politician explained, women cannot participate in politics unless their families – especially their spouses – support them: husbands and children must be willing to withstand gossip.[29] Male politicians typically do not have to ask their families to withstand this type of public scrutiny.

These broader cultural expectations about women's appropriate roles can create significant double binds for female politicians (Murray 2010). As in other regions, female legislators in Latin America cannot be seen as neglecting their familial roles and caregiving duties, but paying too much attention to spouses and children might mean sacrificing opportunities to enter decision-making circles. At the same time, when women do enter these spaces, they face backlash for violating gender roles: a woman attending to her political career can be accused of embarrassing her family. Expectations about motherhood generally, and familial and sexual roles specifically, continue to complicate women's political careers.

Barriers at the Macrolevel

Women's experiences as political actors and mothers are not separate from the social identities reinforced through public policies addressing family, childcare, and work. As late as the 1980s and early 1990s, the family codes of Argentina, Brazil, and Chile still gave fathers full parental rights, denying mothers the same rights. Many Latin American countries also maintained the difference between legitimate and illegitimate children in terms of support and inheritance, and husbands controlled marital property. In Brazil, a husband could annul the marriage if he discovered that his wife was not a virgin (Htun 2003, 113). Despite activists' efforts, modernizing reforms in the democratic era have not yet completely equalized men's and women's legal standing in families. Chile did not legalize divorce until 2004. Its default marital property regime still gives husbands control over marital property; shared control is available but must be chosen at the time of marriage.

In Argentina, the civil code prohibits married couples from having separate domiciles and lists fidelity, respect, and the provision of food as conjugal rights.

Given such laws, scholars of gender have long recognized that public policy constructs and promotes different roles and responsibilities for men and women. Latin America's social and economic policies have long reflected and reinforced a traditional gender ideology that valorizes heterosexual families with male breadwinners and female caregivers (Dore and Molyneux 2000). Although the reality for most families is far from the idealized models in public policies, laws nonetheless retain the power to shape gender roles as well as other social hierarchies. Public policies help to maintain normative beliefs about the centrality of motherhood in women's identities and lives. Public policies also often reflect a vision of motherhood that most closely reflects the race and class privileges of Latin American societies (Mooney 2009). Ultimately, these policies also affect women's prospects for entering electoral politics.

For example, public policies in Latin America have not responded to the problem of the double day. Compared with policies in Western Europe, especially in Scandinavia, policies encouraging paternal leave or male participation in childrearing are virtually non-existent in Latin America.[30] A recent regional survey noted that "there is insufficient recognition for men's role in caring for their children and scant encouragement for them to do so" (CEPAL 2009, 219). Consider, for instance, proposals in Argentina to extend maternity leave and expand state subsidies when women give birth to special needs children, adopt children, or have more than two children (Piscopo 2011). Although these policies ostensibly protect women's access to paid employment, they actually reinforce notions that women's primary responsibilities are domestic and discourage women from returning to work. In Chile, a significant overhaul of maternity leave in 2011 ultimately reinforced expectations that mothers, not fathers, should take the leave. Instead of creating a universal right to parental leave, the reform allowed mothers to transfer a portion (one-quarter) of their entitled leave to fathers. Yet entitlement to this leave is based upon the mother's employment status, revealing that fathers do not enjoy an independent right to take paid leave to care for a child (Staab 2014, 204–5). Thus, work and family policies reinforce the heterosexual family and an ideal model of gendered labour in which men work outside the home and women are the primary caregivers.

Childcare policies also reflect these assumptions. Women are expected to raise children or to make alternative arrangements, typically drawing on the care work of extended family members or low-paid domestic help. Here the Latin American context might be unique: racial and class hierarchies normalize the reliance on domestic workers, available and affordable because of vast class inequality, racial discrimination, and immigration. The lack of stigmatization of employing domestic workers might explain why the state provision of childcare is limited in Latin America. A recent study of efforts to extend labour protections to domestic workers reveals ambivalence from upper- and middle-class women who depend on lower-class women's (often exploited) labour to sustain their careers (Blofield 2012). Political women in Chile and Argentina, when asked about their own strategies for reconciling family obligations and political work, all stressed the importance of domestic help or reliance on mothers or mothers-in-law for childcare (Franceschet 2005).[31] The ability to outsource care grants upper-class (but not lower-class) women freedom from the burden of caregiving while absolving men of greater shared responsibility and the state of its obligation to address the problem.

Public policies in Latin America thus treat childcare and housework as primarily private matters and assume that women will bear the burden of this work. However, growing attention to women's unequal familial responsibilities as a cause of continuing gender inequality has prompted recent policy changes. Some countries – including Costa Rica, Chile, Mexico, and Peru – have expanded preschool education (for children up to the age of five). Chile, Colombia, and Uruguay have extended the school day, making it easier for women to work full time (CEPAL 2009, 217). Yet early childhood education policies are typically framed as mechanisms of poverty alleviation for families in lower socio-economic strata, and – like expanded maternity leave – they do not challenge the notion that women are and should be the primary domestic caregivers (Carrillo, Ripoll-Núñez, and Schvaneveldt 2012).

Finally, the region's public policies have resisted allowing women to choose not to be mothers. Most Latin American countries heavily restrict access to abortion, often penalizing abortion in all circumstances, and in some places policies have become more restrictive. In Nicaragua, for example, a 2006 law removed previous provisions for therapeutic abortions and made all abortions illegal, even in non-viable pregnancies that could result in maternal death. Access to emergency contraception, regarded by Catholic Church authorities as abortive, remains intensely conflict ridden and uneven in availability (Franceschet and Piscopo 2013). For instance, even disseminating information about emergency contraception remains illegal in Honduras. Further, proponents of expanded reproductive rights often rely on maternalist frames, arguing that access to contraception promotes women's ability to choose the timing of motherhood – rather than eschewing motherhood (Mooney 2009; Piscopo 2014b). Likewise, sexual health education has been framed as bolstering traditional families: one of the proposals shaping Argentina's 2006 sexual education law argued that the curriculum must "support the formation of responsible procreation, stable families and the marital love between a man and a woman."[32]

In sum, public policies on maternity leave, childcare, and reproduction in Latin America continue to reinforce maternalist ideologies. These policies ultimately shape the broader social and political contexts in which women can develop political careers. First, state policies on family and work reinforce the expectations and responsibilities of women's maternal roles, creating standards by which female politicians are subsequently judged. Second, these policies reify the gendered division of labour through which caregiving burdens are disproportionately placed on women, thereby leaving them with less time to dedicate to politics, work, and other pursuits. Policies have responded to women's increased labour market participation, but they have not decreased the double day, nor have they addressed how the intersections among race, class, and gender position women differently within society. Even if the availability of domestic workers has freed upper-class women – including female politicians – from the constraints that motherhood places on employment and social life, the reliance on female domestic servants simply perpetuates the idea that hearth and home are women's realm. In this sense, female politicians who are mothers, whether in executive office or in legislative office, face gendered expectations not only at the individual level but also at the structural level.

Conclusion

In this chapter, we have analyzed the continuities and changes in the intersection of maternalism and politics in Latin America. We focused on two areas where motherhood has affected women's political participation in the region: understandings and justifications of women's entry into politics and this work as office-holders, and structural constraints on women's political careers. Our evidence both converges with and diverges from global trends. Consistent with women's experiences throughout the world, our evidence demonstrates that female politicians still grapple with societal gendered expectations about their ability to reconcile political work and family roles. In Latin America, where maternalist ideologies long conditioned how women could justify their political careers, the precise use of gendered ideals has changed: women no longer need to position themselves as national caregivers, but they continue to draw on expectations about women's caregiving capacity, warmth, and compassion to shape their policy preferences and political goals. Women who compete in highly visible presidential contests especially must respond to gendered assumptions about political leadership while also respecting the continued resonance of motherhood. The public still expects female executives and legislators to conform to gender norms, especially in terms of their image and their attention to social policies.

Despite this changing context, we find significant continuity in the structural obstacles that motherhood poses for Latin American women. Political careers strain family lives, and female politicians, on average, have no spouses and fewer children (especially fewer young children) compared to their male counterparts. These barriers are significant. Since female politicians in Latin America are overwhelmingly women with the class privileges that allow them to manage work-family conflicts (i.e., by hiring domestic workers), if *they* cannot reconcile the structural constraints of motherhood, then poor and working-class women will be especially disadvantaged when seeking political careers. Cultural norms that make it acceptable for women to hire domestic help might be unique to Latin America (or other highly class-stratified societies), but even these norms do not prevent Latin American women – like their counterparts elsewhere – from struggling to balance work and family. Despite increasing awareness that caregiving is not just a women's issue and that motherhood is not women's only identity, public policies in Latin America still reflect expectations that women remain primarily responsible for childrearing and caregiving.

What do our findings mean for scholars interested in motherhood, gender, and politics? First, maternalism clearly continues to shape the political opportunities and constraints faced by women who want to pursue political careers. Second, researchers must be aware of the complexity of the intersection of motherhood and politics. Much of the Latin American experience is not unique to the region. Scholars of comparative politics should continue to investigate how motherhood and ideas about women's maternal roles shape women's campaigns for office and their policy priorities once in office. Maternalism also shapes larger social structures that determine how men and women compete for office and which opportunities they have for carrying out policy work once elected. However, scholars must also look for change. As a complex set of norms and practices, maternalism is never static, and female politicians are continually reshaping the connections between motherhood and politics.

Notes

1 While the *quality* of Latin American democracy remains contested, the region has largely met the minimum procedural requirements of free and fair elections (Smith 2012).
2 Authors' calculation using data from Hinojosa (2012, 6).
3 See http://ipu.org/wmn-e/classif.htm. In January 2015, Chile reformed its electoral law, including, for the first time, a 40 percent gender quota that will come into effect for the 2017 elections.
4 Piscopo's communication with Pedro dos Santos, February 27, 2012.
5 Piscopo's communication with Rosemary Castro Solano, March 26, 2012.
6 Piscopo's communication with Beatriz Llanos, July 24, 2012.
7 Author interview with deputy (Chile), November 8, 2006.
8 Author interview with deputy (Chile), November 21, 2006.
9 Author interview with senator (Mexico), December 8, 2009; author interview with former deputy (Mexico), December 16, 2009.
10 Author interview with deputy (Argentina), April 29, 2009.
11 Author interview with senator (Mexico), December 15, 2009.
12 Author interview with legislative analyst (Argentina), August 8, 2009.
13 Author interview with deputy (Argentina), April 15, 2009.
14 Studies linking women's numerical representation to their policy activity are numerous, with our citations offering only a representative sample.
15 Author interview with deputy (Chile), November 21, 2006.
16 Author interviews with deputies (Chile), November 8 and 28, 2006.
17 Author interview with deputy (Argentina), May 9, 2009.
18 Author interview with deputy (Argentina), April 15, 2009.
19 Author interview with deputy (Argentina), September 6, 2006.
20 Author interview with deputy (Argentina), April 7, 2009.
21 Author interview with deputy (Argentina), April 15, 2009.
22 Author interview with deputy (Chile), November 2, 1999.
23 Author interview with deputy (Argentina), April 7, 2009.
24 Data from the Chamber of Deputies were first published in Franceschet and Piscopo (2014). Data from the Senate is original to this chapter.
25 The difference in marital status is statistically significant at the 5 percent level.
26 The difference in parenthood is statistically significant at the 1 percent level for the Chamber of Deputies (Franceschet and Piscopo 2014, 93). The difference is not statistically significant for the Senate.
27 Author interview with legislator (Argentina), May 5, 2009.
28 Author interview with legislator (Argentina), August 15, 2006.
29 Author interview with politician (Mexico), December 8, 2009.

30 Such policies do not mean, however, that European women and men have attained equality in the workforce (Esping-Andersen 2009; Iversen and Rosenbluth 2010).
31 Also author interview with deputy (Argentina), April 29, 2009.
32 Bill 2491-D-2006.

References

Alvarez, Sonia. 1990. *Engendering Democracy in Brazil: Women's Movements in Transition Politics*. Princeton, NJ: Princeton University Press.

Archibold, Randal C. 2012. "Nomination Paves New Path in Mexico." *New York Times*, February 6.

Baldez, Lisa. 2002. *Why Women Protest: Women's Movements in Chile*. Cambridge: Cambridge University Press. http://dx.doi.org/10.1017/CBO9780511756283.

Bayard de Volo, Lorraine. 2001. *Mothers of Heroes and Martyrs: Gender Identity Politics in Nicaragua, 1979–1999*. Baltimore: Johns Hopkins University Press.

Blofield, Merike. 2012. *Care Work and Class: Domestic Workers' Struggles for Equal Rights in Latin America*. University Park: Penn State University Press.

Carrillo, Sonia, Karen Ripoll-Núñez, and Paul L. Schvaneveldt. 2012. "Family Policy Initiatives in Latin America: The Case of Colombia and Ecuador." *Journal of Child and Family Studies* 21 (1): 75–87. http://dx.doi.org/10.1007/s10826-011-9539-z.

Catalano, Ana. 2009. "Women Acting for Women? An Analysis of Gender and Debate Participation in the British House of Commons 2005–2007." *Politics and Gender* 5 (1): 45–68. http://dx.doi.org/10.1017/S1743923X09000038.

Celis, Karen. 2006. "Substantive Representation of Women: The Representation of Women's Interests and the Impact of Descriptive Representation in the Belgium Parliament (1900–1979)." *Journal of Women, Politics, and Policy* 28 (2): 85–114. http://dx.doi.org/10.1300/J501v28n02_04.

CEPAL. 2009. *Social Panorama of Latin America*. Santiago: CEPAL, United Nations.

Chaney, Elsa. 1979. *Supermadre: Women in Politics in Latin America*. Austin: University of Texas Press.

Cruz Pires, Carol. 2011. "Salto no escuro: Stereotyping in Coverage of Dilma Rousseff's Ascent to Power as First Female Brazilian President." MA thesis, Columbia University.

Devlin, Claire, and Robert Elgie. 2008. "The Effect of Increased Women's Representation in Parliament: The Case of Rwanda." *Parliamentary Affairs* 61 (2): 237–54. http://dx.doi.org/10.1093/pa/gsn007.

Dore, Elizabeth. 2000. "One Step Forward, Two Steps Back: Gender and the State in the Long Nineteenth Century." In *Hidden Histories of the State in Latin America*, edited by Elizabeth Dore and Maxine Molyneux, 3–32. Durham: Duke University Press.

Dore, Elizabeth, and Maxine Molyneux, eds. 2000. *Hidden Histories of the State in Latin America*. Durham: Duke University Press.

Eltantawy, Nahed. 2008. "Pots, Pans, and Protests: Women's Strategies for Resisting Globalization in Argentina." *Communication and Critical/Cultural Studies* 5 (1): 46–63. http://dx.doi.org/10.1080/14791420701821773.

Esping-Andersen, Gosta. 2009. *Incomplete Revolution: Adapting Welfare Status to Women's New Roles.* Cambridge: Polity Press.

Franceschet, Susan. 2005. *Women and Politics in Chile.* Boulder, CO: Lynne Rienner Publishers.

Franceschet, Susan, and Jennifer M. Piscopo. 2008. "Gender Quotas and Women's Substantive Representation: Lessons from Argentina." *Politics and Gender* 4 (3): 393–425. http://dx.doi.org/10.1017/S1743923X08000342.

—. 2013. "Federalism, Decentralization, and Reproductive Rights in Argentina and Chile." *Publius* 43 (1): 129–50.

—. 2014. "Sustaining Gendered Practices? Power, Parties, and Elite Political Networks in Argentina." *Comparative Political Studies* 47 (1): 85–110. http://dx.doi.org/10.1177/0010414013489379.

Franceschet, Susan, Jennifer M. Piscopo, and Gwynn Thomas. 2016. "Supermadres, Women's Maternal Legacies, and Political Participation in Contemporary Latin America." *Journal of Latin American Studies* 48 (1): 1–32.

Franceschet, Susan, and Gwynn Thomas. 2010. "Renegotiating Political Leadership: Michelle Bachelet's Rise to the Chilean Presidency." In *Cracking the Highest Glass Ceiling: A Global Comparison of Women's Campaigns,* edited by Rainbow Murray, 177–96. Thousand Oaks, CA: Praeger Publishing.

Heath, Roseanna, Leslie Schwindt-Bayer, and Michelle Taylor-Robinson. 2005. "Women on the Sidelines: Women's Representation on Committees in Latin American Legislatures." *American Journal of Political Science* 49 (2): 420–36. http://dx.doi.org/10.2307/3647686.

Hinojosa, Magda. 2012. *Selecting Women, Electing Women: Political Representation and Candidate Selection in Latin America.* Philadelphia: Temple University Press.

Htun, Mala. 2003. *Sex and the State: Abortion, Divorce, and the Family under Latin American Dictatorships and Democracies.* New York: Cambridge University Press. http://dx.doi.org/10.1017/CBO9780511615627.

Htun, Mala, and Jennifer M. Piscopo. 2014. *Women's Representation in Latin America and the Caribbean.* New York: Social Science Research Council.

Iversen, Torben, and Frances Rosenbluth. 2010. *Women, Work, and Politics: The Political Economy of Gender Inequality.* New Haven, CT: Yale University Press.

Jaquette, Jane S., ed. 1994. *The Women's Movement in Latin America: Participation and Democracy.* Boulder, CO: Westview Press.

Jones, Mark P. 1997. "Legislator Gender and Legislator Policy Priorities in the Argentine Chamber of Deputies and the United States House of Representatives." *Policy Studies Journal: The Journal of the Policy Studies Organization* 25 (4): 613–29. http://dx.doi.org/10.1111/j.1541-0072.1997.tb00045.x.

Kampwirth, Karen. 1996. "The Mother of the Nicaraguans: Doña Violeta and the UNO's Gender Agenda." *Latin American Perspectives* 23 (1): 67–86. http://dx.doi.org/10.1177/0094582X9602300105.

Krook, Mona Lena. 2009. *Quotas for Women in Politics: Gender and Candidate Selection Reform Worldwide.* New York: Oxford University Press.

Lavrín, Asunción. 1995. *Women, Feminism, and Social Change in Argentina, Chile, and Uruguay, 1890–1940*. Lincoln: University of Nebraska Press.
Marx, Jutta, Jutta Borner, and Mariana Caminotti. 2007. *Las legisladoras: Cupos de género y política en Argentina y Brasil*. Buenos Aires: Siglo XXI.
Miguel, Luis Felipe. 2012. "Policy Priorities and Women's Double Bind in Brazil." In *The Impact of Gender Quotas*, edited by Susan Franceschet, Mona Lena Krook, and Jennifer M. Piscopo, 103–18. New York: Oxford University Press. http://dx.doi.org/10.1093/acprof:oso/9780199830091.003.0007.
Mooney, Jadwiga E. Pieper. 2009. *The Politics of Motherhood: Maternity and Women's Rights in Twentieth-Century Chile*. Pittsburgh: University of Pittsburgh Press.
Murray, Rainbow, ed. 2010. *Cracking the Highest Glass Ceiling: A Global Comparison of Women's Campaigns*. Thousand Oaks, CA: Praeger Publishing.
Navia, Patricio. 2009. "La cariñocracia de Bachelet." *La Tercera*, July 4. http://www.latercera.cl.
Pateman, Carole. 1988. *The Sexual Contract*. Stanford: Stanford University Press.
Piscopo, Jennifer M. 2011. "Do Women Represent Women? Gender and Politics in Mexico and Argentina." PhD diss., University of California, San Diego.
—. 2014a. "Beyond Hearth and Home: Female Legislators, Feminist Policy Change, and Substantive Representation in Mexico." *Revista Uruguaya de Ciencia Política* 32 (2): 87–110.
—. 2014b. "Female Leadership and Sexual Health Policy in Argentina." *Latin American Research Review* 49 (1): 104–27. http://dx.doi.org/10.1353/lar.2014.0013.
—. 2016. "When Informality Advantages Women: Quota Networks, Electoral Rules, and Candidate Selection in Mexico." *Government and Opposition* 51 (3): 487–512.
Power, Margaret. 2002. *Right Wing Women in Chile: Feminine Power and the Struggle against Allende, 1965–1973*. University Park: Penn State University Press.
Saint-Germain, Michelle A. 1993. "Paths to Power of Women Legislators in Costa Rica and Nicaragua." *Women's Studies International Forum* 16 (2): 119–38. http://dx.doi.org/10.1016/0277-5395(93)90003-R.
Schwindt-Bayer, Leslie. 2010. *Political Power and Women's Representation in Latin America*. New York: Oxford University Press. http://dx.doi.org/10.1093/acprof:oso/9780199731954.001.0001.
—. 2011. "Women Who Win: Social Backgrounds, Paths to Power, and Political Ambition in Latin America." *Politics and Gender* 7 (1): 1–33. http://dx.doi.org/10.1017/S1743923X10000541.
Smith, Peter H. 2012. *Democracy in Latin America: Political Change in Comparative Perspective*. New York: Oxford University Press.
Staab, Silke. 2014. "Engendering Change and Continuity in Chilean Social Policy: Actors, Ideas, and Institutions." PhD diss., University of Manchester.
Swers, Michelle. 2014. "Unpacking Women's Issues: Gender and Policymaking on Health Care, Education, and Women's Health in the U.S. Senate." In *Representation: The Case of Women*, edited by Maria C. Escobar-Lemmon and Michelle

M. Taylor-Robinson, 158–82. New York: Oxford University Press. http://dx.doi.org/10.1093/acprof:oso/9780199340101.003.0009.

Taylor, Diana. 1997. *Disappearing Acts: Spectacles of Gender and Nationalism in Argentina's "Dirty War."* Durham: Duke University Press.

Taylor-Robinson, Michelle, and Roseanna Michelle Heath. 2003. "Do Women Legislators Have Different Policy Priorities than Their Male Colleagues? A Critical Test." *Women and Politics* 24 (4): 77–101. http://dx.doi.org/10.1300/J014v24n04_04.

Thomas, Gwynn. 2011a. *Contesting Legitimacy in Chile: Familial Ideals, Citizenship, and Political Struggle, 1970–1990.* University Park: Penn State University Press.

—. 2011b. "Michelle Bachelet's Liderazgo Femenino (Feminine Leadership): Gender and Redefining Political Leadership in Chile's 2005 Presidential Campaign." *International Feminist Journal of Politics* 13 (1): 63–82. http://dx.doi.org/10.1080/14616742.2011.534662.

Thomas, Gwynn, and Catherine Reyes-Housholder. 2015. "Latin America's Presidentas: Challenging Old Patterns, Forging New Pathways" at the Women and Leadership in Latin America Conference, April 10. Houston: Rice University.

Towns, Ann. 2010. *Women and States: Norms and Hierarchies in International Society.* New York: Cambridge University Press. http://dx.doi.org/10.1017/CBO9780511779930.

Valdés, Teresa. 2010. "El Chile de Michelle Bachelet ¿Género en el poder?" *Latin American Research Review* 45 (S): 248–73. http://dx.doi.org/10.1353/lar.2010.0036.

Walsh, Denise. 2012. "Party Centralization and Debate Conditions in South Africa." In *The Impact of Gender Quotas,* edited by Susan Franceschet, Mona Lena Krook, and Jennifer M. Piscopo, 119–35. New York: Oxford University Press. http://dx.doi.org/10.1093/acprof:oso/9780199830091.003.0008.

Yoon, Mi Yung. 2011. "More Women in the Tanzanian Legislature: Do Numbers Matter?" *Journal of Contemporary African Studies* 29 (1): 83–98. http://dx.doi.org/10.1080/02589001.2011.539011.

5

"Society Is Balanced, So Local Boards Should Be Balanced Too"

Gatekeeper Attitudes toward the Gender Balance Law in Iowa

REBECCA J. HANNAGAN and CHRISTOPHER W. LARIMER

We recently conducted an in-depth field study of local boards and commissions in Iowa,[1] the first American state to pass a gender balance law at the local level of government. This change means that Iowa has now initiated de facto gender quotas at all levels of government, a unique situation in the United States. The Iowa case is important not merely because it is a unique experiment with quotas in the United States but also because this most recent law applies to the *municipal* level.

Although substantial work in political science focuses on local or urban politics, rarely has such research focused on gender and politics at the municipal level. As Crow (1997) notes, more women in the United States hold office at the municipal level than ever before, and it is an increasingly important site of political participation for women. Municipal politics has been argued to be more attractive to women than state and national politics because it can be less competitive, does not require relocation, might be non-partisan, and can be an important stepping stone for other levels of office (Kopinak 1985; Vickers 1978). This suggests that local political careers can be particularly attractive for women with dependent children given the challenges to mothers with careers in national politics, as outlined in the previous chapters. And though concerns about family responsibilities relating to household tasks and childcare have been shown to be unrelated to decisions about running for elected office (see Fox and Lawless 2014), such factors can be important when considering whether to take on a voluntary position such as membership on a local board or commission.

Existing research on quotas (though not focused on the American state level in particular) suggests that effective application of quotas hinges on elites' willingness to support such legislation and recruit women (e.g., Childs and Krook 2006, 2008; Franceschet, Krook, and Piscopo 2012; Krook 2006, 2007, 2009). The issue of gender quotas for local politics thus has particular importance for the entry of mothers of young children into public service. Responsibility for childrearing and taking care of the home falls largely to women, regardless of whether they work outside the home. This reality was initially cited as one of the reasons that women do not seek political office at a rate equal to that of men (Fox and Lawless 2003), but the relationship between such factors and decisions about running for office has since been shown to be more complex (Fox and Lawless 2014). The gender of a potential candidate certainly matters when it comes to self-perceived qualifications for office and recruitment (Lawless and Fox 2010), but for mothers concerns about family life potentially interfere with the positive effects of quotas, particularly for positions in which salary and status are less visible (e.g., voluntary local boards and commissions). Focusing only on national- or state-level politics in the United States leaves one with the impression that women are not likely to reach gender parity with men any time soon, but the local level might involve different patterns of participation, and Iowa's new law might have an impact on the current situation. Although the work that we present in this chapter is exploratory, we believe that it speaks to all of these issues: the role of quotas in women's entry into politics, the difference that local political service makes for women, the role that parenting plays for both women and men when entering local service, and whether the relationship between parenthood and politics regarding voluntary positions differs from established research on this topic pertaining to elected positions.

Again, the features of municipal service, such as not having to relocate to the state capital, might be why women or men who have young children decide to step up and serve. As an illustration of this logic, a November 4, 2012, article in the *Dickinson Press* reported that the North Dakota legislature does not reflect the electorate, citing that the legislators tend to be older, male, married, and self-employed compared with the general population. One of the challenges cited is the difficulty for women with children at home to leave their families (and perhaps jobs) to serve in the capital for four months at a time. Legislators interviewed for the story cited that the current system makes it difficult for younger people who are working and raising families to run for office (Frank 2012). Previous research shows that such concerns are prevalent among female state legislators (Thomas 2002). Although relative "ease of service" at the local level compared with the state level is not the focus of our study, we do consider the willingness of men and women with young children to serve locally because their interests might coincide with local-level service more than state- or national-level service. Moreover, there is now evidence showing that decisions to run for office (though different from serving on voluntary local boards) are less influenced by family and childcare responsibilities than initially thought (Fox and Lawless 2014). The data presented in this chapter do not provide direct measures of household or childcare responsibilities, but they do address how men and women (parents and non-parents) view gender quotas and, when combined with data on age and group gender composition, speak to how local gender quotas might (or might not) affect gender dynamics among women who are (or are not) parents. The theoretical framework for this chapter draws primarily from political science, our home discipline, but as we argue throughout the chapter the findings have important implications for the intersection of parenthood and politics.

We pose a primary question: will the Iowa gender balance law be successful? We suspect that its success is predicated on the attitudes of currently sitting board members as "gatekeepers" to gender balance. Recruitment to local boards and commissions, particularly in sparsely populated municipalities, is heavily dependent on recommendations from existing board members. Such recommendations are then put to the city council and/or mayor for approval. As an additional query, one that speaks to the content of this volume, we suspect that some aspects of serving one's local community speak to the willingness of women and men with young children to serve. We pursue an answer to our primary question by looking to the framework provided by those who study quota laws cross-nationally, and we rely on a key source of data: our observations and surveys of sitting board and commission members in Iowa prior to implementation of the law. We begin with a brief background on passage of the law in Iowa, including excerpts from proponents and critics, followed by a presentation of the results of our surveys, and we conclude with our assessment of the law's likely success. In short, we present findings suggesting that, though self-identified conservatives currently serving on municipal boards and commissions are much more likely to have negative views of the law, the general sentiment among the gatekeepers whom we surveyed is that "society is balanced, so local boards should be too," and that recruiting and appointing more women to boards is "the right thing to do." In addition, efforts by women's organizations are well under way to educate municipalities on the value of diverse decision-making bodies. The success of the gender balance law in Iowa will no doubt have an impact on women, perhaps mothers in particular, by increasing opportunities to serve their communities. We further illustrate, with qualitative data from our field observations and conversations with board members, our hunch that mothers and fathers of young children serve at the local level because their interests as parents coincide with serving their communities.

Background on the Gender Balance Law in Iowa

Iowa has required gender balance on state-level boards and commissions since 1987. In 2009, the 83rd General Assembly passed HF243, thereby extending this expectation to appointed positions on county and municipal boards and commissions. In the Iowa House, the bill passed 71 to 27, while in the Iowa Senate the bill passed 31 to 19. It was signed into law by Governor Chet Culver on May 26, 2009, requiring all such boards and commissions to be gender balanced by January 1, 2012.

Iowa State Senator Herman Quirmbach (Democrat) and Iowa State Representative Beth Wessel-Kroeschell (Democrat) wrote different versions of a gender balance bill, SF133 and HF243, respectively. The bill sponsored by Wessel-Kroeschell became law, but Quirmbach's concern that board members serving at the time of the law's passage would be removed in order to balance the board or commission was taken into account via Amendment 1144 offered by State Representative Geri Huser (Democrat). Although the implementation date of this law has since passed, the law itself lacks an enforcement mechanism; there is no monitoring mechanism to ensure that municipalities comply with the gender balance requirement, and in its current form the law leaves space for non-gender balanced appointments as long as the municipality made a "good faith effort" to achieve balance. Put another way, though the law directly affects local female representation, the absence of an enforcement mechanism suggests that gender-based recruitment efforts are likely to vary considerably and depend predominantly on the commitment of existing board members. We argue that those efforts are likely to be significantly informed by pre-existing preferences regarding utility of the law.

How the law is written leaves it open to interpretation and is likely to have an impact on its effectiveness (Krook 2007). The language of a good faith effort in the Iowa law is a way for boards and commissions to fill a vacancy without achieving balance. Furthermore, the law states that local governments are to utilize a fair and unbiased method of selecting the best applicants, while providing for gender balance, but the law is vague about what "fair and unbiased" entail. The extent to which gatekeepers (e.g., mayors, city council members, and current board and commission members) see the gender balance law as legitimate, and balance itself as valuable, is likely to impact the law's success. We focus here on two sets of gatekeepers using a mixed method approach: (1) the utility of gender balance legislation as perceived by current board members and assessed through a formal survey, and (2) qualitative assessment of the views of current board members and local elected officials, including council members and mayors. These two groups go hand in hand when it comes to complying with the law. Current board members are directly responsible for recruiting board replacements, and their recommendations go to the city council or mayor for approval. And, though there might be other actors or local cultural norms that will impact the likely success of the law, our analysis is restricted to the views of these two groups since they are most closely associated with ultimate success of the law.

Supporting Views
The rationale for the introduction of the law, according to the Iowa Commission on the Status of Women (ICSW), was that a diversity of experiences is critical in developing representative and balanced local practices and policies.[1] Despite 22 years of best practices from statewide boards and commissions, only a handful of municipalities had adopted gender balance in their appointments prior to passing of the law. State Representative Mary Mascher, who managed HF243 on the floor of the House, stated that "women make up over 50% of the population of Iowa, but make up only 18% of local government boards and commissions. It is time for local governments to double their efforts and ask women to serve their community."[2] In short, the state had already made a commitment to gender balance 22 years earlier, but success of the law at the state level did not trickle down as expected. The rationale for the local law was the same as that for the state law – diverse bodies support better governance by including more viewpoints and being more representative. This reasoning mimics the broader political

science literature on gender and agenda setting showing differences in the types of bills introduced by male and female legislators (Bratton 2005; Bratton and Haynie 1999).

Despite the gender neutrality of language in the bill, those who sponsored and supported the bill argued that more women across Iowa need to be politically engaged – for the good of women and the good of the communities that they serve. They noted that women in Iowa volunteer at significantly higher rates than men and that Iowa is a state of robust civic engagement, ranking seventh in the nation in civic volunteering. They also pointed out that women hold more associate and bachelor's degrees than men in Iowa. Despite their education and volunteerism, however, they are less likely than men to be approached about official leadership opportunities.[3] Furthermore, it was expected by proponents that the gender balance law would benefit future political careers among women. For example, former State Senator Johnie Hammond (Democrat) (2009) stated in an interview that "I believe that the gender balance law [at the state level] has helped women develop a stronger resume to use in running for office. I personally know a few examples where that has happened. Including local boards and commissions in the law should enhance that outcome further."

For over 20 years, the existing state-level law has been successful, and this was pointed out during debate of the bill. In 1974, only 14 percent of all members serving on state boards and commissions were women; by 2006, nearly 50 percent of all members were women. There also appeared to be an impact on the political careers of some women. Barbara Brown notes that she served on the Cedar Falls Planning and Zoning Commission for 13 years, and at times she was the only woman. She left her position on the commission when she won a city council seat in 1995. Brown suggests that it was her experience on the commission that led to her successful bid for a council seat: "After serving on the commission and you see how it's done and you think, 'I can do this'" (quoted in Jamison 2010).

Dissenting Views

Critics of the bill argued that rural areas have a difficult time recruiting individuals to serve on boards and commissions and that the gender balance requirement would make it even more difficult. This type of critique is a "supply-side" argument (Paxton, Kunovich, and Hughes 2007): those whose job it is to fill positions might articulate that there are not enough interested persons, in this case women. Critics of the bill also argued that the choice of who should serve should be based upon qualifications and interests, not upon gender.[4] State Representative Lance Horbach (Republican), for example, offered Amendment 1087, which would eliminate any reference to gender balance and instead articulate that serving should be "open to all members of the community on the basis of their qualifications and without bias or discrimination." This amendment was voted down by the Iowa House. Again, despite the gender neutrality of the language, the bill was written in the spirit of encouraging greater participation of women in politics.

A Field Study of Gender Balance in Iowa

Although supporters of the gender balance law in Iowa certainly reflect political science research on the political ambition of potential male and female candidates (e.g., see Lawless and Fox 2010), arguments at the time generally did not distinguish between simply being a woman and being a woman who is also a parent. Rather, supporters of the bill in Iowa focused on the lack of female representation, regardless of parental status, a factor that we argue can affect the success of recruitment efforts in complying with the law. Particularly for less high-profile and unpaid positions such as voluntary boards and commissions, gender quotas might not be as effective. That is, unlike running for federal office, running for local positions might not offer the net benefits to offset other responsibilities. Susan Thomas (2002, 351) acknowledges as much by suggesting that female state legislators – who have "myriad advantages, including success, prestige, monetary resources, a child who is a teenager rather than an infant, [and] a second parent with whom to share childcare responsibilities" – are likely to view their position (and potentially even the decision to pursue such a position) differently from someone who lacks such advantages.

As mentioned earlier in the chapter, successful compliance with the law is likely to depend on the recruitment efforts of existing board members serving on both gender balanced and gender imbalanced boards. Their views of the legislation and the time commitment required to serve on each type of board are likely to factor into considerations of whether to ask fellow citizens, male or female, parent or non-parent, to serve. Thus, our research design proceeds in two ways: first, by focusing on the views of current members of randomly selected boards and commissions in Iowa; second, by using those findings to speculate on the challenge of successful implementation of the gender balance law in Iowa. If board members do not see a need for such a law, then their recruitment efforts might be minimal or, to use the term in the text of the law itself, not in "good faith." However, even if considerable effort is made, the recruitment of women, particularly mothers, might be difficult given the challenge of recruiting for voluntary positions in sparsely populated communities, the status of the positions needing to be filled, and the lack of an enforcement mechanism for failing to achieve balance. We seek to shed light on this dilemma in the following sections.

Methods

The local gender balance law in Iowa took effect January 1, 2012, but the language of the law allows for those currently serving to complete their terms even if boards remain unbalanced. Future vacancies provide the opportunity to fill the boards with appointees of the gender that would balance them. Further, if boards do not deem applicants suitable, they can retain current members and remain unbalanced as long as they have made a good faith effort to recruit new members to balance them. Thus, implementation of the law is a multi-year endeavour but entirely dependent on the views and recommendations of current board members. We began observation and data collection for selected cities in May 2010 and continued until October 2011. In total, we observed 50 meetings of local boards and commissions in 18 different cities in Iowa and surveyed the members present at each meeting.[5]

Across those 50 meetings, we observed 165 men and 136 women sitting on boards (or 45.2 percent female membership), with meetings chaired by 31 men and 19 women (or 38 percent female leadership). Following each meeting, we distributed anonymous surveys to all members of the group present at the meeting, which they could send back to us in self-addressed, stamped envelopes. The survey consisted of a battery of standard demographic and political questions as well as questions about group decisions and other decision makers on the board/commission.[6] Fundamental to our research question here, the survey also asked an open-ended question about the gender balance law: "Do you think recent legislation requiring 'gender balance' on all local boards and commissions is a good idea? Why or why not?"

Results from the survey were used to examine individual preferences about gender balance. In the following section, we present our findings, focusing on the views of current board members on the law. We further examine some typical categories that could influence views on the law, such as political ideology and religiosity, and we consider the particular boards and commissions and the current status of gender balance on them. We conclude by discussing how board members' views can affect the recruitment of men and women to imbalanced boards as well as the implications for the recruitment of mothers to such boards in light of current research on political ambition.

Results
The economic boards in our field study (i.e., planning and zoning commissions or zoning boards of adjustment) tended to have greater numbers of men than women compared with the non-economic boards (i.e., library boards, parks and recreation boards, and historic preservation boards). Zoning boards of adjustment, on average, had just 26 percent women present, and planning and zoning commissions, on average, had only slightly more, with 29 percent women in their membership. We label such boards "skewed-male" given the gender imbalance favouring men. This is in contrast to non-economic boards, such as historic preservation boards, in which women were 51 percent of the membership, and parks and recreation boards, with 44 percent women. We refer to these boards as "balanced"; such boards should require relatively little adjustment to remain in compliance with the gender balance law. Finally, library boards were "skewed-female," with the average membership being approximately 65 percent women. Thus, based upon our observations, the challenge is for towns and cities in Iowa with unbalanced boards (i.e., library boards and economic boards) to recruit more men or women as necessary.

Using responses to the demographic and political questions in the surveys, we conducted an analysis to see whether there was a correlation between demographic characteristics of board members and attitudes regarding the recently enacted gender balance law. As shown in Table 5.1, a person more inclined to serve on an economic board might have views different from a person more inclined to serve on a non-economic board. Respondents serving on economic boards (i.e., planning and zoning and boards of adjustment) were significantly more conservative, less religious, and less trusting than respondents serving on library boards (skewed-female). Respondents on balanced boards (i.e., historic preservation and parks and recreation boards) were significantly younger and less religious than respondents on library boards. In other words, there seem to be differences (beyond gender) among people serving on different types of boards in terms of political attitudes and personal characteristics.

Based not only upon a general interest in the topics dealt with by the various boards (e.g., city zoning codes, libraries, and parks) but also upon

TABLE 5.1
Demographics by board type

		Age	Ideology[a]	Religiosity[b]	Trusting[c]
Skewed-male	M	55.76	3.10**	3.06**	3.07**
	N	71	70	67	70
	SD	13.10	1.24	1.69	1.29
Balanced	M	53.57**	2.56**	2.66***	2.70*
	N	61	61	62	57
	SD	13.11	1.36	1.70	1.09
Skewed-female	M	58.54**	2.57**	3.62***	2.61**
	N	70	68	68	70
	SD	12.26	1.29	1.52	1.13
Total	M	56.06	2.75	3.13	2.8
	N	202	199	197	197
	SD	12.92	1.31	1.67	1.19

Notes: Race was not included in this analysis since 96 percent of respondents identified themselves as "white." The difference in age between balanced and skewed-female boards is significant ($p < .05$). On ideology, there is a significant difference between skewed-male and balanced boards ($p < .05$) and between skewed-male and skewed-female boards ($p < .05$). On religiosity, there is a significant difference between balanced and skewed-female boards ($p < .01$) and between skewed-male and skewed-female boards ($p < .05$). On trusting, there is a significant difference between skewed-male and skewed-female boards ($p < .05$) and between skewed-male and balanced boards ($p < .10$).

a Ideology measured response to the following question: "In terms of political views, do you consider yourself liberal, conservative, or somewhere in between?" Responses were coded on a five-point scale where 1 = liberal and 5 = conservative.

b Religiosity measured response to the following question: "Approximately how many times a month do you attend religious services? (0, 1, 2, 3, or 4)"

c Trusting measured response to the following question: "Generally speaking, would you say that most people can be trusted, or would you say that you can't be too careful in dealing with people?" Responses were coded on a seven-point scale where 1 = most people can be trusted and 7 = you can't be too careful in dealing with others.

* $p < .10$; ** $p < .05$; *** $p < .01$.

the cultural norms surrounding each within the various communities that we visited, it should not be surprising to find such differences among members on boards. Qualitatively, one thing that we noticed among the younger men and women on parks and recreation boards was that many members spoke of their young children with regard to issues that the boards were addressing, such as "my daughter plays softball, so I am often at that part of the park." Or "I think the 'no dogs policy' at the parks is important for those of us with young children."[7] We got the sense when attending many of these meetings that parents served on parks and recreation boards because their children used the facilities. Although not shown in Table 5.1, women serving on parks and recreation boards, on average, were six years younger than their male counterparts (M = 50.4 for women and M = 56.3 for men), a difference that approaches statistical significance even with a small N (p = .11). In fact, across all board types, the youngest women on average were those serving on parks and recreation boards, though the age difference between women on these boards and those on other boards reaches statistical significance only when compared with library boards ($p < .05$). Qualitatively, the same was true for some meetings of library boards, but libraries varied greatly from place to place in terms of whether they served as a place for early childhood development, a kind of seniors' centre, a place where people could search and apply for employment, and so forth. Among some library boards, however, younger women noted the importance of summer reading programs in which their children participated.

Turning to our key dependent variable – in response to our open-ended question "do you think recent legislation requiring 'gender balance' on all local boards and commissions is a good idea?" – all responses were content analyzed according to whether the statement was positive (+1), neutral (0), or negative (–1). A positive statement was any statement that began with "yes" or some variation thereof, while a negative statement was any statement that began with "no" or some variation thereof. For example, the following comment from a parks and recreation board member was coded positively: "Yes, women should be equally represented. Break up '[o]ld boys club' if there are any." This comment from a planning and zoning board member was coded as negative: "No. Gender balance means an unqualified person may be approved to a board." A neutral statement was one in which the respondent attempted to qualify his or her remarks by stating the pros and cons of gender balance or saying that gender should have no relevance in selecting board members.[8] Neutral responses entailed the board member saying something like "if they are good people, it does not matter."

In Table 5.2, we present the mean responses to the gender balance question based upon the index described above. Overall, board members serving on balanced boards are generally more supportive of gender balance legislation than board members serving on skewed-female boards. The data imply that those serving on mixed gender boards are perhaps more egalitarian in their thinking, or it might be that serving with a mixed group enhances support for gender balance legislation, or more likely it is some combination of the two. Many offered responses such as "yes, I think men and women look at things differently and have different viewpoints and priorities." Those serving on a skewed-female board, perhaps surprisingly, are less supportive of the gender balance law. Why would a group of mostly women not want a law aimed at promoting women as political leaders? Perhaps members believe that enough women are already present (as evident on their board), so no action by the state is needed if the law is interpreted as helping women. From a qualitative standpoint, most of the comments in the survey responses suggest that board members believe that the law is aimed at increasing the number of women. There was no reference to increasing the number of men, so despite the gender neutrality of the language of the law the perception is that the law is aimed at increasing the number of women, unnecessary for skewed-female boards such as library boards.

Turning to differences between men and women in attitudes toward the law, for men the mean response ranged from 0.32 on skewed-female boards to 0.63 on balanced boards. Although men serving on skewed-female boards were considerably less supportive of gender balance legislation than men serving on balanced boards, this difference was not statistically significant. For women serving on skewed-male boards, the mean response was 0.60 compared with a mean response of 0.24 for women on skewed-female boards. Where women were the token female or one of only

TABLE 5.2
Preferences for gender balance legislation by board type and gender (mean response)

Board type	Gender differences	Mean response[a]
Skewed-male	Male	0.37
	Female	0.60*
	Overall	0.44
Balanced	Male	0.63
	Female	0.50
	Overall	0.55**
Skewed-female	Male	0.32
	Female	0.24*
	Overall	0.27**

a Support for gender balance legislation is coded as −1 (negative), 0 (neutral), or +1 (positive). Mean response is the mean level of support using this index for each subgroup based upon the lead coder.

* There is a significant difference between female respondents on skewed-male boards and female respondents on skewed-female boards ($t = 1.86$; $p < .10$).

** The difference between respondents overall on balanced boards and respondents overall on skewed-female boards is significant ($t = 2.19$; $p < .05$). There is no statistical difference between male and female respondents on skewed-male, balanced, or skewed-female boards.

a few women, they were more supportive of gender balance legislation than women on boards surrounded by other women, a statistically significant difference. Women offered responses such as "yes. I feel that male and female perspectives are both needed, just as [are] different age groups."

Pooling all survey responses across all board types, more conservative board members tended to be less supportive of gender balance legislation, offering responses such as "no, the government's role should not be to 'require' gender balance on boards. I'm fed up with the government overstepping in all areas." There was almost a full-point difference (on a five-point scale, with 1 being very liberal and 5 being very conservative) in self-reported ideology between board members who responded negatively (M = 3.48) to the gender balance question and those who responded positively (M = 2.49). This statistically significant difference was borne out when separating members by board type.

On skewed-male boards, those who responded negatively were more conservative than those who responded positively. On balanced boards, we observed no differences on any of the demographic characteristics or other attitudes measured in our survey between board members who responded negatively and board members who responded positively. This is explained, we think, by what we noted above regarding the qualitative "sameness" among those serving on balanced boards who mentioned that they were serving because they cared about parks. On skewed-female boards, board members who responded negatively (M = 3.21) were also significantly more conservative than board members who responded positively (M = 2.41). We performed cross-tabulations of the responses to the gender balance question by board type, gender of the respondent, and ideology of the respondent, and the results are presented in Table 5.3.[9]

Among all respondents on skewed-male boards, we found a significant difference between self-identified conservatives and non-conservatives in terms of attitudes toward the gender balance law. Specifically, non-conservatives responded more positively toward the law. Considering all respondents on skewed-male boards together, 36.4 percent of conservatives responded negatively to the gender balance question, compared with just 6.8 percent of non-conservatives. Among the men on those boards, there was also a statistically significant difference between conservatives and non-conservatives, with the former responding more negatively than the latter and offering responses such as "no. Waste of time and simply another example of government over-regulation – symbolic of the problems with our country and economy." Although 33.3 percent of conservative men gave a

TABLE 5.3
Preferences for gender balance legislation by board type, gender, and ideology

Board type	Gender	Ideology	Negative	Neutral	Positive
	Female	Non-conservative	0.0	23.1	76.9
	Female	Conservative	28.6	14.3	57.1
				$\chi^2 = 4.14$	
Skewed-male	Male	Non-conservative	9.7	22.6	67.7
	Male	Conservative	40.0	26.7	33.3
				$\chi^2 = 6.94^{**}$	
	Total	Non-conservative	6.8	22.7	70.5
	Total	Conservative	36.4	22.7	40.9
				$\chi^2 = 9.79^{***}$	
	Female	Non-conservative	11.5	26.9	61.5
	Female	Conservative	16.7	16.7	66.7
				$\chi^2 = 0.33$	
Balanced	Male	Non-conservative	6.2	6.2	87.5
	Male	Conservative	14.3	28.6	57.1
				$\chi^2 = 2.80$	
	Total	Non-conservative	9.5	19.0	71.4
	Total	Conservative	15.4	23.1	61.5
				$\chi^2 = 0.53$	
	Female	Non-conservative	13.2	31.6	55.3
	Female	Conservative	62.5	37.5	0.0
				$\chi^2 = 11.89^{***}$	
Skewed-female	Male	Non-conservative	16.7	41.7	41.7
	Male	Conservative	20.0	20.0	60.0
				$\chi^2 = 1.21$	
	Total	Non-conservative	14.0	34.0	52.0
	Total	Conservative	38.9	27.8	33.3
		Total		$\chi^2 = 5.12^{*}$	

Note: Cell entries represent the percentage of respondents within each category responding positively, neutrally, or negatively to the question "do you think recent legislation requiring 'gender balance' on all local boards and commissions is a good idea?"
* $p < .10$; ** $p < .05$; *** $p < .01$.

positive response to the gender balance question, 67.7 percent of non-conservative men gave such a response. The only negative responses among women on skewed-male boards were from self-identified conservatives, but the difference between conservative and non-conservative women was not significant. On balanced boards, we found no differences on this issue between conservatives and non-conservatives.

Turning to skewed-female boards, we again observed a difference between conservatives and non-conservatives among all respondents, with conservatives responding more negatively. This difference, however, was primarily driven by differences among women (see also Schreiber, this volume). Conservative women were significantly more negative regarding gender balance legislation compared with non-conservative women: 62.5 percent versus 13.2 percent, respectively. If we look solely at conservative respondents on skewed-female boards, 60 percent of conservative men responded positively to the gender balance question compared with 0 percent of the conservative women. In short, ideology seems to be related to a more negative view of the law. Still, when 60 percent of self-identified conservative men on certain boards were in favour of the law, it is hard to make the case that negative views are likely to have a damning impact on implementation of the law. Our qualitative observations, however, suggest that it might be difficult to recruit younger women (and perhaps men), particularly those with small children, to certain types of boards. This is not because of conservative attitudes that reject women's service as a rule, since we have no real evidence of that from our study, but because of a lack of interest among younger women in serving in particular capacities. It might be that the men and women on the already balanced parks and recreation boards were serving because of interest in their children's activities. Unless there are family-related ties to economic development (or even some of the libraries), there can be challenges in appealing to women with young children to step up and serve.

The Challenge in Iowa

As Mona Krook (2007) notes, the success of quotas hinges on elites' willingness to recruit women and, in the case of Iowa, "balance" the boards. Those already serving in Iowa are the gatekeepers to recruitment and convey the norms accepted by the boards and commissions. Our evidence of the attitudes toward the gender balance law among those serving on the boards, and in many cases acting as the gatekeepers to service on the boards, suggests that there are both positives and negatives in the Iowa case that can impact the success of the law. Overall, the attitudes toward gender parity are positive among those already serving. In addition, many boards in our sample were balanced prior to implementation of the law. We believe that the challenge lies in the attitudes of those serving on boards not yet balanced. The attitudes of both men and women on such boards suggest a challenge to be overcome in implementing the law because those individuals might not see the importance of reaching out to recruit people who would bring gender balance to their boards and might not ultimately vote in support of applicants who could balance the boards.

Our more qualitative observations of what some people articulated in the meetings suggest that where boards are already balanced – parks and recreation boards and historic preservation boards – there is personal interest in service. In the case of the former boards, many parents of young children are willing to serve because doing so provides tangible value for them and their families as well as other families in their communities. This is also likely the case for library boards, but again we note the variations in what libraries provide to communities: summer reading programs for children, job search and placement services, socializing for seniors, and so on. Based upon our sense that many of the currently serving members of balanced boards are likely serving because of concerns with services and facilities for young children, specifically their children, the culture of the boards that have yet to be balanced might not be consistent with the concerns of parents. The challenge might be not merely to recruit women, which the law clearly aims to remedy, but also to recruit women and men with young children at home. Women who responded positively to the gender balance question in our survey who were serving on parks and recreation boards were significantly younger than female board members on library boards and historic preservation boards who also responded positively ($p < .10$); moreover, their mean response to the gender balance question was also significantly greater, indicating more support ($p < .10$). If, as our qualitative analysis suggests, women on parks and recreation boards were more likely to be mothers, then recruiting mothers to serve on other types of boards can improve their balance. Put another way, as mothers become board members and gatekeepers, adherence to balance might increase.

Illustrating some of the realities of the challenge of implementing the gender balance law, the following was reported in a local newspaper in 2012: "On the Allamakee County Zoning Board when Kirby Cahoon was up for reappointment, Colleen Gragg removed herself from consideration because she did not want to be appointed based only on the gender balance requirements. Later the Board met with the County Attorney when faced with reappointing Doug Mullen, whom they considered better qualified than applicant Marlene Imhoff-Duffy" (Beach 2012). The norms of the board conveyed to Gragg were that her appointment would be considered a quota appointment instead of a merit appointment. Those informal norms and cultural signals are the real problem to be overcome, one that the simple attitudes assessed by our survey do not begin to tackle.

This challenge was also recounted in the *Sioux City Journal:* "The [Woodbury County Board of] Supervisors ... bypassed a woman candidate, Rita Elser (a Sioux City school psychologist), for the county Zoning Commission and reappointed a man, Grady Marx, whose experience the majority deemed too valuable to lose. Jackie Smith, the only woman on the five-member board of supervisors, cast the dissenting vote." Smith noted that "we have not done enough to actively recruit women. It has been male-dominated for so long" (Hayworth 2010). Smith had actively recruited Elser and said that not appointing her was a mistake. On the same day in December 2011, just prior to the law's implementation date, the County Board of Adjustment voted to reappoint Corey Meister without considering the application of JoAnn Sadler (Hayworth 2010). From these examples, it seems that even when there are women willing to apply, either they are deemed "not as qualified" as the current board members or other applicants, or they withdraw their applications when they perceive that the current members would see them as merely filling a "balance" position. Such a decision seems to be consistent with the attitudes of some women already serving on boards who do not see the need for the law. A woman might be inclined to see her appointment as based upon her knowledge and expertise, or her willingness to serve, and would not want to be viewed as a less than legitimate applicant or board member under the balance requirement.

Despite such challenges for Iowa (particularly for the economic boards), as well as the lack of enforcement and vagueness of the law, there is reason to be optimistic about the success of the gender balance law. Krook (2007, 382) notes that other actors can have indirect impacts on quotas, such as women's organizations that can pressure elites to comply with the law or work to recruit and train women. In addition, several factors can assist in ensuring the success of a quota or parity law, including responsiveness to the law (or political will) (Woodward 2002). These organizations and efforts aim to change the cultural expectations of who can and should serve on the various boards.

Responsiveness to the Law: Or, Political Will

In many studies of gender quota laws throughout the world, one of the key problems that arises is political will. Does Iowa have it? The information mentioned above on publicly available data and organizations actively discussing and promoting gender balance suggests that, at a general level, Iowa does have the political will. Other evidence of goodwill toward the law comes from media interviews. Interviewed by the *Waterloo–Cedar Falls Courier* in 2010, Councilman David Jones of Waterloo, Iowa, tasked with bringing the city's boards and commissions up to date, said that "it's just the right thing to do [to balance the boards]. I feel very strongly about it whether it's the law or not." In response to the notion that some boards are harder to fill than others, he said that "there are women out there working in the trades and we really hope to accomplish that [recruit and appoint them], not just make an effort" (quoted in Jamison 2010). Echoing the "political will" expressed by Jones, County Supervisor Tom Little said, "I think Black Hawk County is doing a good job and we'll continue to improve based on recommendations we received" (quoted in Jamison 2010). Those recommendations came from a committee made up of representatives from the American Association of University Women and the Black Hawk–Bremer League of Women Voters, who have been meeting with city and county officials to educate them about the gender balance law (Jamison 2010). Such collaborative efforts, both the goodwill expressed by those in a position to recruit and that of groups working to assist municipalities in meeting the goal of the law, are likely to promote success.

It is unclear from our study how much communication and interaction there is among cities and towns in Iowa, but there seems to be a wealth of knowledge and innovative ideas in motion. Towns and cities could learn from each other in terms of strategies for determining potential leaders, identifying other civic groups whose members might have particular talents and expertise, and undertaking civic training or cross-training initiatives to introduce citizens to how a local government works to encourage future willingness to serve. Information shared among communities or mayors could facilitate quicker progress in meeting the challenges of achieving gender balance. Such action is necessary, we argue, to ensure that good faith efforts are less about political posturing than about serious efforts to recruit women and men, mothers and fathers, to serve on and balance gender imbalanced boards.

The resistance articulated earlier in this chapter takes the form of suspicion of top-down directives from state or national governments. That some individuals will disregard the law simply because it is viewed as government intrusion is part of the culture of Iowa's small autonomous towns. Autonomy is great in many ways and gives rise to the "can do" volunteerism that Iowans exemplify, but it can also result in a "separateness" that can pose a challenge for the existing training materials arguing that "this is good for all of us!" We have not yet identified specific training materials that articulate rallying points or a shared language that can assist in overcoming those opposed to gender balance because of perceived government intrusion, nor have we come across any materials that specifically target mothers or parents as appropriate candidates for local boards and commissions. Perhaps as monitoring of the law's implementation progresses, the ICSW or others will identify and disseminate key talking points in an effort to shift away from the focus on government intrusion and toward the value of inclusion and civic engagement that many Iowans prize. Noting that many board positions are consistent with the goals of raising children might encourage participation from those who did not previously consider serving.

The combined preliminary evidence of political will and the presence of many active women's organizations in Iowa bode well for extension of the state-level gender balance law to the local level. It is still in the early stages of implementation, and turnover on boards and commissions is slowly providing opportunities for municipalities to respond. How well they do will have a tremendous impact on local governance and can particularly impact women as leaders and citizens. The efforts in Iowa will also have impacts on other states that might be looking to implement a similar law. In the United States, many eyes are on Iowa regarding the policy experiment of gender balance at the municipal level.

Conclusion

Does gender balance matter for politics? The research to date suggests that it does and not just for reasons of social justice and equal representation (Burns, Schlozman, and Verba 2001; see also Ambrus, Greiner, and Pathak 2009). Women might have different perspectives and policy preferences than men based upon their lived experiences as women and often as mothers, such that more balanced decision-making bodies are more reflective of the populations that they serve. This is particularly critical at the municipal level, where community norms can be more or less successfully embodied in local board decisions and the policies that they recommend to city councils. As we found in our observations of local meetings, men and women alike note that their service is consistent with their interests as parents. Although not shown in the analysis, members of parks and recreation boards were the youngest, on average, members of all five board types. And, across the board types, women on parks and recreation boards were the second youngest group overall. Parents have vested interests in such boards given that the contents and outcomes directly affect the quality of leisure time with their children, and the difference in age by board type suggests that parents are taking advantage of such opportunities. For women with children, serving on such a board with direct implications for children might seem to be linked more closely to childcare responsibilities compared with boards on which the benefits to children are less clear and significant gender imbalance exists.

At the beginning of this chapter, we noted that recent research by political scientists challenged the popular assumption of childcare responsibilities being a hindrance to running for elected office (Fox and Lawless 2014). The question remains open, however, whether such research applies to voluntary positions such as on local boards and commissions, where status is less prominent and monetary benefits are non-existent. For such positions, childcare responsibilities might in fact weigh more heavily on a mother's desire to serve in government. If so, then that is likely to affect recruitment efforts in municipalities where gender balance legislation is in place. Gender balance can ensure that bodies are more democratic, but in the case of our survey of local boards and commissions in Iowa this will be achieved only if economic boards are successful in recruiting more women and library boards are more successful in recruiting more men. Balanced boards, specifically parks and recreation boards, offer an opportunity for parents to be directly involved in policy making related to parenting, and based upon casual observations from such meetings it appears that parents are doing just that. In effect, the gender balance law increases the likelihood of young mothers being involved in local politics, perhaps providing a stepping stone for state- and federal-level involvement. In the political science literature, there is some evidence that women can elicit a different leadership style than men (Rosenthal 2001, 2002; Swers 2002), that women as legislators can be more productive than their male counterparts (Volden, Wiseman, and Wittmer 2010), and that women as leaders can influence citizens' political efficacy (Atkeson and Carrillo 2007; Campbell and Wolbrecht 2006). Further, there is evidence that more women in decision-making groups increases collective intelligence and improves cooperation and efficacy in deliberation (Beaman et al. 2012; Williams Woolley et al. 2010), but of course both men and women can be attracted to certain types of service based upon their interests as parents.

A study of local politics is an attractive way to discern how such interests interact with already identified gender differences in attitude, decision making, and leadership. The gender balance law in Iowa makes no mention of parental status. Recruiting mothers to imbalanced boards such as economic boards might be difficult, particularly if the gatekeepers (current board members) view mothers as not having enough time for board responsibilities. We argue that our research should serve as a starting point for future research on gender quotas in Iowa and elsewhere that focuses not only on female representation but also on parental representation. In the case of Iowa, future research should focus on the extent to which mothers, fathers, and non-parents are being recruited to various boards, particularly those that have historically been gender imbalanced. In conclusion, we believe that gender balance matters for men, women, and parents and will matter for Iowa if municipalities wish to overcome some of the challenges outlined in this chapter.

Notes

Financial support for this project was provided by the Political Science Program of the National Science Foundation (SES 1015406 and SES 1015391). This research was reviewed and approved by the Institutional Review Boards (IRB) at the University of Northern Iowa and Northern Illinois University.

1 According to some discourses on gender quotas or gender parity, there are three main rationales for raising the proportion of women in political bodies. The first is rooted in social justice. This argument purports that men and women are entitled to the same rights and duties in political life. The second is based upon an assumption that politics lacks a considerable resource by relying mainly (or only) on men's participation. This idea suggests that, if men and women were more evenly distributed in public life, then additional participation by women would change both the form and the content of politics. The third argument is based upon policy preferences or political interests. This idea is rooted in the notion that men and women have distinct preferences and even contradictory interests such that, when women are not more involved politically, critical interests – such as the health and education of children – are neglected (Guldvik 2003, 2–3).
2 From http://iowahouse.org/2009/03/18/pay-equity-gender-balance/.
3 The information in this and the preceding paragraph can be found at the Iowa Commission on the Status of Women website, http://www.women.iowa.gov.
4 As an example, these two reasons – difficulty of recruitment and qualifications of appointees over meeting gender balance requirements – were noted in a March 18, 2009, article in the *Gazette* (which serves eastern Iowa, including Iowa City and

Cedar Rapids), http://thegazette.com/2009/03/18/house-approves-pay-equity-gender-balance-bills/.
5. Our sample of cities was based upon a random sorting of all cities in Iowa by congressional district and population. Cities were sorted first by congressional district (as a proxy for geographic location) and then by population. Within each district, four population categories were created (0–1,000 = 1; 1,000–5,000 = 2; 5,000–10,000 = 3; over 10,000 = 4). Within each category, cities were then sorted by a random number, with the first city assigned to our study. Of Iowa's 947 incorporated cities, 910 had a population of less than 10,000 at the time of our study. This randomization process ensured that we selected for observation an appropriate number of such cities. In sum, 20 cities (four [one from each population category] in each of five congressional districts) were selected. We were unable to visit all 20 cities because, in some cities, boards and commissions did not meet regularly or simply did not exist. We were forced to make additional adjustments because of cancellations and cities altering their meeting schedules and travel logistics because of weather, road conditions, and so on. Within each selected city, we observed meetings of one to five different boards or commissions common to most cities in the sample. They were library boards, historic preservation boards, parks and recreation boards, planning and zoning commissions, and zoning boards of adjustment.
6. A copy of the survey is available upon request. The response rate for the survey exceeded 65 percent. Individuals on historic preservation, library, and parks and recreation boards exhibited a higher response rate (> 70 percent) than individuals serving on planning and zoning or adjustment boards. Overall, women were more responsive to the survey than men. Full details on the response rate are available upon request. A thank-you letter to each board or commission was sent approximately three to five days after each observed meeting to thank each board or commission for participation and as a gentle reminder to individual members to complete the survey.
7. We paraphrase here from our field notes.
8. Our computed interrater reliability for two coders was Kappa = 0.805 ($p < .001$; 95 percent CI = 0.729, 0.881).
9. Ideology is operationalized as a dichotomous variable where the variable "conservative" is coded 1 for respondents who indicated that they were conservative or moderately conservative on the five-point ideology scale, whereas liberal, moderately liberal, and moderate responses were coded as 0. Doing so allowed us to more clearly demonstrate whether the ideology of the respondent modified preferences for gender balance legislation by sex.

References

Ambrus, Attila, Ben Greiner, and Parag Pathak. 2009. "Group versus Individual Decision-Making: Is There a Shift?" Working paper.

Atkeson, Lonna Rae, and Nancy Carrillo. 2007. "More Is Better: The Influence of Collective Female Descriptive Representation on External Efficacy." *Politics and Gender* 3 (1): 79–101. http://dx.doi.org/10.1017/S1743923X0707002X.

Beach, Bob. 2012. "Supervisors Discuss Gender Balance Issues in Regard to Planning and Zoning Commission." *Waukon Standard*, September 26. http://www.waukonstandard.com.

Beaman, Lori, Esther Duflo, Rohini Pande, and Petia Topalova. 2012. "Female Leadership Raises Aspirations and Educational Attainment for Girls: A Policy Experiment in India." *Science*, February 3, 582–86. http://dx.doi.org/10.1126/science.121238.

Bratton, Kathleen A. 2005. "Critical Mass Theory Revisited: The Behavior and Success of Token Women in State Legislatures." *Politics and Gender* 1 (1): 97–125. http://dx.doi.org/10.1017/S1743923X0505004X.

Bratton, Kathleen A., and Kerry L. Haynie. 1999. "Agenda-Setting and Legislative Success in State Legislatures: The Effects of Gender and Race." *Journal of Politics* 61 (3): 658–79. http://dx.doi.org/10.2307/2647822.

Burns, Nancy, Kay Lehman Schlozman, and Sidney Verba. 2001. *The Private Roots of Public Action: Gender, Equality, and Political Participation.* Cambridge, MA: Harvard University Press.

Campbell, David E., and Christina Wolbrecht. 2006. "See Jane Run: Women Politicians as Role Models for Adolescents." *Journal of Politics* 68 (2): 233–47. http://dx.doi.org/10.1111/j.1468-2508.2006.00402.x.

Childs, Sarah, and Mona Lena Krook. 2006. "Should Feminists Give Up on Critical Mass? A Contingent Yes." *Politics and Gender* 2 (4): 522–30. http://dx.doi.org/10.1017/S1743923X06251146.

—. 2008. "Critical Mass Theory and Women's Political Representation." *Political Studies* 56 (3): 725–36. http://dx.doi.org/10.1111/j.1467-9248.2007.00712.x.

Crow, Barbara. 1997. "Relative Privilege? Reconsidering White Women's Participation in Municipal Politics." In *Women Transforming Politics: An Alternative Reader*, edited by Cathy J. Cohen, Kathleen B. Jones, and Joan C. Tronto, 435–46. New York: New York University Press.

Fox, Richard L., and Jennifer L. Lawless. 2003. "Family Structure, Sex-Role Socialization, and the Decision to Run for Office." *Women and Politics* 24 (4): 19–48. http://dx.doi.org/10.1300/J014v24n04_02.

—. 2014. "Reconciling Family Roles with Political Ambition: The New Normal for Women in Twenty-First Century U.S. Politics." *Journal of Politics* 76 (2): 398–414. http://dx.doi.org/10.1017/S0022381613001473.

Franceschet, Susan, Mona Lena Krook, and Jennifer M. Piscopo, eds. 2012. *The Impact of Gender Quotas.* New York: Oxford University Press. http://dx.doi.org/10.1093/acprof:oso/9780199830091.001.0001.

Frank, Tracy. 2012. "State Legislature Doesn't Reflect Constituency." *Dickinson Press*, November 4. http://www.thedickinsonpress.com/content/state-legislature-doesnt-reflect-constituency.

Guldvik, Ingrid. 2003. "Gender Quota Regimes and Ideas of Social Justice: The Quota Regime of the Norwegian Local Government Act." Paper presented at the European Consortium for Political Research General Conference, Philipps-Universität Marburg, Marburg, Germany.

Hammond, Johnie. 2009. Cited in "Iowa Extends Gender Balance to City and County Boards." *Voices* 18: n. pag.

Hayworth, Bret. 2010. "Gender-Balance Clock Ticking in Iowa." *Sioux City Journal,* January 17. http://siouxcityjournal.com/news/local/gender-balance-clock-ticking-in-iowa/article_28ef5654-cc62-5c7e-9457-09cc6def48b1.html.

Jamison, Tim. 2010. "Gender Balance on Local Boards Remains Elusive." *Waterloo–Cedar Falls Courier,* July 18. http://wcfcourier.com/news/local/govt-and-politics/article_e73412b0.

Kopinak, Kathryn. 1985. "Women in Canadian Municipal Politics: Two Steps Forward, One Step Back." *Canadian Review of Sociology and Anthropology/La revue canadienne de sociologie et d'anthropologie* 22 (3): 372–89.

Krook, Mona Lena. 2006. "Reforming Representation: The Diffusion of Candidate Gender Quotas Worldwide." *Politics and Gender* 2 (3): 303–27. http://dx.doi.org/10.1017/S1743923X06060107.

–. 2007. "Candidate Gender Quotas: A Framework for Analysis." *European Journal of Political Research* 46 (3): 367–94. http://dx.doi.org/10.1111/j.1475-6765.2007.00704.x.

–. 2009. *Quotas for Women in Politics.* New York: Oxford University Press. http://dx.doi.org/10.1093/acprof:oso/9780195375671.001.0001.

Lawless, Jennifer L., and Richard L. Fox. 2010. *It Still Takes a Candidate: Why Women Don't Run for Office.* New York: Cambridge University Press. http://dx.doi.org/10.1017/CBO9780511778797.

Paxton, Pamela, Sheri Kunovich, and Melanie M. Hughes. 2007. "Gender in Politics." *Annual Review of Sociology* 33 (1): 263–84. http://dx.doi.org/10.1146/annurev.soc.33.040406.131651.

Rosenthal, Cindy Simon. 2001. "Gender Styles in State Legislative Committees: Raising Their Voices in Resolving Conflict." *Women and Politics* 21 (2): 21–45.

–. 2002. *Women Transforming Congress.* Norman: University of Oklahoma Press.

Swers, Michelle L. 2002. *The Difference Women Make: The Policy Impact of Women in Congress.* Chicago: University of Chicago Press.

Thomas, Sue. 2002. "The Personal Is the Political: Antecedents of Gendered Choices of Elected Representatives." *Sex Roles* 47 (7–8): 343–53. http://dx.doi.org/10.1023/A:1021431114955.

Vickers, Jill. 1978. "Where Are the Women in Canadian Politics?" *Atlantis* 3 (2): 40–51.

Volden, Craig, Alan E. Wiseman, and Dana E. Wittmer. 2010. "The Legislative Effectiveness of Women in Congress." Working paper.

Williams Woolley, A., C.F. Chabris, A. Pentland, N. Hashmi, and T.W. Malone. 2010. "Evidence for a Collective Intelligence Factor in the Performance of Human Groups." *Science,* October 29, 686–88. http://dx.doi.org/10.1126/science.1193147.

Woodward, Alison E. 2002. *Going for Gender Balance.* Strasbourg-Cedex: Council of Europe Publishing.

6

Conservative Mothers in Politics

Pushing and Reinforcing Ideological Boundaries

RONNEE SCHREIBER

> Conservatism in America has been painted as rich old white men that hate everyone else and have had it easy for too long. You can't say that with women. Do you really think you're going to come up to me in public and say you're just a rich person that doesn't care about people, when I just recently caught someone's puke that morning?
>
> – SHELBY BLAKELY, TEA PARTY PATRIOT STAFFER

As with the *supermadres* in Latin America, invoking maternalism in public policy debates is a common strategy in US politics. From the fight for women's suffrage to the battle over the Equal Rights Amendment (ERA), women have deployed images of motherhood in an attempt to sway policy makers and the public. Recent political activities and posturing over gun control policy in the United States provide clear examples of this. On January 30, 2013, Gayle Trotter, of the conservative Independent Women's Forum, testified before the US Senate Judiciary Committee about legislation that would increase restrictions on gun access. Urging Congress to oppose the proposal, Trotter argued that "guns make women safer ... [A woman] can protect her children, elderly relatives, herself or others who are vulnerable to an assailant."[1] Conversely, MomsRising, a feminist women's organization that supports efforts to make access to guns more difficult, organized an event on Valentine's Day so that "moms will bring their broken hearts and strong voices to lawmakers and make sure they are heard" about gun violence. Relatedly, the group urged "Congress to have a heart [and] pass common sense gun laws."[2] As these activists make representative claims as and for mothers, they constitute and generate debate over the meaning of mothers' interests.

How activists make claims about gender roles, motherhood, and politics has significance for understanding women's social and political standing and public policy outcomes. For decades, motherhood has also been a key category of contestation between feminists and conservatives. Clashes over motherhood reflect wider ideas about women's familial, political, and economic status – concepts that have been central to many other contests between feminists and conservatives (Burack and Josephson 2002; Luker 1984; Mansbridge 1986; Schreiber 2012b). Whereas feminists argue that gender roles are socially constructed, conservatives consider them to be naturally derived. Feminists have also argued that public and private spheres are mutually constitutive, meaning, for example, that those expected to care for children within the family are affected by public policies and values (Okin 1998). Conservatives generally urge political leaders to think of the family in private terms and allow members of it to make decisions without government "interference," as long as the couple leading the family are married and heterosexual.[3] The expression of "maternal thinking" for them, especially among religious conservatives, does not generate the same debates and tensions as it does among feminists (see, e.g., Dietz 1985; Tronto 1987). Even economic conservatives, who do not tend to espouse traditional views about gender roles, have argued that women are better suited than men to be primary caregivers and have advocated for policies that reflect this sentiment (Schreiber 2012a).

Despite these prevailing beliefs among conservatives, conservative women have a long history of political and workplace participation pointing to inconsistencies in their views about the role of women in the public sphere. Historically, then, conservatives have grappled with a conflict between ideology and political reality when it comes to women's roles in the public sphere, including the realm of professional politics. And this is becoming increasingly true over time. Republican women are running in growing numbers for elected office and thus need support from conservative voters and party leaders.[4] Republicans are also well aware that a gender gap in favour of Democrats means that they must target women voters and encourage political activism among women.[5] George W. Bush's 2004 campaign W Stands for Women featured Republican women leaders touring the country in an effort to mobilize women to vote for him,[6] and more recently conservative women's organizations have organized against the supposed Left's War on Women.[7] In addition, the high-profile candidacies of Republican mothers such as Sarah Palin and Michele Bachmann mean that conservatives must reconcile the espousal of traditional values with the reality that mothers want to be professionally and politically active. The use of motherhood by these high-profile conservative women as a strategic campaign tool (see also Thomas and Lambert, this volume) further highlights this conflict.

Given these tensions for conservatives, I ask here how do conservative women leaders reconcile ideological beliefs about gender roles and motherhood with their interest in promoting conservative women's political careers and getting Republican women, many of whom have children, elected to office? How do conservative women leaders navigate these tensions personally? What impacts might these views and decisions have on how they represent women's interests? As I will show, the conservative women under study articulate views about motherhood and work in ways that attempt to synthesize competing values, and in so doing they ultimately constitute new conceptualizations of motherhood, conservatism, and women's place in politics.

Political Implications of Conservative Women's Views on Motherhood

An important political effect of how conservative women interpret and articulate their views on motherhood is how that translates into representational politics. That is, the conservative women under study here consider themselves to be representatives of women's interests as well as political actors who define and advocate for women's issues. In these capacities, they directly affect policy making, engaging in public debates, media framing, and constituent mobilization, all of which will be shaped by their interpretations of maternal obligations. To this end, I build in this chapter on theories of representation and consider representation broadly and beyond the question of whether or not, for example, elected officials act on behalf of their constituents. Scholars have called on us to evaluate critically how we talk about representation and urge us to think about the concept in less static ways and in a variety of contexts. That is, they argue for moving beyond a linear analysis that merely considers whether or not elected officials represent a set of interests to a broader set of questions that analyze "the multiple possible actors, sites, goals and means that inform processes of substantive representation" (Celis et al. 2008, 99). Relatedly, Michael Saward (2006, 298) argues for "seeing representation in terms of *claims to be representative* by a variety of political actors, rather than (as is normally the case) seeing it as an achieved, or potentially achievable, state of affairs as a result of election." Thus, we should pay careful attention to the effects, purposes, and processes of claims making. Saward also notes that, while some representative claims are made outright, others "are perhaps barely recognizable as representative claims, so implicit are they in familiar institutions, actions and rhetoric" (308).

Building upon this idea of "implicit" representation, I assume here conservative women's narratives about their experiences navigating work and home responsibilities[8] to be those of representational claims making. Such claims, while implicit, are hardly insignificant. The personal accounts that women leaders articulate constitute the substantive interests of those whom they claim to represent and are frequently related to, and indeed shape, organizational missions and policy goals. Personal narratives, or implicit claims, reflect how these political actors understand mothers' interests more broadly and provide insights into how these women leaders, through their actions on behalf of other women, will constitute gender relations. Judith Squires (2008, 188) calls this the "constitutive representation of gender" or "CRG" and argues that representational claims "inevitably privilege particular conceptions of gender relations ... [and] privilege particular policy solutions which in turn privilege particular conceptions of gender." Even when women are not directly engaging in debates over mothers' interests (e.g., what role the federal government should play in providing childcare), they are shaping maternal identities and interests if they make claims as and for mothers. In the opening story about women and gun control, for example, women articulate representational claims as mothers to shape gun laws and suggest that these policies should be of concern to mothers. Thus, mothers' interests are not merely fixed and predefined by activists but also generated as actors make claims about them. The values that women hold about maternal roles and obligations underpin and motivate these processes.

Data and Methods

Data for this chapter come from systematic qualitative analyses of open-ended, in-depth interviews with 12 conservative women leaders who run, or are affiliated with, conservative organizations. Most of these organizations specifically claim to represent women (see the list of interview participants at the end of the chapter for more information). In their professional roles, these leaders shape public discourses about gender roles, conservatism, and women's interests. The interviews are part of a larger research project examining motherhood, ideology, and politics. This chapter highlights one facet of the larger study by addressing the question of how conservative women navigate between conservative views about gender roles and the seemingly contradictory goal of furthering their own and other women's political careers.

Definitions
For my purposes here, conservative women are those who promote social and/or economic conservatism. Social conservatives in the United States are usually Protestant evangelicals who lobby for policies that prohibit abortion, same-sex marriage, and pornography but promote prayer in public schools and a strong and well-funded US military. Economic conservatives favour free-market capitalism, decreased regulations on businesses, and low taxes. Their tendency toward libertarianism means that they generally shy away from supporting laws that ban abortion or same-sex marriage. They contest the existence of intentional or institutional discrimination and specifically challenge the goals and successes of the feminist movement (see also Hannagan and Larimer, this volume). They might also be termed "right wing," but because they explicitly and directly engage with institutions of government (e.g., Congress), other interest groups, and the media I do not consider them to be extremists.

In the interviews examined here, when conservative women talk about motherhood, they specifically refer to women's roles as caretakers of children. Although several credit their ability to be professionally engaged with their husbands' contributions to parenting, their views reflect conservative theories that differences among women and men are naturally, theologically, and/or biologically derived.

Findings
Conservatives must address the changing roles of women generally and conservative women's participation in politics specifically. The narratives below reflect answers to questions about how they balance their personal and professional lives or aim to when and if they have children. Interviewees were also asked to reflect on the popular belief that conservative women condone

mothers' professional and political participation. As noted, leaders denounce this limited view. Subsequent questions and responses suggest that, while conservative women make implicit representational claims that constitute "new conservative mothers," they do so in ways that still signify adherence to other conservative values. Thus, new conservative mothers might defy gender role norms but not other aspects of conservative ideology.

New Conservative Mothers

Conservative organizations and leaders must recognize the potential for change in family dynamics and ultimately gender role ideology. Indeed, conservative interviewees argued that traditional conservative stereotypes of mothers are no longer accurate and explained why in detail. Given that these women make claims to represent conservatism, this is an important finding. It suggests that conservative women leaders constitute maternal activity in broader and more flexible ways than have been associated with this movement (see Schreiber 2012b for more discussion).

When asked whether it was contradictory for her or other conservative mothers to be in the workplace, Stacey Mott, founder of Smart Girl Politics, quickly shut down the idea that conservative ideology prevents mothers from being professionally active:

> I think the premise is wrong to start with. I don't think conservative women are pro stay-at-home moms. I think we run the gamut just as liberal women do. I mean there are plenty of conservative women out there who want to raise a family and have a career as well. I think it's a misconception that conservative women are stay-at-home moms and that's all we want to do. I have my own aspirations, to be something outside of a mom myself. And most of my friends within the organization feel the same way. It's almost offensive. Not coming from you. But it is offensive for people to assume that all of us are cookie-cutters. (Interview with Mott)

Tea Party Patriot staffer Dawn Wildman offered a more complicated assessment of ideology and relative gender role norms, crediting other women for paving the way for conservative women to think that they have more options:

> I guess because I would probably say I benefited from whatever that fight was to make sure that women were quote unquote

equal. So I don't know, I've never considered myself a feminist or a traditionalist in any sense of the imagination because every decision I've made in my life as a woman has been done for myself and family. So it wasn't like my husband expected me to be barefoot and pregnant at home, and I'm a feminist who says screw it, I'm going to go against all societal norms and whatever. So I don't even know what that means. To me, I see women changing things in leaps and bounds in ways that probably wouldn't have happened 20 years ago. Thank God for Geraldine Ferraro. Where would Sarah Palin have been? All those other women who stepped up and said "you know, we should be counted just as important as you are." (Interview with Wildman)

Marjorie Dannenfelser, president of the pro-life Susan B. Anthony List, offered similar sentiments but noted that the conservative women whom her organization supports for elective office tend to enter politics when their children are older, suggesting some compromises:

I interviewed almost a hundred candidates last year ... I would say the percentage of them that have little children is far smaller than the percentage that have children in high school or older. Mostly older. Some of them were in the state Senate; they were doing things a little bit closer to home. And they see a new season in life turning. So it's a slow ratcheting-up rather than ... a particularly conservative female way to do it. It's exactly how it's been for me. (Interview with Dannenfelser)

Dannenfelser added in 2011, however, that the 2010 elections were significant for understanding the role of conservative women in politics:

I really believe this past election was a tipping point in the type of woman that was running. Not only do I believe it, but the numbers back it up. It was what it was. The dominant woman running was a pro-life conservative woman. It was the one getting through the primaries, it was the one doing the best in elections, and the women that did poorly, especially challengers, were women who were of the old model. There really is now a new model. At the very minimum, there is room for both. (Interview with Dannenfelser)

When pushed about why there were still prevailing beliefs that conservative women were opposed to mothers in professional careers, Mott pinned the blame on liberals. As noted, conservatives historically have promoted the idea that women should prioritize stay-at-home mothering (see, e.g., LaHaye 2007), but Mott (and others) did not frame it that way:

> That's why Palin and Bachmann and some of the other conservative women ... are dispelling some of those myths about conservative women, and I don't think that people on the left and some Democrats are ready for that. They had us boxed into a little cookie-cutter category, that we were these women who wanted all women to stay at home and raise the babies, and that's not the case. And I think that because they're shattering that description of who conservative women should be it's kind of caught a lot of people off guard. (Interview with Mott)

The starting place for these conservative women leaders is that conservatism has transformed and is more accepting of mothers' professional goals. These views are consistent with previous research on conservative women's support for Palin's and Bachmann's bids for national offices (Schreiber 2014). Thus, from their point of view, any evaluation of conservative ideology and politics must be understood in this new light. As the next section shows, however, conservative ideology about familial issues has not been completely transformed, for conservative women describe their experiences through the language of individualism and personal choice.

The Personal Might Not Be Political

One component of conservatism that tests the limits of feminism is that of choice. Some argue that the legacy of feminism is that women should be free to make personal decisions appropriate for them regardless of whether or not their actions are "feminist." Ideas about free choice mesh well with conservative ideologies. For example, the Independent Women's Forum argues that the wage gap between men and women derives from women who opt in and out of the workplace in accordance with their maternal obligations (see Furchgott-Roth 2012 for more on this argument). In other words, women are paid less, and are less likely to be promoted, because they choose to be stay-at-home mothers. This conceptualization of choice is a tantalizing way to explain women's decisions without implicating state policies and cultural values and works well within a liberal economic and social order. When asked about their personal lives in reference to their professional goals, conservative women countered with responses framed in the language of choice and personal decision making. Exemplifying the responses of most of my interviewees, Alyssa Cordova of the Clare Boothe Luce Policy Institute told me this:

> Well, I think that definitely is a big challenge for any woman who wants to, I mean liberal or conservative, if a woman has children she wants to be a mother and be a mother to her children ... [I] think it's a personal decision that should be made between you and your family, and nobody else should be telling you that one makes you a stronger woman than another one ... I mean I don't have children. I want children, definitely. And I also care a lot about my career and the work that I do. And I think that's just sort of something I expect I'll just kind of talk about with my husband when I'm married and we'll kind of decide. (Interview with Cordova)

Even women who do not work outside the home have the *option* to be politically active, according to conservative President of Eagle Forum and conservative movement icon Phyllis Schlafly, who told me that "the homemaker isn't chained to the stove. She can do all sorts of things." Indeed, Schlafly suggested that women who work outside the home have fewer choices than women who do not (see also Campbell and Childs, this volume, for additional perspectives on conservative women and childrearing). In talking about her success in defeating the ERA, Schlafly praised the volunteer efforts of "homemakers" and argued that "they were able to be volunteers and had supportive husbands and could take off time to go to the capitol and lobby against the ERA." However, she wavered about the value of mothers working – arguing that women should have the choice but be conscious of the trade-offs. She noted that her mother had to work "out of necessity" because her father lost his job during the Great Depression, but then she added as a warning to women who "choose" to work for other reasons that "the only fulfillment is what you can do reporting to a boss instead of a husband."

Keli Carender, the national coordinator for the Tea Party Patriots and the first person to hold a Tea Party rally in the United States, extended the discussion to cover other conservative mothers in politics and praised them for being role models for women and conservative ideology. In addition, she equated mothers working or running for office with the ability to choose freely one's life goals – a view that meshes with economic conservative ideology:

> I think that's one reason why Sarah Palin and Michelle Bachmann are such enticing figures, because they're incredibly strong and outspoken, and they don't say women are victimized. They give very positive interpretations of what being a woman is today. You can have a big family, you can have a very important career, you can do it all, you can have a great marriage, you're strong and independent, and you're not a victim of anyone. It's that self-governance thing. (Interview with Carender)

In these explanations, women have agency and options, but conservative women also ignore or dismiss the roles of power, institutions, and resources as well as the contexts in which choices are created and must be implemented. Thus, choices are privatized, norms are rationalized, and social/structural relations that undermine mothers' empowerment are considered acceptable if they are "freely" chosen. Within this notion of choice lies no challenge to the role of the state, economic policies, and/or institutional promotion of values about mothers' professional careers.[9]

Juggling Acts

Although conservative women leaders were eager to dispel the notion that mothers do not belong in the workplace, they also readily conveyed that working mothers, including themselves, are likely to encounter difficulties as they navigate their lives. Terms such as "juggling" and "balancing" arose frequently to describe how women managed family and work responsibilities. Leaders commented on the challenges of pursuing career goals while raising children, either because options to help them were unappealing (e.g., daycare) or because they thought that they were making sacrifices in one area to do well in the other. Offering a personal account of these challenges, Dannenfelser, a mother of five, likened addressing tensions to playing a harp:

> As the ... needs in my home have increased, I've just had to sort of adapt. Somebody gave me a great analogy. It's sort of like playing a harp ... To make it all work, sometimes you're playing certain

chords, and that's what you have to do. But at other times in life, you have to shift to another place, and you play those other chords. That's really how it is, and I can't help, I couldn't do it if, frankly, faith weren't driving it, because then it would be way too confusing, keeping the priorities straight ... [I] do have sort of an ideal situation where there's a woman who works for the Susan Anthony List, and she also helps me at home, so it's like another me. (Interview with Dannenfelser)

Tea Party activist Wildman, raising her niece and nephew, was equally frank about her balancing act:

Whoever said you can have it all was full of crap. You can, the unfortunate thing is you don't do a 100 percent at everything. You drop the ball in places. The first year we were doing this I forgot every birthday and anniversary. Which I'd never done. I'm super organized and anal retentive and consider myself kind of the matriarch of the family since my grandma died ... So I think it is the constant conversation we all have. How do you balance it? With the sisterhood that's being built. With helping each other. Women will say "oh, you know what I found at Costco? It's frozen, and it only takes 40 minutes." We start sharing ideas of how to [do things], ... [and] I think things are more in a routine than they used to be, women I think are having an easier time of it. (Interview with Wildman)

Conservative college activist Gabriella Hoffman predicted that she too would feel stress and the need to juggle if and when she had children:

Well, I would like to have a balance between both. I believe, you know, to have a career it's very important. It allows me to do a lot of stuff. To advance myself politically and to network with people and just to enjoy life. Because we're in a society where anyone is capable of achieving their dreams, achieving their goals. So I would ideally like to do that with my respective career. But I also feel it's very important to be a mother, to be responsible to your children, and to be, you know, a devout wife. I don't think that there's anything wrong with juggling and maintaining I guess what people criticize as being the '50s culture ... You know, being a housewife and this and that ... But now, I guess, with society kind of encompassing more, a lot of conservative women will juggle both family and career. (Interview with Hoffman)

Conversely, conservative Pat Weiss, president of the California Federation of Republican Women, whose children are adults, commented that she would not have made what she calls sacrifices if her children were still at home, but she did support women who acted otherwise:

> I will tell you something. If I were raising my children right now, and they were younger, and I was doing what I'm doing now in the federation, I couldn't do it. I just couldn't if I had children at home. Because my time is now so involved with them. So, if you don't have your priorities set right, I don't think you can be a success at doing anything. But, I mean, I know you want to know about running for office. I think it's a huge sacrifice, to tell you the truth ... I think it's a huge sacrifice. (Interview with Weiss)

For representatives of women's organizations, personal narratives about women's choices also have implications for policy debates and outcomes. Fittingly, the organizations that they represent mobilize women to support policies such as tax cuts for businesses that offer flex-time or part-time employment but denounce state-funded family leave, childcare, or similar initiatives (Schreiber 2012a). Indeed, though all interviewees recognized and supported the need for mothers to be involved in politics, several articulated concerns with institutionalized childcare as a resource. Schlafly linked her personal distaste for childcare to an attack on feminists and government support for these institutions: "[Feminists] think that one of the chief examples of the oppression of the patriarchy is that society expects mothers to look after their own children, and this has got to be moved to the taxpayers, and they got [sic] to be provided with daycare."

Like others, Blakely praised her husband's involvement but also stated her opposition to childcare: "Well, I have a husband who knows how to cook and do laundry. That's helpful. He's really the thing that makes it possible for me. I work from home, which is kind of the best and worst of both worlds. On one hand, I don't need to put my kids in daycare, which I am philosophically against." When asked about this opposition, Blakely replied that

> I think that babies need their mommas, and babies need their daddies. That's what I was raised with, and that's what I believe in, and I ... don't think I could stand to drop my kids off to the lowest bidder so I could go do, even if it's saving the world, it's like they're my babies. So to me, when I had kids, I'd never worked outside of the home. This is something I could do from home, and that's actually why I wound up writing for the Tea Party, ... because I could do this basically via the Internet. (Interview with Blakely)

Kerry Healy, a former lieutenant governor of Massachusetts and a co-founder of the Political Parity Project, recognized the need for family involvement, a private solution to women's juggling acts:

> So it really wasn't until they were about three and six that I felt that I could go beyond that and start actually becoming more active in the community and take the chance of running for office. And at that point I need[ed] help from family. My husband's mother [wa]s quite young, and she ha[d] been a high school principal and had directed daycare centres, and she was able to help me with the children while I had my political career. She literally moved into the house next door to us and more or less raised my kids during the years that I was lieutenant governor. I was working anywhere between 14- [and] 16-hour days for probably five years. It was not conducive to spending a lot of family time. (Interview with Healy)

Healy continued by linking her personal account to which policies employers should make, framing her suggestions in conservative economic terms and demonstrating that some conservative women are supportive of childcare if it is not financed by tax dollars but instead offered as an incentive by private businesses. For these conservative women, opposition to childcare is less about gender roles and women's responsibilities and more about what role the state should play in providing services:

> As a conservative, I'm not going to tell a company or employer what sort of benefits they should offer, but I do think that smart employers are going to understand that that's something that will attract women to their enterprise and will also make them loyal.

> So when I started working ... there was a daycare centre there. I didn't have any children, but I certainly admired the vision in that and saw the kind of employee loyalty that you saw. In terms of perhaps providing tax incentives, I think there are ways that you could incentiv[ize] this sort of behaviour, but ultimately I think it's in the rational self-interest of companies to look into providing this sort of support. (Interview with Healy)

Conservative women leaders also connected their personal narratives about motherhood to other mothers seeking professional political status, offering encouragement and support to them. However, perhaps drawing on their own experiences of juggling and balancing, activists consistently invoked the language of sacrifice to discuss political women's careers. For example, Dannenfelser, who runs an organization dedicated to getting more pro-life women elected to office, also recognized for those seeking elected positions that

> the difference now is, in the women who are now running, ... that there is obviously a lot that you do learn by being in public life. So those lessons came slower to more traditional models of women because they were just more reticent to leave home for all the best reasons. The economy changing and frankly ... with more of a need for a different model of woman out there. I almost think of it as a sacrifice. I would be very happy to do everything I do from home. I consider it a sacrificial act to have to drive into Washington every day. (Interview with Dannenfelser)

Consistent with conservative ideas about women's political involvement being akin to a duty (Schreiber 2012a), such sacrifices were also couched in patriotric terms by Weiss:

> I think Sarah Palin does a great job with her family, and she's managed as governor in Alaska. As far as I can tell, she's done a good job with her kids. I think you have to be very special, and most people can't do that. I mean I can't do that. I mean you're working full time and raising kids and writing books ... There's been criticism of Michelle [Bachmann] or Sarah Palin. I certainly wouldn't criticize them for that. I think that they're making

wonderful contributions to their country and sacrificing and doing that. (Interview with Weiss)

Schlafly offered a harsher assessment of the sacrifices and argued that, because of gender differences in priorities, not all women might be up to the task:

> Well, I've spent a good part of my time encouraging women to be active in politics one way or another, and I've encouraged them to run. But I run – I ran for Congress twice, and I can tell you why there are not more women who want to run for Congress. They, it's a, first place, it's a dog's life. You have to put up with all of the nasty remarks by people, those awful chicken dinners, the travelling, away from home, ... endless shaking [of] hands with people, and, uh, it's perfectly obvious why there are not more women who want to do that. If you want to do it, fine, if you've got a supportive husband or if you don't have a husband at all, a lot of women can do it, and we've had a lot of successful women, but any thought that there's got to be as many women as men doing this is just nuts. It just isn't going to happen. (Interview with Schlafly)

All of these leaders declared that women have the right to make choices and that their decisions are personal. And they freely recognized that mothers in the workplace encounter difficulties. However, as noted in the previous section, the remedy for these challenges should not be derived from state involvement. Here leaders offered their own tales of personal sacrifice, spousal involvement, and cobbling together childcare from sitters and family members.

It's a Woman Thing
When explaining why working mothers experienced difficulties, many of the conservative leaders referred to gender differences. That is, they argued that it is in a woman's nature to multitask and feel responsible for caregiving, which in turn generate anxiety and stress. Again, the need to juggle is linked not to structural factors such as workplace policies or cultural expectations about men's roles and responsibilities but to the personal choices that women make. For example, Dannenfelser discussed her experiences in these terms:

> One of the strengths of women is to be conscious of where everybody else in your life is at any given time I think. It's a visceral sense. Just how's everybody in the room here, I mean not just your family, but you go out with the girls, and everybody has a sense of taking care of everybody else. The guys are, like, go get me a beer. We love 'em, but I'm just saying it's a different instinct. (Interview with Dannenfelser)

Wildman offered similar reflections on gendered differences and linked her analysis to why women feel compelled to participate politically:

> I think it's a lot of things. I really hate cliché things, especially [those] that come out of either political people or media. But mama grizzlies. Women really feel a strong sense of stewardship. And what they're handing their kids to be the last generation that did better than their parents is not a pleasant thought. And so mothers, grandmothers, sisters, daughters are looking at – we need to stop it. I think because too they're usually the ones who deal with the family budget. They're the ones clipping the coupons and trying to figure out, okay, how many times can I fix chicken without them realizing it's chicken every night this week? And so I think because they [women] are more influential in the home, that's the ultimate consumer. (Interview with Wildman)

This view is linked strongly to the idea that parents, especially mothers, are more likely to be political consumers (for a more in-depth discussion, see Micheletti and Stolle, this volume) and that political strategies are particularly designed to speak to politicized mothers as a result (see also Langner, Greenlee, and Deason, this volume).

Many of the conservative women under study, as well as the women whom they represent, are conservative Protestant Evangelicals. Articulating a view close to what many of them believe, Charmaine Crouse Yoest, president of Americans United for Life, referenced a Bible verse providing theological support for gendered differences:

> If you really want to drill down to where most conservative people live on this issue, ... a classic reference for most of us is Proverbs 31 ... Coming back to the verse which says that this woman is a huge economic producer. She's going out, she's buying a field, she's

> planting her vineyard. She's ensuring that her family is all well clothed. So she has this very clearly defined role that is not kind of the Hallmark card kitschy mom with the apron on, which I think you were very correct in saying is a caricature of the *Leave It to Beaver* kind of approach to motherhood. So you could certainly find some people out there who have some kind of medieval views, if you will, of what a stay-at-home mom should be, but you're going to find ... an awful lot of even women in that kind of subculture they're doing Mary Kay ... [There] are all kinds of home-based enterprises that even the most traditional stay-at-home kind of mom pursues. (Interview with Yoest)

Although most interviewees invoked gender differences to indicate support for mothers working outside the home, Schlafly was more nuanced and negative. In discussing her views on women's careers and life courses, she exhorted women to focus on childbearing before pursuing other endeavours. However, she added that, when women choose otherwise, it is because feminists have encouraged them to do so. Such antifeminism is consistent with the goals of conservative women to discredit feminism and establish themselves as the more legitimate representatives of women's interests (Schreiber 2012a). As Schlafly noted,

> the first thing that they've got to realize is that God knows what he is doing in sending babies to young women, and you are making a terrible mistake if you think that you can establish a career and then after you're 40 decide you want to have a husband and kids. Life doesn't work that way. You have a biological clock, even though the feminists have often denied it. And the trouble with the women's studies and what the feminist professors are teaching is that the woman should plot her lifetime career without any space for marriage or children. Now, it's okay if you want to do that, but you really ought to realize that if you do that chances are very strong that you're going to wake up after you're 40 and realize you've made a mistake, and it's too late. And so I think that young women ought to plan their life to include marriage and children, and they can do other things too. (Interview with Schlafly)

Like the emphasis on individualism, highlighting gender differences demonstrates that, while there is a "new conservative mother," how and why she acts in her capacity as a politically engaged woman does not completely veer away from conservative beliefs about the role of the state and the biological base of gendered behaviour.

Conclusion

This analysis reveals some important findings about how conservative women leaders understand motherhood, work, and politics and the implications for their representational actions. Most conservative women think about their work-family balance in privatized terms. This language of choice and personal decision making fits well with conservative views on the role of the state and liberal individualism and reflects the policy goals of the organizations that they represent. Given this, these groups might both disagree with and resist the actions and recommendations required to address the gaps identified between women and men in professional politics presented in previous chapters (notably Chapters 2 through 5).

That said, the notion that women should favour their roles as primary caregivers over those of professionals has evolved for conservatives. Whereas the two older interviewees with adult children – Weiss and Schlafly – thought that it is important to focus on mothering when children are younger, the younger women were eager to dispel what they perceived to be myths about conservative views on gender roles. The younger women without children articulated a desire to "have it all," but they had some apprehension about what that would mean in terms of their ability to balance their lives. Of course, my interviewees were selected because they have been involved in professional politics, but they are also women who implicitly and explicitly represent other conservative women and make policy claims that correspond to their views on gender role norms. There is consensus among these leaders on the need for work-at-home options and the personalization of problems that women encounter as mothers in professional politics. Although working at home might be a good option for some, doing so removes some of the responsibility for helping families from policy makers and shifts it to employers. This translates into public policy priorities that correspond to these conceptualizations (Squires 2008). For conservative women, there is an ideological shift in terms of gender roles, but their privatized conceptualizations will lead to policy goals that match.

Although they might ultimately advocate for mothers working outside the home, conservative women also offer slightly distressing accounts of this scenario – though it is acceptable for women to work, it is also hard for them. Few of these leaders focus on why there is so much juggling; instead, they highlight the implications of these balancing acts and how to deal with them. Indeed, gender relations are rarely questioned. In some cases, men's roles are emphasized, but only in the context of granting women the space to be mothers and professionals. The agendas of the organizations represented here indicate that these groups rarely reinforce men's involvement when it comes to public policies, but preliminary findings do suggest a strong correlation between implicit representational claims and explicit organizational actions on behalf of women.[10]

Debates over policies to address mothers' interests reflect how these women constitute gender role norms and will no doubt continue as conservative women vie with feminists over the right to represent women and determine their interests. As noted elsewhere (see Arneil, this volume), such entrenched conflicts reflect wider societal ambivalence about mothers' roles and responsibilities and generate disputes over which policies best address conflicts between workplace and family needs. Future research on this topic should pursue the relative successes of these organizations. In addition, a similar study of men would be enlightening. Do they feel the need to juggle responsibilities? Why have they not organized as fathers to lobby for better family leave and related policies? Would conservative and feminist women support such activism? To what end?

Notes

1 http://iwf.org/media/2790433/#sthash.siuUDwb3.dpuf.
2 http://action.momsrising.org/signup/RSVP_ValentinesDay_GunSafety.
3 I do not mean to diminish the consequences of conservative anti-gay activism and recognize that conservative rhetoric about the relationship between the public and the private is inconsistent with some policy goals of the conservative movement. I am concerned here with mothers' roles vis-à-vis other members of their families and within the workplace, and when talking about these mothers conservative women's organizations assume that they are heterosexual.
4 In 2010, for example, a record number of Republican women ran for and won congressional seats. See http://www.cawp.rutgers.edu for complete data on women running for office.
5 Since 1980, in US presidential elections, women are more likely than men to vote for Democratic candidates.
6 See http://www.gwu.edu/~action/2004/bush/bushorgwomen.html for more information.
7 See, e.g., http://www.cblpi.org/resources/article.cfm?id=221.

8 I use these terms to reflect differences between paid work experiences and those related to personal and familial arrangements. I recognize that these are not perfect terms in that many people, including the women under study, engage in paid work in their homes.
9 Comparatively, feminist leaders also invoked a similar language of "choice" but qualified their statements by referring to the "second shift" for women at home and the lack of state-sponsored family care as factors that shape their options.
10 As part of my larger project, I have examined the mission statements and policy goals of the organizations represented by these women.

Interviews

Blakely, Shelby, journalist coordinator, Tea Party Patriots
Carender, Keli, national coordinator, Tea Party Patriots
Cordova, Alyssa, lecture director, Clare Boothe Luce Policy Institute
Crouse, Janice Shaw, senior fellow, Beverly LaHaye Institute (part of Concerned Women for America)
Dannenfelser, Marjorie, president, Susan B. Anthony List
Healy, Kerry, co-founder, Political Parity, and former Republican lieutenant governor of Massachusetts
Hoffman, Gabriella, Young Americans for Freedom chapter president and UCSD student
Mott, Stacy, founder and president, Smart Girl Politics
Schlafly, Phyllis, founder and president, Eagle Forum
Weiss, Pat, president, California Federation of Republican Women
Wildman, Dawn, national and California state coordinator, Tea Party Patriots
Yoest, Charmaine Crouse, president, Americans United for Life

References

Burack, Cynthia, and Jyl J. Josephson. 2002. "Women and the American New Right: Feminist Interventions." *Women and Politics* 24 (2): 69–90. http://dx.doi.org/10.1300/J014v24n02_04.
Celis, Karen, Sarah Childs, Johanna Kantola, and Mona Lena Krook. 2008. "Rethinking Women's Substantive Representation." *Representation* 44 (2): 99–110. http://dx.doi.org/10.1080/00344890802079573.
Dietz, Mary. 1985. "Citizenship with a Feminist Face: The Problem with Maternal Thinking." *Political Theory* 13 (1): 19–37. http://dx.doi.org/10.1177/0090591785013001003.
Furchgott-Roth, Diana. 2012. *Women's Figures: An Illustrated Guide to the Economic Progress of Women.* Washington, DC: AEI Press.
LaHaye, Beverly. 2007. "Motherhood: Part of God's Plan for the Family." *Christian Examiner,* May 20. http://www.christianexaminer.com/article/motherhood-part-of-gods-plan-for-the-family/43367.htm.
Luker, Kristen. 1984. *Abortion and the Politics of Motherhood.* Berkeley: University of California Press.

Mansbridge, Jane. 1986. *Why We Lost the ERA*. Chicago: University of Chicago Press.

Okin, S.M. 1998. "Gender, the Public, and the Private." In *Feminism and Politics*, edited by Anne Phillips, 115–41. Oxford: Oxford University Press.

Saward, Michael. 2006. "The Representative Claim." *Contemporary Political Theory* 5 (3): 297–318. http://dx.doi.org/10.1057/palgrave.cpt.9300234.

Schreiber, Ronnee. 2012a. *Righting Feminism: Conservative Women and American Politics with New Epilogue*. New York: Oxford University Press.

–. 2012b. "Mama Grizzlies Compete for Office." *New Political Science* 34 (4): 549–63. http://dx.doi.org/10.1080/07393148.2012.729742.

–. 2014. "Motherhood, Representation, and Politics: Conservative Women's Groups Negotiate Ideology and Strategy." In *Gender, Conservatism, and Political Representation,* edited by Karen Celis and Sarah Childs, 121–40. Colchester: ECPR Press.

Squires, Judith. 2008. "The Constitutive Representation of Gender: Extra-Parliamentary Re-Presentations of Gender Relations." *Representation* 44 (2): 187–204. http://dx.doi.org/10.1080/00344890802080464.

Tronto, Joan C. 1987. "Beyond Gender Difference to a Theory of Care." *Signs: Journal of Women in Culture and Society* 12 (4): 644–63. http://dx.doi.org/10.1086/494360.

PART 2
COMMUNICATIONS AND CAMPAIGN STRATEGY

7

Private Mom versus Political Dad?

Communications of Parental Status in the 41st Canadian Parliament

MELANEE THOMAS and LISA LAMBERT

Conventional wisdom suggests that it is difficult, if not impossible, for parents in general and mothers in particular to balance their family lives and careers in electoral politics. Although fewer women than men are elected at all levels of political office, more women sat in the 41st Canadian Parliament than at any other point prior to the 2015 federal election (Parliament of Canada 2012). Women in elected office are less likely to have children than their male counterparts (Thomas 2002), but about 50 percent of the women currently in the House of Commons are mothers. Despite common wisdom, it is possible to balance motherhood and politics, yet the decisions that politicians make about displaying their parental status are certainly influenced by that wisdom. Faced with the fear that potential voters might not think her capable of both mothering and politicking, a woman might downplay her parental status, whereas a man might not think twice about referring to his family in communicating with his constituents.

How a politician either displays her family status or downplays it can be part of a measured strategy informed by deliberate decisions. These decisions link an MP to her party's brand while simultaneously addressing her image as a candidate. For some, overt parental displays can soften a hawkish image, cue the support base, demonstrate adherence to "normal" values, or reinforce a particular policy position. For others, a cursory nod to parental status, or its omission entirely, can represent an attempt to avoid being pigeonholed, stereotyped, or publicly critiqued about their private life. Thus, the strategic decision not to disclose or display parental status can also be about cuing, or controlling, one's political brand.

This chapter makes several valuable contributions to the literature. First, and the most important, is a shift in focus. Much of the literature on gender, political careers, campaigns, and the media focuses on what is done *to* women candidates. Borrowing from Schreiber and from Miller (both in this volume), we take a different tack, focusing instead on the strategic decisions that women make for themselves. Although women in politics face unique constraints often not felt by their male colleagues, they still have agency. What they do with that agency, and how that differs from their colleagues with fewer constraints, helps to improve understandings of elite political participation while simultaneously reflecting back onto theories of representation. Second, we deliberately assess this agency outside election campaigns to capture the bulk of MPs' activities. And third, prior research argues that this question is ripe for comparative research, since past results from candidate/individual-centric contexts such as the United States demonstrate that gender and party interact to shape political strategies (Schneider 2014). Assessing if and how this is the case in a party-centric context such as Canada adds important dimensions to our existing understanding of the actions of women (and men) in politics.

Below we outline the importance of political branding and link this concept to the gender, media, and politics literature. Then, we examine the 41st Canadian Parliament for parental displays on MPs' websites and in mass communications to their constituents, such as householders and holiday cards. We then draw from interviews with MPs and their staff to consider the strategic decision making behind displays of one's family. Our results suggest that MPs are more likely to cue their parental status through texts rather than photos on their websites and to make use of what one called their "gut instinct" when it comes to displays of their parental status in mass communications to their constituents. It is only in holiday cards, a form of communication that lends itself to displays of family photos, that most MPs will display their families. Importantly, these decisions appear to be conditioned by gender, party affiliation, and province.

Political Branding and Parental Status

Political parties, leaders, and candidates in Canada borrow from established marketing techniques to communicate with the electorate. Arguably pioneered by the Conservative Party of Canada, the focus of Canadian political parties is on a "high-level partisan brand" encapsulated by the leader and applied across individual candidates and policies (Cosgrove 2012, 111; see also King 1991).[1] This brand also aids in identifying key constituencies (Giasson, Lees-Marshment, and Marland 2012). In theory, brands help voters to interpret information about the party (Smith 2001) while increasing loyalty and partisanship and facilitating vote choice (Parker 2012).

For candidates and MPs, especially in Canada's party-dominated system, their own brands are based upon party affiliation and supplemented by whichever traits they wish to emphasize (Parker 2012). Provided that it fits with a politician's personality and communication strategy, one's personal life can be politicized deliberately and strategically. Doing so demonstrates that they have the "capacity to offer a 'human' persona" (Langer 2010, 61; Stalsburg 2012). This "politicization of the private persona" is then used to build the political brand and to underwrite political values and legitimize policy (Langer 2010, 61). For party leaders, this means that they must "embody the party brand, [because] their personal lives can personify the party's values and policies ... and function as the unifying narrative" that links policies and platforms (Langer 2010, 61–62). This holds for candidates as well through an expectation that they all strictly adhere to, and communicate, their party's brand. Overall, the party brand framework facilitates an understanding of why displays of various aspects of politicians' private lives, including their parental status, might vary across genders, across and within political parties, and across and within regions.

The role of the family in the political brand is a relatively new phenomenon. Some research suggests that "family" became important in politics only when traditional family structures started to decline. Laurel Elder and Steven Greene (2012) cite the 1992 US presidential election for sparking a political focus on "family values," and notably, a decade later, the fourth most cited word at both American nomination conventions in 2012 was *families* after *jobs, Romney,* and *Obama*. This trend has been mirrored in Canada, exemplified by the focus of the New Democratic Party on "working families" leading up to the 2011 federal election.

Britain offers paradigmatic cases of the political personalization and use of a politician's family as part of the political brand. Tony Blair strategically displayed interactions with his children, both during election campaigns and in the lead-up to the invasion of Iraq (Langer 2010). David Cameron employed similar strategies by using his family to authenticate policy positions and decontaminate his party's brand (Langer 2010, 67). In contrast,

Gordon Brown opted to keep much of his private life private. Thus, parental status can be a cue for a politician's brand or how to interpret a politician under the umbrella or rubric of his or her party's brand.

In light of this, the display of a politician's parental status becomes a key factor in strategic political communications. Political marketing research indicates that image management is directly linked to the selling of political brands and policies to the electorate (Marland 2012). In Canada, Conservative Party insiders state that the prime minister deliberately controlled images to "reinforce the 'common man' brand attributes, and to contradict or negate 'negative image' stereotypes" (Marland 2012, 222). Photos of Stephen Harper with kittens were used judiciously to soften his image: if displays of juvenile felines are deliberately managed, then so too are images and other displays of a politician's spouse, children, and grandchildren. Indeed, as research from the United States shows, on "the biography page [of a candidate's website] ... different aspects of personal history are adjusted in accordance with a strategic plan" (Schneider 2014, 22).

Although prior research was focused either on candidate-centred contexts or on party leaders, it is plausible that the same principles apply to MPs within a party caucus. This raises questions about whether MPs exercise agency in how their personal lives are politicized and whether they do so in a manner consistent with their party's brands. Although the media often respects that choice, the personalization of politics is a reciprocal production between the politician and the media. This can make it more difficult for politicians who are "unhappy or unable to play the personal game" to succeed in politics (Langer 2010, 72–73).

The Gendered Politics of Parental Status[2]

Although anyone in politics can have good reasons for wanting to keep her or his private life private, research indicates that the private lives of female politicians receive a very different kind of scrutiny than those of their male colleagues. This might be partly because politics is a masculine-stereotyped field, for voters tend to rate masculine characteristics more highly than feminine characteristics when evaluating politicians and political jobs (Huddy and Capelos 2002; Huddy and Terkildsen 1993a, 1993b; Sanbonmatsu 2002; Sanbonmatsu and Dolan 2009). Notably, fulsome measures of political stereotypes indicate two things about women in politics. First, they are rated as considerably less masculine than their male peers and, second, they are also about as feminine (Schneider and Bos 2014). Similarly, it is well established that the media coverage of women in politics is very different from that of men: ignored entirely in the past, coverage of women focuses on their appearance, character, or apparent violation of traditional gender roles rather than on their competence (Heldman, Carroll, and Olson 2005; Everitt and Gidengil 2003; Tuchman 1978). Women need to garner considerably more support than their male opponents to receive comparably positive media coverage (Miller, Peake, and Boulton 2010).

Most of the research on gender, politics, and the media does not address the parental status of female or male politicians. The few studies that do suggest that a politician's family arrangements are fairly subject to scrutiny because politicians are public figures. Even so, women in politics face a disproportionate amount of this scrutiny compared with men in politics. This might be a result of traditional gender stereotypes and persistent gender gaps in unpaid labour in the home related to childcare (Eagly and Carli 2007). Men are assumed to have "someone" (read: a wife) at home to look after the children; women are not (Stalsburg 2012; van Zoonen 1998, 2005, 2006). It is therefore not surprising that nearly two-thirds of women in the candidate pool believe that children will make seeking elected office more difficult, compared with a mere 3 percent of men (Lawless and Fox 2005). Importantly, though, parental status and traditional family structures do not explain why women report lower levels of political ambition than men (Fox and Lawless 2011; Lawless and Fox 2010). If women's status as wives and mothers cannot account for the gender gap in political ambition, then the cause must be in something other than their parental status.

The fact that politically ambitious mothers exist highlights a gap in the literature that corresponds to political activity and participation. Most research addresses reactions to female politicians – from both voters and the media – rather than the strategic decisions made by candidates and politicians themselves. Stated differently, the literature highlights what is "done to" women in politics rather than the decisions that women themselves make.

One of the few studies that examine how gender affects how politicians present themselves on their websites finds that political party, not gender, matters most. Women and men from the same party tend to prioritize the same issues; variations appear across, but not within, parties. This "confound[s] expectations of difference based on theories about the stereotyped interests and abilities of women and men candidates" (Dolan 2005, 36). That said, some differences do appear when the priorities of women running against men are contrasted against the priorities of women running against other women. This suggests "strategic behavior on the part of these women to simultaneously counter and benefit from gender-based stereotypes voters may hold about them," though this is done in a "limited fashion" (Dolan 2005, 37). Overall, male and female candidates emphasize the same things. Although this conclusion runs counter to expectations, it is logical when considered in a political marketing framework. Political candidates want to win elections; it follows that they will identify and target the voters and constituencies that will help them to achieve that goal and communicate directly to them. Instead of suggesting that it is *"likely* that women, like men, are rational actors" when seeking public office (Dolan 2005, 42; emphasis added), it is reasonable to assume that female politicians are rational and strategic actors.

This is where women's political ambitions can collide with gender stereotypes about politics. Like male candidates, female candidates have to ask themselves "how do I best present myself to voters?" Yet women in politics face a double bind: do they politicize their personal lives and open themselves up to critique for being "bad mothers," or do they downplay or refuse to disclose aspects of their personal lives and potentially miss out on an effective political brand? Stated differently, do female politicians risk being characterized like Dutch politician Neelie Smit-Kroes, whose teenage son sighed "finally, I have my mother back," when she retired from politics after complaining that he had "learned to prepare [his] own meals" (van Zoonen 2005, 91). Media reports of the son's statements sent a strong cue that "good" politicians are "bad" mothers. Or should political mothers brand themselves as "Mama Grizzlies" rising to protect their offspring from (political) harm (Stalsburg 2012)? For many female politicians, either decision is fraught with risk.

Women might have good reasons to market themselves to voters as mothers. Cuing "mom" also cues stereotypes of altruism, compassion, tolerance, and nurturance (Stalsburg 2012). These stereotypes have positive associations and can be advantageous parts of a political brand. Similarly, men can use children to demonstrate that they are "normal" and heterosexual, that they adhere to social norms, or to play up a "common man" brand (Langer 2010; Marland 2012; Stalsburg 2012). Developing this brand can be more advantageous for women than for men. Participants in an experiment rated childless female candidates the lowest of all, whereas childless male candidates were rated the highest. Among women seeking public office, mothers of young children were rated as favourably as mothers of older children. However, female candidates with small children were rated lower than male candidates with small children (Stalsburg 2010).[3] This suggests that the effects of politicizing the private persona are conditioned by a candidate's gender.

There might be many reasons to present one's family life during a political candidacy, but once a candidate has won the seat it becomes an open question whether the impetus to manage one's political brand remains. We argue that there is for two reasons. First, during the string of minority governments at the federal level between 2004 and 2011, MPs had to be prepared to go into an election campaign on short notice. Similarly, even under a majority government, the context of a constant or perpetual campaign means that MPs' political brands have to be constantly and diligently managed. Second, MPs must be aware of the new media environment and its ability to produce a story in minutes by people who are not professional journalists. For instance, when Vic Toews introduced Bill C-30 (aimed at protecting children from Internet predators), his comments about Internet privacy riled up many Internet-savvy Canadians. His family life – Toews divorced while in office after he fathered a child with a former babysitter – was made public through an anonymous Twitter feed of his divorce affidavits. This proved to be embarrassing for the government and did not fit his political brand as a protector of children. The bill was subsequently withdrawn (Ibbitson 2012). This shows that MPs' political brands affect their ability to do their jobs as well as their candidacies and election campaigns.

Mommy Penalty, Daddy Bonus, and Grandparental Pride

The research outlined above informs several expectations about Canadian MPs and their displays of parental status. We expect that male MPs are more likely than female MPs to be parents. We also expect that, even if both are parents, male MPs will be more likely than female MPs to display images of their children, and female MPs are expected to be more ambiguous about their parental status than the men. Thus, we anticipate that female MPs with young children will not display pictures of them as readily as male MPs will display pictures of their young children. We anticipate that women with adult children and grandchildren will be more likely to present pictures of their role as (grand)mothers than mothers of younger children.

Political parties dominate political brands in Canada (Cosgrove 2012), so MPs' displays of parental status should vary by party affiliation. Although the Conservative Party of Canada might not actively cultivate a traditional "family values" brand, it is broadly perceived to be the party most friendly to this perspective. Local candidates regularly use this messaging, even if the party centre does not (Conservative Party of Canada 2012). Given this, Conservative MPs are expected to be more likely than MPs from other parties to display images of their families. The brand of the New Democratic Party (NDP) is also important here. The NDP often brands its policy as friendly or oriented toward "working families." Its 2011 federal election campaign pushed this part of the NDP brand (Martin 2011). Thus, we expect that NDP MPs will cue this brand by politicizing their private personas.

Data and Methods
We used three different sources of data in this study: websites, paper materials, and interviews with a selection of MPs and party officials.

First, we compiled information about every MP elected to the House of Commons in the 2011 Canadian federal election using publicly available biographical data. We began by examining politicians' websites in the fall of 2011. If an MP mentioned children in any way, we categorized this as a display of parenthood. MPs who presented photographs of their children on their websites were coded as both displays and pictures of parenthood. If an MP's parental status could not be ascertained from the website, then news reports and other biographical sources were used to determine if the politician was a parent. In some cases, the politician was a parent, but there was no display of that status on his or her website. In other cases, the home page and "about me" page were like albums of family photos, complete with names and ages (exact birthdates in some cases) of children and grandchildren.

Second, we solicited paper materials – election leaflets, householders, and holiday cards – usually delivered to a constituent's home via mail from a randomly selected sample of MPs ($N = 103$, 24 percent women). Although these materials are in the public domain, they are typically provided to constituents, a subset of the public. The materials are paid for by public funds made available for communications with constituents. Some MPs shared a great deal of their materials with us, but we supplemented our sample of materials with those available on MPs' websites. Additional holiday cards were collected from the 2014 holiday period.

Third, we conducted interviews with MPs and staffers to gather additional context for a politician's decision either to display or to downplay parental status. These interviews were conducted in January and February 2013.

Results

General Displays of Parental Status on MPs' Websites

Most MPs have websites, each of which has at least some personal information about the MP, such as educational background, previous employment, and volunteer activity. Here we coded mention of children in any form as a display of parenthood. Generally, children do not form a predominant part of any MP's biography; if mentioned at all, they are typically raised in the last paragraph.

That said, parenthood is the norm among Canada's federal politicians. Two-thirds of MPs are parents, 15 percent are not, and the remaining 18 percent are ambiguous. Men are more likely to be parents than women. More than 70 percent of male MPs display parenthood, whereas 55 percent of female MPs appear to be parents. This corroborates research from the United Kingdom and United States suggesting that male politicians use their parental status to communicate that they are "normal" (Langer 2010; Stalsburg 2012). Of the MPs who are clearly not parents, most are women (28 percent of women compared with 11 percent of men). This, too, mirrors research from the United States (Thomas 2002).

We could not determine the parental status of 18 percent of MPs in the 41st Parliament from the information provided on their websites. Contrary to expectations, this does not appear to have been gendered: 17 percent of female MPs and 18 percent of male MPs made no reference to their parental status. This is surprising. It is not possible to assess from their websites if the underlying motivations for this ambiguity were comparable, though our interviews (discussed below) appear to indicate that gendered strategic considerations were at work.

Very few MPs (12 percent) prominently displayed photographs of their family members on their websites. However, male MPs were far more likely to display their families in this manner (14 percent) than women MPs (4 percent).

Parental Status and Party Affiliation

Parental status in Canada's 41st Parliament was certainly conditioned by party affiliation. Parenthood seemed to be more common in the Conservative and Liberal Parties and less common in the NDP and Bloc Québécois.[4] Table 7.1 shows that, within the Conservative and Liberal Parties, more than three-quarters of the MPs indicated on their websites that they were parents. Very few Conservative and Liberal MPs were ambiguous about their parental status, and even fewer did not have children. This was in keeping with our expectations, especially of Conservatives. In contrast, only about half of NDP and Bloc MPs indicated that they were parents. Furthermore, the other half of Bloc MPs were ambiguous about their parental status; no Bloc MP openly admitted not having children. A sizable portion of the NDP caucus was also ambiguous about their parental status (26 percent), and 27 percent of NDP MPs appeared not to have children. This proportion of non-parents in the NDP caucus was more than double that for any other party. This might have been because the caucus was relatively young and because a large portion of it was from Quebec, where all MPs appeared to be reluctant to display any information about their parental status.[5] Perhaps there was little expectation that the private personas of MPs would be politicized in French-speaking Canada as opposed to English-speaking Canada. Furthermore, the unexpected election of many NDP MPs from Quebec in the 2011 election certainly propelled some people into the political limelight who were unlikely politicians and did not fit the cultural "norm" for a politician in terms of age, education, or family status. Regardless, this was not in keeping with our expectations about the NDP and its "working families" brand.

An MP's party was also associated with the propensity to display photos of her or his family. Conservative MPs were the most likely to picture their children (19 percent), though none of the Conservative women with children under 18 pictured them on their websites. The only Conservative

TABLE 7.1
MPs' parental status by party and gender in the 41st Canadian Parliament

Party	Gender	(N)	Parent (%)	Not parent (%)	Unclear (%)
Conservative	Male	(137)	77	9	14
	Female	(27)	74	15	11
Liberal	Male	(28)	86	7	7
	Female	(7)	71	0	29
NDP	Male	(64)	53	17	30
	Female	(40)	38	42	20
Bloc Québécois	Male	(3)	33	0	67
	Female	(1)	100	0	0

women with photos of their children on their websites were those with adult children: Lynne Yelich (SK), Shelly Glover (MB), and Susan Truppe (ON). Even though Liberal MPs were the most likely to mention their families in texts, only 6 percent of them displayed photos of their children on their websites. Only two NDP MPs had photos of their children on their websites, Nathan Cullen and Paul Dewar, both of whom are heterosexual, younger, married men elected in ridings outside Quebec. None of the women or sexual minorities in the NDP caucus posted pictures of their children. This finding is striking: the only female MPs who pictured their children were Conservatives with adult children, whereas men with young children from all parties displayed photos (and sometimes names) of their offspring. These partisan and gender differences suggest that there might be strategic differences in politicizing private personas across MPs and their parties and that these differences relate to how MPs communicate their private lives to constituents.

Displays of Parental Status in Paper Materials
Very few MPs displayed any personal information, including their parental status, in their householders. This is intuitive since householders are printed newsletters that MPs use to inform constituents of their parliamentary activities. That said, all of the MPs in our sample who mentioned their families in their householders were Conservative men.

Holiday cards are somewhat different from websites and householders. Although they display the MP's particular brand, they are less likely to be overtly partisan. Instead, the cards provide a unique opportunity for MPs to reinforce their brands by displaying their families (and politicizing their private personas) in a less cynical way. This was readily apparent in the types of greetings used: over 80 percent of Conservative MPs exclusively wished their constituents a Merry Christmas, whereas MPs from every other party were far more likely to use a more generic or inclusive holiday message. Very few MPs communicated any substantive information in their cards; those who did were most likely to include an office address or information about a family-friendly event in the constituency that the MP planned to host over the holiday period (e.g., a skating party).

Holiday cards are also unique in that, unlike websites or householders, parental status is almost exclusively communicated through a photograph rather than text. Yet, as in other materials, both gender and party condition these displays. Nearly two-thirds of male MPs, but less than one-third of female MPs, included family photos in their holiday cards. This might help to explain why MPs' parental status was clear in only 50 percent of the cards that we analyzed, even though 69 percent of MPs were parents. Nearly four of five Conservative MPs placed images of their families on their holiday cards, regardless of gender. No NDP female MPs (but all NDP male MPs in this sample) displayed their families on their holiday cards. Instead, while the majority of NDP MPs regardless of gender included generic winter scenes on their cards, many NDP male MPs (40 percent) also included family photos. Male MPs, regardless of party, were considerably more likely to include their children's and grandchildren's names in their cards.

Grandparental pride was clearly displayed on holiday cards. Grandparents were more likely than parents to include multiple photos and dedicate more space to photos of their (grand)children. Interestingly, parents and grandparents were equally likely to include the names of the children pictured in their holiday cards. Like parental status, gender and party conditioned grandparental status, since grandparents were most likely to be Conservative male MPs.

"Being an MP Involves Your Whole Family"

To further investigate the rationale employed by parliamentarians for their parental displays, we conducted interviews with six sitting MPs and three staff members.[6] The interviewees offered considerable insights into their strategic thinking on parental displays. Several themes emerged from the interviews. The most prominent is that photos are heuristics for MPs, allowing them to communicate "who" they are to their constituents. This form of communication does not exist in a strategic vacuum: most of the MPs and strategists whom we interviewed indicated that the strategic use of family photos provided a real information shortcut for, and responded to real curiosity from, constituents. One female MP indicated that using family photos is strategic because they are a "short form of who you are and what you're dealing with, if you're a single mom, or in a same-sex relationship, or whether you're looking after an aging parent. I'm sure it's possible to convey that in a picture and save two paragraphs in the brochure [pause] because people are curious about who this person is." This MP went on to lament that, because nuclear families continue to be the assumed norm for politicians, those who are single, LGBTQ, or childless "don't have the quick snapshot I do in the way they communicate who they are in their life." Another MP (male) said that "we get a lot of people in the riding who appreciate seeing the family grow and getting a picture of the family" in various forms of communication from the MP, such as the annual holiday card. In other words, by communicating who they are through displays of parental status, MPs help to establish their own brands.

The interviews reinforced the argument that men in politics use family photos, especially those of children, to soften their image, make them seem more approachable, or give them greater credibility on certain issues. One staffer for a male MP noted that "people do like to see, 'oh, he's a family man!' and he's got kids, and it kind of brings him more down to earth." The same staffer later reiterated that family displays "just bring home that, 'hi, I'm a dad,' or 'I'm a mom,' and 'I've got kids too and the same problems as you.'" Some staffers offered similar advice to women in politics. One reported that he strongly encouraged the (female) MP whom he worked for to talk about her spouse and family on social media. He concluded that "emphasizing the human side of both the candidate and an elected official is an important part of the communication person's job, to remind them that it's okay to show that you're a human being, warts and all." These staffers recommended the strategic use of mentions or photos of their MPs' spouses and children "as long as it's fitting to the message you're trying to get across."

All of the MPs and most of the staffers whom we interviewed argued that the strategic display of family life was a positive, effective strategy for most (but not all) MPs.[7] They further agreed that this strategic advantage was gendered. Some thought that women in politics had the most to gain from this strategy. One staffer said that "it's always nice to see people that have time to manage home, children, and traditional mother/family relationships. That works. That works more for a woman than a man because you know she is a hard worker, and she still goes home and makes dinner for her kids … People would eat that up." However, most of our interviewees took the opposite view, saying that there "still is a double standard when it comes to women, their families, and politics." Several MPs noted that, if a woman politician displayed photos of young children, "somebody's going to say 'who's looking after the children?' [pause] which they don't if you put up the husband with young children." Another MP, on recollecting the experiences of his caucus colleagues, noted hearing, "especially with regard to cabinet ministers both provincial and federal, especially when they have younger children, 'well, I suppose the taxpayers are paying for a babysitter in their office,' because you see a picture of the mother with the young child. [pause] It is usually snarly." It is hardly surprising, then, that several interviewees noted that most female MPs with young families choose not to display them, even on holiday cards, to constituents. Those who do are typically Conservative MPs, and future research could probe whether this reflects greater strategic importance of a "family values" strategy or whether those female Conservative MPs need to undertake additional strategies to tamp down the critique identified here.

A separate but related theme came up with women (MPs and staffers) but not men. Women were concerned about the safety and privacy of their children, especially if they were young. One said that, "when my daughter was young, I was very, very conscious of making sure her privacy was protected. It's just like that with any young child; you're careful of exposing them to that larger community where you don't know who is watching." A staffer candidly stated that she did not refer to her own child by name or location, nor did she post photos of her family, because she was "leery" of the ramifications. Her advice to the MP with whom she worked was that "it's always *safer* to keep younger children out of the spotlight" (emphasis added). Another MP was adamant that she would not display images of or information about her children because "it protects them and their safety." She thought that prioritizing the safety of her children put her at a strategic disadvantage, but any strategic advantage that she might gain otherwise was not enough for her to change her mind. She saw displays of family as "advantageous" because constituents and voters

> see [MPs] humanized in a setting with children, with family, when they can say, "oh, she's more like me because she's a mother, and she deals with teenagers, and she brought up two children, and she's married." I think there is a huge advantage to that actually. But it doesn't change my opinion. I believe that I am at a distinct disadvantage by not using pictures of my family.

This theme was entirely absent in our interviews with male MPs and staffers.

All interviewees, regardless of party affiliation, agreed that politicization of the personal was less fraught with concern for male MPs than for female MPs and that having a "typical" nuclear family, as opposed to a family with same-sex partners or a single parent, was more palatable to the public. All interviewees noted that decisions about displays of an MP's family were made after considering both political and personal advantages and disadvantages. No MP or staff member indicated that his or her party or leader influenced these decisions.

Conclusion

As per our expectations, displays of parental (or grandparental) status in MPs' communications are conditioned both by gender and by party affiliation. Female MPs are more reluctant to display their parental status, and in keeping with results found in other chapters of this volume we find that women in politics are far more likely to be childless than their male peers. Although it is generally uncommon for MPs to display any photos of their families, those who do are more likely to be Conservative men. Female MPs do not, as a rule, picture their children on their websites, and the women who do include their children in their holiday cards are overwhelmingly Conservative too (see Schreiber, this volume). Most female MPs who picture their children have adult children and grandchildren. Our interviewees suggested that there is no clear agreement on the strategic advantage or disadvantage for women in politics of displaying their parental status or politicizing their private lives. Many indicated, as does the literature, that this is more fraught for women than for men. Others argued, though, that this kind of strategy would be as effective, if not more effective, for women than for men. A larger number of female MPs is required to fully infer the effects of gender and the politicization of the private persona in general as well as across parties and regions.

Although the role of Conservative Party affiliation in MPs' displays of parental status was in line with expectations, those for the NDP and its working families brand were not met. NDP MPs are distinctly unlikely to politicize their private personas. This might be partially explained by the larger presence of NDP MPs from Quebec, for few in Quebec across all parties display their parental status. Thus, though the NDP communicates concern for working families and "families at the kitchen table" in platform documents and speeches – notably in Jack Layton's speech – it also appears to eschew the political use of MPs' private lives. The exceptions are NDP men on their holiday cards and younger or past leadership candidates on their websites.[8]

Several clear limitations stem from this study. First, the 41st Canadian Parliament offered great opportunity since the NDP caucus in it was very young. Many were not yet parents, and the results presented here might reflect their stage in the life cycle.[9] This opportunity raised challenges for generalizability to other Canadian Parliaments but could be remedied by examining the communication of parental status by more parliamentarians over more Parliaments. Second, we examined elected MPs only. We were not able to examine fully how these MPs presented their parental status as candidates since their campaign websites were ephemeral, removed shortly after the elections were concluded. We were also unable to compare how displays of parental status varied among candidates. Third, Canada's parliamentary system is characterized by strong party discipline. Although interviewees indicated that their parties did not advise them on whether or not to display their families, partisan differences in the displays imply that there might be some cuing communicated. This, too, could be investigated further by examining other Parliaments, particularly those with different partisan compositions, as well as provincial legislatures. In addition, other political jurisdictions with less rigid party discipline can provide further insights into the balance between MPs' strategic choices in branding themselves via family displays and central party directions. These limitations speak to the need for longitudinal studies in multiple jurisdictions to investigate these questions fully.

Notes

1 Brands formulated in this way can rise and fall on leaders' fortunes (Cosgrove 2012). For example, as a result of weak leadership, the brand of the Liberal Party of Canada has been described in recent years as "fading fast" as it moves away from being "the patriarch" and toward being "the uncaring father" (CBC Radio 2012).
2 We employ a broad definition of parental status here. Anyone who indicated parenting children, be it through birth, adoption, or social relationship, was considered a parent. As is apparent below, we further anticipate that gender will interact with these parenting experiences to produce particular effects of motherhood unique from those of fatherhood.
3 Interestingly, more conservative participants scored female candidates the lowest on all measures (Stalsburg 2010), even though female politicians with small children are more likely to be elected under the same conservative banner (Kuerschner 2011).
4 The lone Green Party of Canada MP, Elizabeth May, is well known as the mother of one young woman. May pictures all of her family, including a two-decade-old picture of her daughter's father, and a woman whom she calls her step-step-daughter on her website.
5 When Quebec is excluded from these counts, parental displays increase and ambiguous displays decrease for both the NDP and the Liberals, especially for female MPs. Outside Quebec, 83 percent of Liberal female MPs disclosed that they were mothers; ambiguous displays dropped to 17 percent. For the NDP, 66 percent of male MPs and 57 percent of female MPs outside Quebec displayed their parental status. The proportion of NDP women who were not parents drops to 29 percent, and the proportion of NDP MPs who were unclear about their parental status falls to 16 percent (male) and 14 percent (female), respectively.
6 Of these nine interviews, four were with male MPs and five with female MPs (or their staff); four interviews were with Conservative MPs, four were with NDP MPs

(or their staff), and one was with a Liberal MP. More information is provided in the reference list.
7   One staffer sharply disagreed with this advice. He argued that voters would "see right through that kind of thing," and he would advise against the strategic politicization of the private persona because he associated that strategy with a great deal of risk: "We are trying to minimize risk here, you know." It is worth noting that this staffer was much younger than most of our other interviewees. This raises questions about whether and how younger cohorts view families as part of the "business" of being an MP in the same way that older generations appear to view them. As newer generations of people enter political life, we might see politicians draw firmer lines between the private persona and the public persona. We might also find that a generation raised in a social media world is less likely to draw those lines at all. Certainly, more research is needed, since some young MPs and staffers have used conventional and social media to announce relationships and births (see Smyth 2013).
8   This link to leadership might be an interesting avenue for future research. Are these displays of parental status by former leadership candidates an artifact of their attempts to build a leader-like personal brand? Future leadership contests in the NDP and other federal parties might provide some clues. This aspect of party leadership needs to be reconciled with the finding from the interviews that party leadership does not direct MPs' strategies for displaying their children.
9   By June 2014, three NDP female MPs had either become new mothers or were pregnant (Burgess 2014). They did not mention their children on their websites in early 2015.

Interviews
Staff to male NDP member, January 19, 2013
Staff to male Conservative member, January 24, 2013
Male Conservative member, January 24, 2013
Staff to female NDP member, January 24, 2013
Male Conservative member, February 1, 2013
Female Conservative member, February 1, 2013
Female NDP member, February 1, 2013
Female NDP member, February 13, 2013
Female Liberal member, February 18, 2013

References
Burgess, Mark. 2014. "Building the Orange Wave, One Caucus Baby at a Time." *Hill Times*, June 30. http://www.hilltimes.com/heard-on-the-hill/hill-life-people/2014/06/30/building-ndps-orange-wave-one-caucus-baby-at-a-time/38950.
CBC Radio. 2012. "Is the Liberal Brand Sick?" *The House*, September 8. http://www.cbc.ca/player/Radio/The+House/ID/2277007307/.
Conservative Party of Canada. 2012. Search results for "family values." http://www.conservative.ca/?lang=&s=family+values.
Cosgrove, Kenneth M. 2012. "Political Branding in the Modern Age: Effective Strategies, Tools, and Techniques." In *Routledge Handbook of Political Marketing*,

edited by Jennifer Lees-Marshment. London: Routledge. https://www.routledge-handbooks.com/doi/10.4324/9780203349908.

Dolan, Kathleen. 2005. "Do Women Candidates Play to Gender Stereotypes? Do Men Candidates Play to Women? Candidate Sex and Issue Priorities on Campaign Websites." *Political Research Quarterly* 58 (1): 31–44.

Eagly, Alice H., and Linda L. Carli. 2007. *Through the Labyrinth: The Truth about How Women Become Leaders*. Boston: Harvard Business School Press.

Elder, Laurel, and Steven Greene. 2012. "Politicians Love to Talk about Family. But Maybe Not Yours." *Washington Post*, September 7. http://www.washingtonpost.com/opinions/politicians-love-to-talk-about-family-but-maybe-not-yours/2012/09/07/0be2edea-f218-11e1-adc6-87dfa8eff430_story.html.

Everitt, Joanna, and Elisabeth Gidengil. 2003. "Tough Talk: How Television News Covers Male and Female Leaders of Canadian Political Parties." In *Women and Electoral Politics in Canada*, edited by Manon Tremblay and Linda Trimble, 194–210. Toronto: Oxford University Press.

Fox, Richard, and Jennifer L. Lawless. 2011. "Gendered Perceptions and Political Candidacies: A Central Barrier to Women's Equality in Electoral Politics." *American Journal of Political Science* 55 (1): 59–73. http://dx.doi.org/10.1111/j.1540-5907.2010.00484.x.

Giasson, Thierry, Jennifer Lees-Marshment, and Alex Marland. 2012. "Introducing Political Marketing." In *Political Marketing in Canada*, edited by Alex Marland, Thierry Giasson, and Jennifer Lees-Marshment, 3–21. Vancouver: UBC Press.

Heldman, Caroline, Susan J. Carroll, and Stephanie Olson. 2005. "She Brought Only a Skirt: Print Media Coverage of Elizabeth Dole's Bid for the Republican Presidential Nomination." *Political Communication* 22 (3): 315–35. http://dx.doi.org/10.1080/10584600591006564.

Huddy, Leonie, and Theresa Capelos. 2002. "Gender Stereotyping and Candidate Evaluation: Good News and Bad News for Women Politicians." In *The Social Psychology of Politics: Research, Policy, Theory, Practice*, edited by Victor Ottati et al., 29–53. New York: Kluwer Academic.

Huddy, Leonie, and Nayda Terkildsen. 1993a. "The Consequences of Gender Stereotypes for Women Candidates at Different Levels and Types of Office." *Political Research Quarterly* 46 (3): 503–25. http://dx.doi.org/10.1177/106591299304600304.

–. 1993b. "Gender Stereotypes and the Perception of Male and Female Candidates." *American Journal of Political Science* 37 (1): 119–47. http://dx.doi.org/10.2307/2111526.

Ibbitson, John. 2012. "How the Toews-Sponsored Internet Surveillance Bill Quietly Died." *Globe and Mail*, May 15. http://www.theglobeandmail.com/news/politics/how-the-toews-sponsored-internet-surveillance-bill-quietly-died/article4179310/.

King, Stephen. 1991. "Brand-Building in the 1990s." *Journal of Marketing Management* 7 (1): 3–13. http://dx.doi.org/10.1080/0267257X.1991.9964136.

Kuerschner, Isabelle. 2011. "Good Mother or Good Politician? Politics and Motherhood in Germany and the United States." Paper presented at the Eighteenth

International Conference of Europeanists, June 20–22, Barcelona. http://dx.doi.org/10.2139/ssrn.1947701.

Langer, Ana Inés. 2010. "The Politicization of Private Persona: Exceptional Leaders or the New Rule? The Case of the United Kingdom and the Blair Effect." *International Journal of Press/Politics* 15 (1): 60–76. http://dx.doi.org/10.1177/1940161209351003.

Lawless, Jennifer L., and Richard Fox. 2005. *It Takes a Candidate: Why Women Don't Run for Office*. Cambridge: Cambridge University Press. http://dx.doi.org/10.1017/CBO9780511790898.

—. 2010. *It Still Takes a Candidate: Why Women Don't Run for Office*. Cambridge: Cambridge University Press. http://dx.doi.org/10.1017/CBO9780511778797.

Marland, Alex. 2012. "Political Photography, Journalism, and Framing in the Digital Age: The Management of Visual Media by the Prime Minister of Canada." *International Journal of Press/Politics* 17 (2): 214–33. http://dx.doi.org/10.1177/1940161211433838.

Martin, Sandra. 2011. "Jack Layton's Legacy Won't End Here " *Globe and Mail*, August 22. http://www.theglobeandmail.com/news/politics/jack-laytons-legacy-wont-end-here/article595869/.

Miller, Melissa K., Jeffrey S. Peake, and Brittany Anne Boulton. 2010. "Testing the *Saturday Night Live* Hypothesis: Fairness and Bias in Newspaper Coverage of Hillary Clinton's Presidential Campaign." *Politics and Gender* 6 (2): 169–98. http://dx.doi.org/10.1017/S1743923X10000036.

Parker, Brian T. 2012. "Candidate Brand Equity Valuation: A Comparison of U.S. Presidential Candidates during the 2008 Primary Election Campaign." *Journal of Political Marketing* 11 (3): 208–30. http://dx.doi.org/10.1080/15377857.2012.699424.

Parliament of Canada. 2012. *Members of the House of Commons*. http://www.parl.gc.ca.

Sanbonmatsu, Kira. 2002. "Gender Stereotypes and Vote Choice." *American Journal of Political Science* 46 (1): 20–34. http://dx.doi.org/10.2307/3088412.

Sanbonmatsu, Kira, and Kathleen Dolan. 2009. "Do Gender Stereotypes Transcend Party?" *Political Research Quarterly* 62 (3): 485–94. http://dx.doi.org/10.1177/1065912908322416.

Schneider, Monica C. 2014. "Gender-Based Strategies in Candidate Websites." *Journal of Political Marketing* 13 (4): 264–90. http://dx.doi.org/10.1080/15377857.2014.958373.

Schneider, Monica C., and Angela L. Bos. 2014. "Measuring Stereotypes of Female Politicians." *Political Psychology* 35 (2): 245–66. http://dx.doi.org/10.1111/pops.12040.

Smith, Gareth. 2001. "The 2001 General Election: Factors Influencing the Brand Image of Political Parties and Their Leaders." *Journal of Marketing Management* 17 (9–10): 989–1006. http://dx.doi.org/10.1362/026725701323366719.

Smyth, Julie. 2013. "Sex and Romance on Parliament Hill: Young MPs Challenge Attitudes about Relationships between Politicians and Staffers." *Maclean's*, January 14. http://www2.macleans.ca/2013/01/14/roses-are-orange/.

Stalsburg, Brittany L. 2010. "Voting for Mom: The Political Consequences of Being a Parent for Male and Female Candidates." *Politics and Gender* 6 (3): 373–404. http://dx.doi.org/10.1017/S1743923X10000309.

–. 2012. "A Mom First and a Candidate Second: Gender Differences in Candidates' Self-Presentation of Family." Working paper.

Thomas, Sue. 2002. "The Personal Is Political: Antecedents of Gendered Choices of Elected Representatives." *Sex Roles* 47 (7–8): 343–53. http://dx.doi.org/10.1023/A:1021431114955.

Tuchman, Gaye. 1978. "The Symbolic Annihilation of Women by the Mass Media." In *Hearth and Home: Images of Women in the Mass Media*, edited by Gaye Tuchman, Arlene Kaplan Daniels, and James Benet, 3–38. New York: Oxford University Press.

van Zoonen, Liesbet. 1998. "'Finally, I Have My Mother Back': Politicians and Their Families in Popular Culture." *International Journal of Press/Politics* 3 (1): 48–64. http://dx.doi.org/10.1177/1081180X98003001005.

–. 2005. *Entertaining the Citizen: When Politics and Popular Culture Converge.* Oxford: Rowman and Littlefield.

–. 2006. "The Personal, the Political, and the Popular: A Woman's Guide to Celebrity Politics." *European Journal of Cultural Studies* 9 (3): 287–301. http://dx.doi.org/10.1177/1367549406066074.

8

Mothers and the Media on the Campaign Trail

MELISSA K. MILLER

When a Washington state legislator dismissed Patty Murray as a mere "mom in tennis shoes" whose political activism couldn't make a difference, he scarcely realized that he was launching a political career (Smolkin 2002). Murray subsequently mobilized thousands of parents to save a vulnerable preschool program, transforming the slight into a winning campaign slogan for the school board, Washington State Senate, and United States Senate.

The evolution of Murray's "mom in tennis shoes" label – from insult to rallying cry – might be a useful metaphor for the changing nature of motherhood and its press coverage on the campaign trail. Scholars of gender have argued that women suffer when coverage of their campaigns focuses on their roles in the private or domestic sphere as opposed to the public sphere (e.g., Braden 1996; Kanter 1977; Woodall and Fridkin 2007). An article that mentions a candidate's young children, for instance, might prompt voters to wonder whether the candidate can successfully balance motherhood and political office. Yet the media-motherhood dynamic might be changing. Not only is press coverage of women on the campaign trail improving overall, but also public attitudes toward mothers running for office might be evolving. Rather than harming women's candidacies, "being a mom" might help them.

Whereas the chapter by Thomas and Lambert (this volume) concerns the strategic decisions made by women in the political arena on whether to politicize their personal lives, this chapter concerns how the media cover such women. It starts from the assumption that parenthood might be treated differently by the media when the candidate under scrutiny is a woman versus a man. Indeed, motherhood is a gendered form of parenthood that could redound to the benefit or detriment of a woman seeking public office. Effects could be twofold. First, mothers can garner different kinds of media coverage than fathers running for office. Second, this coverage can influence public opinion positively or negatively.

This chapter takes stock of the literature on press coverage of women running for public office. It also assesses recent scholarship suggesting that feminine traits, such as being a mother, can have advantages for women among voters. Finally, it examines press coverage of two high-profile mothers who ran for national executive office in the United States in 2008: Hillary Clinton and Sarah Palin. They provide a unique opportunity to compare press coverage of a Democrat and a Republican, a woman with an adult child and a woman with young children, and a woman who downplayed her motherhood and one who showcased it.

Press Coverage of Mothers on the Campaign Trail

The assumption that Murray was just a "mom in tennis shoes" is a familiar one. Examples abound of mothers questioned about their fitness for elective office. As the lieutenant governor of Massachusetts, Jane Swift was vilified in the press when she ascended to the governorship in 2001, eight months pregnant (Loke, Harp, and Bachmann 2011). Palin's status as a mother of five was dissected online and in the mainstream press in 2008; questions were raised about whether she could handle the job of US vice-president while balancing motherhood (Beail and Kinney Longworth 2013). While considering a campaign for governor in 2014, Attorney General of Illinois Lisa Madigan was badgered during an interview with the Chicago *Sun-Times* about whether she could handle raising children while serving as governor (Ross 2012).

Such coverage arguably harms women who run for office by linking them with the private sphere as opposed to the public sphere (Braden 1996; Carlin and Winfrey 2009; Falk 2010; Kanter 1977; Woodall and Fridkin 2007). Stereotypes about the "proper place of women" can be triggered in such cases. Traditionally, campaign professionals have dealt carefully with advising mothers on whether to emphasize their maternal role on the campaign trail. A 1977 handbook written by a former candidate for California's (at that time) all-male Senate cautioned that, "if your candidate has a family, give deep thought about how she will be pictured with them" (Paizis 1977, 106). The handbook offered a cautionary anecdote in a chapter entitled simply "Media" that brings to mind Kathleen Hall Jamieson's articulation of the "double bind" for women of "womb versus brain" (1995, Chapter 3): "One young woman discovered that there was great concern among voters about who would care for her pre-school-age children if she were elected. Because she came across as the mother of small children rather than as a capable and able woman, she found it best to discontinue showing pictures of herself with little ones" (Paizis 1977, 106–7). Such stories generated scholarly interest and eventually led to a considerable literature dissecting how women were treated in the press and whether such treatment focused disproportionately on their parental status.

Women running for the US House, the Senate, or governor traditionally received less coverage than men (Kahn 1992, 1994, 1996; Kahn and Goldenberg 1991). Their coverage was disproportionately negative (Kahn 1994; Kahn and Goldenberg 1991). Most importantly, it focused disproportionately on their appearance, personality, and family status, including their children (Braden 1996; Bystrom, Robertson, and Banwart 2001; Kahn 1996; Norris 1997).

Jamieson (1995) assessed newspaper coverage of all US federal races featuring women in 1990 and 1992 as well as coverage of Kim Campbell, who became Canadian prime minister in 1993. Jamieson found that women were identified by their spousal and parental roles, whereas men were identified by their professional credentials. Likewise, Bystrom et al. (2001) found that women's children were mentioned more than three times as often as men's children in newspaper coverage of US Senate and governor races in 2000.

Recent scholarship suggests that these trends might be improving. Scholars report that women who run for subnational office are beginning to receive coverage in amounts commensurate with men in the United States, Canada, and Australia (Bystrom et al. 2004; Kittilson and Fridkin 2008; Smith 1997). Disproportionate negativity is also coming into balance, with women no more likely to receive negative coverage than men in the United States and elsewhere (Banwart, Bystrom, and Robertson 2003; Bystrom et al. 2004; Kittilson and Fridkin 2008; Smith 1997). Likewise, disproportionate press focus on the gender and family status of women might be receding. Miki Caul Kittilson and Kim Fridkin (2008) compared newspaper coverage of women and men in the 2004 Australian, 2006 Canadian, and 2006 US elections. No significant differences emerged in coverage of their family backgrounds (cf. Bystrom et al. 2004).

However, in contrast to sub-presidential offices, the US presidency has been an all-male bastion. Erika Falk (2010) documents persistent patterns of press bias across three decades of women who have run for president. Compared with men similarly situated in the polls, women (up to and including Elizabeth Dole in 2000) consistently received less coverage. It portrayed them as unviable, disproportionately emphasizing their appearance, gender, and family status (see also Aday and Devitt 2001; Heldman, Carroll, and Olson 2005).

Coverage of Clinton's campaign for the 2008 Democratic presidential nomination countered some of these trends. Clinton received as much coverage as her male rivals (Lawrence and Rose 2010; Miller, Peake, and Boulton 2010; but see Falk 2010), and her issue-oriented coverage was commensurate with theirs (Miller et al. 2010). Nevertheless, her coverage was disproportionately negative (Lawrence and Rose 2010; Miller et al. 2010). Most importantly, her daughter was mentioned significantly more often than John McCain's children (though not Barack Obama's children) in front-page newspaper and prime-time network news stories (Lawrence and Rose 2010). During the fall campaign, Palin's children were mentioned four times as often as those of her Democratic counterpart in newspapers across the country (Miller and Peake 2013).

The amount of coverage and the emphasis on policy issues are standard indicators of press fairness tracked by scholars of gender. Unfortunately, attention to parental status has been spottier. Mentions of parental and marital status are sometimes combined in a single "family status" variable, making it difficult to measure disproportionate press attention to motherhood precisely (e.g., Falk 2010; Kittilson and Fridkin 2008). Even when mentions of the parental status of women versus men are tracked, little is reported beyond differences in percentage. This is unfortunate in light of new evidence suggesting that attitudes about the suitability of feminine traits for elective office, such as those associated with motherhood, might be evolving.

Voters' Views of Mothers on the Campaign Trail

There is a broad consensus among scholars of gender, based upon a significant body of research, that voters use gender stereotypes to gather information about political candidates. For instance, voters tend to attribute stereotypical feminine traits to women and stereotypical masculine traits to men. Kathleen Dolan (2014) summarizes the key distinctions: women are perceived to be more honest, easier to relate to, and more empathetic, whereas men are perceived to be more decisive, stronger leaders, and better able to handle crises (e.g., Alexander and Andersen 1993; Banwart 2010; Huddy and Terkildsen 1993; Lawless 2004; Leeper 1991; Sapiro 1981–82). As well, women are assumed to have greater expertise on issues such as education, health care, and childcare, whereas men are believed to have greater expertise on matters of national security and the economy (e.g., Alexander and Andersen 1993; Huddy and Terkildsen 1993; Koch 1997; Rosenwasser et al. 1987).

This gendered attribution of traits and issue competencies is thought to harm women's candidacies, since voters tend to value stereotypical masculine traits in politics, particularly for offices that hold great power and prestige (Burns, Eberhardt, and Merolla 2013). Yet most of the aforementioned studies rely on data from the 1970s through the 1990s. Attitudes might have changed since then. Moreover, just because voters ascribe stereotypical feminine traits to fictitious female candidates does not mean that they allow such stereotypes to influence their actual votes. Most importantly, these prior studies fail to scrutinize *motherhood* as a possible influence on voters. Only two known studies do so.

Brittany L. Stalsburg (2010) showed study subjects a picture of, short description of, and speech by a mock candidate for governor; the candidate's sex and parental status were varied by Stalsburg. Women *without* children were rated the lowest in terms of being good candidates; being childless was more detrimental than being a mother. Burns et al. (2013) assessed voter evaluations of Palin during the 2008 campaign. Voters exposed to a "mother frame" rated Palin higher on a set of feminine traits, whereas those exposed to a "Mama Grizzly" frame (employing both masculine and feminine markers) rated Palin higher on a set of masculine traits. They further demonstrated that a Mama Grizzly approach was especially effective among Republicans.[1]

Although not directly related to motherhood, additional evidence suggests that voter attitudes toward feminine traits and issues on the campaign trail are changing. For instance, between 2000 and 2004, the survey item "strong leader" became less important in predicting the presidential vote, whereas "candidate cares about you" became more important (Hansen and Otero 2006). Using data collected from nearly 2,000 candidates for subpresidential races in the United States in 1996 and 1998, Paul S. Herrnson, J. Celeste Lay, and Atiya Kai Stokes (2003) found that women benefited when they both targeted women's groups and stressed "feminine" issues such as education, even after controlling for a candidate's party.

Recent work assessing the link between gender stereotypes and voter behaviour holds further promise. Dolan (2014) analyzed 99 congressional districts during the 2010 midterms and found no evidence that gender stereotypes influenced evaluations of candidates or vote choice. Deborah Jordan Brooks (2013) tested whether voters use gender stereotypes when evaluating fictitious candidates for the US Senate. Subjects read fake news stories about "Kevin" and "Karen" Bailey doing things such as crying and expressing anger on the campaign trail. Virtually no difference registered between subjects' assessments of each. There was no evidence that voters employed negative stereotypes when evaluating Karen, though she did benefit from some isolated positive stereotypes.

Nevertheless, questions remain. Brooks (2013, 145) asks whether "all women candidates absolutely never, under any circumstances, face a playing field that is different from what male candidates face." She offers five types of women who continue to suffer from gender stereotyping by voters, including mothers, especially those with young children. They can be especially susceptible to the belief that "a woman's place is in the home." If so, then press coverage similar to that afforded to Swift, Palin, and Madigan, noted above, might be especially harmful.

It is too soon to declare that mothers face a level playing field in seeking press coverage of their campaigns. Recent research suggests growing fairness in how the press treats women on the campaign trail, but the study of coverage of parental status is more limited and shows progress at the subnational level only. Meanwhile, new research on voter behaviour suggests that gender stereotypes are invoked infrequently, though the stereotyping of mothers on the campaign trail has not been systematically tested aside from Stalsburg (2010).

Studying Coverage of Mothers on the National Campaign Trail

The 2008 US presidential campaign offers a unique context in which to assess press coverage of mothers on the campaign trail and its effects on voters. A woman seriously contested the Democratic Party's presidential nomination, and the Republican Party nominated a woman for vice-president. Moreover, Clinton and Palin were a study in contrasts: a Democrat versus a Republican; a political celebrity versus a virtual unknown; the mother of an adult child versus the mother of young children; and a woman who downplayed her motherhood versus one who showcased it. Two data sets are employed to assess their press coverage and its effect on voters.

2008 Presidential Press Coverage Data Set
The 2008 presidential press coverage data set is used to establish whether mentions of Clinton's and Palin's parental status differed quantitatively and qualitatively from those of their male counterparts. I collected the data with Jeffrey Peake of Clemson University.

To assess the coverage of Clinton, the top-circulating newspaper in each state holding its Democratic nomination contest on or before Super Tuesday was included. Two leading newspapers of record were added for a total of 25 newspapers. Data collection spanned from Labor Day through Super Tuesday. A total of 6,600 articles and editorials from the primary stage were coded. For detailed information, see Miller et al. (2010).

To assess the coverage of Palin, the top-circulating newspaper in each of 13 battleground states was included. Four leading newspapers of record were added for a total of 17 newspapers. Data collection spanned from September 1, 2008, through election day. A total of 2,592 articles and editorials from the general election stage were coded. For detailed information, see Miller and Peake (2013).

2008 National Annenberg Election Survey (Phone Edition)
To establish whether press references to Clinton's and Palin's parental status influenced voters, coverage data were merged with public opinion data from the National Annenberg Election Survey (NAES). A total of 57,967 adult residents of the United States were interviewed between December 17, 2007, and November 3, 2008. To test press effects on attitudes toward Clinton, only those 1,448 respondents interviewed between Labor Day and Super Tuesday who reported reading one of the 25 sampled primary stage newspapers were included. To test press effects on attitudes toward Palin, only those 1,931 respondents interviewed on or after September 1 who reported reading one of the 17 sampled general election newspapers were included. Detailed information about the NAES is available online.[2]

Tracking Press References to Candidates' Parental Status
The literature suggests that the press overemphasizes the parental status of women who run for elective office. This was decidedly the case in 2008. Parental status mentions for Clinton and Palin were disproportionately higher than for their male competitors ($p < .001$; one-tailed). The parental status of Clinton was mentioned in just 3.2 percent of articles on her, but this was two to three times as often as similar references for her male competitors, Obama and John Edwards. The parental status of Palin was

mentioned in 18.1 percent of articles on her, four to 10 times as often as mentions for Joe Biden, Obama, and McCain. Palin's parental status resembled Obama's most closely; each candidate had young children, yet her parental status was mentioned seven times more frequently.[3] In addition to these quantitative differences, there were qualitative differences.[4]

Qualitative References to Clinton's Motherhood

Clinton's daughter, Chelsea, was in her late twenties during the 2008 presidential campaign. She had lived in the White House for eight years beginning at age 12 and was arguably a household name. To the extent that she campaigned for her mother, Chelsea might have garnered news coverage typical of other campaign surrogates. Table 8.1 displays summary results of the qualitative coding of all press references to the parental status of the top Democrats.

The vast majority of references to Clinton's parental status pertained to Chelsea either attending a campaign event (52.5 percent) or serving as a campaign surrogate (22.9 percent). For instance, the *Democrat-Gazette* reported on January 27 that "earlier Sunday, Clinton and daughter Chelsea braved slushy sidewalks to go door to door in Manchester for about an hour seeking votes." The *Wall Street Journal* reported on January 29 that "Mrs. Clinton has relied on use of heavyweight campaign surrogates like her husband and daughter, allowing her to spread her influence without physically being present. Last week she ducked out of South Carolina with an election imminent, leaving the campaign to her husband and daughter."

It is difficult to argue that the press wrongly covered Chelsea's activities, since the Clinton campaign used Chelsea as a surrogate. Although Obama's children were too young to use likewise, Cate Edwards (age 18) did campaign actively for her father, and 13.3 percent of his press references reflected that. Notably, the modal category for all three candidates was "child(ren) in attendance/child(ren) present at event."

Also noteworthy are the few references that depict Clinton as a mother in some way other than noting Chelsea's activities on the campaign trail. Only 10 references to Clinton's parental status fit a second category, broadly titled "mother/biographical information." This category is comparable in size (8.5 percent) to Obama's "father/biographical information" category (10 percent). Several of these references to Clinton were positive: "'The Hispanic community is very family oriented, and we respect our mothers,' said Ruben Kihuen, an influential Democratic assemblyman from Las Vegas who supported Mrs. Clinton. 'A lot of middle-aged women see her as a

TABLE 8.1
Parental status mentions during the Democratic primary, 2008

Among articles mentioning candidate *and* candidate's parental status	Parental status mentions %	N
CLINTON		
References to daughter, Chelsea		
Chelsea present at event	52.5	62
Chelsea campaigning on own/acting as surrogate for Clinton	22.9	27
Chelsea mentioned by her parents while on campaign trail	6.8	8
Chelsea quoted directly or indirectly	3.4	4
Chelsea mentioned by someone other than her parents	2.5	3
Mother/biographical information	8.5	10
Other/miscellaneous	3.4	4
Total	100.0	118
OBAMA		
Children present at event	23.3	7
Children incorporated into advertising/Christmas-themed ad	20.0	6
Children mentioned in context of wife, Michelle	20.0	6
Christmas plans with children/plans changed	13.3	4
Father/biographical information	10.0	3
Obama reflecting on fatherhood/Obama's father absent during his childhood/Obama seeks to be good father to his daughters	6.7	2
Other/miscellaneous	6.7	2
Total	100.0	30
EDWARDS		
Child(ren) present at event	30.0	9
Daughter Cate campaigning on own/acting as surrogate for Edwards	13.3	4
Son killed in auto accident	16.7	5
Christmas plans with children/no toys from China for Christmas	16.7	5
Children mentioned in context of wife, Elizabeth	13.3	4
Cate involved in auto accident/fender bender	6.7	2
Other/miscellaneous	3.3	1
Total	100.0	30

(Chelsea references bracketed subtotal: 88.1)

mother, a head of the household, and they can identify with this'" (*New York Times*, January 15, 2008).

Other references in this category were ambiguous in tone or contrasted Clinton's motherhood with her allegedly remote image. Here is an example of the latter: "Shannon Mallozzi of Long Island met Clinton one day when Mallozzi asked for help in finding funds to research her daughter's rare illness. 'I thought she was a bit remote. I didn't know who she was,' said Mallozzi. 'She sat with me, and she was just phenomenal. That day, it was two moms sitting in a car'" (*Washington Post*, December 18, 2007).

Another example comes from the *Los Angeles Times*, in which Clinton was compared with other "unabashed feminists ... raising children" in an article cryptically entitled "Clinton Not an Easy Sell to All Women" (December 7, 2007). Such references comprise a mere handful of the 118 total references to Clinton's parental status.

Qualitative References to Palin's Motherhood

Press references to Palin's motherhood differed dramatically. Table 8.2 displays summary results of the qualitative coding of all press references to the parental status of the major party nominees for president and vice-president. Whereas Clinton's modal category pertained to the campaign activities of her daughter, only 5.1 percent of Palin's parental status mentions did likewise. Palin's modal category comprised scandals involving her children (40.8 percent). References ranged from her teenage daughter Bristol's pregnancy to travel expenses incurred by the State of Alaska for her children's travel and Republican campaign funds spent on their clothes.

Scandal also touched Biden's family during the campaign, yet it barely registered in his press coverage. Only four of the articles on Biden mentioned conflicts of interest generated by his son's lobbying activities – conflicts highly relevant to his campaign for vice-president.

Palin's broad scandal category was dominated by references to Bristol's pregnancy. They comprised 31.6 percent of all parental status references to Palin. One portion announced the breaking news of the pregnancy, often implying that it complicated the Republican campaign, as the following example shows: "Sarah Palin's place on the Republican ticket with John McCain became more complex Monday when, prompted by Internet rumors, she announced that her 17-year-old daughter Bristol is pregnant, would have the child and would marry the child's father" (*Des Moines Register*, September 2, 2008).

TABLE 8.2
Parental status mentions during the general election, 2008

Among articles mentioning candidate *and* candidate's parental status	Parental status mentions %	N
PALIN		
Scandal involving child(ren)		
(Teenage) daughter pregnant	31.6	62
Children travelled at state expense while Palin governor	4.1	8
Atmosphere of scandal surrounding children/other scandal	3.1 40.8	6
Children's wardrobe/party funds spent on clothing for children	2.0	4
Motherhood helps candidacy/attracts voters/being a mother, hockey mom, working mother helps campaign	17.3	34
Hockey mom	15.3	30
Working mother/"everymom"/PTA mother/husband cares for kids	4.6	9
Child(ren) present at event	5.1	10
Son deployed to Iraq	5.1	10
Son has Down's syndrome/son born while Palin governor/might be grandson	5.1	10
Mother/biographical information	3.1	6
Other/miscellaneous	3.6	7
Total	100.0	196
BIDEN		
Daughter died and sons injured in auto accident/raised sons as single dad	37.1	10
Son is attorney general/son in National Guard/son deployed to Iraq	14.8	4
Conflicts of interest/sons involved with companies lobbying Biden	14.8	4
Biden is grandfather/grandchildren on campaign trail	7.4	2
Child(ren) present at event	7.4	2
Father/biographical information	7.4	2
Other/miscellaneous	11.1	3
Total	100.0	27

▶

Among articles mentioning candidate *and* candidate's parental status	Parental status mentions %	N
OBAMA		
Children present at event	37.0	20
Children as campaign message/daughters' future as campaign message	16.7	9
Knows challenge of raising children/cost of raising and educating kids/work-life balance/misses family when working or campaigning	14.8	8
Children mentioned in context of wife, Michelle	11.1	6
Obama as good father/children mentioned in context of praising Obama/Obama's parenting style/will buy dog for children if wins	11.1	6
Other/miscellaneous	9.3	5
Total	100.0	54
McCAIN		
Child(ren) present at event	25.0	8
Wife and children stateside while McCain prisoner of war	15.6	5
Father/biographical information	9.4	3
Son(s) in military/son(s) deployed overseas/son(s) in Iraq	9.4	3
Child(ren) mentioned in context of wife and ex-wife	9.4	3
Child(ren) campaigning on own/acting as surrogate(s) for McCain	6.2	2
Has adopted children/adoptive status informs position on abortion	6.3	2
Hosted with daughter on vacation by corporate executive/ethical issues	6.2	2
Rumour McCain fathered illegitimate child	3.1	1
Other/miscellaneous	9.4	3
Total	100.0	32

Although fewer in number, there were some instances in which the press suggested that Bristol's pregnancy might help Palin's campaign:

> The news that Sarah Palin's 17-year-old daughter is having a baby and marrying the father turned an awkward surprise into an affirmation of the vice presidential candidate's conservative credibility for many GOP convention delegates Monday. (*Minneapolis Star-Tribune*, September 2, 2008)

Gov. Palin's down-to-earth image and her family travails – a pregnant teenage daughter, a baby who she says keeps her up at night, a schedule so busy she says it's often macaroni and cheese for dinner – appealed to young voters who say they had a hard time relating to Sen. McCain. (*Wall Street Journal*, September 11, 2008)

Elsewhere there was further evidence that Palin's parental status was sometimes portrayed positively. Her second largest category was comprised of references to her motherhood as a plus factor for her candidacy (17.3 percent). These references either stated that Palin's motherhood energized voters or quoted voters saying as much:

These days, a lot of Republican women are ecstatic over Sen. John McCain's choice of Sarah Palin, a deeply conservative mother of five, as his running mate. (*Philadelphia Inquirer*, September 8, 2008)

"She does things I relate to," said the 63-year-old grandmother from Glenwood Springs. "She hunts and fishes, and her husband loves the snow machines, and she's about raising kids. I can relate to that." (*Denver Post*, September 9, 2008)

The last sizable category of Palin's parental status mentions (15.3 percent) pertained to the "hockey mom" label that Palin embraced during her speech at the GOP convention. Most of these references were positive:

Republican vice presidential candidate Gov. Sarah Palin Wednesday night told enthusiastic convention delegates that her roots as a "hockey mom," PTA member, and small-town mayor will enable her and Sen. John McCain to change Washington. (*Plain Dealer*, September 4, 2008)

Hundreds held their cellphone cameras aloft as she walked onstage. They brandished signs reading "Palin Power" and "Hockey Mom." (*Virginian Pilot*, September 11, 2008)

Relatively few hockey mom references were negative. They tended to link the label to concerns about the qualifications of Palin, as these examples show:

A self-proclaimed hockey mom and political maverick, she has held her position for less than two years and only one month longer than Barack Obama has been running for president. (*Plain Dealer*, September 15, 2008)

[The debate] was watched by many millions of Americans eager to see how the self-described "hockey mom" with scant national experience would fare against Biden, the chairman of the Senate Foreign Relations Committee and a voluble, gaffe-prone 35-year veteran of Washington. (*Charlotte Observer*, October 3, 2008)

Press references to Palin's motherhood were a mixed bag. Although 4 in 10 concerned scandals, nearly 20 percent portrayed it as benefiting her campaign. Finally, her hockey mom persona was spun both positively and negatively by the press.

Parental Status References and Article Tone

Press references to Clinton's parental status seemed to be fairly innocuous, whereas those for Palin were mixed. Yet both were significantly associated with positive article tone. Articles that mentioned Clinton's parental status were significantly more likely to be positive in tone (46.0 percent) than articles that did not mention it (35.8 percent).[5] Articles that mentioned Palin's parental status were also significantly more likely to be positive in tone (46.5 percent) than articles that did not mention it (27.7 percent).[6] As well, just over 3 in 10 articles noting Palin's parental status also suggested that Palin strengthened the GOP ticket versus a significantly lower 16.4 percent of articles that did not mention it.[7] The only divergent finding pertained to Clinton. Although few articles questioned her viability, those that mentioned her parental status were significantly more likely to do so than those that did not (6.5 percent versus 2.6 percent).[8]

Could parental status references be benign as triggers of harmful gender stereotyping? Alternatively, could an innocuous reference to Clinton's daughter on the campaign trail or Palin's status as a "working mom" cue voters to wonder whether each was suited to national executive office? The NAES permits a test of such possibilities.

Parental Status References and Public Opinion

NAES respondents were assigned coverage measures from the newspapers that they reported reading most often. Four coverage variables specific to each respondent's favoured newspaper are included in the multivariate models reported below. The first measures tone toward each candidate using relative positivity in headline visibility.[9] Three additional variables measure the percentage of references to each candidate's parental status, gender, and clothing/appearance. The latter account for the multiple ways in which press coverage can be gendered. Each coverage measure is cumulative up to the day that each respondent was interviewed, since respondents might not have read the paper daily or on the days of their interviews.

The coverage variables are used to predict favourability toward Clinton and Palin as well as assessments of the former's leadership strength and the latter's readiness to be vice-president. Dependent variables are measured from 0 to 10, with higher scores indicating greater favourability/leadership strength/readiness. Included as controls are respondent sex, race, age, education, partisanship, ideology, level of attention to campaign,[10] and favourability toward McCain (in Palin's models only). A variable recording the week that each respondent was interviewed (1, 2, 3, etc.) is also included to account for unfolding events.

Table 8.3 displays regression models of readers' attitudes toward Clinton and Palin. Clearly, press coverage matters. Although each respondent was exposed to multiple sources of information about Clinton and Palin, coverage tone was positive and significant in three of four models. Greater positivity in headline visibility led to greater positivity toward the candidate, controlling for the other variables in each model. Only opinions on Clinton's leadership strength were impervious to this effect, perhaps because the public already had well-formed opinions about Clinton after her years in the political limelight.

The assumption that press attention to a woman's parental status hampers her campaign receives relatively little support in Table 8.3. Mentions of each candidate's parental status had insignificant effects on reader favourability toward the candidate. Mentions of Clinton's parental status were positively associated, however, with reader assessments of her leadership strength; the effect is small and approaches statistical significance ($p = .10$). Press mentions of Palin's parental status inversely influenced reader assessments of her readiness to be vice-president. The effect is small and negative ($p < .10$).

Additional variables measuring other forms of press gendering proved to be insignificant in Clinton's models. Some, however, did negatively influence reader assessments of Palin. Mentions of her gender negatively influenced her favourability ($p < .01$), whereas mentions of her clothing/appearance negatively influenced opinions about her readiness to be vice-president ($p < .10$).

Conclusion

Much has changed since Patty Murray famously endured the "mom in tennis shoes" slight. There are growing signs of fairness in press coverage of

TABLE 8.3
Predicting attitudes toward Clinton and Palin using respondent and press coverage characteristics, 2008

	Attitudes toward Clinton				Attitudes toward Palin			
	Favourability		Strong leader		Favourability		Ready to be vice-president	
	Slope coefficient	Standard error	Slope coefficient	Standard error	Slope coefficient	Standard error	Slope coefficient	Standard error
RESPONDENT ATTRIBUTES								
Female	0.400****	0.143	0.231**	0.168	−0.101	0.095	0.100	0.092
African American or black	0.506***	0.282	−0.061	0.296	0.283**	0.190	0.178	0.185
Other non-white race	1.154*****	0.329	0.636***	0.380	−0.163	0.184	0.188	0.180
Age	0.002	0.005	0.004	0.005	0.007***	0.003	0.012*****	0.003
Education	0.032	0.036	0.036	0.042	−0.140*****	0.023	−0.181*****	0.023
Party ID (strong Dem→strong Rep)	−0.714*****	0.042	−0.740*****	0.067	0.388*****	0.033	0.310*****	0.032
Ideology (liberal→conservative)	−0.463*****	0.078	−0.294*****	0.092	0.355*****	0.054	0.321*****	0.053
Following campaign (low→hi)	−0.050	0.109	−0.207**	0.126	−0.130**	0.088	−0.213****	0.086
Favourability toward McCain (low→hi)	–	–	–	–	0.597*****	0.021	0.440*****	0.021

NEWSPAPER READ BY RESPONDENT

Coverage tone toward candidate (cumulative relative positivity in headline visibility)	1.912****	0.671	0.885	0.784	1.728*****	0.556	1.358*****	0.543
Candidate's parental status mentioned (cumulative %)	0.013	0.061	0.096*	0.075	-0.001	0.008	-0.011**	0.008
Candidate's gender mentioned (cumulative %)	0.004	0.024	0.010	0.030	-0.015****	0.006	-0.007	0.006
Candidate's clothing/appearance mentioned (cumulative %)	-0.009	0.035	0.002	0.041	-0.009	0.012	-0.018**	0.012
Week of campaign (primary or general)	-0.062**	0.039	-0.135*****	0.045	-0.109*****	0.023	-0.082*****	0.023
Constant	10.099*****	0.880	11.514*****	1.034	1.017***	0.516	1.172***	0.506
Number of cases	1,197		918		1,732		1,719	
Adjusted R^2	.40		.21		.67		.57	
Model F statistic	62.781*****		19.628*****		247.606*****		162.029*****	

Note: Dependent variables are respondent attitudes toward each candidate, ranging from 0 to 10; higher scores indicate greater positivity. Entries are slope coefficients and standard errors derived from OLS regressions.

* $p = .10$; ** $p < .10$; *** $p < .05$; **** $p < .01$; ***** $p < .001$, one-tailed.

Sources: 2008 National Annenberg Election Survey and Presidential Election Press Coverage Study, 2008.

women on the campaign trail. Both the amount and the substance of coverage have improved. Although the evidence is somewhat limited, press emphasis on women's parental status appears to be on the wane at the sub-presidential level. There is also growing evidence that voter stereotyping of women on the campaign trail is declining and that voters might view certain feminine traits (including motherhood) as plus factors.

Scrutiny of the 2008 US presidential campaign yielded results that comport, in part, with these trends. Although Clinton and Palin garnered disproportionate press references to their status as mothers, these references were significantly associated with positive article tone. For Palin, such references were also significantly associated with references to her strengthening the GOP ticket, whereas for Clinton such references were associated with the questioning of her viability.

Clinton's parental status references were substantively different from Palin's. Clinton's largely pertained to her adult daughter's campaign activities. The effects of these references on public opinion about Clinton were insignificant in terms of favourability and positive in terms of leadership strength; the latter approached statistical significance.

Palin's parental status references were decidedly more negative and focused on scandals involving her children, in part because of incongruence with the ideal of conservative motherhood in the United States (see Schreiber, this volume). These references were balanced by a number of other references, including those that linked her motherhood to voter enthusiasm. Together these references failed to influence Palin's favourability ratings, but they dampened public opinion about her readiness to be vice-president. It is not possible to identify the precise causal mechanism at work. Such press attention might have triggered the stereotype that women with young children should not hold demanding jobs outside the home. Alternatively, the specific scandals revolving around Palin's children might have prompted voters to question her ability to lead and/or her ability to both raise children and govern citizens.

Both Clinton and Palin were unique candidates in unique circumstances. Some broad insights can nevertheless be gained from their experiences. Campaign agency, for instance, must be taken into account. Although her daughter campaigned actively, Clinton otherwise spoke relatively little about being a mother. According to Ann C. McGinley (2009, 720), Clinton "offered a tough, masculine approach, downplaying her role as wife and mother." Palin, meanwhile, showcased her maternal status. Remarking on her speech at the GOP convention, Katie L. Gibson and Amy L. Heyse (2010,

245) argue that her "positioning of the 'family story' front and centre ... function[ed] to privilege her maternal identity at the outset." Palin's embrace of the hockey mom label further suggests that campaign organizers believed that a maternal persona would appeal to voters.

These different strategies appear to reinforce Thomas and Lambert's conclusion in this volume that "there is no clear agreement on the strategic advantage or disadvantage for women in politics of displaying their parental status." Clinton's and Palin's contrasting strategies also appear to have led to different outcomes in the press. Clinton largely kept mum about her motherhood and consequently garnered press mentions about it in just 3.2 percent of articles on her. Palin showcased her motherhood and found it mentioned in 18.1 percent of articles on her. Depending on the attitude in question, the effects on public opinion were either absent or positive for Clinton and absent or negative for Palin.

It appears, then, that the strategies of both candidates backfired. Clinton chose to downplay her motherhood, but when it was covered by the press she benefited in the court of public opinion. Palin chose to showcase her motherhood, but when it was covered by the press the effect was negative, presumably because of its focus on scandals involving her children. Notably, the effects were small for both candidates.

Numerous factors influence a candidate's decision to highlight her children and family on the campaign trail, not the least of which is privacy. Family members' willingness and availability to make appearances at events and in advertising are key considerations as well. Certainly, the campaign's overall narrative about the candidate also plays a role in shaping decisions about a family focus on the trail. What this chapter adds to such considerations is the finding that press emphasis on a candidate's motherhood is not an automatic liability, even for the US presidency. The choice to "be a mom" on the campaign trail – in tennis shoes or otherwise – is not strictly dictated by press conventions and public attitudes.

Notes
I wish to thank Jeffrey Peake, with whom the 2008 press coverage data set was collected. Thanks also to Daniel Gordon, who compiled the qualitative press references to parental status and coded them with me. A number of top undergraduate and graduate students at Bowling Green State University completed initial coding of news articles, and their assistance was invaluable. This research was supported by a 2008 grant from the Center for Research Libraries and a 2009 American Political Science Association Small Research Grant.

1. Palin's portrayal as a "hockey mom" conveyed such a Mama Grizzly persona (Burns et al. 2013). A sizable portion of press mentions of her motherhood characterized Palin in this hockey mom manner (see Table 8.2).
2. See http://www.annenbergpublicpolicycenter.org/Downloads/NAES/PhoneSurvey/NAES08-Phone-Codebook.pdf.
3. Palin's five children were ages five months to 19 years, whereas Obama's daughters were seven and 10.
4. If multiple references to a candidate's parental status were made in a single article, then only the first reference was coded. I coded each with the help of a graduate assistant working in isolation. Cases of disagreement were resolved collaboratively. Levels of intercoder agreement were 88.1 percent for Clinton, 80.0 percent for Obama, and 96.7 percent for Edwards. For the general election stage, they were 91.0 percent for Palin, 81.5 percent for Biden, 78.1 percent for McCain, and 85.2 percent for Obama.
5. $p < .01$; chi-squared = 12.0666; $df = 2$.
6. $p < .001$; chi-squared = 29.273; $df = 2$.
7. $p < .001$; chi-squared = 21.736; $df = 2$.
8. $p < .01$; chi-squared = 6.736; $df = 1$. On close examination, this relationship stems largely from articles published in the wake of the Iowa caucus. Such articles tended to raise questions about Clinton's ability to win after her surprise loss to Obama while also noting that the campaign was more actively featuring Chelsea at events.
9. The measure accounts for both the tone of headlines and their relative visibility. See Miller and Peake (2013).
10. The measure ranges from 1 (not following closely at all) to 4 (following very closely). See Miller and Peake (2013).

References

Aday, Sean, and James Devitt. 2001. "Style over Substance: Newspaper Coverage of Elizabeth Dole's Presidential Bid." *Press/Politics* 6 (2): 52–73.

Alexander, Deborah, and Kristi Andersen. 1993. "Gender as a Factor in the Attribution of Leadership Traits." *Political Research Quarterly* 46 (3): 527–45. http://dx.doi.org/10.1177/106591299304600305.

Banwart, Mary Christine. 2010. "Gender and Candidate Communication: Effects of Stereotypes in the 2008 Election." *American Behavioral Scientist* 54 (3): 265–83. http://dx.doi.org/10.1177/0002764210381702.

Banwart, Mary Christine, Dianne G. Bystrom, and Terry A. Robertson. 2003. "From the Primary to the General Election: A Comparative Analysis of Media Coverage of Candidates in Mixed-Gender 2000 Races for Governor and U.S. Senate." *American Behavioral Scientist* 46 (5): 658–76. http://dx.doi.org/10.1177/0002764202238491.

Beail, Linda, and Rhonda Kinney Longworth. 2013. *Framing Sarah Palin: Pit Bulls, Puritans, and Politics*. New York: Routledge.

Braden, Maria. 1996. *Women Politicians and the Media*. Lexington: University of Kentucky Press.

Brooks, Deborah Jordan. 2013. *He Runs, She Runs: Why Gender Stereotypes Do Not Harm Women Candidates*. Princeton, NJ: Princeton University Press.

Burns, Sarah, Lindsay Eberhardt, and Jennifer L. Merolla. 2013. "What Is the Difference between a Hockey Mom and a Pit Bull? Presentations of Palin and Gender Stereotypes in the 2008 Presidential Election." *Political Research Quarterly* 66 (3): 687–701. http://dx.doi.org/10.1177/1065912912471974.

Bystrom, Dianne G., Mary Christine Banwart, Lynda Lee Kaid, and Terry A. Robertson. 2004. *Gender and Candidate Communication: VideoStyle, WebStyle, NewsStyle*. New York: Routledge.

Bystrom, Dianne G., Terry A. Robertson, and Mary Christine Banwart. 2001. "Framing the Fight: An Analysis of Media Coverage of Female and Male Candidates in Primary Races for Governor and Senate in 2000." *American Behavioral Scientist* 44 (12): 1999–2013. http://dx.doi.org/10.1177/00027640121958456.

Carlin, Diana B., and Kelly L. Winfrey. 2009. "Have You Come a Long Way, Baby? Hillary Clinton, Sarah Palin, and Sexism in the 2008 Campaign Coverage." *Communication Studies* 60 (4): 326–43. http://dx.doi.org/10.1080/10510970903109904.

Dolan, Kathleen. 2014. "Gender Stereotypes, Candidate Evaluations, and Voting for Women Candidates: What Really Matters?" *Political Research Quarterly* 67 (1): 96–107. http://dx.doi.org/10.1177/1065912913487949.

Falk, Erika. 2010. *Women for President: Media Bias in Eight Campaigns*. 2nd ed. Chicago: University of Illinois Press.

Gibson, Katie L., and Amy L. Heyse. 2010. "'The Difference between a Hockey Mom and a Pit Bull': Sarah Palin's Faux Maternal Persona and Performance of Hegemonic Masculinity at the 2008 Republican National Convention." *Communication Quarterly* 58 (3): 235–56. http://dx.doi.org/10.1080/01463373.2010.503151.

Hansen, Susan B., and Laura Wills Otero. 2006. "A Woman for U.S. President? Gender and Leadership Traits before and after 9/11." *Journal of Women, Politics, and Policy* 28 (1): 35–60. http://dx.doi.org/10.1300/J501v28n01_03.

Heldman, Caroline, Susan J. Carroll, and Stephanie Olson. 2005. "'She Brought Only a Skirt': Print Media Coverage of Elizabeth Dole's Bid for the Republican Presidential Nomination." *Political Communication* 22 (3): 315–35. http://dx.doi.org/10.1080/10584600591006564.

Herrnson, Paul S., J. Celeste Lay, and Atiya Kai Stokes. 2003. "Women Running 'as Women': Candidate Gender, Campaign Issues, and Voter-Targeting Strategies." *Journal of Politics* 65 (1): 244–55. http://dx.doi.org/10.1111/1468-2508.t01-1-00013.

Huddy, Leonie, and Nayda Terkildsen. 1993. "Gender Stereotypes and the Perception of Male and Female Candidates." *American Journal of Political Science* 37 (1): 119–47. http://dx.doi.org/10.2307/2111526.

Jamieson, Kathleen Hall. 1995. *Beyond the Double Bind: Women and Leadership*. New York: Oxford University Press.

Kahn, Kim Fridkin. 1992. "Does Being Male Help? An Investigation of the Effects of Candidate Gender and Campaign Coverage on Evaluations of U.S. Senate Candidates." *Journal of Politics* 54 (2): 497–517. http://dx.doi.org/10.2307/2132036.

—. 1994. "The Distorted Mirror: Press Coverage of Women Candidates for Statewide Office." *Journal of Politics* 56 (1): 154–73. http://dx.doi.org/10.2307/2132350.

—. 1996. *The Political Consequences of Being a Woman.* New York: Columbia University Press.

Kahn, Kim Fridkin, and Edie N. Goldenberg. 1991. "Women Candidates in the News: An Examination of Gender Differences in U.S. Senate Campaign Coverage." *Public Opinion Quarterly* 55 (2): 180–99. http://dx.doi.org/10.1086/269251.

Kanter, Rosabeth Moss. 1977. *Men and Women of the Corporation.* New York: Basic Books.

Kittilson, Miki Caul, and Kim Fridkin. 2008. "Gender, Candidate Portrayals, and Election Campaigns: A Comparative Perspective." *Politics and Gender* 4 (3): 371–92. http://dx.doi.org/10.1017/S1743923X08000330.

Koch, Jeffrey. 1997. "Candidate Gender and Assessments of Women Candidates." *Social Science Quarterly* 80: 84–96.

Lawless, Jennifer. 2004. "Women, War, and Winning Elections: Gender Stereotyping in the Post-September 11th Era." *Political Research Quarterly* 57 (3): 479–90. http://dx.doi.org/10.1177/106591290405700312.

Lawrence, Regina G., and Melody Rose. 2010. *Hillary Clinton's Race for the White House: Gender Politics and the Media on the Campaign Trail.* Boulder, CO: Lynne Rienner Publishers.

Leeper, Mark Stephen. 1991. "The Impact of Prejudice on Female Candidates: An Experimental Look at Voter Inference." *American Politics Quarterly* 19 (2): 248–61. http://dx.doi.org/10.1177/1532673X9101900206.

Loke, Jaime, Dustin Harp, and Ingrid Bachmann. 2011. "Mothering and Governing: How News Articulated Gender Roles in the Cases of Governors Jane Swift and Sarah Palin." *Journalism Studies* 12 (2): 205–20. http://dx.doi.org/10.1080/1461670X.2010.488418.

McGinley, Ann C. 2009. "Hillary Clinton, Sarah Palin, and Michelle Obama: Performing Gender, Race, and Class on the Campaign Trail." *Denver University Law Review* 86 (Special Election Issue): 709–25.

Miller, Melissa K., and Jeffrey S. Peake. 2013. "Press Effects, Public Opinion, and Gender: Coverage of Sarah Palin's Vice Presidential Campaign." *International Journal of Press/Politics* 18 (4): 482–507. http://dx.doi.org/10.1177/1940161213495456.

Miller, Melissa K., Jeffrey S. Peake, and Brittany Anne Boulton. 2010. "Testing the *Saturday Night Live* Hypothesis: Fairness and Bias in Newspaper Coverage of Hillary Clinton's Presidential Campaign." *Politics and Gender* 6 (2): 169–98. http://dx.doi.org/10.1017/S1743923X10000036.

National Annenberg Election Survey. 2008. Phone Edition (NAES08-Phone). Philadelphia: Annenberg Public Policy Center, University of Pennsylvania.

Norris, Pippa. 1997. "Women Leaders Worldwide: A Splash of Color in the Photo Op." In *Women, Media, and Politics*, edited by Pippa Norris, 149–65. Oxford: Oxford University Press.

Paizis, Suzanne. 1977. *Getting Her Elected: A Political Woman's Handbook.* Sacramento: Creative Editions Publishing.

Rosenwasser, Shirley M., Robyn R. Rogers, Sheila Fling, Kayla Silvers-Pickens, and John Butemeyer. 1987. "Attitudes toward Women and Men in Politics: Perceived Male and Female Candidate Competencies and Participant Personality Characteristics." *Political Psychology* 8 (2):191–200. http://dx.doi.org/10.2307/3791299.

Ross, Tessa. 2012. "*Chicago Sun Times* Asks Whether Woman Can Be Parent AND Candidate." *Name It Change It: Sexism and Equality Don't Mix.* She Should Run, Women's Media Center, and Political Parity. Blog post. September 6. http://www.nameitchangeit.org/blog/entry/chicago-sun-times-asks-whether-woman-can-be-parent-and-candidate.

Sapiro, Virginia. 1981–82. "If U.S. Senator Baker Were a Woman: An Experimental Study of Candidate Images." *Political Psychology* 3 (1–2): 61–83. http://dx.doi.org/10.2307/3791285.

Smith, Kevin B. 1997. "When All's Fair: Signs of Parity in Media Coverage of Female Candidates." *Political Communication* 14 (1): 71–82. http://dx.doi.org/10.1080/105846097199542.

Smolkin, Rachel. 2002. "Once Dismissed as a Lightweight 'Mom in Tennis Shoes,' Senator Patty Murray Leads the Democrats' Bid to Retain Senate Control in November." *Chicago Tribune*, May 10. http://articles.chicagotribune.com/2002-05-10/features/0205100008_1_democratic-senatorial-campaign-committee-tennis-shoes-maria-cantwell.

Stalsburg, Brittany L. 2010. "Voting for Mom: The Political Consequences of Being a Parent for Male and Female Candidates." *Politics and Gender* 6 (3): 373–404. http://dx.doi.org/10.1017/S1743923X10000309.

Woodall, Gina Serignese, and Kim L. Fridkin. 2007. "Shaping Women's Chances: Stereotypes and the Media." In *Rethinking Madam President: Are We Ready for a Woman in the White House?*, edited by Lori Cox Han and Caroline Heldman, 69–86. Boulder, CO: Lynne Rienner Publishers.

9

Identity and Activism in an Era of Politicized Motherhood

CARRIE A. LANGNER, JILL S. GREENLEE, and GRACE DEASON

On Mother's Day in 2000, more than 750,000 moms and advocates convened at the Lincoln Memorial in Washington, DC (Hamm 2010). The Million Mom March organization, a group advocating for stricter gun control policies, brought these women together in an effort to curb gun violence. At the same time on the national mall, the Second Amendment Sisters held the Armed Informed Mothers march in counterprotest; these mothers sought to defend the rights of gun owners. In June 2014, hundreds of activists marched across the Brooklyn Bridge demanding reforms to US gun policy. Among those marching were Lucia Bath, mother of shooting victim Jordan Davis, and other mothers of recent victims of gun violence (Lemire 2014). These marches, and more broadly the movements related to gun policy, emphasize women's parent *identities* and frame the political issue in terms of family roles. There is frequent use of the term "moms," and spokespeople are often parents of victims of gun violence.

We also see many examples of mothers' activism under the banner of motherhood across both the globe and the ideological spectrum. For example, Argentina's Madres de Plaza de Mayo protested for decades against the disappearance of their children during the nation's "dirty war" (Fisher 1989). Conflict in the Middle East has also been long marked by maternal protest, with both Israeli and Palestinian mothers organizing under the banner of motherhood (Hammami 1997; Sharoni 1997). In the United States, and in keeping with Schreiber's analysis (this volume), conservative women participated in groups such as Mothers for a Moral America and were important participants in the early pro-life movement, in which motherhood was central to the identity of anti-abortion activists (Luker 1985; Nickerson 2012).[1] On the left, groups such as Mothers Strike for Peace organized a national movement in the early 1960s to protest nuclear proliferation; marching with babies and strollers, they stressed that US foreign policy endangered future generations (Nickerson 2012; Swerdlow 1993). For these activists, the intersection of gender and parenthood shapes their political engagement.

Generally speaking, can framing a political issue in terms of parenthood lead citizens to politicize their parent identity and in turn foster political activism? We believe that it does. We propose a theoretical model in which activism among mothers can be understood via a politicized parent identity (Langner and Greenlee 2014). Identification with other parents, if politically meaningful (or "politicized"), should predict political behaviour on behalf of the group. We argue that the current emphasis on and politicization of motherhood within American public discourse, which we refer to as Politicized Motherhood (Deason, Greenlee, and Langner 2014), leads to greater politicization of parent identities among women because of increased exposure to maternal images, links between motherhood and politics, and connections to other mothers via the Internet (see Figure 9.1).

In this chapter, we build a theory outlining how the era of Politicized Motherhood can influence mothers' identities and engagement in activism (for a similar analysis of political consumerism, see Micheletti and Stolle,

FIGURE 9.1
Theoretical model of Politicized Motherhood, politicized parent identity, and activism

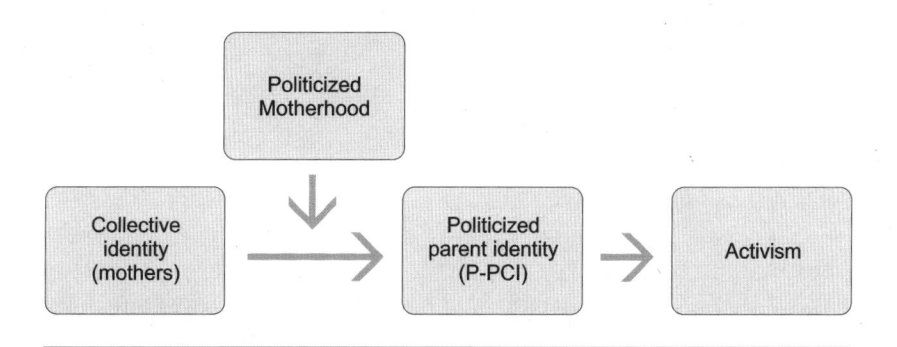

this volume). First, we define politicized parent identity and review related research. Second, we explore how Politicized Motherhood can set the stage for and foster a politicized parent identity and examine how politicized parent identity predicts individual women's engagement with activism. Third, we discuss activism among parents and suggest avenues for future research. Although we use the gender-neutral term "parent" throughout this chapter, particularly in the context of the concept of politicized parent identity, our argument focuses largely on mothers. As we discuss later in the chapter, perhaps in the future, in a different cultural context, our argument could be expanded to fathers.

Collective Identification and Politicization among Mothers

At the centre of our theoretical model, the concept of politicized parent identity links the broader cultural trend of Politicized Motherhood to political activism. Politicized Motherhood moderates the relationship between parent identity and politicization of parent identity, while politicized parent identity is the proximal predictor of an individual mother's activism. Here we review research on collective identity, politicized collective identity, and the recent extension of this work to politicized *parent* identity.

From a psychological perspective, "collective identity" refers to self-categorization within a group that shares some set of characteristics. Collective identities can vary with regard to importance, meaning, evaluation, attachment, and other dimensions (Ashmore, Deaux, and McLaughlin-Volpe 2004). Applying the concept of collective identity to motherhood, there is the potential for self-categorization within the group mothers the moment that a woman becomes a parent. However, mothers can vary in the degree to which identification with that category is important to their overall self-concept and relates to their political preferences and behaviours. Research on gender identity demonstrates that, the more central to self-concept the identity is, the more likely it is to be politicized (Langner 2005). Thus, we would expect individual variation in the importance of mothers' collective motherhood identities and the extent to which those identities are politicized.

Many individuals self-categorize within identity groups, but fewer have political meaning associated with identity. Much research has examined the politicized aspects of collective identities with regard to race and gender (Agronick and Duncan 1998; Cole and Stewart 1996; Gurin and Townsend 1986). As political debates and social movements develop over time, new collective identities will become politicized, and the particular political content associated with a collective identity can shift as well. A conceptualization of politicized collective identity as an individual's perceived association between the collective identity and *any* political content allows for the examination of politicization across identity types (e.g., gender or parent), across eras, and across the ideological spectrum (Langner 2005).

Applied to the group parents, collective identification can become politicized (take on political meaning) when individuals *perceive* an association between parenthood and some political stance or action (Langner 2005). Langner and Greenlee (2012) found that politicized parent identities relate to political preferences; mothers with more politicized parent identities, compared with mothers with less politicized identities, rate certain political issues as more important (e.g., health-care funding or national security).[2] Emerging research demonstrates that politicized parent identity among women can be conceptually and empirically distinguished from politicized gender identity (Langner and Greenlee 2014). This suggests that the act of parenting (and the thoughts and behaviours involved in caring for a child) can lead to a distinct parent identity. Further, initial data from samples of US registered voters who are mothers suggest that parent identity tends to be more politicized than gender identity (Langner and Greenlee 2014). This indicates that a politicized parent identity can be an important and largely unexplored mechanism that motivates political involvement among some women. From the literature reviewed above, we conclude that simple membership in the group parents is unlikely to have predictive power in identifying who might be politically active, whereas individual differences in politicization do have this potential.

In addition to variations among mothers, the politicization of a given individual's identity as a mother can vary over time as her experience of motherhood changes. Currently, we know little about how the stages of motherhood affect political attitudes and behaviours. Some chapters in this volume begin to address this question, but much research is still needed. According to theories of the process of becoming a mother (Hartrick 1997; Mercer 2004; Rubin 1984), the expanding sense of self as a mother is idiosyncratic to each woman's experience and the timing of parenting challenges. However, there can be critical developmental phases in which the expanding sense of identity as a mother would be more likely to incorporate political stances and behaviours. Qualitative data suggest that many women form a maternal identity around the time that an infant reaches four months of age (Mercer 2004), but much less is known about how mothers adapt to motherhood when their children enter school, adolescence, and adulthood. In fact, we know of no research examining how the developmental phases of parenthood might shape political identity and political participation.[3] Initial research suggests that women who have more recently transitioned to parenthood might be more politicized than women who became mothers earlier (Langner and Greenlee 2012), but this politicization might not translate into political action because of the time constraints of caring for an infant. We suspect that, though new mothers might develop a politicized identity, its behavioural effects will be seen farther downstream when the child is older.[4] O'Neill and Gidengil, and Micheletti and Stolle (both this volume), offer additional discussions of the political involvement of mothers with children in different age groups.

Political Meanings Associated with Parent Identity

There are many ways that parent identities can be associated with politics, and we identify two dimensions along which we can organize our understanding of the political content associated with parent identity. The first dimension relates to the beneficiary of the political activism: other-advocacy versus self-advocacy. Activism on behalf of others, particularly children, can be more effective at politicizing mothers because it is seen as a more legitimate activity than self-advocacy, fitting with cultural norms and expectations of women as caregivers. Research indicates that women are more comfortable negotiating on behalf of others compared with negotiating for themselves (Amanatullah and Morris 2010). Indeed, there are numerous examples of mothers who organize events and movements at a grassroots level around specific child well-being-related policy concerns (e.g., nurse-ins, Mothers against Drunk Driving, school funding).

Other theorists have discussed types of parent-related politics that we believe can also be categorized as other-advocacy or self-advocacy. "Motherhood movement politics," as outlined by Patrice DiQuinzio (2006), focuses on political issues that affect mothers and seek to improve the conditions under which mothers and other caregivers do their work (e.g., welfare rights, affordable childcare) and therefore could be framed as self-advocacy. "Maternalist politics," on the other hand, invokes motherhood as a means of justifying, explaining, and propelling political action on a range of issues, some of which might seem to be removed from the practices of parenting (DiQuinzio 2006) but can be framed as other-advocacy (e.g., gun control or gun rights on behalf of the protection of family). See also Franceschet,

Piscopo, and Thomas (this volume) for a discussion of motherhood as political motivation.

The second dimension with which we can organize political content associated with parent identity is ideological orientation. The motherhood movement goals mentioned above align primarily with those of feminists and liberals. Yet maternalist politics can be found at all points on the ideological spectrum. For example, contemporary national groups on the left include Moms Rising and MOMocrats, two groups that combine liberal policy stances with a mother's perspective on politics,[5] and advocating for more restrictive gun laws was the goal of the Million Mom March (Hayden 2003). Right-leaning groups such as Concerned Women of America employ motherhood as a means of framing their political goals and stress the roles of mothering in their advocacy (Schreiber 2008). Smaller groups such as Armed Informed Mothers, a spin-off of Second Amendment Sisters, place motherhood at the centre of their advocacy for gun rights (DiQuinzio 2006).

Maternal activism varies along two dimensions – regarding the beneficiaries of desired political change and regarding ideology – and there are many ways in which mothers can connect politics to a parent identity. Importantly for the theoretical model that we consider here, politicized parent identity refers to an individual-level variable that connects broader cultural discourse to activism. Thus, the question arises, in the identity group mothers, what leads some of these women to have *politicized* mother identities? Next we turn to contextual features that we believe will increase parent identity politicization.

The Effect of Politicized Motherhood on Politicized Parent Identity

Politicized Motherhood is the current emphasis on and politicization of motherhood within American public discourse (Deason et al. 2014). This broader cultural focus on mothers makes the emphasis on family in politics feel more natural, and the Internet provides a space to reinforce links between identity and politics. In this section, we explore how aspects of Politicized Motherhood can influence the process of developing a collective mother identity and the political meanings attached to that identity. We posit that Politicized Motherhood moderates the relationship between membership in the category mothers and politicized parent identity such that Politicized Motherhood makes politicization of parent identity more likely (see Figure 9.1). Of note, Politicized Motherhood helps to explain why mothers, and not fathers, are more likely to develop a politicized parent identity in this current context. Our theoretical perspective suggests that, should the cultural and political context shift, such that fatherhood is similarly politicized within American public discourse, we could see a rise in politicized parent identity among men.

Although motherhood has been emphasized in previous political eras (e.g., the republican motherhood era in the United States in the 18th century and early 19th century and the civic motherhood era of the late 19th century and early 20th century), the current era of Politicized Motherhood emerges from several recent, distinctive trends (Deason et al. 2014). The increased political, policy, and rhetorical emphasis on familial roles beginning in the 1980s (Elder and Greene 2012; Greenlee 2014), the salience of motherhood in broader cultural discourse in the United States (Mezey and Pillard 2012; Podnieks 2012; Warner 2005), and the Internet as a site for mothers' expanded political communication (Lopez 2009) create a unique environment in which motherhood is strongly linked to women's political experiences.

How does the broader environment and cultural discourse influence women's identities? We argue that the era of Politicized Motherhood increases the likelihood that women perceive a connection between collective identification as parents and politics, leading to politicized parent identity. For example, the Breast Is Best public health campaign and associated cultural discourse on the benefits of breastfeeding (Wall 2001) might have set the stage for perceived connections between parent identity and politics. Mothers staged a protest at Target stores in many US states in response to a mother having been told to move to a fitting room to nurse her child (Parents 2011). Women who joined the protests likely perceived a link between their shared identity as mothers and a specific political action, and this might have been more likely to occur because of a cultural environment in which the topic of breastfeeding had moved from the private sphere to the public sphere. Complementarily, during eras when the link between motherhood and politics is not emphasized, we would expect to see less politicized parent identity. However, we theorize that any perceived association between parent identity and politics will lead to identity politicization, whether that is driven by cultural discourse and political elites or by more local and personal experiences. For example, the Community Living movement was formed in Canada by parents of children with disabilities (Panitch 2007), and, in contrast to the current climate of Politicized Motherhood, these mothers were criticized for failing to be at home with their children.[6] Despite these external pressures against politicizing motherhood, these women saw their activism as part of their roles as mothers. Although personal experience can certainly inform politicization, we suggest that a cultural discourse emphasizing the connection between parenthood and politics will amplify politicized parent identity.

The era of Politicized Motherhood's frequent contextual emphasis on motherhood might increase the degree to which women experience this identity as a central aspect of self-concept. As a mother identity becomes increasingly salient, it would stand more of a chance of being linked with political issues and behaviours. For example, Politicized Motherhood might make the family and child-related aspects of policies more salient and thus more likely to be noticed. As mentioned earlier, research on politicized gender identity indicates that the more central to self-concept the identity is, the more likely it is to be politicized (Langner 2005). Translated to the realm of motherhood, this suggests that, the more parent identities are experienced as central to self-concept, the more likely they are to take on political meanings.

Politicized Motherhood can also indirectly affect identity via the images of motherhood emphasized. Although most laws in the United States are sex neutral, the practice of parenting remains deeply gendered (Andrews 2004; Mezey and Pillard 2012; Suk 2010). This subsequently creates a context in which mothers are seen as the "default" parent, which can affect their identities in several ways. Much as mothers in the progressive era were seen as moral authorities, mothers in the Politicized Motherhood era can be seen as authoritative sources for policies related to children. This perspective could provide additional emphasis on the connection between parenthood and politics *for mothers in particular.* The focus on mothers as the primary parent might confer authority on political issues that relate to family and children and thereby foster politicized parent identity.

In the era of Politicized Motherhood, motherhood is also *explicitly* linked to politics. The use of familial themes in politics has increased significantly since the 1980s (Elder and Greene 2012) and is used by political elites on both sides of the aisle to appeal to female voters (Greenlee 2014). Politicians and advocacy groups that attempt to politicize motherhood assume that appeals to it will persuade a large number of voters. Maternal appeals are a risky strategy for female candidates who seek electoral success (Deason 2011), yet we do not know how maternal frames might shape and mobilize citizens' parent identities.[7] Our theoretical model suggests that the increased focus on maternalism in politics, as in the broader cultural context, will politicize mothers' identities and increase the likelihood of activism.

Moreover, multiple identities (e.g., parent, gender, and race) can be primed when politicians make maternal appeals, and these primed identities can then compete with one another to affect political attitudes. Samantha Klar (2013) finds that political rhetoric that threatens an identity can win out over competing primed identities. Extrapolating from her work, we suggest that politicized parent identities, as opposed to other identities, will be particularly responsive to identity priming from elites. Mothers, as the default parent and gatekeeper of children's safety, should be particularly responsive to political rhetoric that emphasizes threats to children and families.

Use of the Internet to connect mothers is another characteristic feature of the era of Politicized Motherhood. This factor is particularly relevant to citizens' participation in activism, since it allows for prolific exposure to the links between motherhood and politics and diversifies the set of voices promoting activism. Although the majority of "mommy blogs" do not pursue a political agenda, the blogosphere has created a fertile space for women to connect and act within the political sphere. These blogs often represent the views of one activist rather than those of an organization and offer a new vehicle to connect motherhood to the issues of the day. Mothers of all political shades share their observations and experiences (some political, some not) with thousands of readers daily (Lopez 2009). On conservative blogs such as Mommentary, MomThink, Jenny Erickson, and the Dana Show, right-leaning views on topics from health-care reform to constitutional interpretation are discussed through the perspective of a mom – often a white, middle-class woman who does not work outside the home. Popular left-leaning blogs, such as Mombian, Viva la Feminista, Pundit Mom, and Ebony Mom Politics, are equally abundant and give voice to perspectives from a multicultural and diverse community, including those of women of colour and lesbians. Groups such as Mothers in Charge and MOTHERS (Mothers Ought to Have Equal Rights) engage primarily African American mothers in addressing issues related to gun violence, poverty, and public schools.

This diversity of voices speaking as mothers demonstrates a pluralism within Politicized Motherhood. Much like third-wave feminisms, there are more organizations attached to these mother-centred efforts on the political left than on the political right. Intersectional perspectives on motherhood and gender are expressed through these communities of mothers. Although white, middle-class, heteronormative views are the most readily available in the political mommy blog realm, views from outside this dominant paradigm can be found through these left-leaning blogs. The Internet might provide a mode in which lines of race and class can be crossed, yet it remains to be seen whether the simultaneous politicization of various mothers will result in coordination of and inclusion in activist efforts. Lessons from social welfare policy in the early 20th century suggest that, even when both black and white women engaged in maternal activism using similar metaphors, black women did not gain as many benefits as did white women (Boris 1993).

The era of Politicized Motherhood includes a number of contextual influences on women's identities: the broader cultural focus on motherhood, connections drawn between motherhood and politics in the political realm, and availability of the Internet to connect mothers. We believe that these contextual influences make it more likely that mothers will be politicized and that a wider variety of mothers will be reached through non-traditional routes of communication (e.g., the Internet).

Politicized Parent Identity and Activism

Prior research indicates that politicized collective identity is predictive of action on behalf of the group (Klandermans et al. 2002; Simon and Klandermans 2001). Politicized collective identity can be conceptually and empirically distinguished from an individual's political orientation by measuring the extent to which the individual perceives an association between the identity and any political content (Langner 2005). Thus, though past research has focused primarily on politicization via ideologies on the left side of the political spectrum, an identity could be politicized in relation to any political belief. The political content of a politicized collective identity could be grounded in progressive policy stances (e.g., Moms Demand Action) or conservative policy stances (e.g., Armed Informed Mothers) or non-partisan policy stances (e.g., Mothers against Drunk Driving). Critically, the degree to which political meaning is associated with a collective identity (i.e., the degree to which it is politicized) predicts political preferences and actions rather than solely the self-categorization within the identity group (Duncan 1999; Gurin and Markus 1988; Langner 2005).

Based upon prior research on other types of politicized collective identities mentioned above (e.g., gender, race), politicized parent identity should also predict political involvement. Yet much of the research literature to date focuses on how parenthood in general, as opposed to *politicized parent identity*, affects political participation. For example, initially becoming a parent can lead to decreased political involvement (Jennings and Niemi 1981). In a climate of intensive parenting, and for women who embrace intensive parenting ideals, parenthood would presumably leave even less time for political involvement. However, political participation can increase at certain points after the transition to parenthood; for example, having school-aged children is associated with more involvement (Bowers 2003; O'Neill and Gidengil, this volume; Verba, Schlozman, and Brady 1995).

Considering mothers' politicized collective identity can shed light on these shifting patterns of involvement among mothers. For example, the degree to which a collective parent identity is politicized can provide greater predictive power of which mothers become more involved and which mothers become less involved over time. In addition to the many structural factors affecting mothers' political participation (income, education, work status), the degree to which the individual connects her acquired maternal identity to political issues likely plays a role. Initial research indicates that mothers who connect their parent identities with political content (politicized parent identity) are more likely to engage in political activism with other parents (Langner and Greenlee 2012).

Political activism can take both traditional forms – marches and events – and newer forms, such as political consumerism or blogging and "clicktivism" (see Micheletti and Stolle, this volume). Signing online petitions can be interpreted as being similar to offline activism but with greater outreach (Bimber 1998; Karpf 2010). The expanded outreach of online modes of activism can be particularly important in the case of mothers. Even if a woman were to experience politicization of a parent identity on becoming a mother, she might find it difficult to participate in traditional modes of political action, such as attending rallies or political group meetings.

In addition, some aspects of Politicized Motherhood can inhibit the link between politicized parent identity and traditional forms of activism or channel mothers into different kinds of activism. For example, the focus on mothers as the primary caregiver can reduce the amount of time that a woman thinks she has to devote to political activities because of the amplified time demands of raising young children (Greenlee 2007; Mercer 2004). Being the default parent, especially in concert with intensive parenting ideals (Hays 1996), can leave less available time for mothers to be politically active. This might be an important way in which politicized parent identity differs from other politicized collective identities in that politicized mothers, especially those with young children, are less likely to engage in some of the traditional forms of collective action (e.g., marches). Indeed, some initial qualitative evidence suggests that some women experience this tension, feeling more compelled to engage in political action after becoming mothers (and finding political meaning in that role) yet experiencing an increase in resource constraints such that political activism is much more difficult (Greenlee 2007).

The Internet might play a role in decreasing the participation gap between men and women (Burns et al. 2001), and we argue that it can play a particularly important role in the mobilization of mothers, and caregivers in general, by helping them to surmount barriers to participation. For example, mothers can blog at home or click on a petition while kids are napping or in between work and daycare pickup. Similarly, political consumerism – that is, choosing producers and products with a political goal or aim in mind – can be another outlet in the era of Politicized Motherhood. For example, a mother with a politicized parent identity might be more likely to advocate for the regulation of Bisphenol-A (BPA)[8] rather than focus solely on her own child's health (e.g., avoiding purchasing products with BPA) if she sees her safety concerns for her children as being connected to other mothers' concerns and other children's well-being. As a result, when researching political activism among parents, it might be important to consider a wide array of non-traditional political actions (e.g., blogging, clicktivism, bumper stickers, yard signs, and political consumerism) that take into account the constraints of caring for young children. An important caveat is that, though more people might be mobilized today compared with the past, there are still many people worldwide who do not have Internet access (Greenlee 2007). Such access can then serve as a moderating factor in the relationship between politicized parent identity and activism.

A wide array of examples of maternal activism can be explained in part, as with other activist movements, via identity politicization. There is preliminary evidence suggesting that politicized parent identity predicts intention to engage in activism, and future research might uncover additional evidence by examining the link between identity and alternative forms of activism. Some important moderators of the link between politicized parent identity and activism that we have mentioned above (e.g., access to the Internet, exposure to intensive parenting ideals) might help to trace important boundary conditions on the theoretical model.

In summary, we argue that activism among mothers can be understood via a process of parent identity politicization such that a climate of Politicized Motherhood amplifies women's perceptions of links between parent identity and politics. When such an important part of the self-concept is strongly linked to political stances, congruent political behaviour is likely to unfold. To conclude the chapter, we consider the implications of the era of Politicized Motherhood and politicized parent identity and outstanding questions in the areas of democratic participation, efficacy of activist efforts, and inclusion of fathers.

Increasing Women's Political Participation

Does activism driven by parent identity narrow these citizens' focus or encourage greater political participation overall? The finding that women have higher levels of parent identity politicization, in contrast to gender identity politicization (Langner and Greenlee 2014), suggests that parent identity can be a fruitful motivator for women's political involvement.

Could the "activist mother" also provide a model for the successful integration of women's formerly "private" and "public" identities? In the realm of candidate evaluations, maternal appeals led to feminine characteristics being weighted more heavily in vote choice (Deason 2011). This suggests that increased visibility of activism among mothers could alter perceptions of political participation. Political elites might conflate gender with motherhood, thereby essentializing women, but female activists could provide a model of how to integrate private and public identities. Women are more likely than men to experience career and parent roles as oppositional and to engage subsequently in cognitively taxing identity shifts (Hodges and Park 2013). The "packaging" of motherhood and politics can provide a domain in which women can surmount the perceived conflict between parent and worker roles. If in fact politics is a space in which women's identities are experienced as complementary rather than oppositional, then future research might examine the features of political environments and the maternal frames that make for a better fit between women's professional identities and their parent identities (see also Miller, this volume, for a discussion of the role of the motherhood frame in campaigns).

Political activism in the era of Politicized Motherhood, despite its liabilities, appears to connect citizens to politics. However, one might ask whether this era is equally encouraging of politicization across lines of class and race. Certain aspects of the political environment might make Politicized Motherhood more salient for women of certain groups, thus making it a stronger driver of activism for that group. Preliminary data are primarily from white samples, so we should not assume that politicized parent identity operates similarly for all women, for there might be important differences across groups. Further, the role of mothering is often assumed by a host of family members, particularly in some communities of colour, thereby complicating our conception of how parent identity might form and take on political meaning. Although we see maternal activism that reaches across racial lines anecdotally (e.g., MomsRising mobilizing mothers to advocate against racial profiling and police violence), the topic needs empirical study.

The Political Efficacy of Activism with a Maternal Frame
In addition to the effects of Politicized Motherhood on women's participation discussed above, we might ask about the efficacy of political activism framed in maternal terms. One critique suggests that the focus on women *as mothers* is dangerous; when motherhood is romanticized, the real social, economic, and political challenges that accompany it go unaddressed by policy makers (Mezey and Pillard 2012). Further, a maternal perspective might be invoked to legitimize women's concerns about a policy issue but can risk alienating women who are not mothers in the process. Thus, linking motherhood to a political issue can activate latent support from some women who see themselves as politically concerned mothers rather than as political actors in their own right, but it can simultaneously squeeze out women who are not mothers and male supporters from the conversation because they find a maternal frame exclusionary. This might be a strategic choice by some advocacy organizations that hope to target mothers, yet the maternal frame can decrease the number of people who could be mobilized to take political action, thereby hindering the group's chances of achieving its policy goals.

The efficacy of maternal activism can also be hindered by stereotypes. Tying political claims to motherhood can essentialize women, emphasizing their reproductive capacities and suggesting that, because of these capacities, they have unique responsibilities that men do not have to protect children, preserve the environment, or promote peace (Hayden 2003; Stearney 1994). Maternalist politics are often a politics of grief, grounded in an emotional response, and as such run the risk of being delegitimized as irrational (DiQuinzio 2006, 61). Political demands connected to issues such as peace and gun control, made in the face of loss, reinforce gender stereotypes about the emotional nature of women, and they are potentially disempowering for women. However, Sara Hayden (2003, 197) argues that, whereas maternal politics highlight attributes that often seem out of place in a political debate, such as nurturance and caring, they are a natural way to package an "alternative vision of society in which the social welfare of citizens is privileged." In this way, maternal politics can offer a more communal approach to politics that can be valuable as political actors (elites and citizens) work to provide for the common good.

It will be important for future research to examine the potentially divergent effects of elite versus activist sources of maternal frames. When political elites frame women's political participation in terms of motherhood, there can be greater activation of harmful gender stereotypes that essentialize women and greater exclusion of women who are not mothers. In contrast, when women themselves emphasize parent identity as a strategy for framing a political issue and mobilizing other mothers, they can be effective in the eyes of the public potentially because they are seen as more legitimate. An additional question is whether differences in efficacy might relate to self-advocacy versus other-advocacy framing.

Politicized Parent Identity among Men

Politicized Motherhood's focus on women as the default parent does not place enough responsibility on men, both in the political world and in the non-political world. An activist community of mothers working under the banner of motherhood could exacerbate this disconnect between parenting and fathers' responsibilities. Although this might intensify the inequities that women face, it might also delegitimize men's increasing efforts as fathers.

Our theoretical model suggests that if messages about the primary parent role shift and there is greater focus on fathers, we would see politicized parent identity increase among men and subsequent activism driven by parent identity. Some research suggests that fatherhood affects the political views of men (Shafer and Malhotra 2011; Washington 2008), though other data suggest that fathers do not vote differently from other men (Elder and Greene 2012). The legalization of same-sex marriage and the shift away from a heteronormative presentation of family in some communities might be where we see greater politicized parent identity among men. We see a potential example of politicized parent identity in the Not One More meme and activist effort begun by Richard Martinez, the father of a shooting victim (Everytown for Gun Safety 2014). Men's increasing efforts as fathers (Parker and Wang 2013) might make politicization more likely as the parent identity becomes more central to men's self-concept. Many men are interested in becoming more involved in parenting, but a cultural context more supportive of a strong, politically relevant father identity might also be needed to encourage men to act alongside other parents.

Conclusion

The process by which mothers become politicized and engage in activism highlights how the personal can indeed become the political. We have argued here that the era of Politicized Motherhood provides a context in which mothers' identities are likely to become politicized via greater cultural emphasis on motherhood, explicit connections between parenthood and politics, and use of the Internet to connect parents (see also Micheletti and Stolle, this volume). Importantly, politicized parent identity, rather than mere identification as a parent, then leads to mothers' activism. Our theoretical model offers a way forward to understand when and among whom we will see maternal activism. Consideration of the links among Politicized Motherhood, politicized parent identity, and activism can generate a number of research questions in the areas of democratic participation, political efficacy of activist efforts, and inclusion of fathers in maternal activism. As broader cultural messages form a backdrop emphasizing the collective identification as parents and the association of parent identity with politics, we expect to see increased activism among parents.

Notes

1 Mothers for a Moral America was created by the Goldwater for President campaign strategists, but it did organically draw support from conservative female activists (Nickerson 2012).
2 Using the term "parent" at conceptual and measurement levels, we can distinguish "politicized parent identity" from gender (the word *mother* likely connotes more than the parenting role) and isolate the effects of parent identity from those of gender identity (Langner and Greenlee 2012).
3 Existing research on this topic examines political participation at moments in time (Burns et al. 2001) and is therefore limited in its ability to help us understand how the differing stages of parenthood influence behaviour.
4 Perhaps the interaction between political identity and political action produces an inverse U-shaped curve, whereby women with very young children are politicized but less politically active than women with school-aged children, who likely have increased contact with other parents and government policies that affect children (e.g., schools), thereby providing greater opportunities for political action. Women with adult children, and thus no longer in the throes of childrearing, likely experience a change in self-concept such that their parent identity is less salient (relative to other identities) in making political decisions. Political action among these older women might be less frequently driven by a politicized mother identity.
5 Moms Rising calls itself a non-partisan organization, but it advocates for left-leaning policy goals.
6 An advocacy movement focused on assisting those with developmental disabilities, the Community Living movement grew from groups of Canadian mothers politically active in the 1960s. These parent groups evolved into a movement aimed at human rights for, and deinstitutionalization of, persons with intellectual disabilities.

7 During this period of Politicized Motherhood, it is an open question whether fathers experience politicization despite, or because of, being excluded from the contemporary cultural emphasis on mothers as the primary parent. This is an important avenue for future research, in addition to thinking about other social forces changing roles within the family (dual-income families, reconceptualization of fatherhood, acceptance of gay partnerships and parenthood) and can affect how parents play a role in politics, regardless of gender.
8 BPA is a substance found in plastics, such as baby bottles, that many consumers believe has negative health effects.

References

Agronick, Gail S., and Lauren E. Duncan. 1998. "Personality and Social Change: Individual Differences, Life Path, and Importance Attributed to the Women's Movement." *Journal of Personality and Social Psychology* 74 (6): 1545–55. http://dx.doi.org/10.1037/0022-3514.74.6.1545.

Amanatullah, Emily T., and Michael W. Morris. 2010. "Negotiating Gender Roles: Gender Differences in Assertive Negotiating Are Mediated by Women's Fear of Backlash and Attenuated When Negotiating on Behalf of Others." *Journal of Personality and Social Psychology* 98 (2): 256–67. http://dx.doi.org/10.1037/a0017094.

Andrews, Edmund L. 2004. "Survey Confirms It: Women Outjuggle Men." *New York Times*, September 15. http://www.nytimes.com/2004/09/15/politics/survey-confirms-it-women-outjuggle-men.html?_r=0.

Ashmore, Richard, Kay Deaux, and Tracy McLaughlin-Volpe. 2004. "An Organizing Framework for Collective Identity: Articulation and Significance of Multidimensionality." *Psychological Bulletin* 130 (1): 80–114. http://dx.doi.org/10.1037/0033-2909.130.1.80.

Bimber, Bruce. 1998. "The Internet and Political Mobilization: Research Note on the 1996 Election Season." *Social Science Computer Review* 16 (4): 391–401. http://dx.doi.org/10.1177/089443939801600404.

Boris, Eileen. 1993. "The Power of Motherhood: Black and White Activist Women Redefine the 'Political.'" In *Mothers of a New World: Maternalist Politics and the Origins of Welfare States*, edited by Seth Koven and Sonya Michel, 213–45. New York: Routledge.

Bowers, Jacob. 2003. *The Dynamics of Political Participation in the Lives of Ordinary Americans*. Berkeley: University of California Press.

Burns, Nancy, Kay Lehman Schlozman, and Sidney Verba. 2001. *The Private Roots of Public Action: Gender, Equality, and Political Participation*. Cambridge, MA: Harvard University Press.

Cole, Elizabeth R., and Abigail J. Stewart. 1996. "Meanings of Political Participation among Black and White Women: Political Identity and Social Responsibility." *Journal of Personality and Social Psychology* 71 (1): 130–40. http://dx.doi.org/10.1037/0022-3514.71.1.130.

Deason, Grace. 2011. "Maternal Appeals in Politics: Their Effectiveness and Consequences." PhD diss., University of Minnesota.

Deason, Grace, Jill S. Greenlee, and Carrie A. Langner. 2014. "Mothers on the Campaign Trail: Implications of Politicized Motherhood for Women in Politics." *Politics, Groups, and Identities* 3 (1): 133–48.

DiQuinzio, Patrice. 2006. "The Politics of the Mothers' Movement in the United States." *Journal of the Association for Research on Mothering* 8 (1–2): 55–71.

Duncan, Lauren E. 1999. "Motivation for Collective Action: Group Consciousness as Mediator of Personality, Life Experiences, and Women's Rights Activism." *Political Psychology* 20 (3): 611–35. http://dx.doi.org/10.1111/0162-895X.00159.

Elder, Laurel, and Steven Greene. 2012. *The Politics of Parenthood: Causes and Consequences of the Politicization and Polarization of the American Family*. Albany: SUNY Press.

Everytown for Gun Safety. 2014. http://everytown.org/press/two-million-postcards-gun-violence-survivors-declare-not-one-more-in-solidarity-with-father-of-ucsb-shooting-victim/.

Fisher, Jo. 1989. *Mothers of the Disappeared*. New York: South End Press.

Greenlee, Jill S. 2007. "The Political Dynamics of Parenthood." PhD diss., University of California, Berkeley.

—. 2014. *The Political Consequences of Motherhood*. Ann Arbor: University of Michigan Press. http://dx.doi.org/10.3998/mpub.5915695.

Gurin, Patricia, and Hazel Markus. 1988. "Group Identity: The Psychological Mechanisms of Durable Salience." *Revue internationale de psychologie sociale* 1 (2): 257–74.

Gurin, Patricia, and Aloen Townsend. 1986. "Properties of Gender Identity and Their Implications for Gender Consciousness." *British Journal of Social Psychology* 25 (2): 139–48. http://dx.doi.org/10.1111/j.2044-8309.1986.tb00712.x.

Hamm, Peter. 2010. "A Decade Later, Million Mom March Endures as a Force to Save Lives." Brady Campaign to Prevent Gun Violence. http://www.commondreams.org/newswire/2010/05/06/decade-later-million-mom-march-endures-force-save-lives.

Hammami, Rema. 1997. "Palestinean Motherhood and Political Activisim in the West Bank and Gaza Strip." In *The Politics of Motherhood: Activist Voices from Left to Right*, edited by Alexis Jetter, Annelise Orleck, and Diana Taylor, 161–68. Hanover: University Press of New England.

Hartrick, G.A. 1997. "Women Who Are Mothers: The Experience of Defining Self." *Health Care for Women International* 18 (3): 263–77. http://dx.doi.org/10.1080/07399339709516280.

Hayden, Sara. 2003. "Family Metaphors and the Nation: Promoting a Politics of Care through the Million Mom March." *Quarterly Journal of Speech* 89 (3): 196–215. http://dx.doi.org/10.1080/0033563032000125313.

Hays, Sharon. 1996. *The Cultural Contradictions of Motherhood*. New Haven, CT: Yale University Press.

Hodges, Allegra J., and Bernadette Park. 2013. "Oppositional Identities: Dissimilarities in How Women and Men Experience Parent versus Professional Roles." *Journal of Personality and Social Psychology* 105 (2): 193–216. http://dx.doi.org/10.1037/a0032681.

Jennings, Kent M., and Richard G. Niemi. 1981. *Generations and Politics: A Panel Study of Young Adults and Their Parents.* Princeton, NJ: Princeton University Press. http://dx.doi.org/10.1515/9781400854264.

Karpf, David. 2010. "Online Political Mobilization from the Advocacy Group's Perspective: Looking beyond Clicktivism." *Policy and Internet* 2 (4): 7–41. http://dx.doi.org/10.2202/1944-2866.1098.

Klandermans, Bert, Jose M. Sabucedo, Mauro Rodriguez, and Marga De Weerd. 2002. "Identity Processes in Collective Action Participation: Farmers' Identity and Farmers' Protest in the Netherlands and Spain." *Political Psychology* 23 (2): 235–51. http://dx.doi.org/10.1111/0162-895X.00280.

Klar, Samantha. 2013. "The Influence of Competing Identity Primes on Political Preferences." *Journal of Politics* 75 (4): 1108–24. http://dx.doi.org/10.1017/S0022381613000698.

Langner, C.A. 2005. "Politicized Collective Identity: Defining the Self in Political Terms" PhD diss., University of California, Berkeley.

Langner, Carrie A., and Jill S. Greenlee. 2012. "Politicized Parent Identity and Its Relation to Gender Identity and Collective Action." Paper presented in Political Motherhood, symposium chaired by G. Deason, annual meeting of the International Society of Political Psychology, Chicago, July 7.

—. 2014. "Gender and Motherhood: Politicized Collective Identities and Action." Paper presented at the Political Psychology Preconference, annual meeting of the Society for Personality and Social Psychology, Austin, February 13.

Lemire, Jonathan. 2014. "Gun Control Group, Including Newtown Families, Marches over Brooklyn Bridge for Tougher Laws." *U.S. News and World Report*, June 14. http://www.usnews.com/news/us/articles/2014/06/14/gun-control-group-marches-across-brooklyn-bridge.

Lopez, Lori Kido. 2009. "The Radical Act of 'Mommy Blogging': Redefining Motherhood through the Blogosphere." *New Media and Society* 11 (5): 729–47. http://dx.doi.org/10.1177/1461444809105349.

Luker, Kristin. 1985. *Abortion and the Politics of Motherhood.* Berkeley: University of California Press.

Mercer, Ramona T. 2004. "Becoming a Mother versus Maternal Role Attainment." *Journal of Nursing Scholarship* 36 (3): 226–32. http://dx.doi.org/10.1111/j.1547-5069.2004.04042.x.

Mezey, Naomi, and Cornelia Nina Pillard. 2012. "Against the New Maternalism." *Michigan Journal of Gender and Law* 18: 229–96.

Nickerson, Michelle M. 2012. *Mothers of Conservatism: Women and the Postwar Right.* Princeton, NJ: Princeton University Press.

Panitch, M. 2007. *Disability, Mothers, and Organization: Accidental Activists.* New York: Routledge.

Parents. 2011. "Michelle Hickman, Mom Organizing Target International Nurse-In to Take Place December 28th." www.huffingtonpost.com/2011/12/19/target-nurse-in_n_1158595.html.

Parker, Kim, and Wendy Wang. 2013. "Modern Parenthood: Roles of Moms and Dads Converge as They Balance Work and Family." Pew Research Center, March 14.

Podnieks, Elizabeth. 2012. *Mediating Moms: Mothers in Popular Culture.* Montreal: McGill-Queen's University Press.

Rubin, R. 1984. *Maternal Identity and the Maternal Experience.* New York: Springer.

Schreiber, Ronnee. 2008. *Righting Feminism: Conservative Women and American Politics.* Oxford: Oxford University Press. http://dx.doi.org/10.1093/acprof:oso/9780195331813.001.0001.

Shafer, Emily F., and Neil Malhotra. 2011. "The Effect of a Child's Sex on Support for Traditional Gender Roles." *Social Forces* 90 (1): 209–22. http://dx.doi.org/10.1093/sf/90.1.209.

Sharoni, Simona. 1997. "Motherhood and the Politics of Women's Resistance: Israeli Women Organizing for Peace." In *The Politics of Motherhood: Activist Voices from Left to Right,* edited by Alexis Jetter, Annelise Orleck, and Diana Taylor, 144–60. Hanover: University Press of New England.

Simon, Bernd, and Bert Klandermans. 2001. "Politicized Collective Identity: A Social Psychological Analysis." *American Psychologist* 56 (4): 319–31. http://dx.doi.org/10.1037/0003-066X.56.4.319.

Stearney, L.M. 1994. "Feminism, Ecofeminism, and the Maternal Archetype: Motherhood as a Feminine Universal." *Communication Quarterly* 42 (2): 145–59. http://dx.doi.org/10.1080/01463379409369923.

Suk, J.C. 2010. "Are Gender Stereotypes Bad for Women? Rethinking Antidiscrimination Law and Work-Family Conflict." *Columbia Law Review* 110 (1): 1–69.

Swerdlow, Amy. 1993. *Women Strike for Peace.* Chicago: University of Chicago Press.

Verba, Sidney, Kay Lehman Schlozman, and Henry E. Brady. 1995. *Voice and Equality: Civic Voluntarism in American Politics.* Cambridge, MA: Harvard University Press.

Wall, Glenda. 2001. "Moral Constructions of Motherhood in Breastfeeding Discourse." *Gender and Society* 15 (4): 592–610. http://dx.doi.org/10.1177/089124301015004006.

Warner, Judith. 2005. *Perfect Madness: Motherhood in the Age of Anxiety.* New York: Penguin.

Washington, Ebonya. 2008. "Female Socialization: How Daughters Affect Their Legislator Fathers." *American Economic Review* 98 (1): 311–32. http://dx.doi.org/10.1257/aer.98.1.311.

PART 3
PARENTHOOD AND OPINION, PARTICIPATION AND BEHAVIOUR

10

The Parent Gap in Political Attitudes

Mothers versus Others

ELIZABETH GOODYEAR-GRANT and AMANDA BITTNER

Parenthood is one of a handful of adult experiences that is both pervasive and consequential in its impact on daily routines, conceptions of self and the world, and, it seems, attitudes toward a range of political issues (e.g., Burns, Schlozman, and Verba 1997, 2001; Elder and Greene 2006, 2007, 2012a, 2012b; Greenlee 2010). Parenthood is a life-changing event for both women and men, but studies suggest that it affects the two sexes differently in a number of ways. Parenthood can affect the campaign decisions of candidates (e.g., Thomas and Lambert, this volume), approaches to conducting legislative business (e.g., breastfeeding and/or toting around young children; see Campbell and Childs, as well as Arneil, this volume), and attitudes (e.g., Elder and Greene 2007, 2012a, 2012b). The chapters in this book assess the role of parenthood in politics, and many of them focus closely on *motherhood* in particular. Motherhood is inextricably linked to both gender and parenthood, and one cannot assess the role of parenthood in shaping attitudes without assessing the gendered dynamics that exist. Past research points to a general parent gap on certain issues, particularly those related to crime and security, but the critical gaps often seem to be gender related, resulting in opinion gaps between mothers and fathers or between parents and their childless counterparts of the same gender (Elder and Greene 2007, 2012a, 2012b). The literature suggests that parenthood often pushes women's attitudes in a liberal direction but has a conservative influence on men's attitudes.

This chapter examines voters' attitudes on three issue dimensions – social welfare, crime and security, and cultural issues – to determine not only whether but also why parent gaps exist in Canada. Building upon existing (largely American) scholarship, we find general parent gaps in attitudes toward both crime and security and cultural issues. We also find a handful of *gender-based* parent effects for particular issues, though the effects of parenthood cannot be described broadly as gender conditional. The patterns that we do find are similar to some of those identified in the American context. Our main objective, ultimately, is to start contributing to the search for explanations, a task that much of the existing literature does not do. Current work often identifies possible causes but does not assess them empirically. We take that work one step further to test two of the most likely explanations: material self-interest and socializing effects of parenthood. Although our data do not permit as thorough an investigation as we would like of the impacts of these forces on parent gaps in opinion, we find scant evidence that either explanatory factor has a consistent impact on such gaps. More research is needed to understand these gaps better and what is fuelling them.

Parenthood and Public Opinion

Recently, a lot of attention has been paid during American elections to "soccer moms," "security moms," and "NASCAR dads" as politicized groups with distinct opinions and preferences (e.g., Burrell 2005; Carroll 2006; Elder and Greene 2012b; MacManus 2006). Recent Canadian federal elections have seen similar thinking about voters, though more so in internal party communications than in media (Goodyear-Grant 2013). Parties and the media are on to something, for parenthood seems to structure public opinion, particularly when conditioned by other social identities, such as gender.

Existing knowledge about parent gaps in attitudes points to three key patterns. First, parenthood sometimes affects opinion, particularly on issues related to social welfare, crime and security and culture, though results are generally not consistent either across these dimensions or for mothers or fathers (Elder and Greene 2006, 2007, 2012a, 2012b; Greenlee 2010). Second, and relatedly, the effects of parenthood on public opinion are often conditional on gender, particularly on social welfare issues (Elder and Greene 2006, 2007, 2012a, 2012b). The critical differences seem to be those between mothers and everyone else, both childless women and fathers (recall the discussion above suggesting that gender and parenthood are intertwined and must be considered together to understand attitudinal patterns). Third, regarding causal forces rather than trends per se, some of the explanations prominent in research on *gender gaps* in public opinion and voting are typically highlighted as explanations of *parent gaps*, including material self-interest, social structural factors, and cuing by parties and media (Chaney, Alvarez, and Nagler 1998; Gidengil 1995; Gidengil et al. 2003; Jennings 2006; Kaufmann and Petrocik 1999; Mueller 1988; Shapiro and Mahajan 1986). In addition, we suggest that adult socialization in which parenthood alters not only the daily routines of individuals but also their outlooks, might be a critical explanation (e.g., Greenlee 2010). We explore existing scholarship here, assessing first the patterns and trends found in the attitudes of parents versus non-parents, including the gendered dynamics of parent gaps, and then discussing the factors that might be causing these patterns. We then build upon this work, extending it to the Canadian context, and focus our efforts on assessing causal factors (where possible).

Attitudes about Social Welfare

Starting with social welfare issues – the dimension in which parenthood seems to have the strongest and most consistent effects on opinion – motherhood is a strong predictor of more liberal attitudes among women on this dimension in every presidential election year from 1984 to 2008 (Elder and Greene 2006, 2007, 2012a; see also Eagly et al. 2004; Howell and Day 2000). This dimension includes issues such as aid to the poor, health care, government provision of jobs, and education. Interestingly, in more recent election cycles, there has been no liberal motherhood effect on education and child care (Elder and Greene 2012a, 2012b), issues that we might presume to be highly salient for parents. Laurel Elder and Steven Greene (2012b) do find consistent liberal motherhood effects from the 1970s to the 2000s on attitudes toward education using the American General Social Survey (GSS). In general, regardless of data source, motherhood effects on social welfare attitudes are sizable, often outpacing the effects of marital status, race, and employment, all of which have received greater attention in the political behaviour literature.

Parenthood commonly has no effect, or modest and conservative effects, on men. No effect was the norm from 1984 to 2000 and again during the 2008 presidential election (Elder and Greene 2006, 2012a), a finding mirrored in other literature showing the few observable effects of parenthood on men's lives (e.g., Nomaguchi and Milkie 2003). Elder and Greene (2012a) do find evidence of a marriage-fatherhood interaction that produces a conservative effect on married fathers' views. It is not entirely clear why having children pushes men to the right and women to the left, but Elder and Greene (2006) argue that it is partly the result of increased politicization of the family, largely along bipartisan lines. They suggest that the two parties have presented polarized messages on related issues, pushing parents in opposite directions. Langner, Greenlee, and Deason (this volume) suggest a similar effect, pointing to increased activism and engagement in the United States as a result of the politicization of parenthood (specifically motherhood).

In discussing the lack of effects for views on education and childcare spending in their analyses of the National Election Study (NES), Elder and Greene (2012a, 2012b) speculate that "motherhood effects are not driven by pure self-interest to support programs immediately benefitting their children, but that having and raising children fosters broader support for a more 'nurturing,' active, and helpful government" (2012a, 435), resulting in a general effect for the social welfare dimension if not for particular issues related to childrearing. This conclusion parallels a typical explanation for gender gaps in public opinion that sees women as more other oriented or "maternal" than men in terms of fundamental values and thereby more willing to expend public resources on social welfare programs. Rather than self-interest or family need as an explanation, in parent gap research there is a lot of explicit attention to maternal thinking as a mechanism underlying attitudinal differences between mothers and childless women, as well as between mothers and fathers, though this proposition is rarely explicitly tested in empirical analyses.

Attitudes about Crime and Security
Crime and security issues are thought to have particular salience for parents because of concerns about their children's safety and well-being. Overall, findings are mixed. In their analyses of attitudes in the 2004 American election, Elder and Greene (2007) report no parenthood effect for either men or women on security and defence issues, a null finding repeated for men in the 2008 election (Elder and Greene 2012a), raising skepticism about the labels security mom and NASCAR dad so pervasive in the post-9/11 climate. For women in 2008, they found a liberal motherhood effect on questions specifically about the Iraq War (Elder and Greene 2012a), similar to the persistent gender gap in opinion on war and conflict in which women are consistently more anti-war than men (e.g., Clark and Clark 1993;

Conover and Sapiro 1993; Eichenberg 2003, 2005; Shapiro and Mahajan 1986; Wilcox, Hewitt, and Allsop 1996).

Most scholars focus on attitudes toward war and defence spending as indicators for the crime and security dimension. What about crime and security in the domestic realm (e.g., drugs, gangs, policing), arguably more relevant to children's immediate safety and well-being? There seems to be a conservative effect on parents of both sexes. Parenthood is associated with tougher stances on the legality of drugs and warmer feelings about security-maintaining institutions (police and military) (e.g., Greenlee 2010), interpreted here as evidence of a general parent gap on domestic security issues. Results are similar for parents generally on this dimension, regardless of gender.

Attitudes about Cultural Issues

This dimension contains classic moral issues that have animated political debate in the United States and Canada for decades: abortion, gay marriage, racial and gender equality, and attitudes toward diversity. Arguably, this dimension has less direct relevance to the daily concerns of parents – less so than social welfare and security issues – so why is it a focus of parent gap research? First, parents might have different attitudes because these issues are "connected to conceptions of the family and 'family values'" (Elder and Greene 2012a, 422) or because of a perceived need for "'defending' their lifestyle choice of marriage and children by increasing their opposition to gay marriage and abortion" (Elder and Greene 2012b, 91). Such a conservative effect does not materialize for mothers in the literature, but it does for fathers regarding gay marriage, a finding, according to Elder and Greene (2012a, 437), suggesting that fathers "seek to protect their children from what they perceive to be negative cultural influences." To put matters simply, some authors expect a defensive, negative stance among parents compared with stances among the childless, particularly on abortion and gay marriage and other so-called family values issues.

At the same time, many of the issues in this dimension speak to equality rights and respect for diversity. Parents sometimes prioritize and hold more liberal opinions on these issues compared with the childless because of aspirations for their children, particularly if they have girls (e.g., Prokos, Baird, and Keene 2010; Warner and Steel 1999).[1] This interest-based account sees the elimination of potential structural barriers to their children's success and happiness as a strong motivator of parents' more liberal attitudes.

Studies to date paint a mixed picture. Sometimes we see parent gaps (or gendered parent gaps), and sometimes we do not. What is not really clear is why these gaps exist (when they do).

Explaining Parenthood Effects on Attitudes

As we suggest above, two broad gaps have been uncovered by past research: the general effects (parents differ from the childless) and the gender-conditional effects (mothers differ from childless women and/or fathers). With both (regardless of the specific issues on which parents differ from non-parents), scholars have focused their explanatory efforts on three sets of factors: socialization, material self-interest, and cuing of parent-based concerns through politicization of the family. We focus on the first two causal factors, but our ability to assess interest-based explanations is far stronger than arguments about socialization, not only because we do not use longitudinal data but also because our indicators for socialization effects are not robust. We set aside cuing and politicization for this chapter because we do not have appropriate data to assess their impacts. Langner Greenlee, and Deason. (this volume) discuss the impacts of cuing and politicization of parenthood on political participation and activism, finding that politicizing motherhood has had an important impact on the propensity of parents (in particular mothers) to be active in the community. We suspect that this effect can also be found on attitudes but lack the data to test this relationship. This is certainly worth pursuing in future research, particularly given the non-decisive findings of past scholarship (as well as our own study here) in explaining the parent gap (or the gendered parent gap).

Socialization as an Explanation of Parent Gaps

Focusing first on the general effect, we can view parenthood as an adult socialization experience, much like marriage, entering the workforce, and retirement, because it alters not only our daily routines but also our outlooks and identities (e.g., Greenlee 2010). Elder and Greene (2006, 451–52), for example, point out that the "emotional and psychological changes parenthood brings," as well as the "day-to-day changes dealing with day-care issues, tighter finances, worries about the quality of schools, and less free time, ... should cause parents to view a variety of political issues in new and different ways." Parenthood is transformative, exerting both salience and directional effects on public opinion. Although an attractive explanation intuitively, socialization effects are difficult to test empirically without longitudinal analyses. Most existing work, including all of Elder and Greene's work, uses cross-sectional data (as do we in this chapter). We think that longitudinal data are essential to uncover this link, but the single longitudinal study on the matter does not provide compelling evidence of a socialization effect (Greenlee 2010).

When it comes to gender-conditional effects of parenthood on opinion, socialization arguments are important. The act of parenting and the expectations for parenthood as a social role are gendered (e.g., Bianchi, Robinson, and Milkie 2006). Although things are improving in terms of the division of childrearing and household labour, gender gaps persist and have been slow to narrow (e.g., Bianchi 2000; Nomaguchi and Milkie 2003). The male breadwinner and female nurturer models continue to influence how society and parents themselves view their roles (Burns, Schlozman, and Verba 2001; Townsend 2002). Indeed, Canadian General Social Survey time-use data show that having children tends to result in more time on paid work for men, but not for women, and leads to growth in the male/female gap in household work (Statistics Canada 2006).

In addition to the work associated with having and rearing children, the psychological processes involved are said to be different for men and women (Meleis et al. 2000). To the extent that women are socialized from childhood to adopt more maternal, other-oriented worldviews – a process that feminist theorists have viewed as producing more liberal, care-oriented attitudes among women (e.g., Elshtain 1983; Gilligan 1982; Ruddick 1989) – the actual experience of being a mother can further liberalize women (Greenlee 2010), creating gaps in attitude both among women and between mothers and fathers. Thus, this socialization effect is both about long-term trends in how family life "looks," combining societal expectations of parents and families more generally, alongside gendered expectations of the role of women as mothers and men as fathers.

Interest-Based Explanations of Parent Gaps

Interest-based explanations for parent gaps are well-trod territory in attitudinal research. That individuals prioritize issues directly relevant to their lives and favour issue positions that will elicit some personal or group benefit permeate the literature. Whether perceived interests stem from a biological influence on perceptions or the caregiving role more generally is not clear. We suspect that it is the latter, that interests are situation based, and that parents/caregivers, whether biologically related or not to their children, have different needs and interests than non-parents. But more research is needed to determine the root cause. Regardless of the source, interests can affect both the *salience* of particular issues among parents and their *position* on those issues.

For parents, issue priorities can emphasize childcare, education, and similar policy fields, so such issues will be more salient for parents than for non-parents. Moreover, their substantive positions on issues can be different from those of the childless because of anticipated benefits for them and/ or their children. They might prefer greater spending on education and childcare, and more generous social welfare policies generally, because they are heavier users of social programs than they were before or because their finances are more burdened as they add dependants. Conversely, financial strain as a result of adding dependants can result in a preference for *less generous* social welfare policies and lower taxes among parents compared with non-parents, an explanation often provided for the few conservative effects on fathers. Indeed, traditional stereotypes about fatherhood slot men into the role of provider or breadwinner, perhaps rendering personal finances key for men on this dimension. The sex of respondents' children can further differentiate their opinions on equality issues, as well as social spending issues, as discussed above, as part of efforts to reduce barriers to their female children's future success.

In the issue domain of law and security, protection of their children will no doubt be of great concern to parents, making this domain more salient for them than for non-parents, and parents might prefer tougher stances on issues such as sentencing and policing expenditures because of a greater orientation to safety. The critical point in all of this is that parents' views on a range of issues might naturally differ from those of the childless because of differences in self-interest generated by the fact of having children. And the interests attached to parenthood are demonstrably both clear and salient, a prerequisite for effects on policy attitudes (Chong, Citrin, and Conley 2001).

Self-interest explanations can also help to account for any gender-conditional effects of parenthood on opinion. Mothers can face greater financial hardships than fathers given that the vast majority of lone-parent families are headed by women. In Canada, 80 percent of single parents are women, and this accounts for 12.8 percent of all census families, compared with the 3.5 percent of families headed by single fathers (Statistics Canada 2012). Moreover, even for women with partners, as they add to their domestic workloads, which often become more gender inequitable when children are added, "mothers ... come to view a generous social welfare state as an asset in their attempts to juggle work and family" (Elder and Greene 2012a, 236).

Socialization- and self-interest-based explanations have been advanced in the literature to date, albeit not very much and inconclusively, and we expand on past research now by assessing those explanations in as much detail as possible given the data.

Data and Method

We used data derived from web-based surveys of representative samples of approximately 1,000 voters in each of six Canadian provincial elections between 2011 and 2013.[2] We pooled the six data sets, yielding a sample of over 6,000 voters. Harris/Decima (Ottawa) programmed and fielded the surveys.

According to the literature, we might expect to find parent gaps in opinions for all three dimensions, producing either a liberal or a conservative parent effect for social welfare, a conservative effect for crime and security, and either a liberal or a conservative effect for social issues. Moreover, the literature provides some support for the proposition that parent gaps are conditional on gender, though effects have been uneven across both elections and studies. This proposition seems to be most supported regarding the social welfare dimension, producing a liberal effect on mothers but a conservative effect on fathers, a divergent effect produced by different parenthood socialization experiences and interest-based considerations among fathers and mothers. These are the primary patterns that we assess with our data, followed by a search for causal patterns underlying any effects that we identify.

We assess attitudes toward three issue domains: social welfare, crime and security, and culture. All of these dependent variables are multi-item indices constructed to capture multiple facets of each dimension.[3] The social welfare index consists of 10 items, primarily about social spending in areas such as education, welfare, and health; the crime and security index includes four items about spending on crime and defence; and the culture index incorporates 24 items, including attitudes toward moral issues, such as abortion and same-sex marriage, as well as attitudes toward equality and diversity (primarily gender and race). In the analyses below, we assess and discuss the indices as a whole and examine the individual issues incorporated into them to get a more detailed picture of where gaps exist.

How and Why Parenthood Shapes Political Attitudes

The Impact of Parental Status on Opinion

To start, we examine the impacts of parenthood on the three issue dimensions. We ran OLS regression models, in two stages, regressing each of the dependent variables on respondents' parental status, gender, and then the interaction between parental status and gender (to test for gendered parent gaps), as well as a set of covariates known to correlate with attitudes toward the three issue dimensions (especially sociodemographic factors and partisanship) but not of particular substantive interest in this chapter (see unnumbered note). The indices representing the issue dimensions are coded 0–1, with 1 representing the most left-leaning position (i.e., strong support for social welfare spending, strong support for reduced crime and defence spending, and permissive, egalitarian responses to cultural issues). Female is coded 1 for women and 0 for men, and parent is coded 1 for people with children (whether adult or young children) and 0 for people without children.

Looking at the first models for each dimension reported in Table 10.1, we see that parenthood correlates with attitudes for two of the three dimensions, including both crime and security and cultural issues. Parenthood does not correlate with views on social welfare, a finding reported in some American studies and puzzling in light of parents' particular interest in gov-

TABLE 10.1
Impacts of parenthood on three issue dimensions

	Social welfare 1	Social welfare 2	Crime and security 1	Crime and security 2	Cultural issues 1	Cultural issues 2
Female	0.043***	0.036**	−0.041***	−0.041**	0.042***	0.041**
	(0.005)	(0.008)	(0.007)	(0.011)	(0.005)	(0.007)
Parent	0.009	0.004	−0.028***	−0.028*	−0.030***	−0.031**
	(0.006)	(0.007)	(0.006)	(0.011)	(0.008)	(0.007)
Female*parent		−0.004		−0.009		−0.002
		(0.006)		(0.008)		(0.006)
Observations	4,711	4,711	4,690	4,690	4,392	4,392
R^2	0.23	0.23	0.19	0.19	0.24	0.24

Note: Standard errors are in parentheses.
** $p < .05$; *** $p < .01$.

ernment spending on education and the like. Perhaps these issues are of such high salience generally in a country such as Canada, where health care is routinely a critical election issue, for example, that social welfare attitudes are not differentiated by parenthood, or perhaps parent gaps are not motivated principally by self-interest in social spending.

Turning to the other dimensions, we see that parents veer to the right of their childless counterparts in their attitudes toward crime and security (coefficient of −0.028) and cultural issues (−0.030), findings reported previously by some American studies (e.g., Greenlee 2010) but not others (e.g., Elder and Greene 2007, 2012a). Bear in mind that age, income, partisanship, and other covariates are included in these models, so these are truly the effects of having children versus not having children.

Gender is also a significant predictor of attitudes on all three dimensions. Women lean to the left of men on social welfare (coefficient of 0.043) and cultural issues (0.042). Indices are coded 0–1, so the gap between men and women is about 4 percent in both cases. This finding is consistent with the literature on gender gaps in political attitudes. Only on crime and security are women to the right of men (−0.041), preferring "tougher" or more conservative stances.

Parents veer to the right of the childless and women to the left of men. The next question, then, is whether the effects of parenthood are conditioned by gender. Do mothers and fathers have different attitudes? These data provide mixed evidence. Looking at the second set of models for each issue domain, not only is the female*parent interaction not significant for any of the dimensions, but also the coefficients for each of the constituent variables remain similar – identical for the crime and security and cultural issues dimensions – in the face of their interactions. Looking at political issue dimensions broadly, we find no gender-conditional effects of parenthood.

That said, there are gender-conditional effects on some of the particular items included in the indices. We broke down the analyses to assess each of the specific items in the indices to see whether there were parent or gendered parent gaps on individual questions, which might be cancelling one another out when assessing the index as a whole.

Table 10.2 presents the results of those analyses, showing only those items for which there were effects (most issues were not affected). For the 10-item social welfare dimension, there is a gender*parent interaction on two items, welfare spending at the provincial level and welfare spending at the federal level, but we do not see effects on any of the other items, including

TABLE 10.2
Gendered parent gaps on three issue dimensions

	Provincial welfare spending	Federal welfare spending	Federal crime spending	Lay off married women first	Same-sex marriage
Female	−0.014	0.002	−0.079***	0.085***	0.072***
	(−0.015)	(−0.015)	(−0.014)	(−0.01)	(−0.015)
Parent	−0.042***	−0.032**	−0.046***	0.021**	−0.073***
	(−0.015)	(−0.015)	(−0.014)	(−0.01)	(−0.016)
Female*parent	0.060***	0.041**	0.037**	−0.034***	0.053***
	(−0.012)	(−0.019)	(−0.018)	(−0.013)	(−0.019)
Observations	5,302	5,280	5,337	5,405	5,030
R^2	0.12	0.12	0.15	0.08	0.28

Note: Standard errors are in parentheses.
** $p < .05$; *** $p < .01$.

health and education spending, both integrally related to childrearing. Focusing on provincial welfare spending for illustrative purposes (the effect is similar for federal spending), we note that parenthood has a small liberal effect on mothers – specifically a marginal effect of 0.018 (−0.042 + 0.060), indicating that mothers' support for welfare spending is about .02 point or 2 percent higher on the 0–1 scale than childless women's support. Parenthood has a conservative effect on men, with a marginal effect of −0.042[4] on attitudes toward welfare spending once men become fathers, a gap twice the size as that for women and in the other direction. These results are consistent with some of the existing American work on the topic, as discussed earlier in the chapter, which has identified a liberal motherhood effect and a conservative fatherhood effect.

These results highlight, moreover, that parenthood seems to differentiate men more than it does women, but they also serve to remind us that men and women, parents and non-parents, are all fairly close in their levels of support for welfare spending, middle of the road, favouring current levels of spending (mean level between 0.4 and 0.5 on the 0–1 scale; see Figure 10.1a).

On the crime and security dimension, one item of the four has a gender*parent interaction: federal crime spending (but not provincial crime spending or defence spending). We view this as a natural response to the fact that threats close to home – in one's neighbourhood, city, or region – seem to be the most relevant to parents rather than general security

FIGURE 10.1
Selected gendered parent gaps

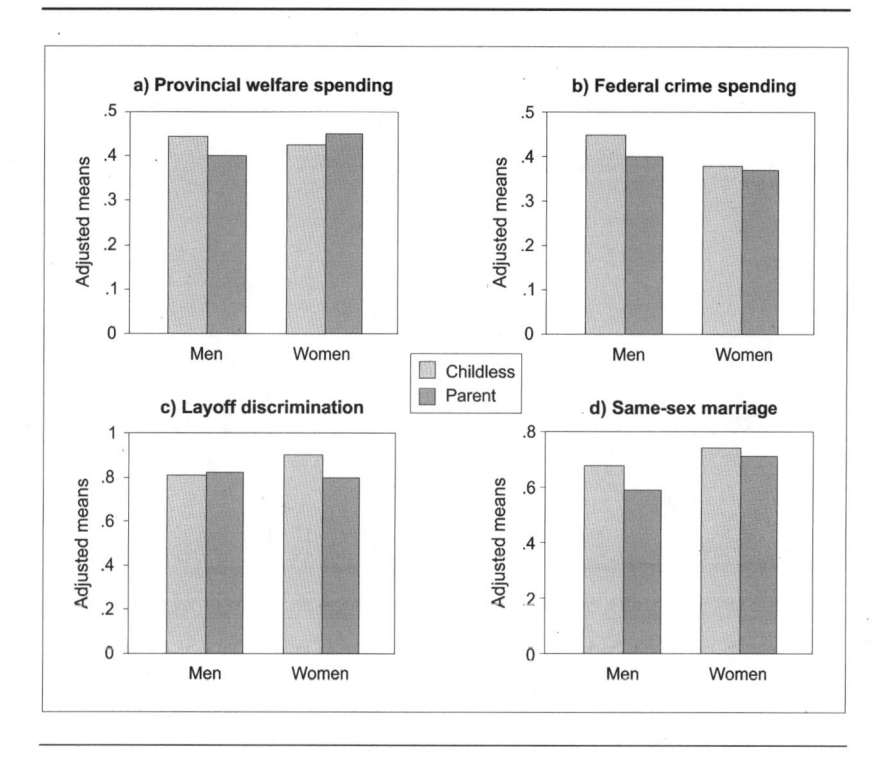

[Figure: Four bar charts showing adjusted means for Childless vs Parent, by Men and Women: a) Provincial welfare spending, b) Federal crime spending, c) Layoff discrimination, d) Same-sex marriage]

considerations on the world stage. Thus, defence spending might not have much potential to differentiate opinion according to parenthood. Respondents were asked whether the federal government should spend more, less, or the same amount on crime and justice, and the variable is coded here on a 0–1 scale, with 1 representing "less" and 0 "more" (thus, negative regression coefficients would denote conservative effects, in favour of more crime spending and a "tough on crime" view). Overwhelmingly, respondents to the survey preferred the status quo or more federal spending on crime, with only 15 percent supporting lower spending. Generally, women prefer more spending than men, by a sizable margin, as do parents than non-parents (not shown). Interacting gender and parenthood produces an effect on this question as well, but this time it is a difference of magnitude, not direction. Parenthood has a conservative influence on attitudes among men in particular (marginal effect of −0.046) but much less so among women (marginal effect of −0.009); in other words, this issue differentiates parents and non-parents more among men than among women, producing a trivial .01 point or 1 percent increase in support for spending on crime and justice among mothers compared with childless women but nearly a 5 percent increase in support among fathers compared with childless men (Figure 10.1b).

Finally, on the social issues dimension, of the 24 items in the index, two have a gender*parent interaction: a question about sex-based discrimination in the workplace and support for same-sex marriage. The question for the former asks for responses to this statement: "If a company has to lay off some of its employees, the first workers to be laid off should be women whose husbands have jobs." The response options comprise a four-point scale from strongly disagree (coded 1) to strongly agree (coded 0), where scores closer to 1 represent more left-leaning or egalitarian positions. Notably, 90 percent of respondents disagree or strongly disagree with the statement (Figure 10.1c). As Table 10.2 illustrates, parenthood is correlated with more conservative responses, on average, among women than among men, resulting in a marginal effect of −0.01 of parenthood on women (again a tiny effect) and a slightly larger and liberal marginal effect of 0.02 among men. Although the effect is weak on both sides, this is the only issue on which parenthood pushes women in a more conservative direction than men. Whereas women overall are more resistant than men to the notion that women with husbands should be the first to go, the interesting question is why women with children should be slightly to the right of women without children, a question that we investigate in the next section.

For attitudes toward same-sex marriage, the results follow the same pattern as attitudes toward federal crime spending. Parenthood has a conservative influence for both men and women, but the magnitude of the effect is larger for men, as Table 10.2 shows, producing a marginal effect of −0.07 for men and −0.02 for women. Indeed, while parenthood has a conservative influence on attitudes generally, mothers are more supportive than childless men of marriage equality rights (see Figure 10.1d).

Explanations of Parent Gaps in Attitudes

We turn now to consider why parent gaps in opinion occur, where our data permit such investigations, focusing on two causal forces: self-interest and socialization. In terms of the general parent gaps on crime and security and cultural issues, interest-based explanations have been used to account for − though not actually to test, as far as we can tell − attitudes on these dimensions. We do not have a great indicator to operationalize self-interest for the crime and security dimension, such as feelings of vulnerability to crime. We do use the sex of parents' children, however, to operationalize one aspect of parental self-interest relevant to this dimension. The idea here is that parents of girls might have a special interest in conservative or tough approaches to crime because of girls' and women's greater vulnerability to certain forms of gender-based violent crime, such as sexual assault, criminal harassment, and certain forms of bullying. We use the same variable, whether or not parents have girls, to operationalize self-interest considerations for the cultural issues dimension. This is motivated by the suggestion in the literature that parents of girls might be more liberal on cultural issues to create or preserve the most autonomy for their children, at risk of being marginalized given gender-based societal stereotypes and prejudices. We do not expect to find much evidence consistent with this sentiment, however, given our finding that parents tend to be more conservative than non-parents on this dimension.

For socialization effects on the general parent gap, our options for indicators are also inadequate, and our lack of longitudinal data is the most important limitation. That said, for both dimensions we interact right-wing ideology with parenthood to see whether this general outlook on politics – which can be affected by the life changes, especially alterations to one's "outlook," introduced by parenthood – accounts for the differences among parents and non-parents. Although ideology is not a perfect proxy for socialization, we know that this basic orientation toward politics is based upon family upbringing and then affected by life experiences, such as education, work, childrearing, and so on. In the absence of more directly related survey questions about socialization in particular (as well as the absence of longitudinal data on this question), we think that this is our best option.

As Table 10.3 demonstrates, the sex of parents' children has no effect on attitudes toward either issue dimension. The variable here codes whether parents have any girls, but substituting a dummy for having *only* girls produces virtually identical results. The sex of one's children does not seem to structure attitudes toward broad issue dimensions, suggesting that personal self-interest in the form of protecting girls in particular from crime and cultural stereotypes and prejudices does not help to explain why parents hold more conservative attitudes than non-parents on both dimensions.

Interestingly, though the sex of parents' children does not have a generalized effect on this dimension, it does have an impact on attitudes toward one of the constituent elements of the dimension most closely related to

TABLE 10.3
Testing interest- and socialization-based accounts of parent gaps

	Crime and security	Cultural issues
Parent	−0.040***	−0.037***
	(0.007)	(0.009)
Girls	−0.012	0.008
	(0.001)	(0.006)
Right ideology	−0.133***	−0.110***
	(0.014)	(0.009)
Parent*right ideology	0.046***	0.005
	(0.017)	(0.011)
Observations	4,642	4,373
R^2	0.21	0.28

Note: Standard errors are in parentheses.
** $p < .05$; *** $p < .01$.

women's rights: abortion rights. Parents who have only girls are more liberal on the issue than those who have only boys or a mix of the two, and the magnitude of this girl-only effect is nearly identical to that of female gender in the model (coefficient of 0.028 versus 0.030, not shown). Compared with men, women are more supportive of women's autonomy, as are parents who have only girls. This is a finding that we interpret as evidence of an interest-based explanation, at least in the context of this single issue, though again having only girls does not explain parents' greater conservatism on the dimension as a whole, as noted above. In other words, on issues related directly to women's issues and their autonomy, perhaps parenting girls will sensitize one to those issues, but not to a broader field of cultural issues, many of which do not involve women's rights directly.

In terms of hints at socialization effects, right-wing ideology seems to affect parents differently than non-parents regarding crime and security issues but not cultural issues. The right-wing ideology variable is a self-identification measure in these data. Initially coded on a 10-point scale, the variable included in Table 10.3's models is coded into three categories representing left-wing, centrist, and right-wing identifications. Naturally, right-wing respondents are generally less liberal on crime and security than their centrist and left-wing counterparts, but the interesting part is that parenthood conditions the effect of ideology on this dimension only for

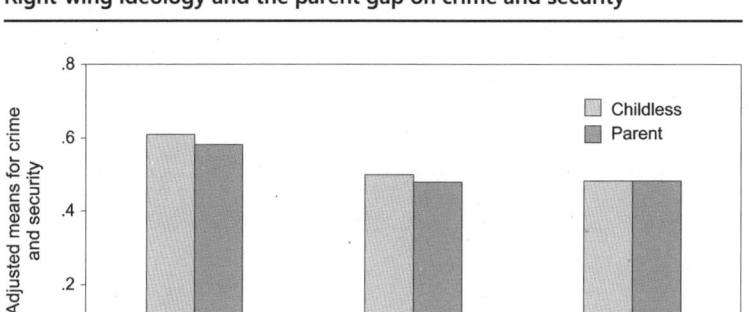

FIGURE 10.2
Right-wing ideology and the parent gap on crime and security

those on the left and in the centre of the spectrum. As Figure 10.2 indicates, right-wing parents and childless individuals have identical attitudes, on average, toward the crime and security dimension; parents on the left, and to a lesser extent those at the centre of the spectrum, are more conservative on crime and security issues than non-parents who identify with the same category (and keeping in mind that this model controls for age, partisanship, and other correlates of crime and security views). So we can say that, even within two of the categories of ideological identification, parents are more conservative or "tough on crime" than non-parents, a finding that we cautiously interpret as providing evidence of a possible socialization effect among parents.

Keeping in mind, of course, that gender does not condition the effect of parenthood for any of the three dimensions broadly, there are a number of key issues on which there is a gendered parent gap in attitudes, as discussed previously. Compared with fathers, mothers are less conservative on federal crime spending and same-sex marriage, more liberal on welfare spending, and more conservative on layoff decisions. Overall, parenthood has a liberal or smaller conservative effect on mothers compared with fathers, a finding reported in much of the American literature.

We operationalize the self-interest explanation in several ways for these issues, depending on the nature of the issue at hand. For crime spending and same-sex marriage, we use the sex of parents' children as indicators again, as we did above for the general parent gaps. For the other two issues, welfare spending and layoff discrimination, we use measures of material self-interest related to socio-economic status and personal economic vulnerability – a dummy variable for low-income respondents and its interaction with parental status and a dummy variable for single parents. These variables test whether economic need motivates mothers' greater liberalism on welfare spending, but greater conservatism on layoff decisions, both consistent with the idea that mothers are keen to protect their abilities to support their children. Indeed, with the layoff issue, perhaps mothers are aware of the economic hardships that some women face, particularly single mothers, who have no partners to help provide for the household, thereby motivating support for the idea that single women should retain their jobs over women who have working husbands when layoffs are necessary.

To search again for hints of socialization effects, we use ideology and its interaction with parenthood, as in the previous section, and we use identification with gendered traits typically associated with parenthood to see if they undergird gendered parent gaps in attitude. The existing literature makes much of the fact that parenthood is a gendered experience that tends to reinforce rather than blur conventional gender roles. So the gendered traits that we use to assess whether this is happening measure the extent to which women identify as sympathetic, an other-focused outlook that puts empathy at the core of one's view, and the extent to which men identify as dependable, also an other-focused outlook or trait but one with a direct tie to the traditional archetype of the masculine provider. We also interact these gendered traits with parental status to see if their effect differs, of course, for parents and non-parents. Indeed, such traits can motivate differences in attitudes generally, but the critical question is this: when mothers and fathers identify strongly with the traits associated with their social roles as gendered parents, does this condition attitudes toward the four issues?

Table 10.4 contains the results of all the models. Regressions for each issue were run separately for male and female respondents, in part to avoid clunky three-way interaction terms in which gender and parental status would be interacted with third variables for ideology, gendered traits, and the like. Starting with welfare spending, none of the interactions is significant, and neither is the effect of single parenthood. Thus, the two self-interest and two socialization indicators fail to produce answers about why the parent gap in attitudes is conditioned by gender. Low-income respondents are more supportive of increasing or maintaining current levels of welfare spending, and gendered traits have an impact on attitudes, sympathy increasing support for welfare spending among women and dependability

TABLE 10.4
Testing interest- and socialization-based accounts of gendered parent gaps

	Welfare spending		Crime spending		Layoff discrimination		Same-sex marriage	
	Women	Men	Women	Men	Women	Men	Women	Men
Parent	0.031 (0.054)	0.021 (0.058)	0.016 (0.049)	−0.04 (0.051)	0.043 (0.034)	0.037 (0.038)	−0.058 (0.052)	0.009 (0.060)
Low income	0.161*** (0.029)	0.155*** (0.029)			−0.065*** (0.018)	−0.070*** (0.020)		
Single parent	−0.026 (0.022)	−0.022 (0.022)			0.023 (0.013)	−0.037** (0.019)		
Girls			0.001 (0.017)	−0.016 (0.018)			0.041** (0.018)	0.009 (0.021)
Gendered traits	0.144*** (0.050)	−0.122** (0.053)	−0.089** (0.044)	−0.007 (0.042)	0.088*** (0.031)	0.131*** (0.033)	0.059 (0.046)	0.146*** (0.050)
Right ideology	−0.070** (0.028)	−0.065** (0.028)	−0.019 (0.025)	−0.083*** (0.021)	−0.043** (0.018)	−0.01 (0.016)	−0.055** (0.026)	−0.072*** (0.024)
Parent*gendered traits	−0.028 (0.066)	−0.012 (0.069)	−0.023 (0.057)	−0.005 (0.058)	−0.062 (0.041)	−0.001 (0.045)	0.004 (0.060)	−0.087 (0.069)
Parent*right ideology	0.002 (0.034)	−0.004 (0.034)	0.027 (0.030)	0.032 (0.025)	0.011 (0.021)	−0.011 (0.020)	0.004 (0.032)	−0.033 (0.030)
Parent*low income	0.006 (0.039)	0.013 (0.039)			−0.014 (0.024)	−0.027 (0.034)		
Observations	2,521	2,520	2,631	2,786	2,589	2,738	2,498	2,604
R^2	0.13	0.13	0.13	0.15	0.07	0.08	0.29	0.26

Note: Standard errors are in parentheses.
** $p < .05$; *** $p < .01$.

diminishing it among men, and for both men and women right-wing ideology is associated with support for lower levels of welfare spending. However, none of these attitudes distinguishes parents from non-parents and thus cannot explain the gendered parent gap identified in Table 10.2.

For attitudes toward crime spending, the models are slightly different, of course, given the different way in which we operationalize self-interest for this issue. Here, too, none of the interactions is significant, and there is no girl-only effect either. Again, the variables identified here to test for causes of the gendered parent interaction on crime spending have no effect.

For the last two items, there are some effects that can help to explain the gendered parent gap. For attitudes toward layoff discrimination, whereby mothers were slightly more conservative than non-mothers and fathers slightly less so, we see that single parenthood has effects on attitudes for men but not women. Interestingly, single fathers are more conservative on the issue, suggesting that they are more open to the idea that women with working husbands should be laid off before single women. This is an interesting outcome and perhaps suggests that single fathers identify with or feel sympathetic toward single women and perhaps single mothers, but it does not help to explain mothers' greater conservatism compared with non-mothers.

Finally, with same-sex marriage, again the interactions are of no assistance in explaining the fairly sizable gender difference in the effect of parenthood on attitudes toward it (Table 10.2). Mothers of girls are more supportive of same-sex marriage, one of the few relevant parent-based effects and, we would argue, an interest-based one in the table. Our interpretation here is that mothers, as women, face vulnerabilities because of cultural stereotypes and prejudices, and they become even more sensitized to such dangers when they have girls, leading to greater support for the equality and autonomy of women and other marginalized people, in this case sexual minorities. This effect is consistent with the one found generally between parents and non-parents on the question of abortion rights, in which having only girls produced a liberal effect on parents of both genders. We interpret both findings as evidence that the gendered effects of parenting stem not only from the genders of the parents but also from those of the children being reared.

Conclusion
Overall, the patterns make sense and are broadly consistent with patterns identified in earlier research. Parents are more conservative on crime and security and cultural issues than non-parents, controlling for a range of

covariates, and mothers are more liberal, or at least less conservative, than fathers on three of four issue areas: attitudes toward welfare spending at both the federal level and the provincial level, crime spending, and same-sex marriage. Mothers, however, are slightly more conservative than fathers on gender-based layoff decisions. In sum, regarding the claim that gender conditions parents' attitudes toward issue dimensions broadly, we find limited evidence that fathers and mothers are all that different. Parenthood affects men and women similarly when it comes to public opinion on the three dimensions tested here, and we identify only a handful of gender-based interaction effects in which fathers and mothers hold different attitudes on issues. Even here, however, some of the differences are small, and mothers' and fathers' views veer in the same direction half the time, separated only by the magnitude of the effect. Although we do not want to minimize the interesting gendered parent gaps that we have identified, we advise taking a cautious approach, for gendered parent gaps are infrequent in our analyses. This is one area where we again lament the lack of longitudinal data, because it is possible that current "norms" in parenting (in which fathers are more active in sharing parental responsibilities than they were in generations past) might have an equalizing effect on attitude change among parents. It is possible that 40 years ago gendered parent gaps were larger, and the reasons for those gaps might have been different.

Our efforts to test some of the causal claims about parent gaps in the literature were limited by the availability of appropriate indicators as well as by our lack of longitudinal data, so we avoid making grand or sweeping conclusions about why parent gaps occur. That said, we encourage other scholars to start assessing causal factors moving forward, and our findings in this part of the chapter are sensible in light of conventional wisdom on public opinion. For example, the idea that having girls or only girls affects parents' views on abortion rights or mothers' support for equality rights for sexual minorities makes sense given that parenting is affected by the gender of one's children – thinking about the particular life experiences and circumstances that they will encounter as adults.

One of the major causal factors identified in the existing American work, but not assessed in this chapter, is the potential for cuing to mobilize parent and gendered parent gaps in the electorate. This can be a powerful force indeed, especially with growing attention to microtargeting strategies by parties. Cuing, however, would presumably have to work in conjunction with one or both of the other two forces (interest and socialization) to produce parent gaps. At least in the short term, cuing should have the potential not to *create* attitudinal differences between parents but to *mobilize* or *activate* them in a context in which parent-based concerns are triggered as salient. Public opinion scholars are well advised to keep searching for interest- and socialization-based accounts of parent gaps as well as considering the conditions under which they might become relevant to public opinion and political decision making.

Notes

In the figures and tables in this chapter, all models also include controls for marital status, age, university degree, full-time employment, income, religiosity, partisanship, and provincial election dummies. Full results are not reported here but are available from the authors.

1 We could easily imagine similar effects for parents of visible minority children, though we do not test this proposition here.
2 Manitoba's election was October 4, 2011; Ontario's election was October 6, 2011; Newfoundland and Labrador's election was October 11, 2011; Alberta's election was April 23, 2012; Quebec's election was September 4, 2012; and British Columbia's election was May 14, 2013. Data were collected during the three weeks prior to each election.
3 Information about variables and coding is available from the authors on request, including details regarding the creation of indices for the three issue areas: attitudes toward government intervention (10-item index, alpha = 0.7477), crime and security (4-item index, alpha = 0.7733), and social issues (24-item index, alpha = 0.8894).
4 This is the coefficient for the variable *parents,* which in the presence of the interaction variable *female*parent* indicates the effect of parenthood when *female* = 0, the effect among men.

References

Bianchi, S. 2000. "Maternal Employment and Time with Children: Dramatic Change or Surprising Continuity?" *Demography* 37 (4): 401–14. http://dx.doi.org/10.1353/dem.2000.0001.

Bianchi, S.M., J.P. Robinson, and M.A. Milkie. 2006. *Changing Rhythms of American Family Life.* New York: Russell Sage.

Burns, Nancy, Kay Lehman Schlozman, and Sidney Verba. 1997. "The Public Consequences of Private Inequality: Family Life and Citizen Participation." *American Political Science Review* 91 (2): 373–89.

–. 2001. *The Private Roots of Public Action: Gender, Equality, and Political Participation.* Cambridge, MA: Harvard University Press.

Burrell, Barbara C. 2005. "Gender, Presidential Elections, and Public Policy: Making Women's Votes Matter." *Journal of Women, Politics, and Policy* 27 (1–2): 31–50. http://dx.doi.org/10.1300/J501v27n01_03.

Carroll, Susan J. 2006. "Moms Who Swing, or Why the Promise of the Gender Gap Remains Unfulfilled." *Politics and Gender* 2 (3): 362–74. http://dx.doi.org/10.1017/S1743923X06231088.

Chaney, Carole Kennedy, R. Michael Alvarez, and Jonathan Nagler. 1998. "Explaining the Gender Gap in U.S. Presidential Elections, 1980–1992." *Political Research Quarterly* 51 (2): 311–39.

Chong, Dennis, Jack Citrin, and Patricia Conley. 2001. "When Self-Interest Matters." *Political Psychology* 22 (3): 541–70. http://dx.doi.org/10.1111/0162-895X.00253.

Clark, Cal, and Janel Clark. 1993. "The Gender Gap 1988: Compassion, Pacifism, and Indirect Feminism." In *Women and Politics: Outsiders or Insiders?*, edited by Lois Lovelace Duke, 32–45. Englewood Cliffs, NJ: Prentice-Hall.

Conover, Pamela Johnston, and Virginia Sapiro. 1993. "Gender, Feminist Consciousness, and War." *American Journal of Political Science* 37 (4): 1079–99. http://dx.doi.org/10.2307/2111544.

Eagly, Alice H., Amanda Diekman, Mary Johannesen-Schmidt, and Anne Koenig. 2004. "Gender Gaps in Sociopolitical Attitudes: A Social Psychological Analysis." *Journal of Personality and Social Psychology* 87 (6): 796–816. http://dx.doi.org/10.1037/0022-3514.87.6.796.

Eichenberg, Richard C. 2003. "Gender Differences in Public Attitudes toward the Use of Force by the United States, 1990–2003." *International Security* 28 (1): 110–41. http://dx.doi.org/10.1162/016228803322427992.

–. 2005. "Victory Has Many Friends: U.S. Public Opinion and the Use of Military Force, 1981–2005." *International Security* 30 (1): 140–77. http://dx.doi.org/10.1162/0162288054894616.

Elder, Laurel, and Steven Greene. 2006. "The Children Gap on Social Welfare and the Politicization of American Parents, 1984–2000." *Politics and Gender* 2 (4): 451–72. http://dx.doi.org/10.1017/S1743923X06060144.

–. 2007. "The Myth of 'Security Moms' and 'NASCAR Dads': Parenthood, Political Stereotypes, and the 2004 Election." *Social Science Quarterly* 88 (1): 1–19. http://dx.doi.org/10.1111/j.1540-6237.2007.00443.x.

–. 2012a. "The Politics of Parenthood: Parenthood Effects on Issue Attitudes and Candidate Evaluations in 2008." *American Politics Research* 40 (3): 419–49. http://dx.doi.org/10.1177/1532673X11400015.

–. 2012b. *The Politics of Parenthood: Causes and Consequences of the Politicization and Polarization of the American Family*. Albany: SUNY Press.

Elshtain, J.B. 1983. "On Beautiful Souls, Just Warriors, and Feminist Consciousness." In *Women and Men's Wars*, edited by J. Stiehm, 342–49. Oxford: Pergamon.

Gidengil, Elisabeth. 1995. "Economic Man – Social Woman? The Case of the Gender Gap in Support for the Canada-United States Free Trade Agreement." *Comparative Political Studies* 28 (3): 384–408. http://dx.doi.org/10.1177/0010414095028003003.

Gidengil, Elisabeth, André Blais, Richard Nadeau, and Neil Nevitte. 2003. "Women to the Left? Gender Differences in Political Beliefs and Policy Preferences." In *Gender and Electoral Representation in Canada*, edited by M. Tremblay and L. Trimble, 140–59. Toronto: Oxford University Press.

Gilligan, Carol. 1982. *In a Different Voice: Psychological Theory and Women's Development*. Cambridge, MA: Harvard University Press.

Goodyear-Grant, Elizabeth. 2013. "Women Voters, Candidates, and Legislators: A Gender Perspective on Recent Party and Electoral Politics." In *Parties, Elections, and the Future of Canadian Politics*, edited by A. Bittner and R. Koop, 119–39. Vancouver: UBC Press.

Greenlee, Jill S. 2010. "Soccer Moms, Hockey Moms, and the Question of 'Transformative' Motherhood." *Politics and Gender* 6 (3): 405–31. http://dx.doi.org/10.1017/S1743923X10000292.

Howell, Susan E., and Christine L. Day. 2000. "Complexities of the Gender Gap." *Journal of Politics* 62 (3): 858–74. http://dx.doi.org/10.1111/0022-3816.00036.

Jennings, M. Kent. 2006. "The Gender Gap in Attitudes and Beliefs about the Place of Women in American Political Life: A Longitudinal, Cross-Generational Analysis." *Politics and Gender* 2 (2): 193–219. http://dx.doi.org/10.1017/S1743923X06060089.

Kaufmann, Karen, and John Petrocik. 1999. "The Changing Politics of American Men: Understanding the Sources of the Gender Gap." *American Journal of Political Science* 43 (3): 864–87. http://dx.doi.org/10.2307/2991838.

MacManus, Susan A. 2006. "Targeting [Specific Slices of] Female Voters: A Key Strategy of Democrats and Republicans Alike in 2004 ... and Most Assuredly So in 2008." *Politics and Gender* 2 (3): 374–87. http://dx.doi.org/10.1017/S1743923X06241084.

Meleis, A.I., L.M. Sawyer, E.O. Im, D.K. Hilfinger Messias, and K. Schumacher. 2000. "Experiencing Transitions: An Emerging Middle-Range Theory." *Advances in Nursing Science* 23 (1): 12–28. http://dx.doi.org/10.1097/00012272-200009000-00006.

Mueller, Carol, ed. 1988. *The Politics of the Gender Gap*. London: Sage.

Nomaguchi, Kei M., and Melissa A. Milkie. 2003. "Costs and Rewards of Children: The Effects of Becoming a Parent on Adults' Lives." *Journal of Marriage and the Family* 65 (2): 356–74. http://dx.doi.org/10.1111/j.1741-3737.2003.00356.x.

Prokos, Anastasia H., Chardie L. Baird, and Jennifer Reid Keene. 2010. "Attitudes about Affirmative Action for Women: The Role of Children in Shaping Parents' Interests." *Sex Roles* 62 (5–6): 347–60. http://dx.doi.org/10.1007/s11199-009-9739-9.

Ruddick, Sara. 1989. *Maternal Thinking: Towards a Politics of Peace*. Boston: Beacon.

Shapiro, Robert, and Harpreet Mahajan. 1986. "Gender Differences in Policy Preferences: A Summary of Trends from the 1960s to the 1980s." *Public Opinion Quarterly* 50 (1): 42–61. http://dx.doi.org/10.1086/268958.

Statistics Canada. 2006. "Caring and Sharing." *Perspectives on Labour and Income* 7 (7): 1–17. http://www.statcan.gc.ca/pub/75-001-x/10706/9268-eng.htm#sharing.

—. 2012. "Portrait of Families and Living Arrangements in Canada." http://www12.statcan.gc.ca/census-recensement/2011/as-sa/98-312-x/98-312-x2011001-eng.pdf.

Townsend, Nicholas. 2002. *The Package Deal: Marriage, Work, and Fatherhood in Men's Lives*. Philadelphia: Temple University Press.

Warner, R.L., and B.S. Steel. 1999. "Child Rearing as a Mechanism for Social Change: The Relationship of Child Gender to Parents' Commitment to Gender Equity."

Gender and Society 13 (4): 503–17. http://dx.doi.org/10.1177/089124399013004005.

Wilcox, Clyde, Lara Hewitt, and Dee Allsop. 1996. "The Gender Gap in Attitudes toward the Gulf War: A Cross National Perspective." *Journal of Peace Research* 33 (1): 67–82. http://dx.doi.org/10.1177/0022343396033001005.

11
Context, Motherhood, and the Gender Gap in Political Knowledge

JANINE GILES

How does parental status affect the gender gap in political knowledge? Multiple studies find a gender gap in such knowledge (Delli Carpini and Keeter 1996; Frazer and MacDonald 2003; Gidengil and Stolle 2012), and previous attempts to understand it have focused on individual-level factors, measured through a survey at a single point in time. Although this approach helps us to understand part of the gender gap in political knowledge, it does not consider how the conditions experienced in the places where people live, work, and vote affect what they know about politics. Nor does it address how this gendered context might affect women's or mothers' levels of knowledge compared with men's or fathers' levels of knowledge. In other words, understanding the social context can help us to understand better why women consistently appear to know less about politics than men.

This chapter starts with two premises. First, the socio-economic context influences how people acquire and store political information. Second, this context is gendered as gender roles, such as those associated with motherhood (see the chapters by Arneil and Schreiber in this volume), encourage women to be less knowledgeable about political facts than with men. These premises lead to the hypothesis that the gender gap in political knowledge will narrow or even reverse in gender progressive contexts that can reduce the cost of acquiring political information for women compared with men. That is, areas with higher employment rates and higher education levels will have more political resources, which are expected to lower information costs for women compared with men.

This approach to studying the gap in political knowledge has a number of theoretical payoffs. By measuring and testing the effects of the local context, scholars can assess how variations in political resources and gender roles affect the size of this gender gap. Similarly, ameliorating group differences in political knowledge is a good normative goal: the more knowledgeable people are about politics, the more likely they are to engage in diverse political activities, such as writing letters to elected representatives, making donations to political parties, and discussing politics with others (Burns, Schlozman, and Verba 2001; Gidengil et al. 2004; Ondercin, Garand, and Crapanzano 2011).

Without measuring and testing the effects of the local context, scholars cannot rule out the effects of variations in political resources across the country on the gender gap. An in-depth analysis of gendered knowledge levels at the constituency level will make a substantive improvement in our knowledge of the gender gap because it can examine gendered political behaviour in a context that has not been examined before in Canada. Furthermore, this study provides an opportunity to test hypotheses related to the role of parenting in relation to political resources at the constituency level.

Results show that a gender gap in political knowledge persists in Canada and that it varies considerably across the country and according to local context. First, both local employment rates and local postsecondary rates are linked to levels of political knowledge for women. Second, cross-level inference shows that women's political knowledge is not affected by their commitment to raising children, providing further evidence to existing research on the gender gap indicating that women's political knowledge is not negatively affected by their role as mothers (Gidengil et al. 2004).

Gender, Parental Status, and Political Knowledge at the Individual Level

Accounts of the gender gap in political knowledge that focus on individual women's political knowledge have had some success. Many studies specifically examine how women's lower socio-economic resources affect their stores of political knowledge compared with those of men. Formal education confers cognitive, social, and organizational skills, and confidence, on individuals that lower the cost of acquiring, analyzing, and storing political information (Dow 2009; Gidengil et al. 2005; Inglehart and Norris 2003).

Similarly, higher levels of material affluence provide access to resources needed to acquire political information (e.g., Internet, cable, print media) and to strengthen an individual's perceived stake in keeping up to date in current affairs (Gidengil et al. 2004, 51). In the Canadian case, accounting for these factors modestly reduced the size of the gender gap in political knowledge, but stark differences between men and women persist, such that "women who had completed some postsecondary education were no better informed than men who had not completed high school" (Gidengil et al. 2004, 51). Other studies show that individual-level factors such as socio-economic resources can account, at best, for half of the gender gap (Delli Carpini and Keeter 1996, 205) and that men gain more political knowledge than women from postsecondary education (Dow 2009; see also Frazer and MacDonald 2003; Kenski and Jamieson 2000). Overall, research that focuses on these resources helps us to produce an important but only partial explanation for the gender gap in political knowledge.

One persistent explanation that has not generated as much empirical support to date is the double day. In theory, time is a valuable, gendered resource with competing public and private dimensions (Gidengil et al. 2004, 5). Many women are responsible for the bulk of unpaid labour in the home, regardless of their employment status outside it (Marshall 2011). Thus, for working mothers, the dual demands of paid employment outside the home and unpaid labour inside it leave them without time to gather and retain information about politics, at least in theory (Burns et al. 2001). Yet individual-level analyses consistently cannot find support for the explanation that the gender gap in political knowledge exists because women in general and mothers in particular are short on time. Some studies find that women and men have equal amounts of free time, yet they occupy their work time differently. Whereas women devote more work hours to the domestic sphere, men with children remain at work longer than men without children (Burns et al. 2001). Although married women do more unpaid labour than unmarried women (Milan, Keown, and Covandanga 2011), both have similar stocks of political knowledge (Gidengil et al. 2004). Similarly, mothers with young children know as much about politics as women without children (Gidengil et al. 2004).

Given how intuitive the argument is, why haven't the dual demands of paid employment and motherhood explained the gender gap in political knowledge? The answer might be at least partly empirical: *conventional models account only for individual-level factors, but the individual has been kept conceptually independent of the information costs associated with the social-political environment.* In other words, however well individual women balance work and family life, there are costs associated with gathering political information that can vary considerably across local environments. The effects of the double day might thus be present but missed when studies examine only individual-level factors.

I argue that investigation of the gender gap in political knowledge ought to include multiple levels of analysis to show both the influence of political resources such as education and employment, as they are distributed across the country, and how women and men benefit from these resources by locality. Both are important because they are crucial factors in bringing women out of the private sphere and into the public fold (Vickers 1997).

Studies of local effects on gendered political engagement are rare; those that do exist examine how feminist activism varies across municipalities (Rankin 1996). These patterns of activism vary across major metropolitan centres, smaller cities, and rural areas in part because of the women's movement's prior experience with the state and in part because of the political opportunities that women confront and the particularities of the places where they organize. Understanding these differences requires linking local political patterns with individual circumstances.

The same logic can be applied to political knowledge. We know that acquiring political information is affected by resources such as education and income as well as by gender (Burns et al. 2001; Gidengil et al. 2004; Ondercin et al. 2011; Sapiro 2005). We suspect, but cannot (yet) demonstrate, that gendered factors such as the dual demands of paid employment and parental status affect women's political knowledge differently than men's. Furthermore, we know that the effects of local social-political factors have been undertheorized and not taken into account in existing examinations of the gender gap (Bowlby, Foord, and MacKenzie 1982). This chapter makes an important contribution by creating a new test of the double day to see how gender works with both individual and community levels of education, employment, and parental status to contribute to the gap in political knowledge.

Contextual Studies in Political Science

Theoretically, contextual studies can be vital to the study of politics and political behaviour. Social context can be described as a force that "arises due to social interaction within an environment" (Huckfeldt, Plutzer, and

Sprague 1993, 298). Individual political experiences are subject to interdependent interactions among members of a community, among coworkers, and within social groups and families. Opportunities to obtain and share political information are embedded in social context, and, though individuals can sometimes control the extent to which they interact with others, there are times when these social processes stem from environmental and social contexts. Logically, these social interactions outside an individual's control can still have an effect on the information that an individual is exposed to and thus shape her or his level of political knowledge.

The idea that the interdependence of individuals in groups, networks, and local contexts can be important in explaining political behaviour, at least in theory, is not new in political science. As Adam Przeworski (1974, 28) notes, "individual behavior is not invariant from one social context to another." A classic study showed that racial hostility in the American South fluctuated as concentrations of African Americans threatened the social, economic, and political power of white people in the respective areas. White people in areas with smaller concentrations of African Americans felt less threatened and were less racially hostile as a result (Key 1949). Importantly, as whites' racial hostility increased, so did their political participation. Our understanding of why this was so is enriched by taking context into account. Similarly, early studies of political behaviour describe mass politics as individuals subjected to a variety of social processes that encouraged "political differences across groups and political homogeneity within groups" (Mettler and Soss 2004, 57). This simplified model focused on the effect of opinion leaders – who paid attention to politics and the media – on those who did not pay attention to political affairs, suggesting that opinion leaders provided information and guidance to less engaged citizens in the course of political discussion (Katz and Lararsfeld 1955).

Given their potential importance, political science studies that deliberately analyze the effect of contextual information on political behaviour are relatively rare. Even fewer examine how context can affect gendered patterns of political engagement. Those studies that do suggest that skills, information, and political recruitment can be gleaned from non-political institutions, such as workplaces and places of worship, partially explain why women are less politically engaged than men (Burns et al. 2001; Verba, Burns, and Schlozman 1997). These findings are particularly important because they provide theoretical underpinnings to justify investigating how local contextual factors facilitate learning political information in general and how gender affects that localized political learning.

Expectations

Education is the strongest predictor of political knowledge at the individual level (Frazer and MacDonald 2003). Formal education cultivates access to political information by fostering cognitive skills that make the complexity of politics easier to understand (Gidengil et al. 2004). As a result, education can also be an important antecedent of knowledge at the aggregate level. As a resource in a local political context, such as a federal riding, formal education helps to develop opportunities for communication and organization. These opportunities, in turn, promote sharing of political information. The higher the level of formal education in a local area, the more likely political learning will occur, for such education lowers the cost of acquiring political information. Politics are more likely to be discussed within social networks, and individuals are more likely to be recruited into political and non-political activities known to help build civic capacity and understanding.

The local employment rate can affect an individual's political knowledge. Like higher levels of education, higher rates of employment are a local resource that acts as a means of lowering the cost of acquiring information. Paid employment varies considerably across Canada, and this variation can produce variation in the political information held and shared by individuals through work-related networks. Areas with high employment are expected to provide individuals with information-rich contexts characterized by more frequent political discussion and information sharing.

Higher local levels of both postsecondary education and employment are expected to have positive effects on levels of political knowledge among both women and men. However, I expect that men more than women will capitalize on these two political resources. Men and women use their formal training and work networks to acquire political information and civic skills in different ways (Beckwith 1986; Dow 2009; Gidengil et al. 2004; Thomas 2012). Men, for instance, are more likely to report an enhanced sense of autonomy from their socio-economic status (Burns et al. 2001), and self-perceived autonomy is critical for political engagement. Men garner more political knowledge from higher levels of education than women in the United States (Dow 2009). Men's political self-confidence, likelihood of discussing politics, and willingness to seize political opportunities when recruited are expected to be stronger compared with those of women and thus help men to acquire relatively more political information. Accordingly, accounting for these gender differences will help to explain a greater portion of the gap in political knowledge.

Other research shows that men more than women have more diverse social networks and pull in more contacts from their workplaces (Erickson 2004; Gidengil et al. 2005). This network diversity helps to transmit political information. In contrast, women have less diverse social networks and are more likely to rely on kin connections to gather political information. The expectation that gender conditions the effects of local levels of education and employment comes from the possibility that men are more politicized and tend to capitalize on political resources more often than women (Ondercin and Jones-White 2011). As a result, men are expected to have an additional benefit compared to women when higher numbers of employed and educated individuals surround them.

Key for this volume, though, is the idea that parental status might exacerbate these effects. As noted above, children take up a great deal of their parents' spare time, and, because women undertake considerably more childcare than men, this is one reason why women might have lower levels of political knowledge than men. Childcare responsibilities require more time and psychological energy for women than men, and mothers might think that they cannot devote their leisure time to political matters because they want to catch up on time missed with their children once they have accounted for their work week (Eagly and Carli 2007; Gidengil et al. 2004). Thus, any information benefits that come from residing in a local context with high education and employment rates might not be conferred equally on women and men. The gendered patterns of information sharing, political discussion, participation in work-related organizations, and political recruitment can thus be structured not only by gender but also by parental status.

I therefore expect that men will know more about politics than women on average. However, employed women without children should know more than mothers, and mothers with jobs should know more than unemployed mothers. Because women perform the lion's share of childcare, the effect of parental status on men should be less acute than it is on women. Finally, net of these individual-level factors, in local areas with high levels of education and/or employment, women without children at home are not expected to benefit as much in terms of political knowledge as men either with or without children.

Potentially different consequences are also anticipated when studying the impact of parental status on political behaviour in Canada. We must consider the unique situation of early childhood care in Quebec. That province is a clear outlier in provincial childcare spending (Friendly et al. 2013). Since the late 1990s, Quebec has contributed disproportionately to regulated childcare services. The allocation jumped from 29 percent of the total provincial/territorial budgets in 1998 to 58 percent in 2001. Still, in 2012, Quebec's share of public spending on childcare represented 60 percent of total allocations (Ferns and Friendly 2014). The disparity between Quebec and the rest of Canada in childcare fees can be enormous. In 2012, for example, the average cost of infant care in Quebec was $1,824 per year, whereas in Ontario it was more than $12,000 per year.

Childcare is a complex issue tied to questions of women's equality, motherhood, labour and employment, and early childhood development. Here I argue that the double day effect is the same in Quebec as in other provinces. A recent study showed that the labour force participation rate for women aged 15 to 64 in Quebec increased from 63 percent in 1996 (prior to the universal childcare policy) to 75 percent in 2011 (Fortin, Godbout, and St-Cerny 2012). Although the labour force participation rate increased in other provinces as well over the same period, the pace in Quebec was faster than the national average. Prior to Quebec's universal childcare program, women's labour force participation rate in Quebec was lower than that in the rest of Canada. The six-point participation gap between women in Quebec and those in the rest of Canada in 1996 closed completely by 2011 (Fortin, Godbout, and St-Cerny 2012). In the data employed in this study, the 2006 Canadian Census shows that, at the riding level, 66 percent of women in Quebec with children six years old and younger were employed, whereas 63 percent of their peers outside Quebec were employed. If employment differences related to parenthood are contributing to the gender gap in political knowledge, then that gap should shrink, even disappear, or become statistically insignificant in the models accounting for a mother's double day.

Measuring Political Knowledge

Understanding the contextual factors that might have an impact on levels of political knowledge requires an examination of both individual and contextual data. I rely on the Canadian Election Studies from 2000 to 2008 for individual-level data, including a measure of political knowledge and individual-level sociodemographic data, and I use the 2006 Canadian Census (using the 2003 representation order) for data aggregated at the constituency level, including aggregated measures of education and employment rates.[1]

Political knowledge is measured at the individual level as a Canadian Election Study respondent's knowledge of the main party leaders.[2] The measure of political knowledge is scored on a 0–1 scale, where 1 represents correct responses to all questions and 0 represents incorrect responses to all questions.[3] To assess community-level knowledge, these mean knowledge scores were calculated at the riding level for women and men to incorporate variations in political knowledge across Canada.[4] The data indicate that on average, among those living outside Quebec, the majority of both women (55 percent) and men (64 percent) can correctly identify federal party leaders. Note, too, that the gender gap in knowledge persists here, since men are nine points more likely than women to be able to name these leaders.[5] In Quebec, approximately 54 percent of women and 67 percent of men know the leaders, which leads to a 13-point gap on average.

As noted above, several individual-level factors are associated with political knowledge. Many are dummy coded. Gender is coded 1 for female respondents. Education is captured by two dummy variables. The first is coded 1 for respondents with some college or university education or a college or technical school degree; the second is coded 1 for university graduates.[6] Income, another key resource, is also captured by two dummy variables. The first captures the tercile with the highest level of income; the second captures the middle tercile.[7] Those gainfully employed are coded 1 (full time, part time, and self-employed), as are those married or living with partners. Similarly, parental status is captured through a dummy variable, which measures the presence of children in the household under the age of 18.[8]

At the local level, two key variables need to be measured: education and employment. To do so, I use data from the 2006 Canadian Census. The riding-level factors measuring the rate of postsecondary education (percentage of the population with a university degree) and the rate of employment have been recoded into deciles to compare the effects among the ridings consistently across each measurement. A control variable for the level of political competitiveness in each riding is also included to account for the variation across Canada in local races, as local campaigns can affect levels of political knowledge (Jones 2013).[9] In addition, the rate of urbanization is controlled for to ensure that the relationships estimated herein are not artifacts of differences between urban and rural Canada (Turcotte 2005).

Assessing Individual and Local Effects

To determine the individual- and riding-level effects of the explanatory variables, I use a random intercept model (Macherenko 2012). This model allows the intercepts to vary. It can therefore estimate the impacts of the intercept that varies at the riding level given the impacts of the individual factors. The model assumes that the slopes, the impacts of the individual-level factors, are fixed across the federal ridings. In addition, it provides information about intraclass correlation, helpful in determining what percentage of the variation is explained by the riding-level factors.

Typically, a regression model[10] is applied only to individual-level data to assess the effects of individual-level explanatory factors on individuals' levels of political knowledge (see Equation A1 in Appendix A). Two problems can arise, though, from this method. First, the standard errors can be estimated incorrectly when the data are not modelled to represent their clustered or hierarchical nature. This is a problem since standard errors are used to assess statistical significance. Second, the single-level regression model cannot estimate how much of what Canadians know about politics can be explained by local factors rather than individual factors.

In a multi-level model, one or more explanatory factors can vary from group to group.[11] I anticipate that this might be the case for rates of post-secondary education and employment. When this occurs, the original effect of that factor is the local average over all groups, and the model estimates the between-group variance (see Equation A2 in Appendix A). When this local model is blended with the individual-level model referred to above, we can estimate both the local-level and the individual-level effects (see Equation A3 in Appendix A).

Summary Statistics

The rate of degree holders and the rate of employment measured at the riding level are reported in Table 11.1. In Quebec, the average employment rate is 60 percent, whereas in the rest of Canada it is 62 percent. The standard deviation of both is six points. This deviation is important because variation in local employment rates means that there is variation in the local context, and this might be important in explaining gender differences in political knowledge. There is also a wide range reported in the minimum and maximum scores. Within Quebec, the difference between the lowest and the highest local employment rates is 27 points. Outside Quebec, that value is 45 points. These summary statistics indicate that the employment situation varies substantially across the ridings.

The rate of university education at the local level is uniform, with 56 percent within Quebec and 55 percent outside Quebec. The standard deviation is very small, two points within Quebec and three points outside Quebec, indicating that Canadians are uniformly educated at the university level.

TABLE 11.1
Summary statistics of riding-level factors, 2006 Canadian Census

		M (%)	SD (%)	Min (%)	Max (%)
Rate of employment	Quebec	60	6	45	72
	Rest of Canada	62	6	39	75
Rate of degree holders	Quebec	56	2	50	67
	Rest of Canada	55	3	44	72

Similar to the local employment rate, the difference between the minimum and the maximum values is large. The range is 27 points in Quebec and 45 points in the rest of Canada.

Results

The persistence of gaps in political knowledge in the first four federal elections of the 2000s is perplexing. The impact of individual factors and the riding-level rates of postsecondary education and employment are reported in Table 11.2. The first row reports the impact of being a parent with children under the age of 18. This explanatory factor is measured at the individual level, coded as a dummy variable. The results show that women in Quebec score four points less on average if they have children at home. Meanwhile, outside Quebec, women score on average five points less. There is no equivalent impact for men since the coefficients are not statistically significant.

The local rate of university degree holders shows a positive impact only on women in Quebec. The coefficient reported for women there shows that, on average, for every percentage point increase in the level of education at the riding level, there is a 0.82 percentage point increase in the level of political knowledge of women. The non-significant findings for the other respondents show that postsecondary education at the local level does not have any bearing on their knowledge of party leaders. The local employment rate has a positive impact for women outside Quebec. The coefficient of 0.24 can be interpreted to mean that a one-point increase in the local employment rate leads to a 0.24 percentage point increase in women's knowledge of party leaders outside Quebec.[12]

The next model adds a cross-level interaction term with motherhood (measured at the individual level) and the riding-level employment rate.

TABLE 11.2
Effects of postsecondary education rates and employment rates at riding level

	Quebec women Model 1		Quebec men Model 2		Rest of Canada women Model 3		Rest of Canada men Model 4	
	Coefficient	SE	Coefficient	SE	Coefficient	SE	Coefficient	SE
Children under 18	-0.041*	(0.024)	-0.009	(0.021)	-0.052**	(0.017)	-0.018	(0.016)
Rate of degree holders	0.819*	(0.451)	0.330	(0.460)	-0.056	(0.197)	-0.230	(0.275)
Rate of employment	-0.134	(0.218)	0.086	(0.219)	0.240**	(0.112)	0.067	(0.127)
Constant	-0.142	(0.218)	-0.015	(0.249)	0.080	(0.118)	0.365**	(0.147)
Between riding SD	-0.032	(0.003)	-0.032	(0.003)	-0.034**	(0.004)	-0.027**	(0.001)
Likelihood ratio test	-81.19		-23.49		-330.99		-149.32	
N	1,373		1,247		2,859		2,585		8,064	

* $p < .10$; ** $p < .05$.

TABLE 11.3
Contextual interactions with women's parental status

	Quebec women		Rest of Canada women	
	Coefficient	SE	Coefficient	SE
Children under 18	−0.433	(0.515)	−0.091	(0.133)
Rate of degree holders	0.550	(0.637)	−0.059	(0.198)
Rate of employment	−0.130	(0.218)	0.338	(0.144)
Rate of degree holders* children	0.694	(0.907)		
Rate of employment* children			−0.226	(0.129)
Constant	0.008	(0.317)	0.021	(0.138)
Between riding SD	−0.037	(0.012)	−0.034	(0.015)
Likelihood ratio test	−80.84		−330.31	
N	1,373		2,859	

This is done to test the double day hypothesis for women in Quebec. The model of women there, as reported in Table 11.3, shows that the interaction term between local employment rate and motherhood is not statistically significant. This means that there is no evidence to support the hypothesis that the impact of the local employment rate is negatively conditioned by having children at home.

At the same time, an interaction term with motherhood and the riding-level rate of degree holders is employed to test the double day hypothesis for women outside Quebec. The model of women in the rest of Canada reported in Table 11.3 shows that the interaction term is not statistically significant either. This means that there is no conditioning effect on mothers. Once again, empirical evidence of the double day effect is elusive.

The Gender Gap in Political Knowledge

At the riding level, the gender differences in knowledge of party leaders without statistical controls are reported in Table 11.4. In Quebec, over the four federal elections from 2000 to 2008, the gender gap was 13 points as 54 percent of women and 67 percent of men correctly identified the party leaders. Likewise, outside Quebec, the gender gap was nine points as 55 percent of women and 64 percent of men correctly identified the party leaders. The sizes of the gender gaps are important as benchmarks of comparison. They will be compared with gender gaps in the models ahead, which include both individual-level and riding-level explanatory factors.

TABLE 11.4
Gender gap in knowledge of party leaders

	No controls %	Gender gap (men/women)	Individual-level factors only %	Gender gap (men/women)	Individual factors and riding-level factors %	Gender gap (men/women)
Quebec						
Women	54	⎤ 13	60	⎤ 6	56	⎤ 8
Men	67	⎦	66	⎦	64	⎦
Rest of Canada						
Women	56	⎤ 9	55	⎤ 6	57	⎤ 5
Men	65	⎦	61	⎦	62	⎦

The gender gap in correctly identifying party leaders decreases slightly when we control for individual-level factors. The gaps in Quebec and the rest of Canada are estimated at six points. Women outside Quebec provided correct responses at a rate of 57 percent, whereas men did so at a rate of 62 percent, for a gender gap of five points. This is a reduction of four points from the gender gap without controls. In Quebec, the average correct response rate was 56 percent for women and 64 percent for men, for a gender gap of eight points. This is a reduction of five points from the gender gap without controls. The change in gender gap demonstrates that political resources such as education, income, and gainful employment at the individual level are critical to reducing the cost of acquiring information about federal politics, but the model does not capture all the explanatory factors that lead to gender differences, particularly in explaining the gender gap in Quebec.

Conclusion

Contextual factors, in theory, might be important to political knowledge, particularly because individual-level factors cannot explain the gender gap in political knowledge. The results presented above show that some contextual factors have a gender-specific effect on knowledge. The full models provide much insight into the gender gap by reducing the gap by five points among the electorate in Quebec and four points among the electorate in the rest of Canada. Neither women's nor men's political knowledge increased because of a local context of higher education outside Quebec, suggesting that an individual's relative level of education has a more immediate impact on keeping long-term stores of political information. Yet the local level of education had a positive impact on women's levels of political knowledge in Quebec. Overall, the substantive gendered effect shows that women benefit from political resources at the local level.

Importantly, for the purposes of this volume, I find that women's levels of political knowledge are negatively affected by the presence of children under the age of 18 in the home. This replicates findings in this volume that highlight how parental status affects political engagement (see the chapters by Goodyear-Grant and Bittner, and Micheletti and Stolle). The negative effect shows that, at the individual level, the commitment to rearing children leads to less knowledge, on average, among women about politics – or at least the names of political leaders – compared with women without children in the house. Yet there was no evidence that the positive effects of higher rates of employment or postsecondary education at the riding level are conditioned by the presence of children. Stated differently, there is no evidence to suggest that context moderates the negative effect of children on women's political knowledge. The gender difference in parenting roles might be caused by time and psychological commitments of mothers compared with fathers to rearing children, though more research is required to confirm this. Indeed, though other research rejects the idea that the double day suppresses women's political engagement, it is unclear how else to explain why children have a persistent negative effect on women's political knowledge. Because women are more likely to be primary caregivers, in both good and bad health, and primary partners running errands and conducting activities involving children, they might have less free time and prioritize less their psychological energy for politics.

The two causal pathways of political resources at the local level differ for women, likely because of the comprehensive public childcare program in Quebec, though more research is required to confirm this (see Harell et al., this volume). Whereas the local rate of employment is a political resource for women in the rest of Canada, the local rate of postsecondary education is a political resource for women in Quebec. One primary limitation of this study is its reliance on cross-sectional data and its aim to determine the causal mechanisms related to acquiring political knowledge. Cross-sectional data can be used to estimate the relationship between the explanatory factors and political knowledge, which is important for testing the hypotheses outlined in this thesis. The limitation of these data, however, is that the estimates reported in the preceding models do not necessarily provide a complete account of the causal mechanisms themselves. Causal mechanisms are the detailed causal reasoning of the relationship between independent variables and dependent variables.

This research points to a need to study in greater depth the patterns of political communication and to assess the costs of acquiring new information. Interpersonal discussion is important because it creates channels through which useful political information and influence pass. Social network research demonstrates that women and men have different information and opportunities available to them through social contacts (Erickson 2004; Erickson and Nosanchuk 1990; Frazer and MacDonald 2003; Gidengil et al. 2005). Women's and men's social networks reflect gendered patterns of employment, recreational activity, associational membership, and kinship, which have potential consequences for the flow of political information. Although social networks and associational involvement have theoretical importance in explaining the spread of political knowledge, there is yet to be a large study done on how gender plays a role in the type and amount of information shared. Relevant measures would capture the types of associational involvement, network diversity, and number and variety of personal contacts. As well, individuals would be asked questions to quantify how much they know about political actors and institutions, social provisions, and public policies across different levels of government. These data would provide information about gendered patterns of political communication and could be used in models to explain gender differences in political knowledge.

The study of local context moves beyond individual-level models that do not explain the gender gap completely. This multi-level approach to understanding the gender gap in political knowledge satisfies major methodological and theoretical concerns about that gap. Gendered political knowledge varies greatly across Canada at the riding level, indicating that generalizations across the country might not be accurate without accounting for contextual factors. This study demonstrates that political resources do not necessarily have the same impacts on the accumulation of women's and men's political information across different local contexts. This suggests that some factors are better detected in a contextually specified model that accounts for variations across the geographical landscape.

Appendix A: Regression Equations

Formula A1: Simple Regression Model

$$y_i = \beta_0 + \beta_1 x_i + e_i$$
$$e_i \sim N(0, \sigma^2)$$

Formula A2: The Random Component

$$y_{ij} = \beta_0 + u_j + e_{ij}$$
$$u_j \sim N(0, \sigma_u^2)$$
$$e_{ij} \sim N(0, \sigma_e^2)$$

Formula A3: Random Intercept Model

$$y_{ij} = \beta_0 + \beta_1 x_{ij} + u_j + e_{ij}$$
$$u_j \sim N(0, \sigma_u^2)$$
$$e_{ij} \sim N(0, \sigma_e^2)$$

Notes

I would like to thank Brenda O'Neill and the editors and reviewers of this volume for helpful comments in preparing this chapter. This research was partly funded by the Social Sciences and Humanities Research Council (SSHRC).

1 The individual-level and aggregate-level data sets were merged according to respondents' particular ID number and the federal riding number. The pooled Canadian Election Studies from 2000 to 2008 comprise 11,025 respondents. I would like to thank Jason Roy for assisting me with merging the data sets.
2 Although there are other types of questions on political knowledge in the Canadian Election Studies, such as identifying party promises and prominent politicians past and present at different levels of government, the knowledge measure of party leaders used here is the only set based upon questions consistently asked across these election studies. The 2006 Canadian Census was chosen because it overlaps the most with the individual-level data in the 2000–8 Canadian Election Studies.
3 The political knowledge index of recalling the names of party leaders included identifying Bloc Québécois leader Gilles Duceppe for respondents from Quebec. Scores were standardized from 0 to 1 for all respondents. A question asking respondents to identify Green Party leader Elizabeth May was included in the 2008 measure.
4 The analysis of 305 ridings excluded the three ridings in the northern territories. The pooled elections provided at least 30 respondents in each district with the exception of four electoral districts (ridings 35106, 35081, 59034, and 46003). Ridings with fewer than 30 respondents were given average values of political knowledge for men and women so that the low sample size did not skew the average values of political knowledge or the estimates in the multivariate analysis.

5   When I assess responses of "don't know," the patterns are similar: the average score for women is 39 percent and for men 28 percent (an 11-point gap). The main underlying question is whether the "don't know" item format results in masking women's political knowledge, compared with men's, or distorts the level of political knowledge because of the propensity for men to guess more than women. The results of studies addressing the effects of guessing on the gender gap in political knowledge are mixed (Sturgis 2006; Sturgis, Allum, and Smith 2008).
6   The reference category is comprised of respondents with high school education or less.
7   The reference category is comprised of low-income earners.
8   Other individual-level factors known to be associated with political knowledge are also included in this study. Immigration within the past 10 years is dummy coded 1 for those who have recently started to live in Canada. Religiosity is coded 1 for those who believe that religion is very important in their lives. Partisanship is also coded 1 for strong identifiers with any political party and 0 for weak identifiers and those who do not identify with any political party. Media attention is measured by adding together a respondent's consumption of four types of news media: television, radio, newspaper, and online. This variable ranges from 0 (no attention) to 10 (high attention). Interest in the election campaign is also measured by a variable ranging from 0 (low interest) to 10 (high interest). The last individual-level variable captures how often an individual discusses politics and is coded on a scale of 1 (never discussed politics during the campaign) to 3 (discussed politics several times during the campaign).
9   A dynamic measure of district competitiveness is used in the analysis that takes into account both short-term and long-term information about riding competitiveness. Ridings are classified as either a party stronghold or a party battleground. Here information about the 2004 and 2006 elections is used to measure the competitiveness of the riding in the 2008 election. (For more information about this measure and its calculation, consult Bodet 2013; Thomas and Bodet 2013).
10 This choice is based upon a larger discussion on the multiple ways in which to model the dependent variable. Political knowledge can be treated as an ordinal variable that requires a different method of estimation. Treating the variable as having ordered response categories such as "don't know," "incorrect," and "correct" lends itself to estimation methods such as ordered logit or probit (Ondercin et al. 2011). Ordered logit or probit relaxes the assumption that the distances among the three categories are equal. In addition, political knowledge can be treated as an interval-level variable that has a value of 0 and equal distance between values. Equivalent research in the American case has shown that the substantive results using ordered probit are the same as the results using the OLS estimates. OLS is preferred because there are potential drawbacks to ordered logit and probit models, in which it is easy to violate the independence of irrelevant alternative assumptions when categories of the dependent variable are similar to each other. Violation of such assumptions can occur when using political knowledge as an ordinal level of measurement when one response category (e.g., "don't know") is a close substitute for another response category (e.g., "correct" or "incorrect"), particularly if respondents make blind guesses at answers (Ondercin et al. 2011).

11 The statistical power of multi-level models examining second-level effects dependent on the number of groups is included. To conduct research with sufficient statistical power, sample sizes of at least 20 groups are required (Leeuw and Fkreft 1998).
12 Across the models, the intraclass correlation is 2 percent. This means that total variance explained at the riding level accounts for 2 percent of variance in the dependent variable, knowledge of party leaders. The controls for urbanization and local political competition were not statistically significant in the models, with the exception of a positive effect of urbanization on women outside Quebec. The coefficient and standard error were reported at 0.054 (0.003), and the p value is less than 0.05.

References

Beckwith, K. 1986. *American Women and Political Participation: The Impacts of Work, Generation, and Feminism.* New York: Greenwood Press.

Bodet, M.A. 2013. "Strongholds and Battlegrounds: Measuring Party Support Stability in Canada." *Canadian Journal of Political Science* 46 (3): 575–96. http://dx.doi.org/10.1017/S000842391300067X.

Bowlby, S.R., J. Foord, and S. MacKenzie. 1982. "Feminism and Geography." *Royal Geographical Society* 14: 19–25.

Burns, N., K.L. Schlozman, and S. Verba. 2001. *The Private Roots of Public Action: Gender, Equality, and Political Participation.* Cambridge, MA: Harvard University Press.

Delli Carpini, M.X., and S. Keeter. 1996. *What Americans Know about Politics and Why It Matters.* New Haven, CT: Yale University Press.

Dow, J.K. 2009. "Gender Differences in Political Knowledge: Distinguishing Characteristics-Based and Returns-Based Differences." *Political Behavior* 31 (1): 117–36. http://dx.doi.org/10.1007/s11109-008-9059-8.

Eagly, A.H., and L.L. Carli. 2007. *Through the Labyrinth: The Truth about How Women Become Leaders.* Boston: Harvard Business School Press.

Erickson, B. 2004. "The Distribution of Gendered Social Capital in Canada." In *Creation and Returns of Social Capital: A New Research Program*, edited by H. Flap, 19–37. New York: Routledge.

Erickson, B., and T.A. Nosanchuk. 1990. "How an Apolitical Association Politicizes." *Canadian Review of Sociology and Anthropology/La revue canadienne de sociologie et d'anthropologie* 27 (2): 206–19. http://dx.doi.org/10.1111/j.1755-618X.1990.tb00451.x.

Ferns, C., and M. Friendly. 2014. *The State of Early Childhood Education and Care in Canada 2012.* Guelph: University of Guelph.

Fortin, P., L. Godbout, and S. St-Cerny. 2012. "Impact of Quebec's Universal Low-Fee Childcare Program on Female Labour Force Participation, Domestic Income, and Government Budgets." Chaire de recherché en fiscalité et finances publiques Working Paper 2012/02, University of Sherbrooke.

Frazer, E., and K. MacDonald. 2003. "Sex Differences in Political Knowledge in Britain." *Political Studies* 51 (1): 67–83. http://dx.doi.org/10.1111/1467-9248.00413.

Friendly, M., S. Halfon, J. Beach, and B. Forer. 2013. *Early Childhood Education and Care in Canada 2012.* Guelph: University of Guelph.

Gidengil, E., A. Blais, N. Nevitte, and R. Nadeau. 2004. *Citizens*. Vancouver: UBC Press.

Gidengil, E., E. Goodyear-Grant, A. Blais, and N. Nevitte. 2005. "Gender, Knowledge, and Social Capital." In *Gender and Social Capital*, edited by B. O'Neill and E. Gidengil, 241–72. New York: Routledge.

Gidengil, E., and D. Stolle. 2012. "What Do Women Know about Government Services and Benefits?" *Canadian Public Policy* 38 (1): 31–54. http://dx.doi.org/10.3138/cpp.38.1.31.

Huckfeldt, R., E. Plutzer, and J. Sprague. 1993. "Alternative Contexts of Political Behavior: Churches, Neighborhoods, and Individuals." *Journal of Politics* 55 (2): 365–81. http://dx.doi.org/10.2307/2132270.

Inglehart, R., and P. Norris. 2003. *Rising Tide: Gender Equality and Cultural Change around the World*. New York: Cambridge University Press. http://dx.doi.org/10.1017/CBO9780511550362.

Jones, P.E. 2013. "The Effect of Political Competition on Democratic Accountability." *Political Behavior* 35 (3): 481–515. http://dx.doi.org/10.1007/s11109-012-9203-3.

Katz, E., and P. Lararsfeld. 1955. *Personal Influence: The Part Played by People in the Flow of Mass Communications*. New York: Free Press.

Kenski, K., and K.H. Jamieson. 2000. *Everything You Think You Know about Politics and Why You Are Wrong*. New York: Basic Books.

Key, V.O.J. 1949. *Southern Politics in State and Nation*. New York: Knopf.

Leeuw, I., and J.D. Fkreft. 1998. *Introducing Multilevel Modeling*. London: Sage Publications.

Macherenko, Y. 2012. *Multilevel and Mixed Models in Stata*. College Station, TX: Stata Press.

Marshall, K. 2011. *Generational Change in Paid and Unpaid Work*. No. 11–008–X. Ottawa: Government of Canada.

Mettler, S., and J. Soss. 2004. "The Consequence of Public Policy for Democratic Citizenship: Bridging Policy Studies and Mass Politics." *Perspectives on Politics* 2 (1): 55–73. http://dx.doi.org/10.1017/S1537592704000623.

Milan, A., L.-A. Keown, and R.U. Covandanga. 2011. *Families, Living Arrangements, and Unpaid Work*. No. 89–503–X. Ottawa: Government of Canada.

Ondercin, H.L., J.G. Garand, and L. Crapanzano. 2011. "Political Learning during the 2000 U.S. Presidential Election: The Impact of the Campaign on the Gender Gap in Political Knowledge." *Electoral Studies* 30 (4): 727–37. http://dx.doi.org/10.1016/j.electstud.2011.06.016.

Ondercin, H.L., and D. Jones-White. 2011. "Gender Jeopardy: What Is the Impact of Gender Differences in Political Knowledge on Political Participation?" *Social Science Quarterly* 92(3):675–94. http://dx.doi.org/10.1111/j.1540-6237.2011.00787.x.

Przeworski, A. 1974. "Contextual Models of Political Behavior." *Political Methodology* 1: 27–61.

Rankin, P. 1996. "Experience, Opportunity, and the Politics of Place: A Comparative Analysis of Provincial and Territorial Women's Movements in Canada." PhD diss., Carleton University.

Sapiro, V. 2005. "Gender, Social Capital, and Politics." In *Gender and Social Capital*, edited by B. O'Neill and E. Gidengil, 151–84. New York: Routledge.

Sturgis, P. 2006. "Measuring Political Knowledge: Gender, Partial Information, and the Propensity to Guess." Paper presented at the Annual Meeting of the American Political Science Associaton, Philadelphia, August 31.

Sturgis, P., N. Allum, and P. Smith. 2008. "An Experiment on the Measurement of Political Knowledge in Surveys." *Public Opinion Quarterly* 72 (1): 90–102. http://dx.doi.org/10.1093/poq/nfm032.

Thomas, M. 2012. "The Complexity Conundrum: Why Hasn't the Gender Gap in Subjective Political Competence Closed?" *Canadian Journal of Political Science* 45 (2): 337–58. http://dx.doi.org/10.1017/S0008423912000352.

Thomas, M., and M.A. Bodet. 2013. "Sacrificial Lambs, Women Candidates, and District Competitiveness in Canada." *Electoral Studies* 32 (1): 153–66. http://dx.doi.org/10.1016/j.electstud.2012.12.001.

Turcotte, M. 2005. *Social Engagement and Civic Participation: Are Rural and Small Town Populations Really at an Advantage?* Ottawa: Government of Canada.

Verba, S., N. Burns, and K.L. Schlozman. 1997. "Knowing and Caring about Politics: Gender and Political Engagement." *Journal of Politics* 59 (4): 1051–72. http://dx.doi.org/10.2307/2998592.

Vickers, J. 1997. *Reinventing Political Science: A Feminist Approach*. Winnipeg: Fernwood Press.

12

Attitudes toward Work, Motherhood, and Parental Leave in Canada, the United States, and the United Kingdom

ALLISON HARELL, STUART SOROKA,
SHANTO IYENGAR, and VALÉRIE LAPOINTE

In most Western societies, biological sexual differences have provided a pretext for various forms of discrimination against women. Women's bodies, especially in regard to motherhood and reproduction, have been used to justify inequalities in the labour market. Indeed, the extensive debate among feminist scholars to distinguish and define sexual differences and gender has centred in part on the link between the biological ability to reproduce and the social norms that have developed that link this ability to women's roles in societies, their values and attitudes, and their skills (de Beauvoir 1949; Gilligan 1982; Scott 1986). Motherhood, then, is understood as both a defining characteristic of women based upon biological differences and a gendered form of parenting.

Development of the modern welfare state was based, in part, upon a gendered division of work within the family, in which a male breadwinner was in the paid workforce and a female partner was responsible for unpaid labour in the home. Contribution-based state welfare programs such as employment insurance were in place to support the household through the male breadwinner (Fraser 1994) and arguably garnered some of their support because of their association with popularly accepted gender norms and a view of the worker as both white and male (Winter 2008). Yet, as more women entered the workforce, there was a corresponding development of maternity benefits, family allowances, and childcare regimes that disproportionately benefited women, and these benefits were often tied to their roles as mothers (Bock and Thane 1991; Fraser 1989, 144–60). This two-tiered or gendered system within the welfare state has served both to promote women's entry into the workforce and to reinforce a gendered division of labour within the family (Gordon 2012; Orloff 1996).

In this chapter, we focus on men's and women's attitudes toward motherhood, specifically the role of women vis-à-vis childcare and work in three liberal welfare states: Canada, the United States, and the United Kingdom. In a first step, we explain how men's and women's personal situations are tied to more traditional views of women's roles, and we then demonstrate how traditional gender role ideology affects support for parental leave. Most research on the consequences of gender role attitudes focuses on how they affect the division of labour in the home, women's employment, and relationships in the family (for a review, see Davis and Greenstein 2009), yet much less has focused on how such attitudes shape support for family policies.

Parental leave policies provide an interesting case because they are intended to provide working parents (especially working mothers) with opportunities to care for their children full time in the home for a preset length of time. Parental leave benefits are inherently gendered in contemporary democracies, in which, despite their increasing participation in the workforce, women continue to be disproportionately responsible for childcare, and program design continues to make distinctions between mothers and fathers in terms of policy benefits (Fusulier, Laloy, and Sanchez 2007; Kulik 2011). At the same time, there has been a shift to make such policies more gender neutral and to provide more access to fathers (e.g., Duvander 2014), though such policies do not necessarily translate into more paternal involvement (Wells and Sarkadi 2012). We ask here how traditional gender role ideologies influence support for parental leave benefits.

Our analysis draws on the survey Race, Gender, and the Welfare State undertaken in 2011 ($N = 3,600$) across Canada, the United States, and the United Kingdom. We identify those most likely to hold more traditional gender norms and demonstrate that such attitudes are intimately tied to gender policy domains.

Attitudes toward Motherhood and Gendered Division of Work

Since the 1970s, there has been extensive research on how the public views working mothers and the consequences of work for women's traditional role as caregiver in the family. These gender role or gender ideology measures tend to focus on how traditional attitudes toward gender roles view motherhood and work as incompatible while privileging the male breadwinner model (for a review, see Davis and Greenstein 2009).

Over time, analyses have shown that attitudes toward gender roles have become more egalitarian, with increasing numbers of people rejecting the idea that women's primary responsibility should be to the home (Bolzendahl and Myers 2004; Brooks and Bolzendahl 2004; Campbell and Marsden 2012; Cotter, Hermsen, and Vanneman 2011; Cunningham 2008). The largest shifts seem to have occurred from the 1970s to the 1990s, followed by a stabilization of attitudes (Cotter, Hermsen, and Vanneman 2011). According to Campbell and Marsden (2012), however, attitudes specifically toward employed mothers and childrearing continued to liberalize into the 2000s in the United States, despite the larger trend toward stabilization. The sources of this change are partly in cohort replacement, with younger generations tending to hold more egalitarian views (Brooks and Bolzendahl 2004; Ciabattari 2001; Scott, Alwin, and Braun 1996). Changes in social structure are also linked to changes in attitude, especially regarding women's entry into paid employment, strongly related to more liberal gender role ideologies (Bolzendahl and Myers 2004; Cunningham 2008; Fortin 2005; Harris and Firestone 1998).

At the individual level, many factors tend to be consistently linked to less conservative attitudes toward motherhood and work. Gender itself is an important factor, with women tending to be more egalitarian in their views of work and motherhood (Bolzendahl and Myers 2004; Ciabattari 2001; Davis and Greenstein 2004; Knudsen and Waerness 2001; Sunström 1999; Valentova 2013). What people think about gender roles is also related to the gendered roles that they actually hold. For example, people with children tend to have more traditional gender role attitudes, and this is particularly true for first-time mothers (Katz-Wise, Priess, and Hyde 2010; Koivunen, Rothaupt, and Wolfgram 2009; Goodyear-Grant and Bittner, this volume).[1] Those in married relationships also tend to hold more conservative attitudes (Chauffaut and Domingo 2011; Vespa 2009).[2]

Furthermore, factors associated more generally with conservative attitudes tend to be strongly related to such attitudes toward gender, including living in rural areas and greater levels of religiosity (Campbell and Marsden 2012; Knudsen and Waerness 2001). In contrast, youth and higher levels of education are associated with more liberal gender role attitudes (Knudsen and Waerness 2001; Sunström 1999). Not surprisingly, conservative political ideology is also related to conservative gender role ideology (Bolzendahl and Myers 2004; Schnittker, Freese, and Powell 2003).

Race has a complicated relationship to gender role ideology in the literature. For example, Karen Dugger (1988) argues that the history of black women makes them more likely to reject traditional (white) gender roles, and she shows that this is largely the case across a host of gender attitudes. Kathleen M. Blee and Ann R. Tickamyer (1995) similarly show that African American men tend to have more liberal attitudes, at least toward women's employment. The underlying argument is that these more liberal attitudes stem from experiences in black families, in which less traditional family structures are more common.

Finally, there is also reason to believe that institutional contexts matter as well (Alwin, Braun, and Scott 1992; Banaszak 2006; Knudsen and Waerness 2001; Scott et al. 1996; Sunström 1999). Comparative studies of gender role ideologies tend to find that wealthier and more egalitarian welfare states are associated with more liberal attitudes toward motherhood and employment, though whether attitude changes or institutions come first is a question that remains unanswered. Jing Guo and Neil Gilbert (2012) provide a cross-national test of welfare state regimes and show that gender role attitudes are largely consistent with state policies. Using the case of the former East and West Germany, Lee Ann Banaszak (2006) argues that state policies have both a direct – through rhetoric and ideology – and an indirect – by influencing women's overall employment levels – effect on gender role attitudes.

Gendered Division of Labour and the Welfare State

Clearly, modern welfare programs targeted at working mothers can shape attitudes toward motherhood and work because such parental leave programs aim to give working mothers (and increasingly fathers) the opportunity to stay at home with their children for a period of time after the birth of a child. Such programs can reconcile (in part) the perceived conflict between work and motherhood at the heart of more traditional gender ideologies. Yet, as mentioned, such programs can also reify the role of women as mothers by institutionalizing that role through public programs.

This tension in the role of the welfare state with respect to gender relations is clearly laid out by Orloff (1996, 53), who argues that there are two broad approaches to gender relations within the welfare state. The first perspective, which she calls the social reproduction perspective, views social policies as reproducing gender inequalities through three mechanisms:

(1) by reinforcing the gendered division of labour in which men are considered the economic breadwinners and women are responsible for caregiving and childrearing; (2) by creating a system in which wages and benefits for men are based upon the dependence of women and children on their incomes; and (3) by reinforcing traditional definitions of marriage. Traditional gender roles are thus reinforced and reproduced by state programs in which "men tend to make claims on the welfare state as workers while women make claims as members of families (as wives or mothers)" (Orloff 1996, 54).

Orloff (1996) also points out that a second perspective, the amelioration approach, sees the welfare state as remediating gender inequalities. Programs aimed at fighting poverty (increasingly) used by women, especially by single mothers, can help to attenuate gender-based economic inequalities. Clearly, the work of women's movements and organizations to secure benefits for women suggests that such policies are considered a legitimate avenue to address inequality, and this is particularly the case with programs aimed at ensuring benefits and job security for working mothers.

Yet it could also be argued that shifts to make family policies more gender neutral also aim to improve gender equality by challenging the gendered nature of care work and providing opportunities for fathers to fulfill parental duties (Dubeau, Devault, and Forget 2009). "Dual-caring" models are designed to promote paternal engagement in childrearing while also supporting female employment (Alwin et al. 1992).

The relationship between gender role ideologies and family policies within the welfare state, however, has received little scholarly attention. A wealth of literature shows that women tend to be more supportive of the welfare state in general. Gender gaps in support for social welfare programs are consistently noted across industrialized democracies (Gidengil 1995; Inglehart and Norris 2000; Kaufmann and Petrocik 1999). Although there are competing theories to explain this support, it has been partly linked to women's self-interest: women are disproportionately employed in, and benefit from, welfare state programs. The welfare state has important gendered dimensions in how it promotes (or discourages) women's engagement in the workforce (Koven and Michel 1993; Mink 1998; Orloff 1993). For example, many welfare state programs, such as childcare, have specific policy legacies tied to gendered discourses about motherhood and femininity (White 2002). In other words, there is good reason to view a host of welfare state policies as being targeted at women, and this perception might well influence citizens' levels of support.

As we outlined in the previous section, it is precisely the perceived tension between motherhood and work that underpins more traditional gender ideologies. Parental leave policies in particular address this tension, yet we know almost nothing about how gender ideologies influence support for this policy. On the one hand, such policies are (at least historically) tied specifically to women's roles as mothers, and those holding more traditional attitudes might support some policies because they promote women leaving the workforce (at least temporarily) to fulfill this role. On the other hand, such policies are necessarily tied to women as workers (and indeed employment is a requirement for access to such benefits), so the effect of gender role ideology might be muted. Furthermore, as parental leave policies increasingly promote leave by fathers, thus breaking down the traditional gender divide in care work, we might expect that those holding more traditional gender role ideologies would be less supportive of leave policies, at least when applied to male recipients.[3]

In the remainder of this chapter, we provide an overview of the levels and sources of more traditional attitudes toward motherhood and work, and then we examine in detail how such attitudes are related to support for parental leave policy.

Data and Methods

The data used for this analysis are drawn from the survey Race, Gender, and the Welfare State administered in July 2012 with online panels in the United States, Canada, and the United Kingdom ($N = 1{,}200$ per country). Each survey was fielded by YouGov-PMX, which uses a matching methodology for delivering online samples that mirror target populations on key demographics (for details on the sampling procedures and composition of the YouGov online panels, see Rivers and Bailey 2009; Vavreck and Iyengar 2011).

These three countries were selected because they are considered liberal welfare states. They also have the practical commonality of having large English-speaking populations, meaning that the survey instrument can be conducted in the same language in each country, minimizing the risk of differences caused by survey instrument translation. That said, in Canada the survey was conducted in both English and French to ensure representativeness as well as to allow us to examine important intra-country variation in policy attitudes within that context.

Our primary variable of interest is traditional gender role ideology, which we measure using a four-item scale.[4] The additive scale runs from 0 to 1 and has high internal reliability (Cronbach's alpha = .82).[5] Higher scores represent more conservative attitudes toward gender roles. The four items are drawn from classic gender ideology questions related to women's roles in the home and as mothers, in contrast to the paid workforce. Response categories are a four-point agree-disagree scale, recoded to vary from 0 to 1. The items include the following.

1. A woman's place is in the home, not in the office or shop.
2. A mother who carries out her full family responsibilities doesn't have time for outside employment.
3. The employment of mothers leads to more juvenile delinquency.
4. Women are much happier if they stay at home and take care of their children.

In the first step of the analysis, we examine the distribution and correlates of traditional gender role ideology. This analysis focuses primarily on gender and situational differences. In the second step, we examine how traditional gender role ideology relates to support for parental leave policies and whether it disproportionately influences support for gender-typical (married, female) versus gender-atypical (single female, married and unmarried male) parental leave takers. In this analysis, we are able to distinguish between the two constituent categories of motherhood (women, parent) to examine how more conservative gender role attitudes influence support for "parents" of each gender as well as embed motherhood within the institution (marriage) with which it tends to be associated.

Our measure of support for parental leave is based upon survey responses to experimental vignettes that describe the personal situation of a potential leave taker and the amount of leave to which she or he is entitled in each country. It then asks the respondent to assess how much he or she thinks the recipient should receive (from nothing to twice the actual level of benefits). The vignettes experimentally vary the gender and marital status of the recipient.[6] The dependent variable is the amount attributed to the fictional leave taker, centred on current levels and converted to US dollars based upon purchasing power parity (PPP). Further details on the vignette can be found in the appendix.

Results

Table 12.1 provides the mean responses to the individual gender role questions as well as the aggregate gender role ideology scale. Across all three countries, and across each item, the general tendency is for respondents to

TABLE 12.1

Traditional gender role ideology in Canada, the United Kingdom, and the United States

	Canada	United Kingdom	United States
A woman's place is in the home, not in the office or shop.	0.21	0.22	0.22
A mother who carries out her full family responsibilities doesn't have time for outside employment.	0.41[UK, US]	0.43[US, CAD]	0.36[UK, CAD]
The employment of mothers leads to more juvenile delinquency.	0.33	0.36	0.35
Women are much happier if they stay at home and take care of their children.	0.39	0.41[US]	0.37[UK]
Gender role ideology (total)	0.33[UK]	0.35[US, CAD]	0.33[UK]

Note: Superscript indicates pairs that are significantly different (minimum $p < .10$ level).
Source: Race, Gender, and Support for the Welfare State Survey.

disagree with more traditional conceptions of gender roles. Distributions across the countries are relatively similar, though UK respondents appear to be slightly more conservative on two of the four items, especially compared with US respondents. In general, though, the three publics appear largely to reject the view that a woman's employment is detrimental to her perceived duty in the home, as expected from past research showing a general trend toward more liberal gender role attitudes.

Although overall levels reflect more liberal views, there is clearly variation among respondents. Table 12.2 provides a breakdown of the principal demographic factors associated with gender role attitudes. We expect being a woman, having a university education, holding employment, being a minority, and being younger to be associated with more liberal gender role attitudes, whereas those who are married, have children, and are older are expected to hold more conservative views. We also include an attitudinal control: namely, the respondents' attitude toward government intervention, which we use as a proxy for more conservative political attitudes (particularly related to redistribution). We expect those with more conservative political attitudes to hold more conservative gender role attitudes as well.

The results in Table 12.2 are largely in line with expectations. The most consistent effects come from gender, employment, and education. In the full

TABLE 12.2
Determinants of traditional gender role ideology in Canada, the United Kingdom, and the United States

	All countries		Canada		United Kingdom		United States	
Female	−0.046	(.01)***	−0.047	(.01)***	−0.053	(.01)***	−0.041	(.01)***
Married	0.025	(.01)***	0.036	(.02)**	−0.001	(.01)	0.035	(.02)**
Kids	0.037	(.01)***	0.021	(.02)	0.043	(.02)***	0.038	(.02)**
Employment	−0.058	(.01)***	−0.048	(.02)***	−0.062	(.01)***	−0.053	(.02)***
University	−0.067	(.01)***	−0.074	(.02)***	−0.064	(.02)***	−0.072	(.02)***
White	−0.006	(.01)	−0.063	(.02)***	−0.026	(.03)	0.024	(.02)
Under 30	−0.013	(.01)	−0.021	(.02)	−0.042	(.02)**	0.007	(.02)
Over 55	−0.031	(.01)***	−0.037	(.02)**	0.001	(.02)	−0.046	(.02)***
Government intervention	−0.098	(.01)***	−0.015	(.03)	−0.017	(.03)	−0.166	(.02)***
Country								
United Kingdom	0.014	(.01)						
United States	−0.032	(.01)***						
Constant	0.450	(.02)***	0.451	(.03)***	0.441	(.03)***	0.420	(.03)***
R^2	0.07		0.05		0.07		0.12	
N	3,450		1,166		1,127		1,157	

* $p < .10$; ** $p < .05$; *** $p < .01$. Columns include coefficients for an OLS regression, with standard errors in parentheses.

Source: Race, Gender, and Support for the Welfare State Survey.

model, as well as in the model for each country, these factors have a consistent and significantly negative effect on conservative gender role ideology. Although the differences are not enormous (in the range of .04 to .07 on a 0–1 scale), they are in the expected direction. Marital status and children tend to relate to more conservative attitudes, though both effects are not always significant in the country models and are about half the size of the effect of gender, employment, and education. Age is also related to more conservative gender role attitudes, with those over 55 being more conservative across three of the four models. Note that, somewhat surprisingly, this effect does not appear in the British model, and in fact there is evidence that those under 30 were more inclined toward conservative gender role responses. This suggests that, at least in the British context, the underlying cohort replacement that has led to a liberalization of gender role attitudes might have come to an end, though further research is needed to explain the slightly more conservative gender role ideas among those under 30 in the United Kingdom.

Political ideology is also a long-standing correlate of gender role ideology, yet this effect seems to be largely confined to the US context, where attitudes toward government intervention are the strongest predictor by far of gender role attitudes. Moving from the most conservative position to the most liberal position on the scale results in an estimated shift of 16 points on the gender role ideology scale. Yet we do not find the same effect in Canada or the United Kingdom, where there is no evidence of an association between positions on political ideology and positions on gender ideology. This might be a result of the distribution on this scale in these contexts. The mean response on the government intervention scale in the United States is .44, suggesting an overall tendency toward more conservative responses, and a closer look at the distribution shows a large percentage of respondents clustered at the two extremes, suggesting rather polarized views.[7] In Canada and the United Kingdom, the mean response is approximately .63, suggesting a tendency toward more liberal political attitudes toward state intervention and a more normal distribution compared to the United States. The strong effect of political ideology in the United States might stem partly from the presumably more intense (and potentially more coherent) ideological positions of those on the conservative end of the spectrum.

One of the important correlates in the literature not included in Table 12.2 is religiosity. Unfortunately, religious variables were not included in the survey Race, Gender, and Support for the Welfare State. However, the US data included additional profile data available from the survey firm about religious attendance.[8] When this variable is included in the model, it proves to be a powerful predictor of gender role attitudes. The difference between those who never attend religious services compared with those who attend such services more than once a week is .12 ($p < .01$) and increases the predictive power of the model by about a third (model not shown). Its inclusion does not have any meaningful impact on the other variables in the model.

In sum, then, our analysis of attitudes toward women's roles as both mothers and workers suggests relatively liberal attitudes across all three countries under consideration here. Furthermore, we largely found the expected relationship at the individual level between salient demographic and attitudinal factors and gender role attitudes. The question now is whether such attitudes have concrete implications for support for public policies aimed at addressing family/work conflicts.

Our approach to answering this question is to examine whether citizens are more or less generous toward parental leave takers based upon their gender role attitudes as well as the gender stereotypicality of leave takers. Gender norms related to childrearing continue to have two specific and interrelated components in contemporary Western democracies: the gender of the primary caregiver as well as her status within the family unit. Women in married relationships with men tend to be viewed as the cultural norm for primary caregivers despite the liberalization of attitudes on these dimensions.

Table 12.3 indicates the direct effects of gender role ideologies on the generosity of respondents toward parental leave as well as the direct effects of the experimental treatment that manipulates the gender and marital status of leave takers. The literature provides mixed expectations for the impacts of gender role ideologies on support for parental leave. On the one hand, they can reinforce women's roles as mothers since women are the primary users of parental leave policies; on the other, they can support women's entry into and retention in the workforce.

Our analysis suggests that those who hold more conservative gender role attitudes tend to be less generous toward leave takers, at least in the US and UK contexts. The results in Table 12.3 suggest that those who hold more conservative gender role attitudes (highest tercile of the scale) report giving the fictional recipient about $68 (in the United Kingdom) and $124 (in the United States) less (calculated based upon PPP). This is after controlling not only for the characteristics of these leave takers but also for the more general ideological orientation of the respondent toward government

TABLE 12.3
Support for parental leave by gender ideology and gender typicality of leave takers in Canada, the United Kingdom, and the United States

		All countries	Canada	United Kingdom	United States
Gender role ideology (terciles)	Mid	−24.2 (23.2)	45.5 (48.1)	−40.4 (16.2)**	−50.6 (46.9)
	High	−50.1 (22.6)**	55.5 (46.7)	−68.1 (16.0)***	−124.1 (45.7)***
Leave-taker characteristics	Female	175.9 (18.5)***	209.0 (38.6)***	101.5 (13.0)***	207.7 (36.8)***
	Married	71.4 (18.5)***	80.1 (38.6)**	28.2 (13.0)**	119.6 (36.9)***
Respondent characteristics	Female	19.3 (19.1)	40.5 (40.1)	2.7 (13.4)	15.1 (37.9)
	Married	25.4 (21.2)	23.8 (45.5)	2.1 (14.6)	47.9 (41.5)
	Children	24.8 (22.0)	46.1 (45.5)	49.2 (15.7)***	2.1 (43.5)
	Employment	13.2 (20.6)	−8.6 (42.8)	8.0 (14.6)	43.9 (41.8)
	University	36.2 (20.9)*	51.7 (41.7)	22.2 (15.6)	41.2 (42.4)
	White	−57.1 (26.6)**	15.7 (56.9)	−41.9 (26.4)	−70.8 (43.8)
	Under 30	38.9 (27.6)	−10.5 (55.5)	89.8 (19.4)***	69.4 (57.7)
	Over 55	−118.8 (22.8)***	−200.2 (50.2)***	−75.3 (16.5)***	−85.2 (42.8)**
	Government intervention	514.6 (31.5)***	434.0 (75.4)***	243.6 (25.5)***	658.6 (53.0)***
Country	United Kingdom	−191.1 (22.8)***			
	United States	−140.2 (24.0)***			
Constant		−309.8 (48.0)***	−377.8 (97.0)***	−285.5 (37.3)***	−543.0 (80.1)***
R^2		0.18	0.09	0.22	0.23
N		3,005	2,013	985	997

* $p < .10$; ** $p < .05$; *** $p < .01$. Columns include coefficients for an OLS regression, with standard errors in parentheses.

Source: Race, Gender, and Support for the Welfare State Survey.

intervention in the economy. No similar effect is apparent in Canada, where the overall model tends to be weaker in predicting parental leave support.

When it comes to the stereotypicality of the leave taker, we find strong evidence that typicality affects support levels more generally, across all three countries, even after controlling for attitudes toward gender roles. The direct effect of the gender of the leave taker is by far the strongest, with women on average receiving about $175 more in benefits than men. The marital status of the leave taker is also important, though, with married leave takers receiving about $70 more than single parents. Although one might think that single parents are particularly in need of state support, our respondents were more likely in general to enforce expectations for the family compositions of leave takers. Thus, regardless of people's expressed attitudes toward work and gender roles, there seems to be a general tendency to enforce gender norms in terms of who benefits from family leave policies.

In a final analysis, we examine whether gender role attitudes accentuate this enforcement of gender norms in parenting by repeating the analysis in Table 12.3 but allowing our attitudinal measure to interact with the two leave-taker characteristics. Rather than presenting the full model here, we show the effect of three-way interaction for the full sample (Figure 12.1) and in each of the three countries (Figure 12.2). Our expectation, based upon the previous analysis, is that those who endorse more conservative gender norms will be particularly likely to make distinctions across the stereotypicality of leave takers, with married women receiving the highest levels of support and single men receiving the lowest levels of support. The results in Figure 12.1 reflect, in part, this expectation. Although the ordering across leave takers is consistent with expectations (primarily with respect to gender) across all levels of gender role ideology, the spread is greatest among those with the highest levels of conservative gender role attitudes. However, the differences across leave-taker characteristics are largely insignificant, with the exception of single male recipients, who receive significantly less among those with high levels of traditional gender role attitudes. Married women, on average, received about $55 more than current levels, whereas single men were given almost $275 less, for a difference of about $330 (PPP). In contrast, among those at lower levels on the traditional gender role ideology scale, the difference between married women and single men is over $100 less. The primary reason is that traditional gender ideology leads people to be less generous toward gender-atypical leave takers (whereas there is little difference in amounts attributed to female leave takers, regardless of respondents' attitudes toward gender roles).

FIGURE 12.1
Traditional gender role ideology, gender typicality of leave takers, and support for parental leave, all countries

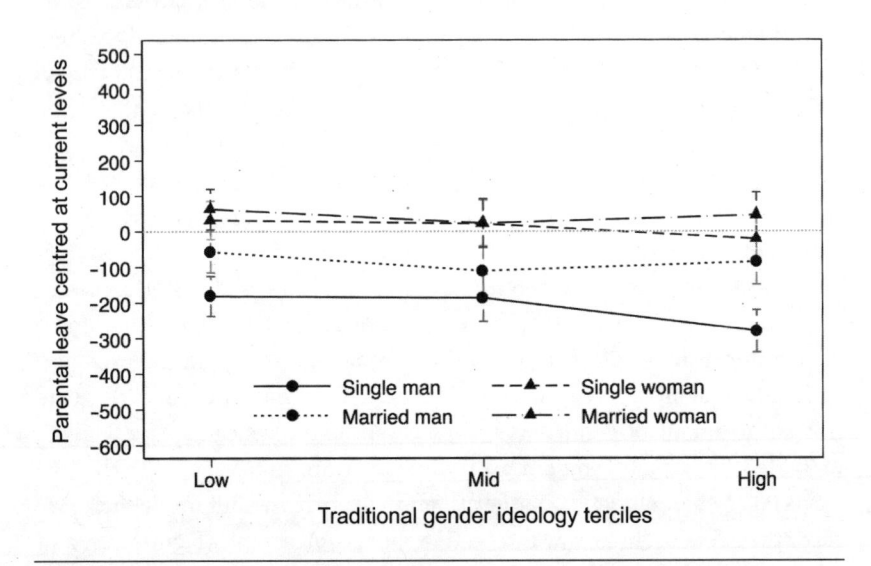

This general pattern can be observed across countries as well. In every case in Figure 12.2, the amounts given for parental leave vary more among those with more conservative attitudes toward gender roles, and as we observed in Figure 12.1 this is particularly the result for support given to single fathers, except in the Canadian case, in which married men seemed to receive a boost among those with more conservative gender ideologies.

Conclusion

This chapter has considered the sources of more traditional attitudes toward women in the workplace as well as how these more general attitudes influence support for family-friendly leave policies. As we have argued here, the tension between motherhood and work underpins what we call traditional gender role ideologies. The establishment of welfare programs, which include parental leave policies, addresses those tensions. However, the relationship

FIGURE 12.2 (facing page ▶)
Traditional gender role ideology, gender typicality of leave takers, and support for parental leave, by country

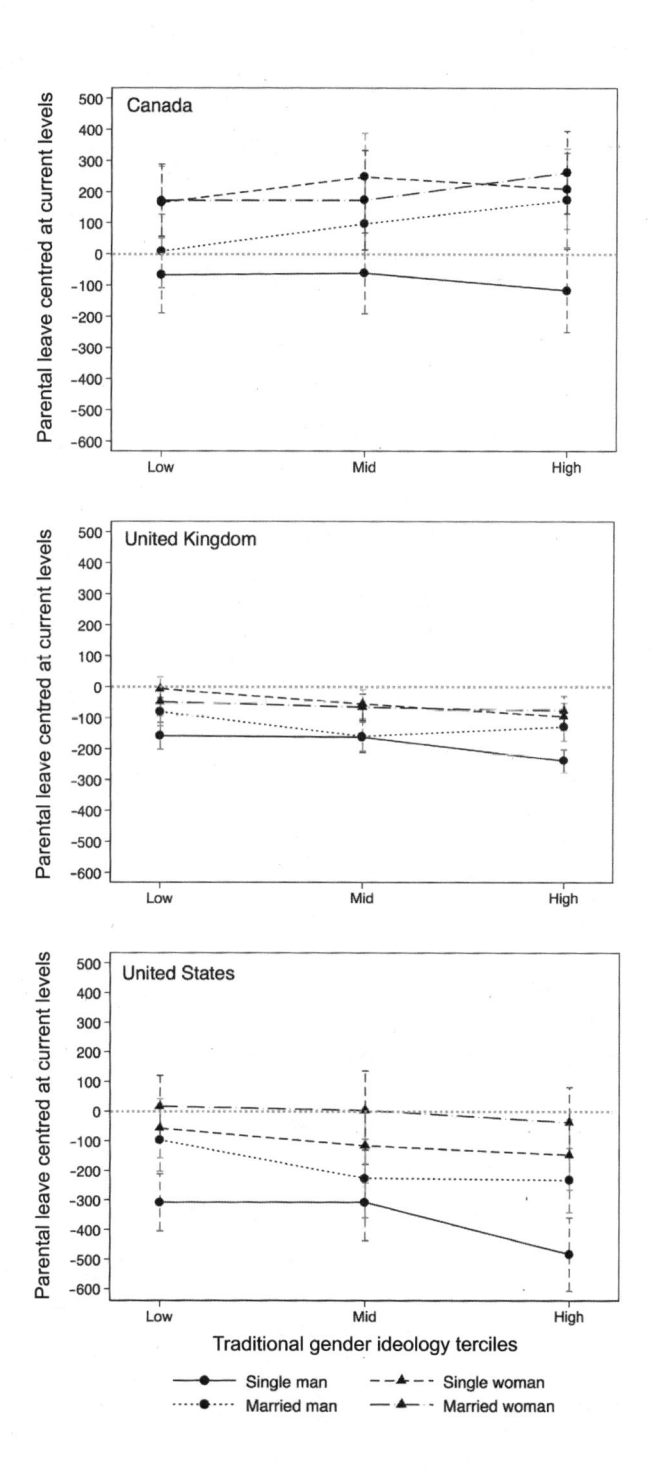

Attitudes toward Work, Motherhood, and Parental Leave

between conservative attitudes toward motherhood and work, on the one hand, and policies that make it easier to reconcile the two, on the other, is unclear. We have tested this tension in this chapter by examining how traditional gender role ideologies influence support for parental leave of various types of leave takers – from the stereotypical married woman to the least stereotypical single father.

Our findings suggest that those who hold the most traditional gender role ideologies – such as those who believe that motherhood and work are incompatible – are the least likely to support more generous parental leave. Furthermore, our results suggest that those who hold more conservative attitudes are also the most likely to enforce gender norms for taking parental leave or to enforce the gendered aspect of parenting fundamental to modern conceptions of motherhood. Not only are those with more traditional gender norms less generous overall, but also they tend to be particularly punitive to non-stereotypical leave takers.

These findings are particularly interesting because we show that, though women are more likely to reject traditional gender roles, having children and being married tend to increase (or are at least correlated with) such beliefs (see also Goodyear-Grant and Bittner, this volume). In other words, those who reflect the stereotypical category of married mothers are also more likely to endorse traditional gender ideologies. The same people are less willing, then, to support policies that extend welfare benefits to the non-gender-stereotypical parent. From a policy perspective, we thus expect that the extension of benefits to fathers will meet resistance in part because (married) mothers believe in the gendered division of parenthood. This is in keeping with the ideas associated with some forms of conservative activism (see Schreiber, this volume).

Our findings also point to some interesting cross-national variations in these trends. Although we cannot fully address the sources of these cross-national variations with the data available here, this is an interesting avenue for future research to examine how welfare state policies themselves can shape values among the population about work and motherhood. Do long-standing generous leave policies allow citizens to see how work and motherhood can be successfully reconciled? A broader sample that includes a wider range of welfare-state regimes would allow for a more serious test of this hypothesis.

Appendix

Vignette for Male Recipient (Canadian Version)

X is 32 years old, and he is [married/single]. He has been working full time for the past two years. He works for a small business designing websites, and he makes about $2,400 a month. Recently, X's [wife/ex-girlfriend] found out that she is pregnant. The baby's mother works part time in construction.

X would like to apply for parental leave benefits to be able to take time off work after the birth of his baby. The average benefit in this situation is about $1,300 per month for up to eight months.

Vignette for Female Recipient (Canadian Version)

X is 32 years old, and she is [married/single]. She has been working full time for the past two years. She works for a small business designing websites, and she makes about $2,400 a month. Recently, X found out that she is pregnant. The baby's father works part time in construction.

X would like to apply for parental leave benefits to be able to take time off work after the birth of her baby. The average benefit in this situation is about $1,300 per month for up to eight months.

Dependent Variable

How much, if any, do you think X should be entitled to receive per month from parental leave benefits? (The response scale runs from $0 to $2,600, and respondents are able to move it in $10 increments.)

Country Variations

Vignettes were nearly identical across the countries. The only difference was that the level of "average benefits" in the United Kingdom was set at £700 to reflect the benefit level there. In the United States, since there is no current federal paid maternal, paternal, or parental leave benefits program open to employed people, we set the benefit level at $1,200 for a "new program in her state" based upon an average of the approximate levels available under temporary disability benefits in the five states that offer such programs. The name of the recipient varied by gender and ethnicity.

Notes

1 Along with gender, there is an important literature on how gender norms are produced and reproduced within the family context, partly through sex-typing household work (e.g., Blair 1992; Cunningham 2001).
2 Although note that Jonathan Vespa (2009) shows that these effects are not uniform for all groups. More traditional views are related to marriage for whites (but not blacks), whereas parenthood tends to have a conservative effect only for married parents.
3 Although work in this area is limited, previous studies have shown that men with more egalitarian views on gender roles are more likely to use parental leave benefits (Duvander 2014) and that both men and women holding more traditional views tend to report more work/family conflict (Davis 2011).
4 The items are drawn from the gender role ideology battery of the National Longitudinal Survey of Youth but are commonly found in a number of other surveys. See Davis and Greenstein (2009) for a review.
5 Note that the internal validity is equally high in each case country.
6 The racial background of the recipient was also varied but is not included in the analysis here.
7 In the United States, over 30 percent of respondents have a 0 on the government intervention scale, compared with only 2–3 percent of respondents in the other two countries. The highest two response categories across all three countries contain about 25 percent of respondents.
8 The question is based upon the standard Pew Research Center wording about how often one attends a religious service, and responses vary from never to more than once a week. For the analysis reported here, we have standardized the six responses to vary from 0 to 1, with higher scores representing more frequent attendance.

References

Alwin, Duane F., Michael Braun, and Jacqueline Scott. 1992. "The Separation of Work and the Family: Attitudes towards Women's Labour-Force Participation in Germany, Great Britain, and the United States." *European Sociological Review* 8 (1): 13–37.

Banaszak, Lee Ann. 2006. "The Gendering State and Citizens' Attitudes toward Women's Roles: State Policy, Employment, and Religion in Germany." *Politics and Gender* 2 (1): 29–55. http://dx.doi.org/10.1017/S1743923X06060016.

Blair, Sampson Lee. 1992. "The Sex-Typing of Children's Household Labor: Parental Influence on Daughters' and Sons' Housework." *Youth and Society* 24 (2): 178–203. http://dx.doi.org/10.1177/0044118X92024002004.

Blee, Kathleen M., and Ann R. Tickamyer. 1995. "Racial Differences in Men's Attitudes about Women's Gender Roles." *Journal of Marriage and the Family* 57 (1): 21–30. http://dx.doi.org/10.2307/353813.

Bock, Gisela, and Pat Thane, eds. 1991. *Maternity and Gender Policies: Women and the Rise of the European Welfare State*. London: Routledge.

Bolzendahl, Catherine, and Daniel Myers. 2004. "Feminist Attitudes and Support for Gender Equality: Opinion Change in Women and Men: 1974–1998." *Social Forces* 83 (2): 759–89. http://dx.doi.org/10.1353/sof.2005.0005.

Brooks, Clem, and Catherine Bolzendahl. 2004. "The Transformation of U.S. Gender Role Attitudes: Cohort Replacement, Social Structural Change, and Ideological Leaning." *Social Science Research* 33 (1): 106–33. http://dx.doi.org/10.1016/S0049-089X(03)00041-3.

Campbell, Karen, and Peter Marsden. 2012. "Gender Role Attitudes since 1972: Are Southerners Distinctive?" In *Social Trends in American Life: Findings from the General Social Survey*, edited by Peter Marsden, 84–116. Princeton, NJ: Princeton University Press. http://dx.doi.org/10.1515/9781400845569-006.

Chauffaut, Delphine, and Pauline Domingo. 2011. "Évolutions familiales et stabilité des opinions concernant les enfants." *Politiques sociales et familiales* 103 (1): 47–63. http://dx.doi.org/10.3406/caf.2011.2577.

Ciabattari, Teresa. 2001. "Changes in Men's Conservative Gender Ideologies: Cohort and Period Influences." *Gender and Society* 15 (4): 574–91. http://dx.doi.org/10.1177/089124301015004005.

Cotter, David, Joan M. Hermsen, and Reeve Vanneman. 2011. "The End of the Gender Revolution? Gender Role Attitudes from 1977 to 2008." *American Journal of Sociology* 117 (1): 259–89. http://dx.doi.org/10.1086/658853.

Cunningham, Mick. 2001. "The Influence of Parental Attitudes and Behaviors on Children's Attitudes toward Gender and Household Labor in Early Adulthood." *Journal of Marriage and the Family* 63 (1): 111–22. http://dx.doi.org/10.1111/j.1741-3737.2001.00111.x.

—. 2008. "Changing Attitudes toward the Male Breadwinner, Female Homemaker Family Model: Influences of Women's Employment and Education over the Lifecourse." *Social Forces* 87 (1): 299–323. http://dx.doi.org/10.1353/sof.0.0097.

Davis, Shannon N. 2011. "Support, Demands, and Gender Ideology: Exploring Work-Family Facilitation and Work-Family Conflict among Older Workers." *Marriage and Family Review* 47 (6): 363–82. http://dx.doi.org/10.1080/01494929.2011.594216.

Davis, Shannon N., and Theodore N. Greenstein. 2004. "Cross-National Variations in the Division of Household Labor." *Journal of Marriage and Family* 66 (5): 1260–71.

—. 2009. "Gender Ideology: Components, Predictors, and Consequences." *Annual Review of Sociology* 35 (1): 87–105. http://dx.doi.org/10.1146/annurev-soc-070308-115920.

de Beauvoir, Simone. 1949. *The Second Sex*. New York: Bantam.

Dubeau, Diane, Annie Devault, and Gilles Forget. 2009. *La paternité au XXIe siècle*. Québec: Presses de l'Université Laval.

Dugger, Karen. 1988. "Social Location and Gender-Role Attitudes: A Comparison of Black and White Women." *Gender and Society* 2 (4): 425–48. http://dx.doi.org/10.1177/089124388002004002.

Duvander, Ann-Zofie. 2014. "How Long Should Parental Leave Be? Attitudes to Gender Equality, Family, and Work as Determinants of Women's and Men's Parental Leave in Sweden." *Journal of Family Issues* 35 (7): 909–26. http://dx.doi.org/10.1177/0192513X14522242.

Fortin, Nicole M. 2005. "Gender Role Attitudes and the Labour-Market Outcomes of Women across OECD Countries." *Oxford Review of Economic Policy* 21 (3): 416–38. http://dx.doi.org/10.1093/oxrep/gri024.

Fraser, Nancy. 1989. *Unruly Practices: Power, Discourses, and Gender in Contemporary Social Theory.* Minneapolis: University of Minnesota Press.

–. 1994. "After the Family Wage: Gender Equity and the Welfare State." *Political Theory* 22 (4): 591–618. http://dx.doi.org/10.1177/0090591794022004003.

Fusulier, Bernard, David Laloy, and Émilie Sanchez. 2007. "L'acceptabilité sociale de l'usage de congés légaux pour raisons parentales: Le point de vue des cadres d'une grande entreprise." *Recherches sociologiques et anthropologiques* 38 (2): 83–103. http://dx.doi.org/10.4000/rsa.464.

Gidengil, Elisabeth. 1995. "Economic Man – Social Woman? The Case of the Gender Gap in Support for the Canada–United States Free Trade Agreement." *Comparative Political Studies* 28 (3): 384–408.

Gilligan, Carol. 1982. *In a Different Voice: Psychological Theory and Women's Development.* Cambridge, MA: Harvard University Press.

Gordon, Linda, ed. 2012. *Women, the State, and Welfare.* Madison: University of Wisconsin Press.

Guo, Jing, and Neil Gilbert. 2012. "Public Attitudes and Gender Policy Regimes: Coherence and Stability in Hard Times." *Journal of Sociology and Social Welfare* 39 (2): 163–81.

Harris, Richard J., and Juanita M. Firestone. 1998. "Changes in Predictors of Gender Role Ideologies among Women: A Multivariate Analysis." *Sex Roles* 38 (3–4): 239–52. http://dx.doi.org/10.1023/A:1018785100469.

Inglehart, Ronald, and Pippa Norris. 2000. "The Developmental Theory of the Gender Gap: Women's and Men's Voting Behavior in Global Perspective." *International Political Science Review* 21 (4): 441–63.

Katz-Wise, Sabra L., Heather A. Priess, and Janet S. Hyde. 2010. "Gender-Role Attitudes and Behavior across the Transition to Parenthood." *Developmental Psychology* 46 (1): 18–28. http://dx.doi.org/10.1037/a0017820.

Kaufmann, Karen M., and John R. Petrocik. 1999. "The Changing Politics of American Men: Understanding the Sources of the Gender Gap." *American Journal of Political Science* 43 (3): 864–87.

Knudsen, Knud, and Kari Waerness. 2001. "National Context, Individual Characteristics, and Attitudes on Mothers' Employment: A Comparative Analysis of Great Britain, Sweden, and Norway." *Acta Sociologica* 44 (1): 67–79. http://dx.doi.org/10.1177/000169930104400106.

Koivunen, Julie M., Jeanne W. Rothaupt, and Susan M. Wolfgram. 2009. "Gender Dynamics and Role Adjustment during the Transition to Parenthood: Current Perspectives." *Family Journal* 17 (4): 323–28. http://dx.doi.org/10.1177/1066480709347360.

Koven, Seth, and Michel Sonya, eds. 1993. *Mothers of a New World: Maternalist Politics and the Origins of Welfare States.* New York: Routledge.

Kulik, Liat. 2011. "Developments in Spousal Power Relations: Are We Moving toward Equality?" *Marriage and Family Review* 47 (7): 419–35. http://dx.doi.org/10.1080/01494929.2011.619297.

Mink, Gwendolyn. 1998. *Welfare's End.* Ithaca, NY: Cornell University Press.

Orloff, Ann S. 1993. "Gender and the Social Rights of Citizenship: The Comparative Analysis of Gender Relations and Welfare States." *American Sociological Review* 58 (3): 303–28.

—. 1996. "Gender in the Welfare State." *Annual Review of Sociology* 22 (1): 51–78.

Rivers, Douglas, and Delia Bailey. 2009. "Inference from Matched Samples in the 2008 US National Elections." In *Proceedings of the Joint Statistical Meetings*, 627–39. Alexandria, VA: American Statistical Association.

Schnittker, Jason, Jeremy Freese, and Brian Powell. 2003. "Who Are Feminists and What Do They Believe? The Role of Generations." *American Sociological Review* 68 (4): 607–22. http://dx.doi.org/10.2307/1519741.

Scott, Jacqueline, Duane F. Alwin, and Michael Braun. 1996. "Generational Changes in Gender-Role Attitudes: Britain in a Cross-National Perspective." *Sociology* 30 (3): 471–92. http://dx.doi.org/10.1177/0038038596030003004.

Scott, Joan. 1986. "Gender: A Useful Category for Historical Analysis." *American Historical Review* 91 (5): 1053–75.

Sunström, Eva. 1999. "Should Mothers Work? Age and Attitudes in Germany, Italy, and Sweden." *International Journal of Social Welfare* 8 (3): 193–205. http://dx.doi.org/10.1111/1468-2397.00083.

Valentova, Marie. 2013. "Age and Sex Differences in Gender Role Attitudes in Luxembourg between 1999 and 2008." *Work, Employment, and Society* 27 (4): 639–57. http://dx.doi.org/10.1177/0950017013481638.

Vavreck, Lynn, and Shanto Iyengar. 2011. "The Future of Political Communication Research: Online Panels and Experimentation." In *Oxford Handbook of American Public Opinion and the Media*, edited by R. Shapiro and L. Jacobs, 156–68. Oxford: Oxford University Press.

Vespa, Jonathan. 2009. "Gender Ideology Construction: A Life Course and Intersectional Approach." *Gender and Society* 23 (3): 363–87. http://dx.doi.org/10.1177/0891243209337507.

Wells, Michael B., and Anna Sarkadi. 2012. "Do Father-Friendly Policies Promote Father-Friendly Child-Rearing Practices? A Review of Swedish Parental Leave and Child Health Centers." *Journal of Child and Family Studies* 21 (1): 25–31. http://dx.doi.org/10.1007/s10826-011-9487-7.

White, Linda A. 2002. "Ideas and the Welfare State Explaining Child Care Policy Development in Canada and the United States." *Comparative Political Studies* 35 (6): 713–43.

Winter, Nicholas. 2008. *Dangerous Frames: How Ideas about Race and Gender Shape Public Opinion*. Chicago: University of Chicago Press. http://dx.doi.org/10.7208/chicago/9780226902388.001.0001.

13

Motherhood's Role in Shaping Political and Civic Participation

BRENDA O'NEILL and ELISABETH GIDENGIL

Parenthood is a potentially critical aspect of adult political socialization, yet there has been surprisingly little attention paid to the effect of parental status on women's political and civic activities (see also Langner, Greenlee, and Deason, this volume). Much of what we know is based upon data collected more than two decades ago. It is clearly time to revisit motherhood's role in shaping women's participation in political and civic life. This chapter addresses two fundamental questions about the impact of parental status on women's political and civic activities. Does being a mother influence women's participation in political and civic life? And, if so, to what extent is this dependent on the ages of children in the home?

Our focus is on motherhood, by which we mean the state experienced by women who have given birth to and/or are raising a child. Motherhood brings with it a number of responsibilities that necessarily affect the resources available – notably time – for devoting to political activities. In addition, modern society continues to hold a set of expectations regarding what constitutes good mothering, expectations that might well influence whether, how, and when women will engage in political activities. Good mothers are expected to place the needs of their children above all.

Women's role as mothers has undergone significant changes since the early 1960s, when the impact of motherhood on political and civic activities first attracted the attention of political scientists. Women are having fewer children nowadays, and they are waiting longer to have their first child.

Women's fertility rate has declined dramatically from almost 4.0 children per woman in 1960 to only 1.68 per woman in 2008 (Statistics Canada 2012, 350). Women in the 1960s typically gave birth to their first child at age 23.5 years, compared with 28.1 years in 2008 (36). Women are delaying having their first child for a number of reasons, including a focus on higher education and workforce participation as well as the trend toward delaying marriage and common-law relationships. At the same time, women with children are more likely than they once were to return to work when their children are younger. In 1976, only 27.6 percent of women with children under three years of age were employed; by 2009, that figure had more than doubled to 64.4 percent. There have also been major changes in conceptions of gender roles. Women are much less willing now than they were in the 1970s to believe that women's place is in the home, and they are more willing to believe that women with children have a right to work (Everitt 1998). There are good reasons, then, to expect that the effect of motherhood on women's political and civic participation has changed in recent years.

We focus here on women because the effects of parental status appear to be gendered. Becoming a parent seems to be more consequential for women than men, both in the home and in the political realm. Kei M. Nomaguchi and Melissa A. Milkie (2003) report that parenthood has relatively little effect on married men. Married women with children, however, do more housework and experience more marital conflict than married women without children. Turning to politics, Marieke Voorpostel and Hilde Coffé (2012) find that women's interest in participating in some political and civic activities increases when their children start school; there is no comparable effect for men.

Our findings suggest that the presence of children in the home, regardless of their number, has little impact on women's political and civic participation. What does seem to matter are the ages of the children. Women with children between five and 12 are more likely to engage in some activities than other women. There is also some evidence that single mothers and mothers in the workforce exhibit a political and civic participation profile that differs somewhat from that of other mothers.

The Impact of Motherhood on Women's Political and Civic Participation

Early studies concluded that motherhood tended to depress women's political participation (see, e.g., Almond and Verba 1963; Campbell et al. 1960; but see Welch 1977). Gabriel A. Almond and Sidney Verba (1963) offered two reasons why motherhood would impede women's involvement in political activities: time constraints and social isolation (see also Campbell et al. 1960).

The time constraints hypothesis suggests that the demands of caring for their homes and families leave mothers with less time than fathers to undertake political activities, especially the more time-consuming ones. This explanation seems to be plausible when we consider how much time women devote to caring for their children. According to the 2010 General Social Survey, women spent an average of 50.1 hours per week on unpaid childcare in the home, more than twice the average for men (Statistics Canada 2012, 42). The average rises to 67.5 hours for women with preschool-age children in the home but drops to 37.7 hours for women with children between the ages of five and 14. Women with preschool children in the home also spend an average of about 20 hours per week on domestic work, compared with 17 hours for women with children between the ages of five and 14 and just over nine hours for women with children between the ages of 15 and 18 in the home (Statistics Canada 2012, 44). If the time constraints explanation holds, then we should expect mothers with preschoolers at home to be the least involved in political and civic activities. We should also expect women's political and civic involvement to increase progressively with the ages of their children (see Beckwith 1986).

Karen Beckwith (1986) found that the presence of preschool-age children was associated with lower voter turnout and less electoral activism among women. Apart from this, though, the presence of children in the home made little difference to women's electoral participation. Having four or more children did have a dampening effect, but this was true for men and women alike. Nancy E. McGlen (1980) found some support for the time constraints hypothesis, but it was limited to college-educated mothers, among whom the most time-consuming political activities were most affected by motherhood. However, Nancy Burns, Kay Lehman Schlozman, and Sidney Verba (2001) report that even married women who have children and work full-time typically have only a little less free time than their husbands, who tend to spend more time at work. In any case, they found little connection between the amount of leisure time and political activity. Accordingly, they reject the time constraints hypothesis: "Try as we might, we could find no evidence that an absence of free time handicaps women as citizens. Not only are women, on average, not disadvantaged when it comes to leisure, but neither the amount of free time nor the number of hours devoted to household tasks and child care has an independent impact on political activity" (333).

The social isolation explanation assumes that caring for young children entails spending more time in the home, which limits women's opportunities to develop social networks that encourage political discussion and spur people to become politically active (Kay et al. 1987; Lynn and Flora 1974). Child-centred caring networks, in particular, have been identified as having a dampening effect on the development of a political identity among women (Lynn and Flora 1973).

The work of Allison Munch, J. Miller McPherson, and Lynn Smith-Lovin (1997) offers some confirmation of the social isolation hypothesis. They note that "intensive childrearing during the preschool years" (518) negatively affects women's social networks by limiting the time available for contact with others. However, more recent work contradicts these findings. Nomaguchi and Milkie (2003) suggest that parenthood brings an increase in social integration with friends, neighbours, and relatives. Although not the focus of their investigation, the implication is that motherhood can have a positive impact on political and civic activities.

Another common explanation suggests that the socialization of women into motherhood roles negatively impacts their political participation given the importance assigned to these roles (Jennings 1983; Lynn and Flora 1974; Ruddick 1989). According to the role constraints hypothesis, social expectations keep mothers focused on the needs of their families rather than issues and activities that seem to be of little direct consequence for the family unit. This is the phenomenon that Virginia Sapiro (1983, 73) refers to as privatization, "the domination of women's lives by private roles, concerns, and values. Even where women are involved in public life, as in the workforce and politics, their activities and concerns are expected to be imbued with the private significance of being a woman."

McGlen (1980) found evidence of conflict between political and motherhood roles, but this conflict was confined to the college educated. According to work by Nancy Romer (1990), this conflict begins early; young female political activists were found to be more likely than their male counterparts to express doubts that they would be able to continue their political activities once they were married, had children, and were employed full time.

Finally, studies have highlighted the importance of civic skills and other participatory resources. These studies suggest that the influence of motherhood is indirect through its impact on decisions about whether and how much to work for pay, especially for mothers of preschoolers (Burns et al. 2001). In one of the first studies to identify a link between paid employment and political participation, Kristi Andersen (1975) noted that women's increasing entry into the workforce between 1952 and 1972 had led to a closing of the gender gap in rates of political participation. The workplace can be an important source of skills, such as organizing meetings and making public presentations, that facilitate involvement in political and civic activities. In line with this explanation, Burns and her colleagues (2001) find that mothers who are working full time and have school-age children tend to be more politically active than their stay-at-home counterparts. However, the dynamics of work and family are constantly changing, so findings now more than two decades old might not be indicative of current realities. For example, the average amount of time spent per day on paid work has become more similar for men and women since the 1980s (Marshall 2011; the study was limited to comparisons of 20 to 29 year olds). At the same time, research in the United States reveals that the amount of time that parents spend on childcare has increased dramatically since the mid-1990s. This suggests that it is time to revisit the effects of the so-called double day of full-time employment and domestic responsibilities (Ramey and Ramey 2009). See Giles (this volume) for a discussion of the impact of the double day on women's political knowledge.

Although much of the literature has focused on reasons why motherhood might curtail women's political and civic activities, there has been some recognition that motherhood might stimulate greater activity. Parenthood brings a number of significant and immediate changes to one's life, including new responsibilities, greater time commitments, and psychological demands (Nomaguchi and Milkie 2003). Socialization theory suggests that such changes would alter the salience of certain issues, especially those connected to the well-being of one's family. As Burns and her colleagues (2001, 317) argue, "having children might reinforce a sense of social responsibility or create a stake in a broader set of political issues – for example, child care or school funding – and generate political participation, especially among those with school-age children."

An early exploration of this possibility found that parenthood was associated with much greater involvement in school politics, especially among mothers (Jennings 1979). More recently, Marieke Voorpostel and Hilde Coffé (2012) found that having children turn five and start school has a significant effect on women's political and civic participation. Women whose youngest child turned five between different waves of their panel study were twice as likely to undertake voluntary work as women who remained childless. They were also somewhat more likely to consider political activism in the future. However, this transition had no effect on their probability of voting. The importance of having children start school is highlighted by the fact that there were no comparable effects associated with children entering or leaving the household.

The Impact of Motherhood on Political and Civic Activities

To explore the impact of motherhood on women's political and civic participation, we combine data from two surveys: the 2007 Women's Political Participation Survey and the 2010 Quebec Women's Political Participation Survey (see Appendix A). We examine four types of political and civic activity: voting in elections, signing petitions, engaging in political consumerism, and volunteering for a group or organization. We can expect the effect of parenthood to vary with the type of participation in question (Voorpostel and Coffé 2012).

Voting is the most fundamental form of political participation in an electoral democracy. Turning out to vote seems to require little time or effort, but for a woman with young children it can mean having to find a babysitter so that she can go to the polling place or finding the time to learn about the issues and where the parties stand on them. Having young children can impede women's turning out to vote. Our survey asked women whether they had voted in the most recent federal, provincial, and municipal elections. More than half of the women in the sample (58 percent) reported that they had voted at all three levels, 17 percent had voted in two of the three elections, and 9 percent had voted in one election; 16 percent had not voted in any of the elections. Our voting measure is based upon whether women had reported voting in at least one of the three elections.

There are many ways of participating politically beyond voting in elections. Women can make their views known, for example, by signing petitions. The women in our surveys were asked whether they had signed a petition in the past 12 months. Thirty-two percent of the women had done so. This serves as our measure of petition signing.

Whether aimed at a government or corporation, political consumerism is a profoundly political act. When people buy – or refuse to buy – a product as a way of pressuring powerful political actors to change their behaviour, they are using the market as "an arena for politics" (Stolle and Micheletti 2013, 28; see also Micheletti and Stolle, this volume). Accordingly, our survey asked women whether they had bought and/or boycotted any product for political, ethical, or environmental reasons in the past 12 months. Our political consumerism measure distinguishes between women who had engaged in either form of political consumerism and those who had not.

TABLE 13.1
Motherhood and political and civic activities

	Children at home ($N = 1,079$)	No children at home ($N = 1,405$)
Voted	83.0***	86.8
Signed a petition	35.1***	30.0
Engaged in political consumerism	50.6**	46.4
Volunteered time	59.8****	53.2

Note: The table entries indicate the percentage of women who have undertaken each activity.
** $p < .05$; *** $p < .01$; **** $p < .001$. (Significance levels are based upon the chi-square test.)

Forty-eight percent of the women reported that they had buycotted and/or boycotted a product.

Finally, we look at a form of activity at the local level. Volunteering makes much heavier demands on a mother's time than signing a petition or boycotting a product. Our measure is based upon a question asking women whether they had volunteered for a group or organization other than a political party in the past 12 months. Fifty-six percent of the women reported that they had done so.

Our interest, of course, is in how parental status affects women's political and civic activities. Table 13.1 compares women who have one or more children at home with those who have none. There is only one activity – voting – for which having children at home appears to have a negative effect. The gap in voter turnout, however, is small, and when it comes to signing petitions, engaging in political consumerism, and volunteering for a group or organization women with children at home are significantly more likely to engage in these activities. Note, though, that the differences are modest.

The number of children living at home does not seem to matter much. Women with three or more children at home are almost as likely to vote (83.4 percent) as those with only one child at home (84.3 percent). Similarly, they are almost as likely to sign petitions (35.8 percent) as the latter (36.5 percent), and they are actually more likely to engage in political consumerism (50.9 percent) and to volunteer for a group or organization (61.0 percent) compared with 47.5 percent and 49.8 percent for women with one child at home.

Bigger differences emerge when we look at the ages of the children (Table 13.2), suggesting that it is not the mere presence of children in the home that matters but their ages, at least for some political and civic activities. Women

TABLE 13.2
Ages of children and political and civic activities

	Preschoolers at home (N = 297)	Children ages five to 12 at home (N = 317)	Older children at home (N = 465)	No children at home (N = 1,405)
Voted	74.6****	81.6	89.2	86.8
Signed a petition	35.9	40.1**	31.2	30.0
Engaged in political consumerism	46.7	54.8*	50.1	46.4
Volunteered time	52.0	73.4****	55.5	53.2

Note: The table entries indicate the percentage of women who have undertaken each activity. Tests of statistical significance indicate whether women in the named category are significantly different from those with no children at home.
* $p < .10$; ** $p < .05$; *** $p < .01$; **** $p < .001$. (Significance levels are based upon Table 13.B1 in Appendix B.)

with at least one preschooler at home are significantly less likely to vote than other women. Meanwhile, women who have children aged between five and 12, but no younger children, are the most likely to sign petitions, engage in political consumerism, and volunteer for a group or organization. The difference is especially large in the case of voluntary activity at around 20 percentage points. This is consistent with the results obtained by M. Kent Jennings (1979) and is likely linked to the fact that women are often drawn into these activities when their children enrol in school. However, having children in elementary school appears to draw women into more than volunteering. With the exception of voting, political and civic activity appears to drop off when women have only older children. These women participate at much the same level as women with no children at home.

It is possible, though, that the differences that we have observed do not really reflect the impact of having children at home (see Burns et al. 2001; Wolfinger and Wolfinger 2008). For example, there are well-documented life cycle and generational differences in voter turnout (Blais, Gidengil, and Nevitte 2004): younger people are much less likely to vote in elections than older people. Voter turnout increases as people move into middle age and begins to drop off only among the elderly. Given that women with preschool-age children at home are likely younger, this might explain why they are less likely to vote than women with older children at home. In other words, it is not the fact of having young children that depresses their turnout but simply the fact that they tend to be younger. Similarly, women with school-age children might be more politically active because they are more likely to be working outside the home or because they are suddenly part of a new social network that centres on their children's school. Both expanded social networks and greater civic skills are positively associated with greater political and civic engagement (Burns et al. 2001).

To explore these possibilities, we estimated a series of regression models. In addition to parental status, age, and labour force participation, the models included controls for education, marital status, and attendance at a place of worship. These models enabled us to isolate the impact of having children at home, net of other factors that could be associated with both the presence of children and women's political and civic activities. The first models included only the parental status variables. Adding the other variables enabled us to see how much of the impact of parental status is explained by these social background characteristics. The full results for both sets of models are presented in Appendix B.

Like Nicholas H. Wolfinger and Raymond E. Wolfinger (2008), we find no evidence that having children at home reduces the likelihood of turning out to vote, once other social background characteristics are taken into account. When these characteristics are added to the models, having preschoolers at home ceases to have a significant impact on women's turning out to vote. On closer examination, the effect observed in Table 13.2 is almost entirely explained by the fact that women with preschool-age children at home tend to be younger. Age is by far the most important predictor of voting. Education and marital status also matter. The more educated women are, the more likely they are to vote. Being married or living common law with a partner also enhances the probability that a woman will vote. However, unlike age, neither factor explains away the empirical association between having preschool-age children at home and voting since women with very young children are more likely to be university graduates and less likely to be single.

The introduction of other social background characteristics completely fails to explain away the association between having children aged five to 12 at home and signing petitions. Younger women are more likely to sign petitions, as are women aged 55 and older. Women with less than a high school education are less likely to undertake this political activity; university graduates are significantly more likely to do so. Meanwhile, women who are not married or living with a partner are less likely to sign petitions. However, none of these factors can explain why women with elementary school–age children are more likely than other women to sign petitions.

This is not the case when we look at the association between having children in this age group at home and engaging in political consumerism. The introduction of other social background characteristics completely explains the association observed in Table 13.2. The vast majority (83 percent) of women with children aged five to 12 at home are aged between 35 and 54. This is the age group most likely to buy – or refuse to buy – products for ethical, environmental, or political reasons. Moreover, a high proportion (72 percent) of these women have completed some postsecondary education, also strongly associated with political consumerism.

Finally, the association between having children aged five to 12 at home and volunteering is only partially explained by other social background characteristics. As we saw in Table 13.2, the probability of volunteering for a group or organization is 20 points higher for women with children in this age group, compared with women who have no children at home. When other social background characteristics are taken into account, the gap shrinks to 13 points. In other words, about one-third of the gap can be explained by other factors. Once again the key factors are age and education. Older women are less likely to have school-age children and less likely to volunteer for a group or organization. The same is true for women with lower levels of education. However, even taking differences in age and education into account, a significant gap remains to be explained. Religious attendance has a significant impact on women's propensity to engage in voluntary activities (see O'Neill 2006, 2009), but women with children aged five to 12 at home do not attend a place of worship any more frequently than women with no children at home, so religious attendance does not help to explain why they are so much more likely to engage in voluntary activity than other women.

Taking all these results together, what is striking is how little difference motherhood and its associated responsibilities make to women's political and civic activities. Having preschoolers or teenagers at home makes little or no difference to women's propensity to vote, sign petitions, engage in political consumerism, or volunteer for a group or organization. These women are as likely to engage in these activities as women who have no children at home. The effects of motherhood are confined to women who have children aged five to 12 at home. These women are no more likely to vote or engage in political consumerism than other women, but they are significantly more likely to sign petitions and volunteer, even taking other social background characteristics into account.

The Impact of Marital Status

It is possible, though, that motherhood hampers the political and civic engagements of single mothers. With no one to share household chores, the demands on a single mother's time and energy are much heavier. Half of the mothers who were married or living with partners said that household chores were divided equally in their homes. Presumably, this arrangement leaves them with more time for political and civic activities than most single mothers enjoy. Moreover, as we have just seen, single women are less likely to vote and sign petitions. This might reflect the fact that single people tend to have smaller social networks (Erickson 2004), exposing them to fewer discussions about politics or invitations to sign petitions. Taken together, these considerations suggest that single mothers will be less likely to engage in political and civic activities than other mothers. To explore this possibility, we added interaction terms to the regression models (see Table 13.B3).

Contrary to expectations, single mothers of school-age children are actually more likely to vote than their married counterparts. The probability of voting is 4.1 points higher for single mothers of five to 12 year olds, and 3.8 points higher for single mothers of older children, compared with mothers who are married or living with partners and have children of the same age.

However, their probability of signing petitions is much lower: an estimated 15.9 points lower for single mothers of five to 12 year olds and 15.1 points lower for single mothers of older children. In the case of single mothers of five to 12 year olds, much of the difference stems from the fact that their married counterparts are so much more likely than other women to sign petitions. Even allowing for the impacts of other social background characteristics, married mothers of children in this age group have a 44.3 percent probability of signing a petition, compared with only 32.2 percent for married women with no children aged five to 12 at home. Being single has a more negative effect on mothers of older children. Their probability of signing a petition is only 22.2 percent, compared with 30.4 percent for single women who do not have older children at home.

Marital status has little or no effect on the propensity of mothers to engage in political consumerism, regardless of the ages of children in the home. Voluntary activity is a different matter. Single mothers of preschoolers are much less likely (32.1 percent) to volunteer for a group or organization than their counterparts who are married or living with partners (53.9 percent). Similarly, single mothers with older children at home are less likely (45.1 percent) to undertake voluntary activities than their married counterparts

(56.4 percent). However, whether they are single or not, mothers of children aged five to 12 are more likely to volunteer than other women.

The Impact of the Double Day

Working outside the home does not have a significant effect on women's political and civic activities (see Table 13.B2), though it might matter for women with children at home. Women who work full time spend an average of 49.8 hours per week caring for their children if they are part of a dual-earner couple and 50.8 hours if they are part of a single-earner couple (Statistics Canada 2012, 42). These hours are on top of the time spent on unpaid domestic work: 13.9 hours per week for women working full time who are part of a dual-earner couple and 15.2 hours per week for those who are part of a single-earner couple. Juggling these domestic responsibilities with the demands of a job can leave little time or energy for political and civic activities (see Giles, this volume; McGlen 1980). Adding interaction terms to the regression models once again enables us to see if this is so (see Table 13.B4).

The effects of working outside the home are limited to volunteering for a group or organization. However, the effects run directly contrary to the double day thesis. Mothers who have preschoolers and are not employed outside the home are much less likely (39.2 percent) to undertake a voluntary activity than their counterparts who are employed or self-employed (53.8 percent). The latter are almost as likely to volunteer as working women who do not have young children at home. A similar pattern holds for mothers who have teenagers at home. Among those working outside the home, 57.7 percent have volunteered for a group or organization, compared with only 44.5 percent of those who remain in the home. Mothers who work outside the home are as likely to volunteer as their counterparts who do not work a double day. These results might have interesting implications for other forms of civic participation, as noted by Hannagan and Larimer in this volume. Meanwhile, being employed or self-employed makes little difference to the propensity of mothers with children at home to vote, sign petitions, or engage in political consumerism.

Conclusion

Our goal in this chapter was to answer two questions. Does being a mother matter for women's political and civic participation? And, if so, to what extent is this dependent on the ages of any children in the home? The short answer to the first question is that being a mother does have an impact on women's political and civic activities (see also Langner, Greenlee, and Deason, this volume). Women who have at least one child in the home are more likely to sign petitions, engage in political consumerism, and volunteer for a group or organization. On the other hand, they are less likely to vote in elections. However, all of these effects are modest. The number of children in the home matters even less. More interesting differences emerge when we consider the second question. The short answer to this question is that the ages of children in the home do matter; more precisely, having children aged five to 12 matters.

Contrary to the time constraints hypothesis, women with young children at home are no less likely to participate in political and civic activities than women with teenaged children or women who have no children at home. The apparent difference in voter turnout is explained by the fact that these women tend to be younger. The only exception relates to single mothers, who are much less likely to volunteer for a group or organization if they have young children at home. Volunteering requires a bigger investment of time and energy than the political activities that we examined here, in line with the time constraints hypothesis. However, it seems that time constraints do not impede voluntary activity among women who are part of a couple.

The findings with respect to women who have children aged five to 12 at home are in striking contrast. Even allowing for the effects of other social background characteristics, these women are significantly more likely to sign petitions and to undertake voluntary work. These findings are consistent with those of Voorpostel and Coffé (2012). Moreover, they indicate that having school-age children not only influences involvement in school district politics (Jennings 1979) or anticipated political activism (Voorpostel and Coffé 2012) but also extends to actual political activity, at least in the form of petition signing. More consequentially, they strongly indicate that there is something distinctive about having children of elementary school age at home; no comparable effects are found for women who have teenaged children at home. Clearly, future studies need to try to understand what it is about having children in this age group that stimulates political and civic activities. One possible explanation is that having young children in school expands women's social networks.

The lack of significant associations between labour force participation and political and civic activities is surprising given the importance assigned to such associations in much of the literature (see Giles, this volume). To the extent that we did uncover effects, they ran completely counter to the double day thesis. Mothers of preschoolers are more likely to volunteer for a group or organization if they are working outside the home. The same is true of mothers with teenagers at home. This increased activity likely stems from the expanded social network and/or resource boost associated with participation in the labour force. At the least, it suggests that the time constraints associated with the double day are not so heavy as to keep working mothers from engaging in volunteer activities, to which they presumably assign high priority.

The good news to emerge from this chapter is that motherhood appears to make relatively little difference to women's political and civic activities. The only instances in which having children at home impedes political and civic participation involve single parents, but even here the news is by no means all bad. Overall, as also posited by Langner, Greenlee, and Deason in this volume, there is more evidence of motherhood boosting women's political and civic involvement than the reverse.

Some important questions remain. First, additional research is needed on the effects of pregnancy. Becoming pregnant typically brings women into greater contact with the health-care system and prompts concern about issues such as food and drug safety and can thus have politicizing effects. Second, more study is needed of the effects of teenage parenthood on political and civic activities. Julianna Pacheco and Eric Plutzer (2007), for instance, argue that early parenthood, particularly among whites in the United States, decreases voter turnout later in life given the increased likelihood of dropping out of high school. Third, future studies should focus on more time-intensive activities such as volunteering for a political party or candidate, activities that can pave the way for more elite-level participation. Findings for one political activity do not translate across other activities, so attention to a broad range of activities could offer additional insight into women's political and civic participation.

Appendix A: The Surveys

The 2007 Women's Political Participation Survey (WPPS) and the Quebec Women's Political Participation Survey (QWPPS) were both administered by telephone. Only female interviewers were employed to avoid sex-of-interviewer effects. The same questionnaire was used in both surveys. The WPPS was conducted in English, and the QWPPS was conducted in French.

The Institute for Social Research at York University (http://www.isr.yorku.ca) conducted the fieldwork for the WPPS. The survey was undertaken between July 18 and October 2, 2007. The response rate was 59 percent. In total, 1,264 telephone interviews averaging approximately 18 minutes in length were completed with a random sample of women 18 years of age and older in nine provinces (Quebec was excluded).

The fieldwork for the QWPPS was conducted by CROP (http://www.crop.ca). The survey was fielded between June 2 and July 3, 2010. The response rate was 34 percent. In total, 1,201 telephone interviews averaging approximately 23 minutes in length were completed with a random sample of women 18 years of age or older in Quebec.

The WPPS and QWPPS samples were combined and weighted to reflect national population figures. Assistance with the calculation of weights for the combined samples was provided by CROP. The questionnaires and technical information on the surveys are available from the authors on request.

The Social Sciences and Humanities Research Council (Grant #410-2003-1822), the Institute for Advanced Policy Research, a University Research Grants Committee (Calgary), and McGill University provided funding for the WPPS. The Social Science and Humanities Research Council (Grant #410-2009-0285) funded the QWPPS.

Appendix B: Regression Models

TABLE 13.B1
Motherhood and political and civic activities

	Voting	Signing petitions	Political consumerism	Volunteering
Has a child at home	−0.49 (.13)****	0.22 (.12)*	0.15 (.11)	0.26 (.11)**
Number of children	−0.14 −(.08)*	(0.09) (.06)	0.08 (.06)	0.19 (.06)****
Preschoolers	−0.79 −(.23)****	0.22 (.18)	−0.00 (.17)	−0.05 (.17)
Children aged five to 12	−0.34 −(.25)	0.43 (.17)**	0.31 (.17)*	0.89 (.19)****
Older children	0.22 (.27)	0.08 (.16)	0.13 (.16)	0.08 (.16)
Number of cases	2,310	2,349	2,346	2,379

Note: The column entries are logistic regression coefficients with robust standard errors shown in parentheses. The coefficients are derived from three separate models.
* $p < .10$; ** $p < .05$; *** $p < .01$; **** $p < .001$.

TABLE 13.B2
Impact of motherhood on women's political and civic activities

	Voting	Signing petitions	Political consumerism	Volunteering
NO CONTROLS				
Preschoolers	−0.79 (.23)****	0.22 (.18)	−0.00 (.17)	−0.05 (.17)
Children aged five to 12	−0.34 (.25)	0.43 (.17)**	0.31 (.17)*	0.89 (.19)****
Older children	0.22 (.27)	0.08 (.16)	0.13 (.16)	0.08 (.16)
WITH CONTROLS				
Preschoolers	−0.13 (.27)	0.08 (.21)	−0.33 (.21)	−0.31 (.21)
Children aged five to 12	−0.22 (.27)	0.43 (.20)**	0.00 (.20)	0.62 (.22)***
Older children	−0.04 (.28)	0.06 (.18)	−0.14 (.17)	−0.12 (.18)
Under 35 years of age	−1.08 (.23)****	0.29 (.18)*	−0.22 (.18)	−0.11 (.18)
55 years and older	1.76 (.31)****	0.39 (.17)**	−0.19 (.16)	−0.34 (.16)**
Less than high school	−0.56 (.31)*	−0.87 (.25)****	−0.41 (.22)*	−0.57 (.21)***
Some postsecondary	0.58 (.24)**	0.21 (.16)	0.59 (.16)****	0.53 (.16)****
University graduate	0.75 (.28)***	0.43 (.17)**	1.11 (.17)****	1.10 (.17)****
Paid labour force	0.04 (.24)	0.23 (.14)	0.22 (.14)	0.18 (.14)
Single	−0.53 (.20)***	−0.24 (.14)*	−0.19 (.13)	−0.00 (.14)
Religious attendance	0.04 (.07)	0.00 (.04)	−0.05 (.04)	0.30 (.04)****
Constant	1.53 (.31)****	−1.24 (.22)****	−0.40 (.20)	−0.61 (.21)***
Number of cases	2,310	2,349	2,346	2,379

Note: The column entries are logistic regression coefficients with robust standard errors shown in parentheses.
* $p < .10$; ** $p < .05$; *** $p < .01$; **** $p < .001$.

TABLE 13.B3
Motherhood, marital status, and women's political and civic activities

	Voting	Signing petitions	Political consumerism	Volunteering
Preschoolers	−0.26 (.31)	0.04 (.22)	−0.30 (.22)	−0.09 (.22)
Children aged five to 12	−0.50 (.31)	0.54 (.21)**	0.01) (.22)	0.73 (.24)***
Older children	−0.36 (.34)	0.20 (.20)	−0.08 (.20)	0.04 (.19)
Under 35 years of age	−1.04 (.23)****	0.26 (.18)	−0.22 (.18)	−0.14 (.18)
55 years and older	1.73 (.31)****	0.42 (.17)**	−0.18 (.16)	−0.32 (.16)**
Less than high school	−0.54 (.31)*	−0.88 (.26)****	−0.42 (.22)*	−0.59 (.21)***
Some postsecondary	0.61 (.24)**	0.21 (.16)	0.58 (.16)****	0.51 (.16)****
University graduate	0.76 (.28)***	0.45 (.17)***	1.10 (.17)****	1.07 (.17)****
Paid labour force	0.01 (.23)	0.25 (.14)*	0.23 (.14)*	0.19 (.14)
Single	−0.80 (.26)***	−0.14 (.16)	−0.15 (.16)	0.19 (.16)
Single*preschoolers	−0.03 (.63)	0.69 (.56)	−0.04 (.59)	−1.07 (.55)*
Single*ages five to 12	1.02 (.65)	−0.57 (.43)	0.07 (.47)	−0.36 (.49)
Single*older children	1.01 (.55)*	−0.64 (.42)	−0.27 (.37)	−0.54 (.40)
Religious attendance	0.05 (.07)	0.00 (.04)	−0.05 (.04)	0.30 (.04)****
Constant	1.68 (.33)****	−1.30 (.22)****	−0.42 (.20)**	−0.69 (.21)****
Number of cases	2,310	2,349	2,346	2,379

Note: The column entries are logistic regression coefficients with robust standard errors shown in parentheses.
* $p < .10$; ** $p < .05$; *** $p < .01$; **** $p < .001$.

TABLE 13.B4
Motherhood, labour force participation, and women's political and civic activities

	Voting	Signing petitions	Political consumerism	Volunteering
Preschoolers	−0.44 (.49)	0.22 (.42)	−0.02 (.39)	−0.70 (.40)*
Children aged five to 12	−0.43 (.57)	0.09 (.39)	−0.08 (.40)	0.28 (.36)
Older children	−0.36 (.61)	−0.11 (.36)	−0.41 (.33)	−0.46 (.32)
Under 35 years of age	−1.07 (.23)****	0.30 (.18)*	−0.21 (.18)	−0.10 (.18)
55 years and older	1.71 (.33)****	0.38 (.18)**	−0.18 (.16)	−0.38 (.16)**
Less than high school	−0.58 (.30)*	−0.90 (.26)****	−0.43 (.22)*	−0.60 (.21)***
Some postsecondary	0.57 (.24)**	0.20 (.16)	0.58 (.16)****	0.52 (.16)****
University graduate	0.73 (.28)***	0.42 (.17)**	1.10 (.17)****	1.09 (.17)****
Paid labour force	−0.14 (.32)	0.16 (.18)	0.19 (.17)	−0.02 (.16)
Labour force* preschoolers	0.42 (.54)	−0.17 (.45)	−0.19 (.13)	0.54 (.44)
Labour force* ages five to 12	0.27 (.63)	0.44 (.42)	−0.37 (.42)	0.47 (.42)
Labour force* older children	0.43 (.69)	0.24 (.41)	0.13 (.44)	0.50 (.38)
Single	−0.54 (.19)***	−0.25 (.14)*	−0.20 (.13)	−0.01 (.14)
Religious attendance	0.04 (.07)	0.00 (.04)	−0.05 (.04)	0.30 (.04)****
Constant	1.68 (.34)****	−1.18 (.24)****	−0.38 (.22)*	−0.48 (.22)**
Number of cases	2,310	2,349	2,346	2,379

Note: The column entries are logistic regression coefficients with robust standard errors shown in parentheses.
* $p < .10$; ** $p < .05$; *** $p < .01$; **** $p < .001$.

Note

We wish to thank Julie Croskill for her research assistance and the multiple graduate students at the University of Calgary and McGill University who assisted with the WPPS and QWPPS survey projects.

References

Almond, Gabriel A., and Sidney Verba. 1963. *The Civic Culture: Political Attitudes and Democracy in Five Nations*. Princeton, NJ: Princeton University Press. http://dx.doi.org/10.1515/9781400874569.

Andersen, Kristi. 1975. "Working Women and Political Participation, 1952–1972." *American Journal of Political Science* 19 (3): 439–53. http://dx.doi.org/10.2307/2110538.

Beckwith, Karen. 1986. *American Women and Political Participation: The Impacts of Work, Generations, and Feminism.* New York: Greenwood Press.

Blais, André, Elisabeth Gidengil, and Neil Nevitte. 2004. "Where Does Turnout Decline Come From?" *European Journal of Political Research* 43 (2): 221–36. http://dx.doi.org/10.1111/j.1475-6765.2004.00152.x.

Burns, Nancy, Kay Lehman Schlozman, and Sidney Verba. 2001. *The Private Roots of Public Action: Gender, Equality, and Political Participation.* Cambridge, MA: Harvard University Press.

Campbell, Angus, Philip E. Converse, Warren E. Miller, and Donald E. Stokes. 1960. *The American Voter.* New York: John Wiley and Sons.

Erickson, Bonnie H. 2004. "The Distribution of Gendered Social Capital in Canada." In *Creation and Returns of Social Capital: A New Research Program,* edited by Henk Flap and Beate Völker, 27–50. London: Routledge.

Everitt, Joanna. 1998. "Public Opinion and Social Movements: The Women's Movement and the Gender Gap in Canada." *Canadian Journal of Political Science* 31 (4): 743–65. http://dx.doi.org/10.1017/S0008423900009628.

Jennings, M. Kent. 1979. "Another Look at Politics and the Life Cycle." *American Journal of Political Science* 24 (4): 755–71. http://dx.doi.org/10.2307/2110805.

–. 1983. "Gender Roles and Inequalities in Political Participation: Results from an Eight Nation Study." *Western Political Quarterly* 36 (3): 364–85. http://dx.doi.org/10.2307/448396.

Kay, Barry J., Ronald D. Lambert, Steven D. Brown, and James E. Curtis. 1987. "Gender and Political Activity in Canada, 1965–1984." *Canadian Journal of Political Science* 20 (4): 851–63. http://dx.doi.org/10.1017/S0008423900050435.

Lynn, Naomi B., and Cornelia Flora. 1973. "Motherhood and Political Participation: The Changing Sense of Self." *Journal of Political and Military Sociology* 1 (1): 91–103.

–. 1974. "The Implications of Motherhood for Political Participation." In *Pronatalism: The Myth of Mom and Apple Pie,* edited by E. Peck and J. Senderowitz, 227–48. New York: Crowell.

Marshall, Katherine. 2011. *Generational Change in Paid and Unpaid Work.* 11–008–X. Ottawa: Government of Canada. http://www.statcan.gc.ca/pub/11-008-x/2011002/article/11520-eng.htm.

McGlen, Nancy E. 1980. "The Impact of Parenthood on Political Participation." *Western Political Quarterly* 33 (3): 297–313. http://dx.doi.org/10.2307/447257.

Munch, Allison, J. Miller McPherson, and Lynn Smith-Lovin. 1997. "Gender, Children, and Social Contact: The Effects of Childrearing for Men and Women." *American Sociological Review* 62 (4): 509–20. http://dx.doi.org/10.2307/2657423.

Nomaguchi, Kei M., and Melissa A. Milkie. 2003. "Costs and Rewards of Children: The Effects of Becoming a Parent on Adults' Lives." *Journal of Marriage and the Family* 65 (2): 356–74. http://dx.doi.org/10.1111/j.1741-3737.2003.00356.x.

O'Neill, Brenda. 2006. "Canadian Women's Religious Volunteerism: Compassion, Connections, and Comparisons." In *Gender and Social Capital,* edited by Brenda O'Neill and Elisabeth Gidengil, 185–211. New York: Routledge.

—. 2009. "Religion, Political Participation, and Civic Engagement: Women's Experiences." In *Faith in the Public Realm: Controversies, Policies, and Practices*, edited by Adam Dinham, Robert Furbey, and Vivien Lowndes, 123–42. Bristol: Policy Press. http://dx.doi.org/10.1332/policypress/9781847420305.003.0007.

Pacheco, Julianna, and Eric Plutzer. 2007. "Stay in School, Don't Get Pregnant: The Impact of Teen Life Transitions on Voter Turnout." *American Politics Research* 35 (1): 32–35. http://dx.doi.org/10.1177/1532673X06292817.

Ramey, Garey, and Valerie A. Ramey. 2009. "The Rug Rat Race." NBER Working Paper 15284. Cambridge, MA: National Bureau of Economic Research. http://www.nber.org/papers/w15284.

Romer, Nancy. 1990. "Is Political Activism Still a Masculine Endeavor?" *Psychology of Women Quarterly* 14 (2): 229–43. http://dx.doi.org/10.1111/j.1471-6402.1990.tb00016.x.

Ruddick, Sara. 1989. *Maternal Thinking: Towards a Politics of Peace*. Boston: Beacon Press.

Sapiro, Virginia. 1983. *The Political Integration of Women: Roles, Socialization, and Politics*. Urbana: University of Illinois Press.

Statistics Canada. 2012. *Women in Canada: A Gender-Based Statistical Report*. 6th ed. Ottawa: Minister of Industry. http://www.statcan.gc.ca/pub/89-503-x/89-503-x2010001-eng.htm.

Stolle, Dietlind, and Michele Micheletti. 2013. *Political Consumerism: Global Responsibility in Action*. New York: Cambridge University Press. http://dx.doi.org/10.1017/CBO9780511844553.

Voorpostel, Marieke, and Hilde Coffé. 2012. "Transitions in Partnership and Parental Status, Gender, and Political and Civic Participation." *European Sociological Review* 28 (1): 28–42. http://dx.doi.org/10.1093/esr/jcq046.

Welch, Susan. 1977. "Women as Political Animals? A Test of Some Explanations for Male-Female Political Participation Differences." *American Journal of Political Science* 21 (4): 711–30. http://dx.doi.org/10.2307/2110733.

Wolfinger, Nicholas H., and Raymond E. Wolfinger. 2008. "Family Structure and Voter Turnout." *Social Forces* 86 (4): 1513–28. http://dx.doi.org/10.1353/sof.0.0031.

14

Toying Around with the Future

Sustainability within Families

MICHELE MICHELETTI and DIETLIND STOLLE

Sustainability involves balancing economic, environmental, and social equity development to ensure that future generations can achieve wellbeing (so-called intergenerational justice) (Howarth 1992; UNCED 1987). Governments in different countries as well as a wide variety of NGOs stress in their sustainability campaigns that families as collectivities and family members individually have important roles to play in helping states reach their policy goals for sustainability (OECD 2009; Wier et al. 2005). Considerable academic and even public effort has been put into studying and changing household practices when it comes to transportation, water and energy use, and waste generation. However, much less public attention has been paid to the role of toys in sustainability policy and practice: that is, how toys are chosen and how they can become more integral parts of sustainable development. Instead, the focus has been on toy safety and the role of toys in socializing and educating children to become good adults. Indeed, little public concern has been raised about the environmental and social equity consequences of toy production and consumption or the impact of toy preference and selection on reproducing or challenging traditional gender roles. Although such lacunae in public thinking and action are surprising, the question arises about whether being a parent, especially a mother, is linked in any way to considerations of both environmental sustainability and social equity and how such considerations come into play in family life.

This chapter uses unique Swedish surveys and focus group data to investigate whether and how parents are mobilized into the sustainability discourse through their relationships with toys for their children. Do adults in general and parents in particular have sufficient resources and information to make sustainable choices when buying toys? Which aspects of sustainability, if any, do they think about when shopping for toys? Are mothers more engaged than fathers on these matters? How does the age of a child matter to this kind of engagement? These questions address how parents, especially mothers, might become engaged in a form of political action to address political and environmental problems in ways that do not involve traditional political actors (see more in Stolle and Micheletti 2013; see also Langner, Greenlee, and Deason; Goodyear-Grant and Bittner; O'Neill and Gidengil, all in this volume).

Family Life and Sustainable Development
The combined impact of household behaviour and habits is seen as "an important contributor to a number of environmental problems" and a wide variety of social equity concerns associated with less sustainable consumption (Zacarias-Farah and Geyer-Allély 2003, 819; see also OECD 2009). Different national and international institutions ponder which incentives and public policies might trigger new views about household consumption and therefore how families can develop greener lifestyles by changing their transportation, energy, and water use, by choosing foods less reliant on chemical use, and generally by consuming less. Sustainability is also a focus for other large family consumer items, such as clothing and textiles, electronics, and toys (Georg 1999; Spangenberg and Lorek 2002). Such examples demonstrate the salience of household consumption as part of a large political project for realizing sustainable development.

Thus, the question about how sustainability is transmitted within families through consumption is important for both everyday political life and for policy-implementing targets and strategies. Parents are seen as key (political) socializing agents who can instill sustainable values and practices in their children through their daily practices. The role model effects provided by parents, as well as family conversations about issues such as sustainability, can be carried by children into their adult lives (Heft and Chawla 2006), thus contributing to efforts to promote intergenerational justice. Parental values, standards, and practices concerning sustainability are assumed to be one important gauge of the actions of future generations (Grønhøj and Thøgersen 2009). Political socialization research confirms these insights

(Jennings and Niemi 1968), for the transmission of values and behaviours is found to be stronger when parents are politically engaged and frequently discuss politics with their children (Jennings et al. 2009; McIntosh, Hart, and Youniss 2007). However, recent socialization studies suggest that political socialization is not unidirectional, because children might also shape the behaviours and values of their parents (McDevitt and Chaffee 2002). Therefore, academic attention has begun to focus more on what happens to adults politically and in other ways when they become parents.

Several studies indicate that people change when they become parents. A number of scholars show that women's participation in the workforce (England 2005; Population and Development Review 2006), time spent in volunteer work (Kovács 2007), and interactions with relatives and friends (Bost et al. 2002) are affected when they become mothers. Studies even find that parents are politically more active than non-parents (Voorpostel and Coffé 2012). See also Goodyear-Grant and Bittner, and O'Neill and Gidengil (this volume), for additional discussion on the impact of parenthood on attitudes and behaviours. However, though there is some evidence that women and men change politically when they have children, there is little research on how this political awareness and "sensibilization" process takes place and how it might both directly and indirectly affect their values, attitudes, and actions and whether it does so differently for mothers and fathers. Less is known about how this process occurs in the context of sustainable consumption, and even less is known about how toy consumption and use play roles in transmitting sustainability-related values.

Do Toys Trigger Sustainable Thoughts and Actions?

Toys are a major family consumer item since they are central as birthday and holiday gifts. Sometimes they are used to appease children or even to relieve guilt about how mothers and fathers conduct parenthood (Elsäkerhetsverket 2012; Handell 2012; Schor 2005; Statista 2013). The toy industry is more than a US$80 billion industry and growing globally (Euromonitor 2014; IPEN and GRID-Arendal 2013, 3). Thus, toys appear to comprise a key product to study how ideas, attitudes, and actions on sustainability are prioritized by and transmitted through families.

Toys are also one of the most dangerous consumer products. The European Union's rapid alert system on marketing and products posing serious risks to consumer health and safety reports that toys and clothing are the two most dangerous products in the European Union (European Voice 2014). Several toy brands have been found to be non-compliant with legal regulations and bans, such as powerful small (and easily swallowed) magnets in toys for infants and flammability problems with doll wigs. Governments use their regulatory powers at times to recall dangerous toys (US PIRG 2013), but some consumers purchase and use them anyway (ABC News 2013; Kemikalieinspektionen 2008).[1] A policy institute working with the United Nations declares that "we are unwittingly placing the future of our children in jeopardy" (IPEN and GRID-Arendal 2013, 3) when consumers make less informed toy purchases and governments lag on controlling toy manufacturing more strictly. Therefore, public bodies, NGOs, and other institutions plead with consumers to take responsibility for their families and "be vigilant" (Swedish Consumer Agency n.d., 3; see also European Voice 2014; US PIRG 2013), since "toxic or dangerous toys can still be found on store shelves despite tough new federal regulations" (Healthy Day 2013).

Toys are important in politics in other ways because there are other identified problems with them beyond children's physical safety because of risks with injury, choking, and strangulation. Scholars, public bodies, and NGOs warn about their environmental hazards because of the use of chemical-based plastics in toys and their packaging (Mulder 1998). Others worry about toy overconsumption, the throw-away character of toys, and their short lifespans, all of which contribute to the general environmental problem of household waste (Becker, Edwards, and Massey 2010; Cooper 2005; Langer 2005; Pugh 2009; Schor 2005). Human rights are also an issue since toy workers, particularly in China (the largest manufacturer of toys under licence from large Western and Japanese conglomerates), have been denied benefits, rights, and safety measures and are forced to work long hours (Inter Press News Agency 2002; People's Daily Online 2008). Their situation is compared with that of workers in the "sweatshop" global garment industry (Fairtrade Center 2011; SACOM 2011). Toys are also part of larger international political issues, such as the boycott of goods manufactured in the Israeli settlement territory.[2]

Attention is also drawn to the increased prevalence of gender-typed toys. Here educators, social movements, and others argue that the "pinkification" of girlhood through the selling of pink princesses and other toys "prescribe[s] heavily stereotyped and limiting roles to young girls" (Pink Stinks, http://pinkstinks.org.uk; see also Blakemore and Centers 2005). Similarly, playing with weapons, action hero figures, and other "boys' toys" contributes to the development of aggressive behaviour in boys (Benenson, Carder, and Geib-Cole 2008). Some activism against toy brands has commenced on the basis of these different political reasons. In sum, it is reasonable to assume that toys play a role in transmitting different values associated with sustainability, since that discourse strongly emphasizes values and behaviours for the future of the planet (Baretto et al. 2013) and intergenerational justice.

Does this awareness of the "politics of toys" matter to parents and their choices of toys in any direct or indirect way? Some help in answering this question and understanding the importance of being a parent for socialization into sustainability can be found in scholarship that attempts to establish the factors that predict which toys parents select for their children. A survey of 230 parents of children from two to five years old reported that the most important criteria for toy choice for both mothers and fathers were safety, entertainment value, and educational quality (Christensen and Stockdale 1991, 29). Other research investigates how concerns about gender equality within sustainability (part of social equity) influence parents' choices of toys for their children.[3] For example, clear differences are found in how toys gender-typed for girls or boys are rated, though toy selection for infants and toddlers does not follow this pattern (Campenni 1999; Wood, Desmarais, and Gugula 2002; see also Nelson 2005). This might reflect the less gendered nature of toys for very young children. These studies claim that the toys that parents select for boys and girls can "serve as primary influences in the learning of 'appropriate' gender roles" (Wood et al. 2002, 39).

The question that emerges from past research is whether conscious and inadvertent choices of toys affect how families learn about various matters of sustainability. In general, this question is understudied in social science. The few scholars studying the environmental and equity aspects of sustainability more directly tend toward an advocacy or policy approach. They focus on how toys can be intentionally designed to instill sustainable values (Baretto et al. 2013) or on the use of toy libraries to encourage collaborative toy ownership and less consumption (Hughes 2013). Others argue that the most significant problem with toys is that they unintentionally reproduce certain political values because "they are embedded within a Western social logic that nurtures materialistic consumerism ... perpetuated into adult life" (Wain 2014, 2). The rare studies on the corporate social responsibility of the toy industry find that it generally lags behind others also catering to families (Sethi et al. 2011) in addressing issues of sustainability and that toy suppliers are not completely following corporate codes of conduct (Egels-Zandén 2007).

In sum, previous research touches on the relationship between family life and sustainability but rarely on how toy consumption can reflect sustainable actions. Required are more investigations of the contemplations, choices, and trade-offs made at individual and family levels on various values involved in toy consumption – the prices and physical qualities of toys (the economic side of toys), their chemical and other elements (the environmental side of toys), and how toy consumption affects toy workers, gender roles, and other societally oriented values (the social equity side of toys).

This chapter helps to fill this knowledge gap. We compare parents with non-parents since previous research suggests that being a parent might lead to new worries, thoughts, attitudes, and actions regarding household consumption. There are several reasons for this link. Concerns about family safety might draw parents into thinking more about and engaging in the sustainable consumption discourse than non-parents. Furthermore, it is likely that the dominant presence of toys in the lives of parents with babies and small children (NPD Group 2014), compared with parents with older children, makes them more concerned about working conditions in the toy industry, materials used in toys, and whether they are generally "good" for their children and society in general. In addition, parents' networks with other parents or conversations with their older children can help to socialize them into sustainable habits. Alternatively, they might be too busy with the practicalities of parenthood to care about the sustainability politics of toys. The questions are how much information parents have about the identified problems of toy production and consumption and whether they use the available information to become sustainable consumers. Finally, as suggested in research on political consumerism, we study the intersection between gender and parenthood by examining more carefully whether mothers and fathers engage differently in these matters. These questions structure the empirical analysis reported in the remaining part of this chapter.

Sweden is a good case for studying how parents view the importance of toys for sustainable development. Swedish parents show relatively high awareness of toy sustainability. First, Sweden has a well-developed, family-oriented welfare state with policies such as a tax-free child allowance and a gender equality bonus for parents who split the parental leave evenly.[4] Second, Sweden is one of the most equal societies, and gender equality is an important element in most policy sectors, including the labour market, education, and childcare. Third, Swedes show high awareness of and concern about the environmental, political, and ethical qualities of consumer goods. As a result, Swedish consumers are continually found to practise political consumerism, a special form of market-based political activism, more than consumers in other comparable countries (Stolle and Micheletti

2013, 96–97). Thus, if parents link toys to sustainable and political consumerism, evidence of this should be found in Sweden.

Methods

Three different data sources helped us to study the awareness of Swedish parents regarding matters of toy sustainability as well as their actual practices. First, the Consumption and Societal Issues Survey (conducted in 2009) with 1,053 nationally representative respondents included various attitudinal and behavioural dimensions of sustainable consumption.[5] Second, another survey (conducted in 2012–13) of 1,002 parents throughout Sweden tapped directly into attitudes toward the role of toys in sustainable development. Third, four focus groups of parents with young children (up to 10 years of age) were conducted in 2013 as a follow-up to the second survey. These focus groups were stratified on gender and education since these factors play significant explanatory roles in research on political consumerism.[6]

Swedish Families and Sustainable Consumption

The surveys included various questions on motivations for decisions on buying toys, ranging from safety concerns, to the educational value of toys, to concerns about sustainability, including environmental considerations, corporate social responsibility, as well as concerns about the gender neutrality of toys. Table 14.1 includes all of these motivations in the first column and shows that most parents in our sample think about the toy's safety, price, and material quality. (See the discussion below on the differences between mothers and fathers on these measures.) This reflects a more typical consumer orientation to material quality and costs rather than one geared to sustainability per se. Respondents also highly rank the toy's educational value. The roles of these particular aspects were further emphasized in the four focus groups. When participants were asked early in the discussion to list the aspects that they think about when choosing toys, the first responses were safety, durability, cost, and value for money. One father in the focus group of participants with only high school education contrasted durability with what he called the "throw-away" quality of most toys sold today. Different focus groups also highlighted the quality of toys available when they or older relatives were young and complained about the general material quality of toys and other household items sold today, which break easily and cannot be repaired. This was viewed as a negative side of consumer society.

TABLE 14.1
Parents and sustainable toy shopping, 2013

There are many reasons for choosing to buy one toy over another. How important are the following reasons when choosing which toy to buy? Please indicate on a scale of 1 to 5, with 1 being very unimportant and 5 very important.	All	Mothers	Fathers	Gender significance
Whether they break	93.9	95.8	91.2	***
Whether they are safe	88.9	91.1	85.7	***
Price	84.0	87.7	78.6	***
Educational value	64.1	67.7	58.7	***
Corporate social responsibility of toy company	49.6	59.0	35.9	**
Environmental consequences of toy production	47.8	54.3	38.3	***
Toys my child convinced me to buy	34.1	32.4	36.6	
Special brands	25.5	26.9	23.6	
Toys that keep my children entertained	23.6	24.7	22.1	
Gender-neutral toys	17.3	21.0	11.8	***
Those promoted in children's books	11.8	13.9	8.6	**
Those advertised in films	11.3	10.9	11.8	
Toys that the friends of my kids have	6.2	5.5	7.1	
Toys advertised	4.7	4.7	4.7	
Valid N	1,002			

Notes: Cell entries are percentages of groups of people mentioning these considerations as very important or important when shopping for toys. The grey-shaded cells indicate measures of strong forms of sustainable toy consumption. The item on corporate social responsibility reflects the interaction between the economic and two strong elements of sustainable development, whereas the one on gender-neutral toys is more an indication of concerns about social equity broadly speaking.
** $p < .01$; *** $p < .001$. (Statistical significances are between fathers and mothers.)

Table 14.1 also shows that other matters of sustainability, such as thinking about the toy's environmental impact or the toy company's corporate social responsibility (CSR), were not as high on the agenda. Nevertheless, nearly 50 percent of the sample thought about CSR and the environmental consequences of production. The focus group discussions offered some additional insights here. In two of the groups – one comprised of women with only high school education and the other comprised of men with at least some university or college education – concerns about toxic and plastic toys were spontaneously mentioned as important when thinking about which toys to purchase. When the focus groups were asked directly about chemicals in toys, they discussed how toxins in plastics (especially plasticizers) can harm particularly young children as a prominent worry. Some participants referred to relevant media reports, whereas others stated that people close to them kept them informed. One additional green sustainability matter, toy overconsumption, was mentioned in all four focus groups. Participants complained about the number of toys that entered their homes, observing that their children tired of them quickly.

In contrast, there was only rare spontaneous mention of working conditions in toy factories. When asked about this issue directly, many participants in all of the focus groups did not associate the word *sweatshop* with toy manufacturing. Instead, they mentioned the garment industry. Interestingly, both the mother and the father focus group participants stressed other matters related to social equity sustainability; most did not approve of toy weapons and war toys for their children, no matter if they were boys or girls.

The analysis further suggests that concerns about sustainability are more likely to motivate the purchase of food and clothes than toys (results not shown). This suggests that toys do not mobilize the same level of concern about sustainability as other family-oriented products. When such concerns do influence toy purchases, environmental or green considerations are more important than social equity considerations. The same holds for food, though not for clothing. Given the common understanding of gender equality as a cornerstone of modern Swedish society, gender neutrality or alternatively gendered toys are not found to be an important consideration in these data, since only 20 percent of Swedes mentioned this as a motivation for some toy purchases. Similarly, gender neutrality was rarely raised as a concern in spontaneous discussions in the focus groups, though lively discussions were sparked by direct questions on the topic. Finally, neither the survey nor the focus groups showed that general worries about the effects of advertisements and forceful toy marketing particularly close to the Christmas season figured into parents' purchasing decisions.

Research suggests that relatively low levels of concern about key sustainability issues for household consumption are explained in part by an information deficit (Hobson 2003). For toy consumption generally, the problem might be that information about toys and sustainability is not widely available through the media and other institutions; or, if it is available, it might be presented in a confusing way. Similarly, some consumers might not be sufficiently informed about the role that their consumption can play in developing better general practices of sustainability (Stenborg 2013). After all, a conscientious shopper who wants to buy sustainably needs to find such information on brand labels or elsewhere and be able to understand what the labels mean.

Our survey shows that over 70 percent of Swedish parents can easily find information about the brand of a product, and half of the respondents do price comparisons. However, fewer than one in four respondents can easily identify a toy's country of origin, and most find it nearly impossible to locate information about a toy's environmental impact or the working conditions under which it was made. The survey and focus groups also show that Swedish parents lack basic knowledge about the most prevalent label on toys and other household goods, the Conformité Européene (CE) mark (a mandatory conformity mark for certain products sold within the European Economic Area). Only 15 percent of the parents in our survey knew what the label stands for; dads and moms gave indistinguishable answers. From the national survey, we learn that there is a gender difference when other consumer labels are brought into the analysis: men knew more about the more technical labels, and women knew more about ecolabels and particularly those associated with food.

Thus, though parents indicate that they wish to choose toys based upon their safety, durability, and educational value, it is difficult for them to do so, since they find sustainable shopping for toys difficult, time consuming, and confusing. This might be one reason why only 11 percent of parents surveyed said that they actively seek information about toy companies' social responsibilities. As noted above, the toy industry is comparatively less transparent and less active in CSR than many other household-oriented industries. Toy sustainability activism has a much lower public profile than food and apparel sustainability activism, since higher concern about toys' physical safety dominates media reports and is the focus of many toy recalls. The focus group data confirm that this public discussion directs parents' attention to toy safety more than to other aspects of toys and CSR. Participants indicated that they were reliant on primarily the media and authorities to inform them about these issues; thus, if this kind of information is not easily forthcoming, then both mothers and fathers might not feel a need to worry about sustainability problems associated with toys. Parents in the focus groups stated that public scandals and toy recalls mobilize them to seek more information and to make different choices in their toy purchases. Because these scandals and recalls are primarily safety related, it is perhaps less surprising that other aspects of CSR do not factor much into mothers' and fathers' toy purchases.

Are parents more involved in sustainable consumption than non-parents? To answer this question, we present nine shopping motivations for food, clothes, and toys and compare the responses of Swedes without children to those with both younger and older children. Of the nine motivations, parents use five significantly more than non-parents (see the results in the first two rows of Table 14.2). Importantly, the differences are largest for toy shopping, in which parents are much more concerned about the environmental consequences than non-parents (also less likely to buy toys). Similar patterns are found for other products, including food.

However, these results cannot yet reveal whether parenthood in general or becoming a mother or father in particular is a mobilizing factor. It could be, for instance, that people practise sustainable shopping before becoming parents or that other indicators of high levels of political consumerism – such as age or education – explain some of the differences. Indeed, when including controls for education and age, the differences between parents and non-parents vanish for food and clothes. Differences remain, though, for toy shopping, in which parents are more concerned about (and involved in) sustainability issues than non-parents.

Which parents are more prone to shop sustainably? Here we conduct two comparisons. First, we compare parents with young children to parents with children older than five years. Second, we compare parents of children over 18 to parents with children younger than 18. This comparison can reveal whether having young children mobilizes parents to undertake sustainable practices or whether such mobilization is a long-term process of parenthood over a child's development from toddler to teenager to young adult (see the third and fourth rows in Table 14.2). Results clearly show that parents with young children do not drive the practice of sustainable shopping; rather, they are less concerned with sustainability issues. This might be because mothers and fathers with young children might not have sufficient time to think about which stores carry organic baby food or diapers, ecological clothing, and/or sustainable toys. This time crunch can be exacerbated for parents of young children who also work outside the home. Similarly, parents of young children might not have sufficient resources to consider more sustainable shopping as a viable option. "Who can afford them?" queried one mother in the focus group with only high school

TABLE 14.2
Sustainable shopping between parents and non-parents

Children status	Environmental considerations for food	Working conditions for food	Animal conditions for food	Environmental conditions for clothes	Working conditions for clothes	Animal conditions for clothes	Environmental conditions for toys	Work conditions for toys	Animal conditions for toys
No kids	77.36	49.32	63.39	35.07	37.08	28.52	25.00	24.14	13.16
Kids	83.01**	55.71*	65.73	41.52*	42.51	29.29	42.31***	35.07**	19.82
No young kids	83.36	56.47	66.05	44.40	45.57	32.78	47.11	39.09	24.07
Young kids	81.30	52.03	64.23	27.83***	27.83***	12.39**	28.32***	23.21***	07.27***
No old kids	78.05	49.76	59.71	25.13	28.43	14.43	28.75	24.53	09.55
Kids over 18	85.01**	58.09**	68.17**	48.39***	48.41***	35.48***	50.00***	40.99***	25.63***

Notes: Cell entries are percentages for three types of motivation for sustainability when shopping for food, clothes, and toys using the Swedish Sustainability Survey. The first pair of rows includes parents and non-parents, whereas the remaining two pairs include only parents. (Statistical significances are among the various groups within each pair.)

* $p < .05$; ** $p < .01$; *** $p < .001$.

education. Some focus groups touched on how a trade-off between economic reality and environmental and social equity can occur in real-life shopping settings, even if there is sufficient household economy to make sustainable shopping viable for a family. For instance, a 32-year-old father employed as a police officer sketched an envisioned priority list for sustainable shopping that did not include toys for his toddler. Rather, it ranked less expensive food items highly (with a specific mention of organic milk) before prioritizing more expensive food items (e.g., organic meat) and ending with unspecified fair trade goods.

Parents with adult children (over 18 years of age) are most concerned with sustainable shopping practices, especially for food and clothes. This effect holds beyond controlling for age, education, and income of the respondents. Again, we can only speculate about reasons. The focus groups suggest that the greater range of sustainable food and clothing alternatives for older children might trigger their parents to think more broadly about making sustainable choices. Similarly, it might matter that food and clothes are generally consumed at higher rates than toys. It might also be that parents in general, especially those of younger children, trust Swedish public authorities and the welfare state to protect their children from threats to their well-being. If this is the case, then parents might not be publicly identified or consider themselves as actors who need to take responsibility (see Stenborg 2013). This implies that parents might not need to take a more direct or personal role by seeking information about toys or changing their shopping practices. This speculative explanation received support from all focus groups, which emphasized that government agencies monitor toy sustainability and safety. The parents who participated also believed that reputable toy brands are careful about what they sell because public scandals damage their reputations. In short, they trust reputable brands. But the focus groups disagreed about the role that parents need to play here: the two groups with higher education tended to believe that consumers should engage more actively in monitoring toy companies' practices, whereas the groups with lower levels of education spoke most about government authorities and toy brands. The gender of the parent did not matter here. Rather, this result reflects the importance of education and income for becoming a political and sustainable consumer. In addition, it might be that parents become more concerned about sustainable consumption because their children learn about sustainable development in school and bring the discussions home, especially as these children age. This can cause a reverse socialization effect comparable to that noted above.

Finally, women are generally more involved than men in political and sustainable consumerism. In Sweden at least, this is not because women are more likely than men to shop for their families (see Stolle and Micheletti 2013, Chapter 3). This gender gap mostly has historical roots and motivational reasons. For instance, women are more likely than men to be motivated to shop sustainably out of concerns for animal treatment and child labour (Stolle and Micheletti 2013, 83). Women can also be more concerned than men about toy safety since dangerous toys directly affect their children's welfare. Prior research also suggests that mothers more than fathers might think about other sustainable aspects, such as the environment and CSR (Mackendrick 2014) commitments by the companies whose products they purchase on a regular basis. Going back to Table 14.1, we see that this appears to be the case for purchasing toys. Mothers are significantly more concerned than fathers about toy safety, price, and educational value. The gender differences are largest, however, when it comes to concerns about the environment and CSR, our measures of sustainable toy shopping. More than half of all mothers care about these issues compared with a third of fathers. This gender effect remains in multivariate analyses (see below).

Other interesting gender differences appeared in the focus groups. Fathers gave more spontaneous weight to the fun aspect of toys (whether or not they liked to play with the toys with their children) and to some extent the durability aspect of toys. Interestingly, given the emphasis in Sweden on gender equality and orientation as part of social equity and human rights, the focus groups comprised of fathers with some college education expressed serious worries about the negative effects of boys playing with toys identified for girls. The colour pink and "girly toys" as factors leading to bullying were mentioned specifically. The survey also revealed that fathers were more hesitant about purchasing princess toys, costumes, and jewellery for boys (results not shown). The data did not show any comparable concern about girls playing with "boys' toys." Instead, several fathers saw this as important for socializing and empowering girls. Some mothers with some college education spontaneously noted in their focus group that they attempted to steer their daughters away from princess-related toys, also for reasons of socialization, but survey results showed that mothers also purchase such toys more for girls than boys.

As Table 14.3 shows, mothers remain significantly more engaged in sustainable toy shopping than fathers, regardless of age, education, income, type of housing (as a measure of economic status), and number of young children in the family. Age does not make a difference, likely because of the truncated age range in this sample of parents with children up to 10 years old. As expected, higher education and higher income increase, whereas living in a house decreases, political consumerism through sustainable toy shopping.[7] A higher number of young children at home is also negatively related to sustainable shopping, confirming earlier insights that young children do not really mobilize parents to practise sustainability in their shopping. Sustainable toy shoppers are also significantly more interested in human rights, the environment, consumption, and developing countries. This confirms the basic pillars of sustainability at work on the family level of consumption. Yet, even when these interests are taken into account, mothers are still more likely than fathers to engage in political consumerism for toys. The focus groups confirmed this result. Fathers referred to women in their lives as important informers about green and social equity sustainability matters associated with toys; mothers discussed toy sustainability ideologically in association with the relationship between capitalism and consumption (mothers with high school education) and through an environmentally oriented conversation about chemicals, plastics, and labour conditions in toy factories (mothers with some college education).

Conclusion

This chapter has asked how the family environment shapes current political commitments and attitudes. We have examined sustainable consumption, focusing on how purchases of toys might have mobilizing effects. Toy consumption is embedded within the broader public context that sets as goals the modification of household consumer preference and practice toward sustainability. Although the focus is primarily on encouraging families to use less energy and produce less waste, getting them to consider more generally how their consumer desires and habits affect the environment and workers today and in the future is a growing concern of social activists and many governments. How sustainability first enters family life and is then transmitted within it is therefore a critical topic not only for academic theorizing about the importance of families for political mobilization but also for movement research and public policy.

Our study finds that being a parent matters in several ways and that intersectionality between gender and parenthood matters (for similar discussions with respect to the welfare state and public opinion, respectively, see Harell et al., and Goodyear-Grant and Bittner, this volume). First, when parents are compared with non-parents, the national survey shows that parents care more about the environmental aspects of purchases of toys and

TABLE 14.3
Correlates of sustainable toy shopping among parents

Variables	Model 1		Model 2	
Constant	.315**	(.122)	.119	(.111)
Age	.001	(.003)	.000	(.003)
Mother	.197***	(.029)	.130***	(.027)
Lives in house versus apartment	−.063*	(.030)	−.042	(.027)
Higher education	.068*	(.030)	.008	(.028)
Higher income	.067*	(.030)	.050	(.027)
Number of young children	−.037*	(.018)	−.025	(.017)
Interest in Swedish politics			.059	(.031)
Interest in environmental issues			.152***	(.032)
Interest in consumer issues			.104***	(.029)
Interest in human rights issues			.118***	(.033)
Interest in developing countries			.111***	(.033)
N	934		934	
Adjusted R^2	.063		.232	

Note: Cell entries are unstandardized regression coefficients with standard errors in parentheses.
* $p < .05$; ** $p < .01$; *** $p < .001$.

food. They are wary of bringing certain products into their families, as illustrated in the focus groups' expressions of worry about toys containing toxic chemicals and plastics. However, parents are much less concerned about the working conditions of toy workers. They relate the "sweatshop issue" (which also involves the effects of chemical use on workers) more to clothing than to toys, reflecting how this problem of sustainability has been discussed publicly. Second, parents with older children – but not those with younger children – are most concerned about sustainable consumption. Third, mothers are more likely than fathers to show general concern about sustainable consumption and toy sustainability; however, mothers do not always have more knowledge than fathers about labelling schemes. Still, gender, as shown in political consumer practice, matters. The gender of parents even appears to affect how they assess their children's socialization into gender roles: the toy survey and focus groups clearly find that mothers are more open to boys playing with toys typically meant for girls. Fathers are more hesitant; in one focus group, they explicitly stated that they feared their sons would be bullied if they played with girls' toys and wore pink clothing. In sum, it appears that being a parent, particularly being a mother, is related in some way to concerns about green and social equity sustainability.

Yet the direction of causality is still an open question. Controlling for sociodemographic differences between parents and non-parents is only one limited way to ascertain causal direction; it might be the case that those who decide to have children are also generally more concerned about sustainability than those who decide not to have children. Trying to understand whether parents of young children are more engaged in sustainable living was one way of establishing that having children nudges parents to act more responsibly. This might be the case, but many countervailing factors at work do not allow parents of young children to practise fully their concerns about sustainability.

Thus, if children are supposed to "trigger" political engagement associated with a sustainable lifestyle, then our research uncovers two plausible mechanisms. First, the politically mobilizing effect of having children does not work instantaneously and linearly; rather, it works slowly over time. It might reveal itself occasionally only when children are grown-ups. Second, it might be possible that concerns about chemicals and dangerous side effects will nudge parents to think about larger issues of sustainability. If media reports about various problems of sustainability with toys increase, then we might see how parents will become the forerunners of sustainable lifestyles. The focus groups confirmed the importance of such information; participants stated spontaneously at the ends of their discussions that they felt the need to become more aware of and to devote more time to reading product labels and content information. However, parental involvement here is limited since parents might not give much thought to how they figure into discussions and practices of sustainability. An important conclusion is that the lack of self-motivation to seek information is a barrier to more sustainable consumer practices. It is indeed likely that only information about the damaging effects of toys on children's health can get mothers and fathers motivated and interested in additional aspects of sustainability.

Thus, even people with consistently high levels of political consumerism and public discussions of sustainability, such as Swedes, find it difficult to be sustainable toy consumers. Although being a mother might trigger more sustainable living, parents in general need more readily available information about sustainable toys. More knowledge about various labelling schemes is required to make decisions about purchasing sustainable toys and other products. Past studies (Berlin 2011) and our focus groups showed that government and other institutions that consumers trust play clear roles here. Socialization into sustainable development through parenthood requires considerable efforts by mothers, fathers, governments, corporations, and civil society in general.

Finally, let us add a few reflections on future research on the mobilizational role of parenthood. Our study has relied on two very different data sources – surveys and focus groups – to explore how political attitudes and behaviours can be affected by parental status. Although the methods are compatible and can clarify some of the questions raised by either method alone, they are still insufficient to understand fully the complex phenomenon of adult socialization. Our analysis indicates that we need at least two important innovations in this research area. First, panel studies that include adults before and after they have children and possibly while they are expecting them might help us to understand better how political beliefs and attitudes change with the life event of having children. The few panel studies that exist often do not include suitable political indicators, let alone measures of sustainable living. Second, more behavioural indicators are necessary. Although it is important to study parental awareness of sustainable issues, for example, it is crucial to trace how mothers and fathers act on this awareness. Asking respondents what motivates them while shopping might cause a host of social desirability problems, so actual observed behaviour in terms of purchases or other political acts is more useful. Suggested approaches include longitudinal study with the help of additional methods, such as toy inventories, wardrobe and kitchen studies, participatory shopping observations, and experiments.

Notes
The Swedish Research Council has funded the data collection for this chapter through the project Sustainable Citizenship: Opportunities and Barriers for Citizen Involvement in Sustainable Development.
1 Toy companies notify consumers about recalls of the toys that they produce (e.g., http://www.toysrusinc.com/safety/recalls/), and online parenting magazines and forums (e.g., http://www.parents.com/baby/safety/toy/kid-toys/), NGOs (e.g., http://www.safekids.org/product-recalls, http://www.toyinfo.org/ToyInfo/RECALLS/2014_RECALLS/ToyInfo/Recalls/2014_Recalls.aspx), and government agencies (e.g., http://www.recalls.gov/cpsc.html, https://www.recalls.gov.au/content/index.phtml/itemId/952869) list recalled toys.
2 http://pressreleases.religionnews.com/2014/11/13/israels-settlements-expand-church-boycotts-grow/.
3 See, for instance, the mobilization against the large toy store Toys 'R' Us on gender-specific marketing at http://newyork.cbslocal.com/2013/09/23/parents-petition-toys-r-us-to-do-away-with-gender-specific-marketing/.

4 Information from the Swedish Social Insurance Agency at http://www.narhalsan.se/upload/Primarvarden/Rekrytering/barnbidrag_flerbarnstillagg_eng.pdf.
5 See more technical information about this survey in Micheletti, Stolle, and Berlin (2014).
6 The four focus groups were comprised of women with only high school education, women with at least some college or university training, men with only high school education, and men with at least some college or university training. Focus group participants were recruited from the IPSOS database of approximately 8,800 respondents and screened via telephone interviews before being invited to participate in the groups. IPSOS Sweden is part of an international research group that conducts market and public opinion research.
7 This effect of living in a house holds despite controlling for education and income and thus might capture the higher rates of living in houses in less urbanized areas of Sweden.

References

ABC News. 2013. "Five NY Firms Charged with Importing Toxic Toys." February 6. http://abcnews.go.com/blogs/business/2013/02/ny-firm-charged-with-importing-toxic-toys-from-china/.

Baretto, Mary, Michelle Scott, Ian Oakley, Evangelos Karapanos, Nuno J. Nunes, Sofia Gomes, and Joana Gomes. 2013. "Playing for the Planet: Designing Toys that Foster Sustainable Values." Proceedings of the 31st European Conference on Cognitive Ergonomics Article 16. http://dl.acm.org/citation.cfm?id=2501947.

Becker, Monica, Sally Edwards, and Rachel I. Massey. 2010. "Toxic Chemicals in Toys and Children's Products: Limitations of Current Responses and Recommendations for Government and Industry." *Environmental Science and Technology* 44 (21): 7986–91. http://dx.doi.org/10.1021/es1009407.

Benenson, Joyce F., Hassina P. Carder, and Sarah J. Geib-Cole. 2008. "The Development of Boys' Preferential Pleasure in Physical Aggression." *Aggressive Behavior* 34 (2): 154–66. http://dx.doi.org/10.1002/ab.20223.

Berlin, Daniel. 2011. "Sustainable Consumers and the State: Exploring How Citizens' Trust and Distrust in Institutions Spur Political Consumption." *Journal of Environmental Policy and Planning* 13 (3): 277–95. http://dx.doi.org/10.1080/09640568.2011.603207.

Blakemore, Judith E. Owen, and Renee E. Centers. 2005. "Characteristics of Boys' and Girls' Toys." *Sex Roles* 53 (9–10): 619–33. http://dx.doi.org/10.1007/s11199-005-7729-0.

Bost, K., M. Cox, M. Burchinal, and C. Payne. 2002. "Structural and Supportive Changes in Couples' Family and Friendship Networks across the Transition to Parenthood." *Journal of Marriage and the Family* 64 (2): 517–31. http://dx.doi.org/10.1111/j.1741-3737.2002.00517.x.

Campenni, C. Estelle. 1999. "Gender Stereotyping of Children's Toys: A Comparison of Parents and Nonparents." *Journal of Sex Roles* 40 (1–2): 121–38. http://dx.doi.org/10.1023/A:1018886518834.

Christensen, Karen E., and Dahlia F. Stockdale. 1991. "Predictors of Toy Selection Criteria of Preschool Children's Parents." *Children's Environments Quarterly* 8 (1): 25–36.
Cooper, T. 2005. "Slower Consumption: Reflections on Product Life Spans and the 'Throwaway Society.'" *Journal of Industrial Ecology* 9 (1–2): 51–67.
Egels-Zandén, Niklas. 2007. "Suppliers' Compliance with MNCs' Codes of Conduct: Behind the Scenes at Chinese Toy Suppliers." *Journal of Business Ethics* 75 (1): 45–62. http://dx.doi.org/10.1007/s10551-006-9237-8.
Elsäkerhetsverket. 2012. *Barn ska ha säkra leksaker.* http://www.elsakerhetsverket.se/privatpersoner/barn-och-elsakerhet/.
England, P. 2005. "Gender Inequality in Labor Markets: The Role of Motherhood and Segregation." *Social Politics* 12 (2): 264–88. http://dx.doi.org/10.1093/sp/jxi014.
Euromonitor International. 2014. *Toys and Games: Global Trends, Developments, and Prospects.* http://www.euromonitor.com/toys-and-games-global-trends-developments-and-prospects/report.
European Voice. 2014. *RAPEX Continues to Find Dangerous Clothes and Toys.* http://www.europeanvoice.com/article/rapex-continues-to-find-dangerous-clothes-and-toys/.
Fairtrade Center. 2011. *Leksaksföretagen har agerat efter kritiken: Branschen bättre men många problem kvarstår.* http://www.fairtradecenter.se/sites/default/files/leksaksuppfoljning_slutrapport_april_2011_1.pdf.
Georg, Susse. 1999. "The Social Shaping of Household Consumption." *Ecological Economics* 28 (3): 455–66. http://dx.doi.org/10.1016/S0921-8009(98)00110-4.
Grønhøj, A., and J. Thøgersen. 2009. "Like Father, like Son? Intergenerational Transmission of Values, Attitudes, and Behaviours in the Environmental Domain." *Journal of Environmental Psychology* 29 (4): 414–21. http://dx.doi.org/10.1016/j.jenvp.2009.05.002.
Handell, Svensk. 2012. *Julhandeln 2012.* http://www.svenskhandel.se/globalassets/_gammalt-innehall/rapporter/svensk-handels.
Healthy Day. 2013. *Cross These Dangerous Toys off Kids' Christmas List, Experts Say: Annual 'Trouble in Toyland' Report Cites Playthings that Could Choke or Poison a Child.* http://consumer.healthday.com/general-health-information-16/emergencies-and-first-aid-news-227/trouble-in-toyland-what-not-to-get-your-kid-this-christmas-682555.html.
Heft, Harry, and Louise Chawla. 2006. "Children as Agents in Sustainable Development: The Ecology of Competence." In *Children and Their Environments: Learning, Using, and Designing Spaces,* edited by Christopher Spencer and Mark Blades, 199–216. Cambridge: Cambridge University Press.
Hobson, K. 2003. "Thinking Habits into Action: The Role of Knowledge and Process in Questioning Household Consumption Practices." *Local Environment* 8 (1): 95–112. http://dx.doi.org/10.1080/135498303200041359.
Howarth, Richard B. 1992. "Intergenerational Justice and the Chain of Obligation." *Environmental Values* 1 (2): 133–40. http://dx.doi.org/10.3197/096327192776680124.

Hughes, Nicole. 2013. "Toy Libraries: Toys that Won't Cost You or the Earth." *Every Child* 13 (4): 28–29.

Inter Press News Agency. 2002. *RIGHTS-CHINA: Young Workers Toil to Churn out Santa's Toys*. http://www.ipsnews.net/2002/12/rights-china-young-workers-toil-to-churn-out-santas-toys/.

IPEN and GRID-Arendal. 2013. *Toxic Metals in Children's Products: An Insight into the Market in Eastern Europe, the Caucasus, and Central Asia.* http://www.grida.no/publications/toxic-metals/.

Jennings, M. Kent, and Richard G. Niemi. 1968. "The Transmission of Political Values from Parent to Child." *American Political Science Review* 62 (1): 169–84. http://dx.doi.org/10.1017/S0003055400115709.

Jennings, M. Kent, Laura Stoker, and Jake Bowers. 2009. "Politics across Generations: Family Transmission Reexamined." *Journal of Politics* 71 (3): 782–99. http://dx.doi.org/10.1017/S0022381609090719.

Kemikalieinspektionen (Swedish Chemicals Agency). 2008. "Att arbeta med produktval i praktiken." http://www.kemi.se/global/rapporter/2008/rapport-2-08-produktval-i-praktiken.pdf.

Kovács, B. 2007. "Mothering and Active Citizenship in Romania." Studia Universitatis Babes-Bolyai Serie. *Politica* 1: 107–27.

Langer, Beryl. 2005. "Consuming Anomie: Children and Global Commercial Culture." *Childhood* 12 (2): 259–71. http://dx.doi.org/10.1177/0907568205051907.

Mackendrick, Norah. 2014. "More Work for Mother: Chemical Body Burdens as a Maternal Responsibility." *Gender and Society* 28 (5): 705–28. http://dx.doi.org/10.1177/0891243214529842.

McDevitt, Michael, and Steven Chaffee. 2002. "From Top-Down to Trickle-Up Influence: Revisiting Assumptions about the Family in Political Socialization." *Political Communication* 19 (3): 281–301. http://dx.doi.org/10.1080/01957470290055501.

McIntosh, Hugh, Daniel Hart, and James Youniss. 2007. "The Influence of Family Political Discussion on Youth Civic Development: Which Parent Qualities Matter?" *PS: Political Science and Politics* 40 (3): 495–99. http://dx.doi.org/10.1017/S1049096507070758.

Micheletti, Michele, Dietlind Stolle, and Daniel Berlin. 2014. "Sustainable Citizenship: The Role of Citizens and Consumers as Agents of the Environmental State." In *State and Environment: The Comparative Study of Environmental Governance*, edited by Andreas Duit, 202–33. Cambridge, MA: MIT Press. http://dx.doi.org/10.7551/mitpress/9780262027120.003.0008.

Mulder, Karel F. 1998. "Sustainable Consumption and Production of Plastics?" *Technological Forecasting and Social Change* 58 (1–2): 105–24. http://dx.doi.org/10.1016/S0040-1625(97)00129-7.

Nelson, Anders. 2005. "Children's Toy Collections in Sweden: A Less Gender-Typed Country." *Journal of Sex Roles* 52 (1–2): 93–102. http://dx.doi.org/10.1007/s11199-005-1196-5.

NPD Group. 2014. *Evolution of Play 2014.* https://www.npd.com/lps/pdf/TOYS-EOP-2014.pdf.

OECD. 2009. *OECD Conference on Household Behaviour and Environmental Policy.* http://www.oecd.org/env/consumption-innovation/oecdconferenceonhouseholdbehaviourandenvironmentalpolicy.htm.

People's Daily Online. 2008. "China Toy Factory Board Agree to Renew Labor Contracts after Violent Protests." http://en.people.cn/90001/90776/90882/6541343.html.

Population and Development Review. 2006. "Policies to Reconcile Labor Force Participation and Childbearing in the European Union." *Population and Development Review* 32 (2): 389–93.

Pugh, Allison. 2009. *Longing and Belonging: Parents, Children, and Consumer Culture.* Berkeley: University of California Press.

SACOM (Students and Scholars against Corporate Misbehaviour). 2011. *Making Toys without Joy: ICTI CARE Covers Labour Rights Violations for Global Toy Brands like Disney, Walmart, and Mattel.* http://sacom.hk/making-toys-without-joy-icti-care-covers-labour-rights-violations-for-global-toy-brands-like-disney-walmart-mattel/.

Schor, Juliet B. 2005. "Prices and Quantities: Unsustainable Consumption and the Global Economy." *Ecological Economics* 55 (3): 309–20. http://dx.doi.org/10.1016/j.ecolecon.2005.07.030.

Sethi, Prakash, Emre Veral, H. Shapiro, and Olga Emelianova. 2011. "Mattel, Inc.: Global Manufacturing Principles (GMP) – A Life-Cycle Analysis of a Company-Based Code of Conduct in the Toy Industry." *Journal of Business Ethics* 99 (4): 483–517. http://dx.doi.org/10.1007/s10551-010-0673-0.

Spangenberg, Joachim H., and Sylvia Lorek. 2002. "Environmentally Sustainable Household Consumption: From Aggregate Environmental Pressures to Priority Fields of Action." *Ecological Economics* 43 (2–3): 127–40. http://dx.doi.org/10.1016/S0921-8009(02)00212-4.

Statista (Statistics Portal). 2013. *Average Amount Spent on Toys Per Child by Country 2013.* http://www.statista.com/statistics/194424/amount-spent-on-toys-per-child-by-country-since-2009/.

Stenborg, Emelie. 2013. "Making Sense of Risk: An Analysis of Framings in Media of the Chemical Risks of Textiles, Toys, and Paint." PhD diss., Lund University.

Stolle, Dietlind, and Michele Micheletti. 2013. *Political Consumerism: Global Responsibility in Action.* Cambridge: Cambridge University Press. http://dx.doi.org/10.1017/CBO9780511844553.

Swedish Consumer Agency. N.d. *Leksaker och säkerhet.* http://www.konsumentverket.se/Vara-omraden/Sakra-varor-och-tjanster/Leksaker/.

UNCED (United Nations World Commission on Environment and Development). 1987. *Our Common Future* (the Brundtland Report). Oxford: Oxford University Press.

US PIRG (United States Public Interest Research Group Education Fund). 2013. *Trouble in Toyland: The 28th Annual Survey of Toy Safety.* Washington, DC: US PIRG. http://www.uspirgedfund.org/sites/pirg/files/reports/USP%20Toyland%202013%201.3.pdf.

Voorpostel, M., and H. Coffé. 2012. "Transitions in Partnership and Parental Status, Gender, and Political and Civic Participation." *European Sociological Review* 28 (1): 28–42. http://dx.doi.org/10.1093/esr/jcq046.

Wain, Brendan. 2014. "Toys: More than Just Child's Play." *Journal of the National Centre for Sustainability* 1 (82): 1–8.

Wier, Mette, Line Block Christoffersen, Trine S. Jensen, Ole G. Pedersen, Hans Keiding, and Jesper Munksgaard. 2005. "Evaluating Sustainability of Household Consumption: Using DEA to Assess Environmental Performance." *Economic Systems Research* 17 (4): 425–47. http://dx.doi.org/10.1080/09535310500284276.

Wood, Eileen, Serge Desmarais, and Sara Gugula. 2002. "The Impact of Parenting Experience on Gender Stereotyped Toy Play of Children." *Journal of Sex Roles* 47 (1–2): 39–49.

Zacarias-Farah, Adriana, and Elaine Geyer-Allély. 2003. "Household Consumption Patterns in OECD Countries: Trends and Figures." *Journal of Cleaner Production* 11 (8): 819–27. http://dx.doi.org/10.1016/S0959-6526(02)00155-5.

CONCLUSION

15

Gender, Parenthood, and Politics
What Do We Still Need to Know?
AMANDA BITTNER and MELANEE THOMAS

What We've Learned
The chapters in this book have all contributed to a nascent literature on the role of parenthood in politics by approaching the question from different angles, different countries, and different issues facing women (and men) and parents. A few generalizations, however, can be made.

First, we can reasonably say that women's participation in politics is becoming "normal" and expected and that voters do not discriminate against female candidates (Goodyear-Grant 2010). Yet women in politics are less likely to be mothers than men in politics are to be fathers (Campbell and Childs, this volume) as well as less likely to display their parental status (Thomas and Lambert, this volume). Women's participation in politics, especially in elite-level electoral politics, is seen to be less serious or committed if the women are explicit about balancing their political work and family obligations (Campbell and Childs, this volume; Franceschet, Piscopo, and Thomas, this volume), and some care-related activities, such as breastfeeding, become problematic for women in legislatures (Arneil, this volume).

Second, parenthood is political, but how it is political can vary for mothers and fathers. Mothers are more likely to be politically engaged when their children are aged five to 12 (O'Neill and Gidengil, this volume); overall, politicizing parental status, with the addition of Internet mobilization, can motivate mothers to engage in political action (Langner, Greenlee, and Deason, this volume). Parents are generally more conservative than non-parents on crime and security, as well as cultural issues (Goodyear-Grant and Bittner, this volume), but more liberal about environmental considerations, especially with respect to toy and food production (Micheletti and Stolle, this volume). Interestingly, these trends are further conditioned by gender, for fathers are more conservative on crime than mothers, whereas mothers are more concerned than fathers about sustainable consumption. Those who hold more conservative attitudes about gender roles support less generous parental leave policies, especially for parents in non-traditional relationships (Harell et al., this volume).

The research presented here, like the research conducted in the past, struggles to find evidence of double day effects (Giles, this volume; O'Neill and Gidengil, this volume). Thus, though intuitive, the idea that women are underrepresented in politics, or know less about politics because of the dual demands of paid employment outside the home and a greater share of unpaid labour inside the home, especially with respect to childcare, does not garner much support. Indeed, a few of the chapters in this book, including those by O'Neill and Gidengil and Micheletti and Stolle, indicate that having children can actually mobilize parents, including mothers.

Third, expectations for parenthood are different today than they were 50 (or even 25) years ago: fathers are generally more involved in care activities and spend more time doing household chores than was once the norm (Pew Research Center 2013). This suggests that stereotypes and norms surrounding motherhood/fatherhood are likely evolving; it also suggests that issues facing contemporary mothers are likely to be faced by contemporary fathers more so than in the past. Indeed, though a good portion of this book deals with motherhood and politics, fatherhood is an important variable that needs to be given attention as well.

As norms are changing, including norms surrounding the public/private divide, what it means to be a caregiver, and expectations for equality and representation, greater pressures are placed on the state to facilitate the participation of not only women but also parents, both in the workplace and in politics. Many state benefits and programs that support parents in the workplace can also help parents in public office, including parental leaves, childcare, and flexibility in work-time arrangements. Yet the political "job" is different from jobs in other sectors, and different types of support would also be of assistance to parents who juggle work and life.

Thus, in this chapter, we examine (some) global trends, assessing women, work, families, and care; parental benefits and programs; and attitudes toward women, engagement in politics and work, and family values. Most of our aggregate data come from OECD countries because the data are readily available, and our individual-level data come from the World Values Survey. We then focus on attitudes reported from residents of OECD countries, not only to keep things consistent but also because the bulk of the chapters here focus on OECD countries. We make some observations but draw few concrete conclusions. We see this chapter as contributing to the discussion and making some suggestions for what we might expect in the future, given some of the findings in this book and elsewhere. Our goal is to identify a research program for moving forward, particularly valuable for what is really a budding area of research.

Women and Participation in Politics

Since suffrage, the role of women in politics has increased tremendously. The global average of women's presence in legislatures, according to the Interparliamentary Union, is currently about 21 percent.[1] There is still some disparity around the world, and some countries have substantially higher numbers of women in legislatures than others. In no way, however, does the "norm" approach parity. The bulk of the countries examined in this book hover around the global average, whereas Sweden has been far ahead since before the early 1990s. Scholars have noted the Scandinavian trend for years (Dahlerup 1988; Paxton and Kunovich 2003), and many attribute the much higher numbers to the electoral system, the gender quotas in place, as well as other "cultural" factors (Krook 2010).

As numbers of women in legislatures grow, we can expect changes in public policy and the workings of legislatures themselves. Research shows that women's presence in legislatures makes a difference to both legislation and the legislative process (Campbell and Childs, this volume; Franceschet et al., this volume; Kathlene 1994; Mendelberg, Karpowitz, and Goedert 2014). Indeed, we anticipate that, as a result of women's participation in politics today and in the past, a greater number of women will participate in the future for a few reasons. First, the role model effect is likely to encourage future generations of women to participate in politics (Campbell and Wolbrecht 2006; Thomas 2012; Wolbrecht and Campbell 2007). This effect has been repeatedly documented, and we fully expect it to continue. Second, we believe that legislators today are likely to create policies that will facilitate women's participation in the future, including different "types" of women who might not be participating now in high numbers, given childrearing and other caregiving responsibilities. Third, women's presence in politics is tied (albeit loosely) to their presence in the workforce, and as workplace policies become more women and family friendly we anticipate increased participation in politics, partly because of norm diffusion, partly because of policy diffusion. The focus of this book is on the dual effects of gender and parental status on politics; we cannot escape the conclusion that parenthood has different effects on women and men and that, traditionally, women have been the primary caregivers. Whether parental status will continue to have different effects on women and men in the future remains to be seen. More research is needed in these areas to identify clearly the nature of these relationships.

Women, Families, and Work

As is the case in legislatures, women are now more present in the workforce than they were in the past. Admittedly, their progression in the workforce has been much quicker than that in formal politics. For example, women's labour force participation in the United States increased from 34 percent in 1950 to 60 percent in 1998;[2] during the same period, their participation in Congress increased from just under 2 percent to just over 12 percent. This trend of women participating in paid work at considerably higher levels than electoral politics is consistently found throughout OECD countries.

It is also important to note that the workforce participation rates of mothers do not always match the participation rates of childless women around the world. Figure 15.1 demonstrates the proportion of mothers working in paid employment across OECD countries (where data are available). As Figure 15.1 demonstrates, approximately 70 percent of mothers work in paid employment, a number slightly higher among single mothers than partnered mothers, though some countries do not match this trend. This suggests that mothers' participation in paid work is a ubiquitous international pattern.

Although birth rates in most countries have decreased substantially over time, across OECD countries at least one-third of all households have children in them, as indicated in Figure 15.2. In some countries, it is much higher (e.g., Korea, with nearly 75 percent of households having children). On average in OECD countries, over 46 percent of households have children in them, and among those households nearly 20 percent are led by single parents.

Although these numbers reflect OECD countries rather than global averages, they still indicate relatively high rates of family life for workers. Indeed, when we combine the numbers presented in Figures 15.1 and 15.2, we see that, with an average of 65 percent of mothers in paid work and 46 percent

Gender, Parenthood, and Politics

FIGURE 15.1
Proportion of mothers working in paid employment, OECD countries

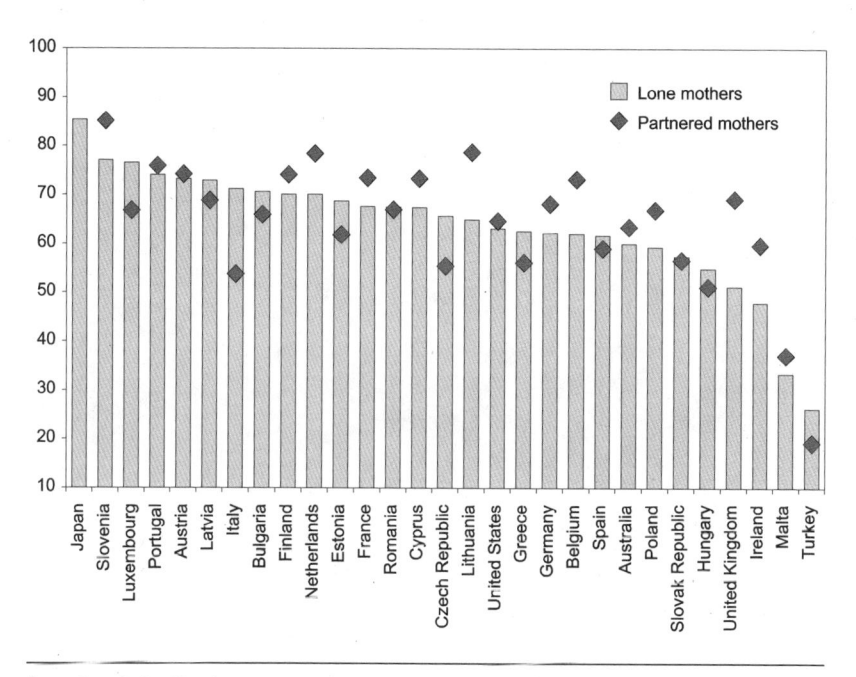

Source: Data obtained from https://www.oecd.org/els/soc/LMF_1_3_Maternal_employment_by_partnership_status.pdf.

of all households having children, mothers constitute roughly one-third of the OECD country workforce.

The data suggest, therefore, that having children is a normal part of life for many people and that working is a normal part of life for both women and men, even for mothers. This means that the inclusion of mothers in the workforce will have long-term effects for societies (both across OECD countries and elsewhere) as work becomes normalized and society adapts to the norms, seeking to facilitate and promote work/life balance for parents.

Indeed, such balance is not simply a concern for mothers. Although women are still the primary caregivers for both children and elderly/disabled relatives across OECD countries, men also spend a good portion of their time involved in caregiving activities. Table 15.1 lists the average number of weekly hours allocated to family care activities of both sexes, including childcare and elder/disabled care. Numbers vary by country, and the male/female breakdown varies by country. On average, women spend approximately 28

FIGURE 15.2
Proportion of children living in single- and two-parent households, OECD countries

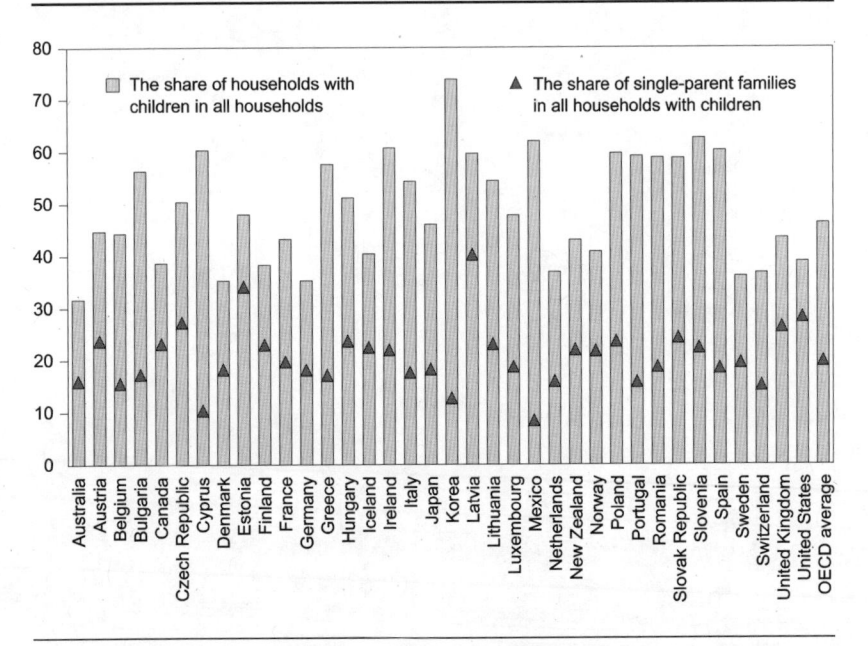

Note: Data reflect "latest year" collected for each country, ranging from 2005 to 2011.
Source: Data obtained from https://www.oecd.org/els/family/SF_1_1_Family_size_and_composition.pdf.

hours per week on childcare and men 17 hours. On elder/disabled care, the sex disparity is not quite as large: women spend about 10 hours a week on average and men nine hours.

Finland has the smallest sex-based difference in household care, and both women and men spend the least number of hours caring for family members overall, among all OECD member states for which data were available. In contrast, in both Estonia and the Netherlands, there are gaps of more than 20 hours between women and men, where the average time spent in care activities is also the highest. These patterns suggest that there is room for the state to assist with care and that this assistance can reduce the sex-based inequality of the workload. Indeed, research examining the welfare state confirms this by suggesting that the state's role can either ameliorate or exacerbate the time that each sex spends in care work (Esping-Andersen 2002; Orloff 1996). This suggests at least one point of connection across mothers in politics and mothers in the workplace.

TABLE 15.1
Time spent performing care duties, adults aged 18 and over, OECD countries

	Caring for and educating children		Caring for elderly/disabled relatives	
	Women	Men	Women	Men
Estonia	44	23	9	9
Netherlands	48	22	5	9
Germany	35	19	15	7
Poland	37	23	12	9
United Kingdom	35	19	14	8
Ireland	32	20	16	28
Spain	28	16	17	9
Norway	40	23	5	5
Czech Republic	35	17	9	10
Greece	25	14	18	8
Luxembourg	32	20	10	9
Sweden	33	26	5	5
Austria	29	11	8	5
Cyprus	27	17	10	7
Malta	23	12	14	10
Slovenia	26	19	11	12
France	29	17	7	6
Lithuania	29	18	7	6
Hungary	26	15	10	9
Portugal	23	16	11	14
Slovakia	22	11	12	12
Bulgaria	20	13	13	8
Romania	19	13	14	10
Latvia	22	16	10	8
Hungary	22	16	8	5
Belgium	23	15	6	5
Italy	20	15	9	7
Denmark	23	19	5	10
Turkey	21	10	7	9
Finland	17	15	5	4

Note: Countries are ordered by decreasing percentage of time dedicated to childcare activities by women.

Sources: Adapted from http://www.oecd.org/social/family/LMF2_5_Time_use_of_work_and_care.pdf. Data obtained from the Second European Quality of Life Survey, 2007.

Other connections to work and/or politics are less obvious. Do countries with higher levels of state support for care also have higher levels of parental employment? How does that support affect the daily lives of parents? How does it affect parents' – in particular mothers' – decisions to enter politics? And what is the relationship among care, representation, and child-friendly or family-friendly policies? These questions have not been answered yet; instead, research thus far has focused on how the presence of women in a legislature or cabinet leads to more family- or women-friendly policies (Atchison and Down 2009; Caiazza 2004) rather than on how those policies affect women's and parents' recruitment into politics. We suspect that there are connections between these "lifestyle" factors and mothers' entrance into politics, and these links need more exploring. To that end, we turn now to the provision of parental benefits and programs.

Parental Benefits and Programs

Parental benefits are widely seen as tools to increase gender equality, largely because the bulk of care work has been conducted by women for some time, and the gender distribution of care work does not appear to change much with women's entrance into the labour force. Women still bear the larger burden when it comes to both childcare and care for elderly or disabled relatives. Given that nearly 65 percent of mothers are also involved in paid employment, this speaks to a fairly heavy workload, which can impinge on mothers' willingness or ability to participate in politics, particularly with young children, when time is the most precious and children need the most care. There are plenty of ways that states can support women, parents, and families, including (but not limited to) health care, housing support, childcare, early childhood education, funding to encourage children's participation in art or sport, and maternity and paternity leave (or more generic parental leave).

We look at four areas of parental/family programs in this section, including public spending on family benefits, childcare programs, flexibility in work-time arrangements, and parental leave for fathers. We look at these four areas in particular for two main reasons. First, in the case of public spending on family benefits writ large, we think that this is the most comprehensive way to compare countries. Second, in relation to the latter three programs, we think that they speak most directly both to contemporary patterns in employment and care and to contemporary discussions about which benefits governments and employers should consider if they want to encourage citizens and employees to be engaged in both the economy and

FIGURE 15.3
Public spending on family benefits in cash, services, and tax measures, OECD countries

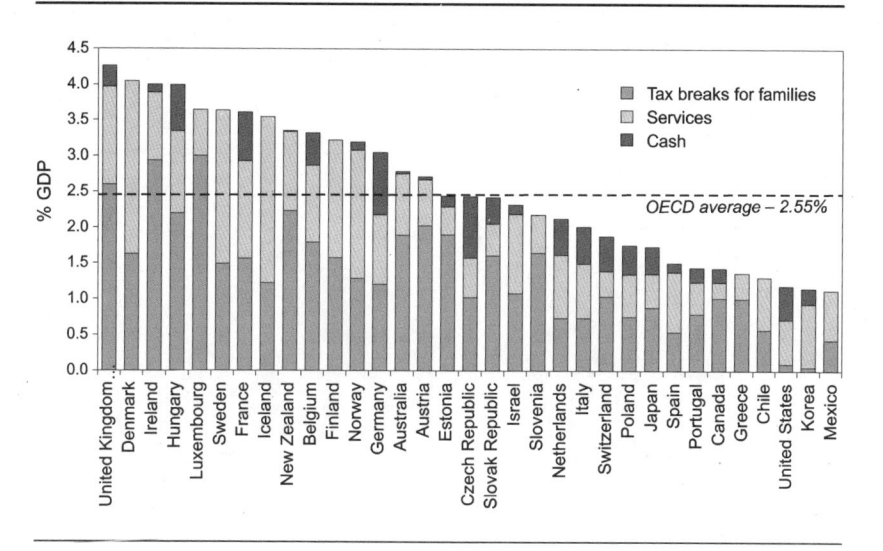

Source: Replicated from http://www.oecd.org/els/soc/PF1_1_Public_spending_on_family_benefits_Oct2013.pdf.

politics. Many countries (though not all) have maternity leave for mothers; indeed, many countries introduced paid leave in the 1970s and some even earlier, such as Italy in 1950.[3] The latter three programs, including flexibility in work-time arrangements, childcare, and parental leave for fathers, are less established and raised more frequently as programs that should be standard today.

There is substantial variation across countries in public spending on family benefits. We look only at OECD countries, and though they vary in their provision of programs to families none dedicates a large portion of the budget to family benefits. As depicted in Figure 15.3, the average amount of public spending on family benefits across the 33 countries for which there are data available is 2.55 percent of GDP, and it ranges from as low as about 1 percent in Mexico to as high as about 4.25 percent in the United Kingdom. Both Canada and the United States fall below the average and near the bottom of the group, while Scandinavian countries can be found near the top.

Interesting as well is the breakdown among spending on tax benefits for families, services, and cash. Countries vary widely in how they transfer benefits to families, and even those that spend more heavily do not necessarily do

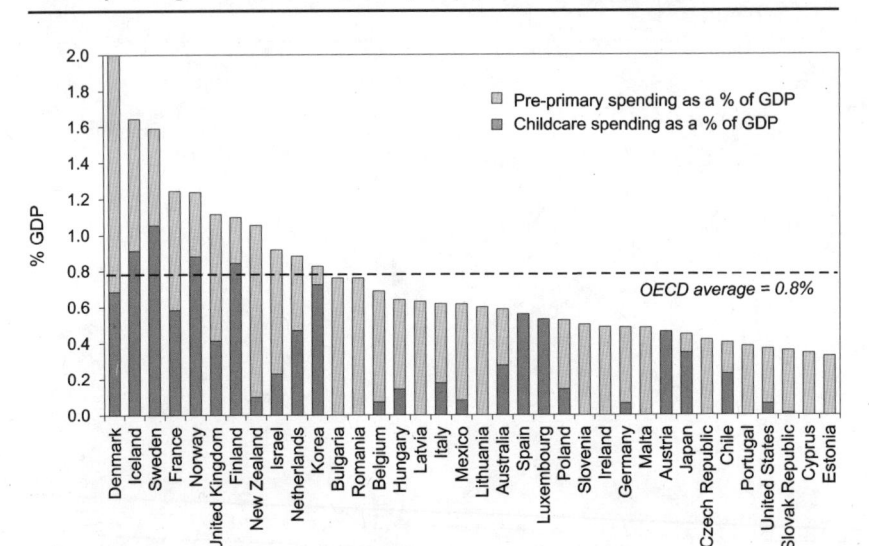

FIGURE 15.4
Public spending on childcare and pre-primary education, OECD countries

Source: Replicated from http://www.oecd.org/els/soc/PF3_1_Public_spending_on_childcare_and_early_education.pdf.

so in the same ways: the United Kingdom and Denmark are examples of higher spenders and have very different ratios across the three areas. Similarly, Korea and Mexico, the two countries that spend the least on family benefits, also have very different ways of transferring funds to parents. There is no "one way" that states confer benefits on families.

Childcare is one way that states can provide relief and support to families, and Figure 15.4 presents data on childcare and pre-primary education spending across the OECD countries. Not surprisingly, Denmark, Iceland, and Sweden are found at the top of the list when it comes to spending in this category, though of the three Sweden spends the most on childcare, whereas Denmark spends substantially more on pre-primary education.

Spending rates across OECD countries are not astronomical in this category overall, with an average of 0.4 percent of GDP spent on childcare and 0.5 percent of GDP spent on pre-primary education. Countries with the highest spending on childcare specifically, in addition to Sweden, Iceland, and Denmark, include Norway, Finland, and Korea. Again, we see the leadership of Scandinavian countries in supporting policies that facilitate gender equality.

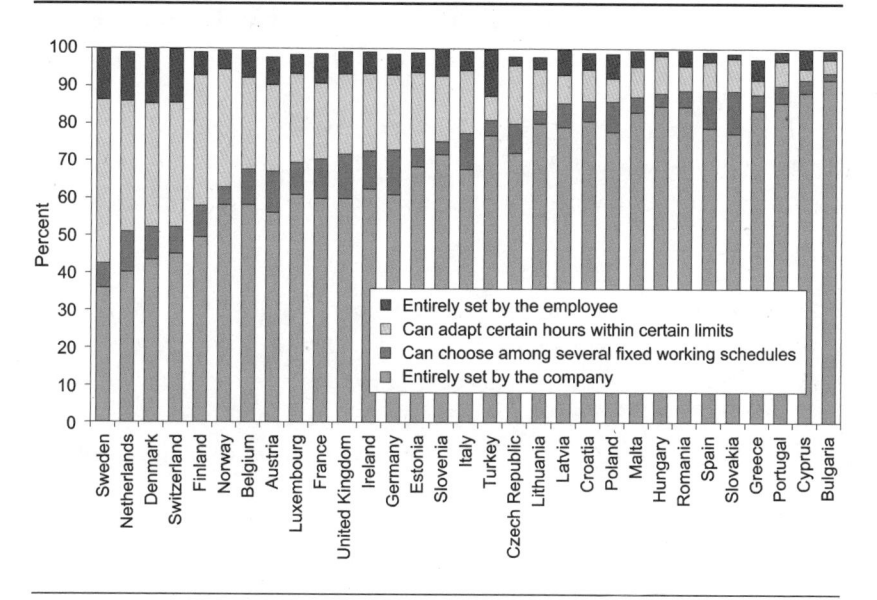

FIGURE 15.5
Flexibility in work-time arrangements, OECD countries, 2010

Source: Replicated from http://www.oecd.org/social/family/LMF-2_4_Family_friendly_workplace_practices_Sep2014.pdf.

Denmark and New Zealand spend the most on pre-primary education (1.3 percent and 1.0 percent of GDP, respectively), and a number of these countries spend only on pre-primary education and not on childcare. At the bottom of the OECD countries are Estonia, Cyprus, and the Slovak Republic. The United States is only slightly ahead of the three, spending 0.1 percent of GDP on childcare and 0.3 percent on pre-primary education.

Without state support for childcare and pre-primary education, many families look to "private" options for managing their work and childcare responsibilities. One idea that has gained in popularity as the result of a high-profile op-ed piece written by Anne-Marie Slaughter in the *Atlantic* magazine in 2012 is that flexibility in and autonomy over one's schedule can make major differences in women's abilities to "have it all." Slaughter compares her job as an academic to her job as the director of policy planning at the State Department, and she notes the incredible privilege of her challenging academic job, which gives her control over her schedule. As academic women ourselves, we can attest to this ability to manage our timetables and tend to our families when need be. On a number of occasions, we have been thankful that we are not required to punch a clock.

Although we lack more recent data, we do have information about flexibility in work-time arrangements across OECD countries for years as recent as 2010. Figure 15.5 presents the information available from some of these countries on the levels of autonomy that employees have over such arrangements.

As is clear from Figure 15.5, most employee hours are entirely set by companies: a little over 68 percent of employees have no autonomy over their work hours, and 7 percent of employees can choose from among several fixed work schedule options.

In some countries, companies offer more flexibility, and about 17 percent of employees in them can adapt their work hours within certain constraints. Only 6 percent of employees across OECD countries have complete autonomy over their schedules, and this freedom varies substantially by country: workers have the most autonomy (unsurprisingly) in Scandinavian countries (at the top, 14.4 percent of Swedish employees have complete control over their work hours).

This raises two important questions. First, is this flexibility still gendered? Studies suggest that flexibility in the workplace appears best when it is "faked": men are less likely than women to ask for permission to use flexible time to accommodate family responsibilities. Stated differently, whereas women ask for permission first from their employers to accommodate family responsibilities during work hours (and are often punished as a result), men are more likely to take the flex time and ask for forgiveness later, if required (New York Times 2015; Reid 2015). This suggests that although flexible time is a great addition to the workplace, more is required to ensure that women and men can access flexible time in comparable ways. Second, how can flexibility be integrated into politics? Slaughter's argument noted above rests on the difficulties that Slaughter encountered trying to balance work life and family life when transitioning from a flexible job (academics) to an inflexible job (politics). Chapters in this volume, notably the chapter by Campbell and Childs, highlight how the inflexibility of politics is hard on mothers in politics, for work-based expectations have developed around masculine norms and the assumption that there is a caregiver (wife) at home to look after the children while the (male) politician goes to the legislature or out into the constituency. These norms do not work particularly well for women in dual-earner homes who wish to participate in electoral politics; similarly, as expectations for gender, care, and unpaid labour in the home continue to change, we doubt that they will work well for men.

FIGURE 15.6
Paid leave reserved for fathers, OECD countries, 2014

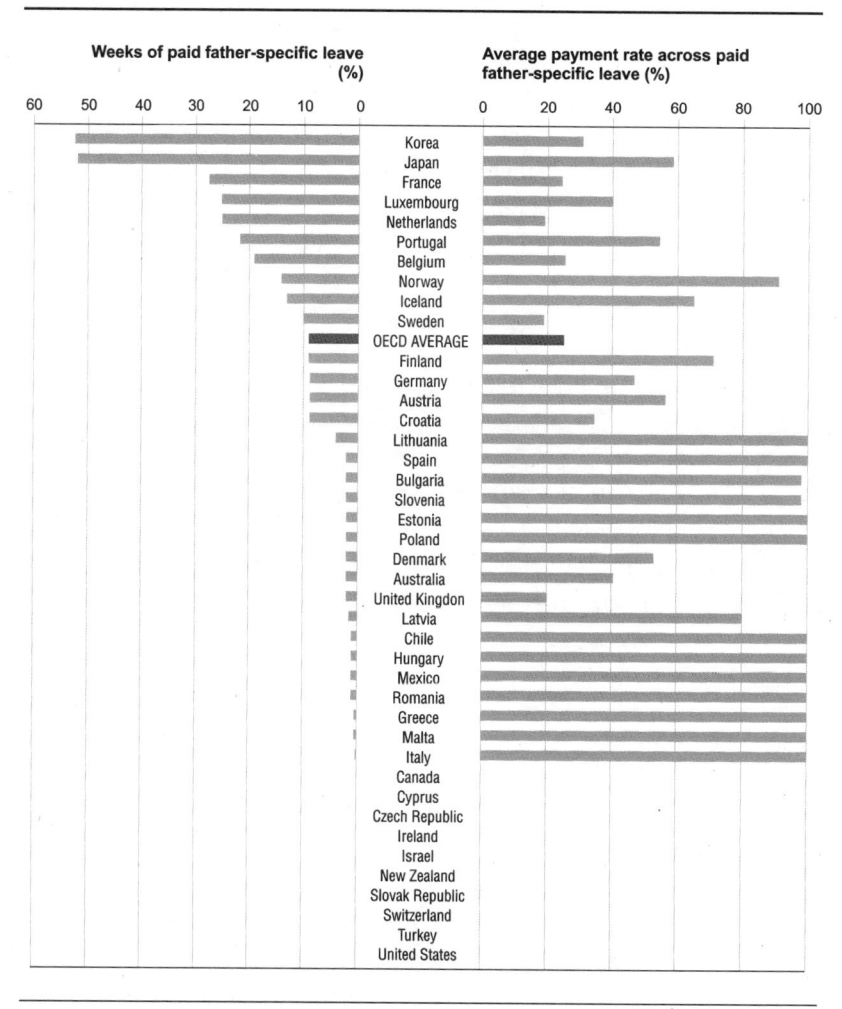

[Bar chart with two panels. Left panel: "Weeks of paid father-specific leave (%)" with x-axis from 60 to 0. Right panel: "Average payment rate across paid father-specific leave (%)" with x-axis from 0 to 100. Countries listed between panels:]

Korea
Japan
France
Luxembourg
Netherlands
Portugal
Belgium
Norway
Iceland
Sweden
OECD AVERAGE
Finland
Germany
Austria
Croatia
Lithuania
Spain
Bulgaria
Slovenia
Estonia
Poland
Denmark
Australia
United Kingdom
Latvia
Chile
Hungary
Mexico
Romania
Greece
Malta
Italy
Canada
Cyprus
Czech Republic
Ireland
Israel
New Zealand
Slovak Republic
Switzerland
Turkey
United States

Source: Replicated from http://www.oecd.org/els/soc/PF2_1_Parental_leave_systems.pdf.

Policies that encourage both parents to play strong roles in childrearing also encourage higher levels of gender equality. Paternity leave, or parental leave for fathers, is one such state policy, and again we see wide variation in provision of it across OECD countries. Figure 15.6, replicated from OECD reports, compares countries in terms of both the number of weeks of father-specific leave available and the average rate of payment across the time of leave. Countries are ordered according to how many weeks of leave are available to fathers.

We see substantial variation across the countries. For many countries, we lack data, but a clear trend is visible for those for which we do have information: countries that have the shortest durations of leave set aside specifically for fathers have the highest payment rates (presumably because it is relatively inexpensive to pay fathers 100 percent of their salaries for two weeks or less). Countries with the longest parental leaves available specifically for fathers are Korea and Japan, and they have widely different payment rates (31 percent and 58 percent, respectively). The OECD average is about nine weeks of leave with a payment rate of about 45 percent of normal annual income.

Again, though these policies are incredibly important for gender equality in the workforce, applying them to political work raises new challenges. Several chapters in this volume (Arneil, Campbell and Childs) explicitly note that new mothers in politics do not think that it is appropriate for them to take maternity leave. It follows that fathers in politics might think the same about paternity leave. Determining how best to help parents balance political careers, especially those predicated on democratic elections, is important if we wish to ensure that women and men of childbearing/rearing age can access this kind of work.

As has been the case for most of the data presented in this chapter, Scandinavian countries tend to fall above the average, both in relation to leave time available for fathers and in relation to payment rates during leave. The picture starting to emerge is one in which Scandinavian countries have the highest rates of female participation in legislatures, and the highest levels of support for women in the workplace, including spending on family benefits, childcare and pre-primary education, employee autonomy over work hours, and parental leave. What remains is something of a chicken/egg question: did support for women- or family-friendly policies come as a result of women's participation in politics, or did women's participation in politics follow as a result of state support? What is the role of values in all of this? Is Scandinavia just "different"? It is to attitudes that we now turn, though we do not really answer these questions, at least not to our satisfaction, and more research is necessary.

Values about Women, Work, Political Engagement, and Family

Cross-national opinion data analysis is not easy at the best of times, and longitudinal (over-time) analysis of attitudes across countries is nearly impossible. Still, we believe that incorporating attitudes about women's roles in work, politics, and the home is essential to understanding the trajectory of women's (and mothers' and fathers') participation in politics in the future. We assessed values about women, political engagement, and the family using World Values Survey (WVS) data collected between 1981 and 2014. These data are interesting in that they incorporate the attitudes of countries around the world, since different waves of the survey poll respondents in different sets of countries. Sometimes a country is included in the survey only once; at other times a given country is included in multiple waves.

Here we present basic statistics from OECD countries included in the WVS cumulative file (six waves from 1981 to 2014). We present data collected in three broad "categories" of attitudes, including those toward politics and engagement, gender equality, and the family and childrearing. As with the aggregate/state-level statistics presented earlier, there is substantial variation over time and across countries for all of the variables that we incorporate into our analysis.

Table 15.2 presents mean attitudes across 16 questions included in the WVS. Each wave of the survey includes a separate data point to track values over time.[4] All variables are coded on a 0–1 scale, where 1 reflects more progressive attitudes (e.g., support for equality).[5]

As indicated in the table, the most progressive attitudes can be seen on questions related to gender equality: both women and men should contribute to household income; university is *not* more important for boys than girls; men do *not* make better leaders or business executives; and men do *not* have first rights to jobs when they are scarce. Furthermore, there is widespread agreement that working mothers can establish warm and secure relationships with children just like mothers who do not work.

On other family-related questions, respondents are slightly less progressive, and the majority believe that children need homes with both mothers and fathers; that women need children to be fulfilled; that women want homes and children; and that being a housewife is just as fulfilling as working.[6]

On the dimension of politics and engagement, most agree that work is very important, but fewer believe that politics are important, fewer claim to be interested in politics, and very few report discussing politics with friends and family.

Across OECD countries on all of these dimensions, there is little change indicated in attitude over the past 30 years, though where there is change we do see an upward trend (as individuals become more progressive over time). For example, people disagree in greater numbers with the idea that men

TABLE 15.2
Average attitudes toward women, engagement, and family across waves of the WVS

	1981–84	1989–93	1994–98	1999–2004	2005–9	2010–14
POLITICS AND ENGAGEMENT						
Discuss politics with friends and family	.35	.44	.43	.37		
Interested in politics	.44	.49	.49	.44	.46	.49
Importance of politics		.44	.46	.46	.46	.49
Importance of work		.84	.82	.83	.78	.77
GENDER EQUALITY						
When jobs are scarce, men have first rights		.53	.60	.58	.73	.69
Men make better leaders			.56	.56	.63	.63
Men make better executives					.67	.66
University is more important for boys			.68	.71	.75	.72
Both women and men should contribute to household income		.65	.69	.70		
Jobs make women independent		.55				.70
FAMILY VALUES						
Children need homes with both mothers and fathers	.15	.07	.16	.14	.24	
Preschool children suffer when mothers work outside the home		.35				.57
Women need children to be fulfilled	.38	.35	.57	.47		
Women want homes and children		.36				
Working mothers can establish warm and secure relationships with children just like mothers who do not work		.57	.64	.67		
Being a housewife is just as fulfilling as working		.39	.37	.32	.36	.42

Gender, Parenthood, and Politics

have first rights to jobs when they are scarce, and they are less likely to agree that men make better leaders or executives than women in later years. Similarly, there is an upward shift reflecting ideas that children do not necessarily need homes with both mothers and fathers, that women do not necessarily need children to be fulfilled, that working mothers can establish warm and secure relationships with children, and that being a housewife might not be as fulfilling as paid work outside the home. When we look at all individuals and countries pooled together, citizens are becoming more progressive over time.

When we break citizens into subgroups, however, we see some variation. Figure 15.7 presents the results of *t* tests comparing average opinions among women to men and average opinions among parents and non-parents.

FIGURE 15.7

Comparing women and men, parents and non-parents (pooled data from WVS, 1981–2014)

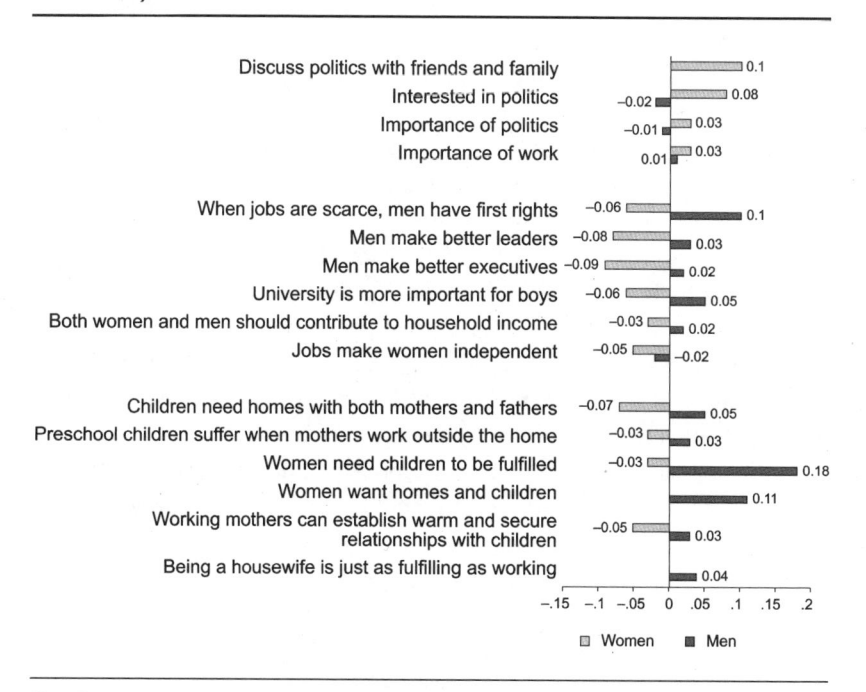

Question	Women	Men
Discuss politics with friends and family		0.1
Interested in politics	−0.02	0.08
Importance of politics	−0.01	0.03
Importance of work	0.01	0.03
When jobs are scarce, men have first rights	−0.06	0.1
Men make better leaders	−0.08	0.03
Men make better executives	−0.09	0.02
University is more important for boys	−0.06	0.05
Both women and men should contribute to household income	−0.03	0.02
Jobs make women independent	−0.05	−0.02
Children need homes with both mothers and fathers	−0.07	0.05
Preschool children suffer when mothers work outside the home	−0.03	0.03
Women need children to be fulfilled	−0.03	0.18
Women want homes and children		0.11
Working mothers can establish warm and secure relationships with children	−0.05	0.03
Being a housewife is just as fulfilling as working		0.04

Notes: Reports mean responses to questions. Positive values indicate that men and non-parents are more progressive; negative values indicate that women and parents are more progressive

Again, we caution that these are basic summary statistics, and we do not control for any other intervening variables likely to influence attitudes. Our goal here is to point to areas for further research rather than to make conclusive arguments one way or the other. Also, we are not comparing parents and women. The category "women" includes parents, and the category parents includes women. The reference groups in the graph are men and non-parents. Positive values indicate that parents/women are less progressive than their counterparts, whereas negative values indicate that parents/women are more progressive than their counterparts.

What is fascinating is that in almost all instances parents are less progressive than non-parents, and women are more progressive than men. This is in keeping with Goodyear-Grant and Bittner's findings in this volume and with research conducted elsewhere (Klar, Madonia, and Schneider 2014). Figure 15.7 depicts the gender gap and the parent gap across the same 16 questions included in Table 15.2. As the figure shows, men are more likely than women to be engaged in and prioritize politics and work, and parents are more likely than non-parents to be interested in and believe that politics are important.

When it comes to attitudes toward gender equality, again there are important gaps between the sexes and between parents and non-parents. Women are more progressive on all of the questions included in the gender equality dimension, and in relation to family values, where there are differences between women and men, women are more progressive. In contrast, parents are less progressive than non-parents on all of the same dimensions. They are more likely than non-parents to agree that men should have first rights to scarce jobs, that men make better leaders and executives, and that university is more important for boys; they are less likely to believe that both women and men should contribute to household incomes. Furthermore, they are more likely to agree that children need homes with both mothers and fathers, that children suffer when mothers work outside the home, that women need children to be fulfilled, and so on. Clearly, more research is needed to understand these more conservative tendencies among parents. We believe that controls are necessary to really tease apart the relationships among gender, parenthood, and attitude. Many of these patterns might disappear if controls are introduced, but at first blush we think that this is interesting and worth pursuing further.

One necessary control, for example, is country of origin. Indeed, when we look at overall attitudes of respondents across countries, we see substantial diversity in opinion. Table 15.3 presents mean responses to the same

TABLE 15.3
Average attitudes toward women, engagement, and family, OECD countries

	Australia	Canada	Czech Republic	Finland	France	Hungary	Italy	Japan	South Korea	Mexico	Holland	New Zealand	Norway	Poland	Spain	Sweden	Turkey	Great Britain	United States
POLITICS AND ENGAGEMENT																			
Discuss politics with friends and family	.42	.34	.55	.38	.43	.43		.32	.45	.39	.53	.49	.53	.48	.32	.50	.36	.39	.45
Interested in politics	.53	.46	.69	.42	.49	.49	.40	.56	.49	.38	.44	.54	.59	.42	.31	.53	.43	.42	.56
Importance of politics	.50	.46	.36	.33	.32	.32	.40	.61	.57	.47	.68	.46	.50	.38	.31	.54	.43	.43	.53
Importance of work	.73	.77	.79	.76	.79	.79	.86	.79	.84	.90	.84	.75	.82	.85	.82	.82	.82	.67	.72
ATTITUDES TOWARD GENDER EQUALITY																			
When jobs are scarce, men have first rights	.76	.82	.49	.83	.63	.63	.69	.44	.44	.64	.71	.80	.87	.53	.73	.95	.38	.75	.80
Men make better leaders	.64	.69	.47	.70	.53	.53	.65	.51	.48	.58	.74	.66	.81	.48	.69	.77	.42	.64	.63
Men make better executives	.71	.73		.68	.62	.62	.67	.56	.54	.65	.80	.69	.79	.60	.74	.80	.45	.67	.72
University is more important for boys	.75	.79	.58	.79	.76	.76	.72	.60	.64	.63		.76	.90	.64	.74	.86	.67	.74	.74
Both women and men should contribute to household income	.59	.67	.80	.72	.82	.82		.52	.62	.70	.76	.59	.72	.80	.71	.83	.74		.65
Jobs make women independent	.62		.53					.72	.51	.65		.57		.78	.71	.58	.76		.63

FAMILY VALUES	Australia	Canada	Czech Republic	Finland	France	Hungary	Italy	Japan	South Korea	Mexico	Holland	New Zealand	Norway	Poland	Spain	Sweden	Turkey	Great Britain	United States
Children need homes with both mothers and fathers	.24	.34	.02	.39		.04	.07	.09	.06	.17		.27	.24	.04	.14	.36	.04		.32
Preschool children suffer when mothers work outside the home	.65		.32					.55	.39	.43	.69	.61		.41	.52	.61	.41		.62
Women need children to be fulfilled	.70	.81	.17	.86		.09		.30	.23	.52		.82	.81	.30	.54	.83	.30	.82	.83
Women want homes and children			.25					.34	.31	.41					.44				
Working mothers can establish warm and secure relationships with children just like mothers who do not work	.60	.68	.65	.91		.72		.72	.58	.59		.61	.68	.52	.64	.73	.59		.67
Being a housewife is just as fulfilling as working	.38	.30	.53	.26			.46	.31	.31	.39	.47	.38	.42	.47	.45	.47	.33	.38	.32

Note: All variables are coded on a 0–1 scale, where 1 reflects more progressive attitudes.

16 questions, and it becomes clear that there is no "one way" of perceiving politics and engagement, attitudes toward gender equality, or family values across OECD countries.

Not surprisingly, values tend to be most progressive in Scandinavia, and we suspect that this is the case for both women and men as well as for parents and non-parents. More nuanced research is needed to understand the gaps seen in Figure 15.7 and determine whether they are "real" gender/parent gaps or something else.

There is substantial diversity across these dimensions even in comparing Canada, Australia, New Zealand, Great Britain, and the United States. Canadians appear to be less engaged with politics, for example, than Americans, Australians, or New Zealanders, but they appear to hold more progressive attitudes toward gender equality.

To what extent are these attitudes linked to aggregate patterns in state support for women and parents or to patterns in legislative participation? On the surface, it seems to be clear that mothers in Scandinavia have substantial advantages in state supports facilitating political participation over mothers in the United States, and indeed more Scandinavian women participate in politics than American women and by a large margin. Are there values about equality or family values to thank for the participation gap across countries? Or is it about state support and policies supporting gender equity?

These questions point to a need to understand the causal arrow: does state support precede value change, or does value change precede state support? Addressing this question is next to impossible with these cross-sectional data, and it is unlikely that the necessary longitudinal data exist. In the absence of an empirically confirmed time order, we offer the hypothesis that, once the process is under way, value change and state support reinforce each other. Indeed, cross-national research on the relationship between public opinion and policy suggests that it operates much like a thermostat (Soroka and Wlezien 2004, 2005, 2010), that public demand precedes government action and then responds to government action accordingly. These studies do not assess, however, broader attitudes toward equality and participation in their analysis; they focus on public demand and state provision of services through spending. The story is complex, and the path to greater participation is likely to involve both supportive state policies and changes in values. But more comparative and cross-time research is needed to assess these relationships fully.

Conclusion

State policies on women and work are different now than they were a century ago. Indeed, post-suffrage, a number of changes have led to women's increased presence in the workforce as well as formal politics. Yet there are substantial differences around the world, as reported by the Interparliamentary Union, not just overall but also within OECD countries.

The Scandinavian countries stand out as the gold standard, with high levels of state support for family-related policies, including childcare, parental leave, and higher levels of flexibility in work arrangements. In terms of values, we see some of the most progressive attitudes toward gender equality and "traditional" family ways. We also see high levels of political participation among women, which arguably have something to do with both attitudes and state supports. A number of countries follow in the Scandinavian wake, including western European countries, but much further down the line we see the Anglo-American democracies and central and eastern European countries.

Overall, though, more research is required to understand the relationship between state support for family- and women-friendly policies, values, and women's/mothers' participation in politics. Does state support precede value change? If yes, then governments can help to create more egalitarian societies through value leadership. Conversely, women's and mothers' participation in both work and politics might be required before policy changes occur. If so, then perhaps more generous parental leave policies will lead to value change via increases in women's representation in legislatures. All of this is highly speculative, however, and points to a number of interesting avenues of future research.

Another avenue of normative research that stems from this project addresses the question of how best to balance parental status and politics. Like others, we believe that it is deeply problematic to ask citizens in a democracy to leave politics voluntarily and/or delay exercising all of their democratic rights (e.g., running for or holding political office) because the responsibilities of being a parent are incompatible with the job. As shown by the data presented in this chapter, most societies now agree that parents will work outside the home and that the state can help families to balance their work and care responsibilities. Given that, the discrepancy between support provided for *working* families throughout OECD countries and lack of support provided for mothers/parents in *politics* is stark. Put simply, politics is work.

This volume has been focused on parenthood, but we highlight women's workforce and political participation here because of the intimately gendered nature of parenthood, which has had differential impacts on women and men in the past and is likely to have differential impacts on both in the future (though we recognize that the effects are shifting organically with the times). We are only starting to unpack the complex nature of the public/private and political/household divides, and, given that we are comfortable asserting that increased diversity in legislatures is desirable, we argue that understanding the nature of parenthood and its relationship to the political is essential because it provides an avenue to boost the representation of traditionally marginalized groups, such as women. We do not begin to ask (or answer) questions addressing these topics for sexual or racial minorities, though we think that these questions are just as important and likely to be even more complex for other historically underrepresented groups. More research is necessary, and we hope that this volume helps to spark some of it.

The contributors in this book have helped to launch a conversation about the role of parenthood in politics, seeking to understand better its influence on political careers, media and party/candidate strategic communications, and public opinion and political participation among "ordinary" citizens. We have learned that the role of parenthood in politics is complex, nuanced, gendered, and in no way straightforward. Parenthood affects men and women differently, thus influencing their political careers, their strategic choices as political candidates, and their basic values, attitudes, and political engagements as citizens. Furthermore, societal expectations for parents, while evolving and changing, are also gendered, thus influencing both media coverage and our perceptions of mothers and fathers in politics.

We began this book with a discussion on the complex relationship among gender, participation, and politics. In particular, we focused on the effects of stereotypes of motherhood and the "mommy problem" for women who have children but might be interested in pursuing political careers. This might be one area where politics and work are not seen the same way. As this concluding chapter has shown, most people seem to agree and understand that women and mothers are an important part of the workforce and that families are not better off when mothers stay home. As a result, the assumption is that the state should assist *working families* to allow them to flourish in society. At the same time, there still appears to be something different about how we think about parents involved in politics. On this front, we are left with a paradox.[7]

We are also left with a number of unanswered questions that could not be addressed in this volume. We have barely scratched the surface of the relationships among gender, parental status, and politics. Investigation of how race and ethnicity influence these relationships is urgently needed, particularly given their implications for political careers, media analysis, and vote choice (Tolley 2015). Similarly, interactions among sexual orientation and gender, parental status, and politics merit study, for there are increasing numbers of those who work in politics and declare themselves as LGBTQ. Given the range of reactions in this volume to more traditional presentations of gender and parental status in politics, it will also be key to determine when, why, and how various parental and gender identities are activated, suppressed, and valued in political careers and the political behaviour of individual citizens.

Notes

We would like to thank Josh Smee for his excellent research assistance.

1 http://www.ipu.org/wmn-e/world.htm.
2 http://www.fas.org/sgp/crs/misc/RL30261.pdf.
3 http://www.oecd.org/els/family/PF2_5_Trends_in_leave_entitlements_around_childbirth.pdf.
4 Recall, however, that not all waves include the same countries: these are not panel data, so this is not a true "tracking" table and does not follow the same group of respondents (or even countries) over time.
5 All coding details, Stata data files, and syntax are available from the authors.
6 This last question (about whether or not being a housewife is just as fulfilling as working) is difficult to code in that no clear "stance" is the most progressive. Some might argue that it is more progressive to believe that paid work outside the home is more satisfying than unpaid work inside the home, whereas others might suggest that both types of work are equally important and therefore should be equally satisfying. In our coding decisions, we opted to label the former as "most progressive." That is, those who said that the two types of work are equally satisfying were coded as the least progressive (value of 0 on the 0–1 scale). The low numbers in the table thus indicate that most people believe that being a housewife is just as satisfying as doing paid work outside the home.
7 Much of the research in this book points to the challenges faced by political parents as well as the roles of cultural attitudes toward gender, families, and the importance of care. However, part of the explanation might also be that, in addition to not really valuing care, society does not really value parenthood. We have pointed to the importance of removing barriers to political participation through the provision of services, but changing cultural norms to make society more family friendly might also change the relationship between parenthood and politics. More research on the subject is needed (and we thank one of our anonymous reviewers for this observation).

References

Atchison, A., and I. Down. 2009. "Women Cabinet Ministers and Female-Friendly Social Policy." *Poverty and Public Policy* 1 (2): 1–23. http://dx.doi.org/10.2202/1944-2858.1007.

Caiazza, Amy. 2004. "Does Women's Representation in Elected Office Lead to Women-Friendly Policy? Analysis of State Level Data." *Women and Politics* 26 (1): 35–70. http://dx.doi.org/10.1300/J014v26n01_03.

Campbell, D.E., and C. Wolbrecht. 2006. "See Jane Run: Women Politicians as Role Models for Adolescents." *Journal of Politics* 68 (2): 233–47. http://dx.doi.org/10.1111/j.1468-2508.2006.00402.x.

Dahlerup, D. 1988. "From a Small to a Large Minority: Women in Scandinavian Politics." *Scandinavian Political Studies* 11 (4): 275–98. http://dx.doi.org/10.1111/j.1467-9477.1988.tb00372.x.

Esping-Andersen, Gosta, ed. 2002. *Why We Need a New Welfare State*. Oxford: Oxford University Press. http://dx.doi.org/10.1093/0199256438.001.0001.

Goodyear-Grant, Elizabeth. 2010. "Who Votes for Women Candidates and Why? Evidence from the 2004 Canadian Election Study." In *Voting Behaviour in Canada*, edited by C. Anderson and L. Stephenson, 43–64. Vancouver: UBC Press.

Kathlene, Lyn. 1994. "Power and Influence in State Legislative Policymaking: The Interaction of Gender and Position in Committee Hearing Debates." *American Political Science Review* 88 (3): 560–76. http://dx.doi.org/10.2307/2944795.

Klar, Samara, Heather Madonia, and Monica Schneider. 2014. "The Influence of Threatening Parental Primes on Mothers' versus Fathers' Policy Preferences." *Politics, Groups, and Identities* 2 (4): 607–23.

Krook, M.L. 2010. "Why Are Fewer Women than Men Elected? Gender and the Dynamics of Candidate Selection." *Political Studies Review* 8 (2): 155–68. http://dx.doi.org/10.1111/j.1478-9302.2009.00185.x.

Mendelberg, T., C.F. Karpowitz, and N. Goedert. 2014. "Does Descriptive Representation Facilitate Women's Distinctive Voice? How Gender Composition and Decision Rules Affect Deliberation." *American Journal of Political Science* 58 (2): 291–306. http://dx.doi.org/10.1111/ajps.12077.

New York Times. 2015. "How Some Men Fake an 80 Hour Workweek and Why It Matters." http://www.nytimes.com/2015/05/05/upshot/how-some-men-fake-an-80-hour-workweek-and-why-it-matters.html?_r=0&abt=0002&abg=1.

Orloff, Ann. 1996. "Gender in the Welfare State." *Annual Review of Sociology* 22 (1): 51–78. http://dx.doi.org/10.1146/annurev.soc.22.1.51.

Paxton, P.M., and S. Kunovich. 2003. "Women's Political Representation: The Importance of Ideology." *Social Forces* 82 (1): 87–113. http://dx.doi.org/10.1353/sof.2003.0105.

Pew Research Center. 2013. "Modern Parenthood Roles of Moms and Dads Converge as They Balance Work and Family." http://www.pewsocialtrends.org/2013/03/14/modern-parenthood-roles-of-moms-and-dads-converge-as-they-balance-work-and-family/8/.

Reid, Erin. 2015. "Embracing, Passing, Revealing, and the Ideal Worker Image: How People Navigate Expected and Experienced Professional Identities." *Organization Science* 26 (4): 997–1017. http://dx.doi.org/10.1287/orsc.2015.0975.

Slaughter, Ann-Marie. 2012. "Why Women Still Can't Have it All." *Atlantic Monthly*, July–August. http://www.theatlantic.com/magazine/archive/2012/07/why-women-still-cant-have-it-all/309020/.

Soroka, Stuart, and Christopher Wlezien. 2004. "Opinion Representation and Policy Feedback: Canada in Comparative Perspective." *Canadian Journal of Political Science* 37 (3): 531–60.

–. 2005. "Opinion-Policy Dynamics: Public Preferences and Public Expenditure in the UK." *British Journal of Political Science* 35 (4): 665–89.

–. 2010. *Degrees of Democracy: Politics, Public Opinion, and Policy*. Cambridge: Cambridge University Press.

Thomas, Melanee. 2012. "The Complexity Conundrum: Why Hasn't the Gender Gap in Subjective Political Competence Closed?" *Canadian Journal of Political Science* 45 (2): 337–58. http://dx.doi.org/10.1017/S0008423912000352.

Tolley, Erin. 2015. *Framed: Media and the Coverage of Race in Canadian Politics*. Vancouver: UBC Press.

Wolbrecht, C., and D.E. Campbell. 2007. "Leading by Example: Female Members of Parliament as Political Role Models." *American Journal of Political Science* 51 (4): 921–39. http://dx.doi.org/10.1111/j.1540-5907.2007.00289.x.

Contributors

Barbara Arneil is a professor of political science at the University of British Columbia. She has a specialization in the intersection between liberalism and colonialism, and she is interested in gender and political theory. Her most recent work is in the areas of social trust and diversity, global citizenship and cosmopolitanism, the role of disability in political theory, and domestic colonies.

Amanda Bittner is an associate professor of political science at Memorial University. She studies elections and voting in both Canadian and comparative contexts. In addition to her ongoing work on party leaders, she has published research on voter turnout, immigration, and the impacts of social cleavage and political sophistication on political attitudes. Her current research includes voters' attitudes about immigration, the influence of gender on public opinion and voting, and Canadian parties and elections.

Rosie Campbell is a professor of politics at Birkbeck University of London. She has recently written on parliamentary candidates, the politics of diversity and gender voting behaviour, and political recruitment. She was the principal investigator of the ESRC-funded Representative Audit of Britain, which surveyed all candidates standing in the 2015 British General Election, and a co-investigator of a Leverhulme-funded study of British parliamentary candidates and MPs from 1945 to 2015 (see http://www.parliamentarycandidates.org).

Sarah Childs is a professor of politics and gender at the University of Bristol. Her research expertise centres on women's representation, political parties, and parliaments. She is currently researching feminized institutions with the UK Parliament and writing a book on substantive representation theory. In 2016, she published *The Good Parliament* report, outlining necessary reforms to achieve a diversity-sensitive House of Commons. She is the special adviser to the new House of Commons Reference Group on Representation and Inclusion.

Grace Deason is an assistant professor of psychology at the University of Wisconsin–La Crosse. She is currently working on several research projects that examine stereotypes of mothers and the impacts of motherhood on American politics. Her recent work has appeared in the *Journal of Personality and Social Psychology*, *Basic and Applied Social Psychology*, and *Public Opinion Quarterly*.

Elisabeth Gidengil is the Hiram Mills professor in the Department of Political Science at McGill University and the founding director of the Centre for the Study of Democratic Citizenship. Her research centres on public opinion, voting behaviour, and political engagement, with a particular focus on gender and diversity.

Janine Giles is a recent graduate of the PhD program in political science at the University of Calgary. Her doctoral research examined gender, political knowledge, and campaign learning in Canadian federal elections.

Elizabeth Goodyear-Grant is the director of the Queen's Institute of Intergovernmental Relations, the director of the Canadian Opinion Research Archive, as well as an associate professor in the Department of Political Studies at Queen's University. Her research focuses on elections, political behaviour, political communication, methods of measuring gender in survey research, and the political representation of women.

Jill Greenlee is an associate professor of politics and women's, gender, and sexuality studies at Brandeis University. Her current scholarship investigates the relationships between major life cycle events, such as becoming a parent, and the political attitudes and behaviours of ordinary citizens. She has published work in journals such as *Political Psychology, Politics and Gender,* and *Politics, Groups, and Identities.*

Rebecca J. Hannagan is an associate professor of political science at Northern Illinois University. Her research focuses on gender group dynamics and leadership. She is a National Science Foundation grant recipient as well as an Excellence in Undergraduate Teaching Award winner.

Allison Harell holds the UQAM Research Chair in the political psychology of social solidarity at the Université du Québec à Montréal, where she is an associate professor in the Department of Political Science. She also co-directs the Public Opinion and Political Communication Lab (LACPOP) and is a member of the Centre for the Study of Democratic Citizenship.

Shanto Iyengar holds the Chandler Chair in communication at Stanford University, where he is also a professor of political science and the director of the Political Communication Laboratory.

L.A. (Lisa) Lambert is a sessional instructor at the University of Lethbridge and works for the Legislative Assembly of Alberta. Her research interests are social movements, gender politics, and political parties.

Carrie Langner is an associate professor of psychology at California Polytechnic State University–San Luis Obispo. She investigates social hierarchy, collective identity, and political activism. Her work has been published in journals such as the *Journal of Personality and Social Psychology, Journal of Experimental Social Psychology,* and *Politics, Groups, and Identities.*

Valérie Lapointe is a doctoral candidate in the School of Political Studies at the University of Ottawa.

Christopher W. Larimer is an associate professor of political science at the University of Northern Iowa. His research focuses on the psychology of voting behaviour and state politics. He is the author of *Gubernatorial Stability in Iowa* and the co-author of *The Public Policy Theory Primer.*

Michele Micheletti holds the Lars Johan Hierta Chair of political science at Stockholm University.

Melissa K. Miller is an associate professor of political science at Bowling Green State University. Her research focuses on the intersection of gender and politics, voter behaviour, and political participation. Her work appears in *Public Opinion Quarterly, Political Research Quarterly, Politics and Gender*, and *PS: Political Science and Politics*, among other journals.

Brenda O'Neill is an associate professor of political science at the University of Calgary. Her research focuses on political engagement, public opinion, gender and party leadership, and Canadian feminism.

Ronnee Schreiber is a professor and the chair of political science at San Diego State University. She has published widely on conservative women and politics, and her book *Righting Feminism: Conservative Women and American Politics* has been reviewed extensively. Her recent projects include examining how motherhood and ideology intersect in politics, the status of conservative feminism, and how women fare in electoral politics.

Stuart Soroka is the Michael W. Traugott Collegiate Professor of communication studies and political science at the University of Michigan and a faculty associate in the Center for Political Studies at the Institute for Social Research.

Dietlind Stolle is a professor in the Department of Political Science at McGill University and the director of the inter-university Centre for the Study of Democratic Citizenship.

Melanee Thomas is an associate professor of political science at the University of Calgary. Her research centres on the causes and consequences of gender-based political inequality in Canada and other post-industrial democracies, with a particular focus on political attitudes, behaviour, and engagement.

Index

Age, 249, 254-56, 258, 298, 301-3; of children, 117, 122, 128, 269-70, 272-80, 282-85, 294, 298-300, 302-3, 320; and civic participation, 274-75; and political participation, 274-75, 320; and voter turnout, 270, 273-75
agency, of women, 136
Alvarez, Sonia, 64, 67
Americans United for Life, 126
Anglo-American democracies, 334
antifeminism, 127
Argentina, 67, 69, 72-78, 178
Armed Informed Mothers, 178, 183
Australia, 47, 49-52, 54, 157, 332

Bachmann, Michele (US), 113, 118, 124
balance, work/life, 115, 120-21, 123-25, 128-29, 313, 324
Batchelet, Michelle (Chile), 6, 69-71
Biden, Joe (US), 162, 164-65
bidirectional socialization, 290, 295, 300
Blair, Tony (UK), 137
Blakely, Shelby (US), 111, 122

Blanchette-Lamothe, Lysane (Canada), 56
Bloc Québécois, 143-44
Bolivia, 68
Boothroyd, Betty (UK), 48
breastfeeding, 9, 46, 184, 313; and lactating, 46-47; and public opinion, 50, 53; as public or private activity, 46-47, 52, 55, 58, 60, 184; sexualized breast, 55; societal norms, 46, 47, 56-57; in workplace, 47, 55-57
breastfeeding, advocacy of, 9, 54; pressure to be role model, 47, 57-58
breastfeeding, constituency care and, 46, 50, 53; and maternity leave, use of, 47, 50, 53-54, 57, 59
breastfeeding, in political institutions, 46-60; accommodation of, 46, 47, 51, 53, 60; best interests of child argument, 48, 51-52, 56, 59; emergency rule, 52, 59; facilities provision, 47-49, 56, 59; during legislative voting, 47, 52, 58, 60; refreshment rule, 48, 54, 57; scheduling challenges,

46, 54, 57, 60; and self-contained worker, 55-56; strangers rule, 47, 49-54, 57; workplace efficiency argument, 48, 55, 57
Brown, Barbara (US), 92
Brown, Gordon (UK), 137-38

California Federation of Republican Women, 122
Cameron, David (UK), 137
Campbell, Kim (Canada), 6, 157
Canada, 47, 52-56, 136, 142-46, 149, 157, 184-85, 202, 205, 207, 209-22, 227-28, 231-36, 248-49, 252, 254-56, 258-61, 269-85, 321-32
Canadian Census, 233
Canadian Election Study, 233
Carender, Keli (US), 119-20
carework, 28, 40, 79-80, 248, 313-15, 317-20; of disabled relations, 317, 319; of elderly relations, 317, 319; fathers, 317, 325; gendered, 320; hours per week, 318-19; mothers, 317; and political participation, 320; as private function, 28, 79; as unpaid labour, 324, 327; and women in labour force, 320
"caring-ocracy," 71
Central European countries, 334
Chamorro, Violeta (Nicaragua), 70
Chaney, Elsa, 64, 67
child well-being policy, 182
childcare, 7, 52, 65, 208, 232, 270, 314; 317, 319-21, 326
childcare programs, 320
childcare spending, 232-33, 322, 326
children, with disabilities, 184-85
children, number per household, 274, 276, 278, 282, 303
Chile, 67-69, 73-74, 76-77, 79
Chinchilla, Laura (Costa Rica), 69, 72
civic skills, 271, 276
Clare Boothe Luce Policy Institute, 119
Clark, Helen (NZ), 6
Clinton, Chelsea (US), 162-63

Clinton, Hillary (US), 12, 156, 158, 160-64, 168-73
collective identification, 179-80; and gender, 180; individual variation, 180-81; and motherhood, 180; and parenthood, 180; self-categorization, 180
Colombia, 76, 79
Community Living Movement, 184-85
Concerned Women of America, 183
Conformité Européene (CE), 297
conservatism 115, 118, 122; economic, 115; and feminist movement, 115, 118, 122; social, 115
conservative attitudes, 249-50, 253-54, 256-57, 259, 262, 330
conservative effects, 205, 208-9, 212-21
Conservative Party of Canada, 136, 142-46, 149
Consumption and Social Issues Survey, 294
Cordova, Alyssa (US), 119
Costa Rica, 68-69, 72, 76, 79
crime and security, 204-5, 209-12, 314; in domestic realm, 205; and gender gap, 204; salience to parents, 204, 208, 212-13; war and conflict, 204-5
Crouse Yoest, Charmaine (US), 126-27
cuing, 14, 136, 140, 206, 222; and parental issues, 206
Cullen, Nathan (Canada), 145
cultural issues, 205-6, 209-16, 220, 314; abortion, 205; diversity, 205; gender equality, 205; racial equality, 205; same-sex marriage, 205, 220
Cyprus, 323

Dannenfelser, Marjorie (US), 117, 120, 124, 126
democracy, 9, 25, 67, 69
Democratic Party (US), 156, 158, 160, 162-64
Denmark, 322-23
Dewar, Paul, Canada, 145
DiQuinzio, Patrice, 182

Index

division of labour, gendered, 9, 25, 65, 67, 75, 80, 207, 251
Dole, Elizabeth (US), 158
"double bind" for women, 157
double day, 7, 75, 78, 228-29, 233, 238, 240, 272, 279, 281, 314
Drown, Julia, United Kingdom, 48, 55
dual-caring model, 251
dual-earner couple, 279, 324; and political participation, 324

Eagle Forum, 119
early childhood education, 79, 320, 322-23, 326
Eastern European countries, 334
East Germany, 250
Ecuador, 68
education level, 208-10, 249, 254-56, 258, 276-77, 283-84, 294-95, 298, 300-3
Edwards, Cate (US), 162-63
Edwards, John (US), 161
electoral systems, 315
employment, 228-29, 254-56, 258, 271-72, 276, 279-80, 283-84; and political participation, 271-72, 276, 279-80; self-employment, 279
environmental issues, 314
Equal Rights Amendment 111, 119
Estonia, 318, 323
European Economic Area, 297
European Union, 290

families, working, 335
family, 204, 288, 292; conceptions of, 205; and consumer items, 289-90, 296-97, 299-300; polarization of, 204; politicization of, 204, 206; social program usage, 208-9
family benefits, 293, 320-21; as allowance, 293; as cash, 321; and public spending, 320-21; as services, 321; as tax benefits, 321
family responsibilities, 30; lack thereof as resource, 30

family values, 205
fatherhood, 190, 192, 201, 203; and marital status, 203-4; and political participation, 313; and social expectations, 207-8, 218; and social welfare attitudes, 203
female politicians, 4, 76, 138-41, 146-48; and appearance, 139; and caregiving needs, 39; and character, 139; with children, 4, 76; without children, 4, 76; and competency, 139; family size, 76; and gender violations, 139; marital status, 76; and maternal guilt, 28, 37; media representation of, 11, 138-39; and privacy concerns of, 148; and safety concerns of, 148; and strategic communications of, 139-40, 143; and voter reactions to, 139
feminine stereotypes, 139-40, 147-48, 156, 158-59, 172, 335; as benign triggers, 168; as caregivers, 78; and branding, 11-12, 140, 147-48; and expertise, assumptions of, 159; grandmotherhood, 141, 146; impact of, 7; and maternal identities, 67; motherhood, 140-41; and motherhood (in)compatibility, 6, 50, 71; and women's (in)compatibility, 6, 7, 35-37
feminism, 25, 66, 118; and free choice, 118
Fernández de Kirchner, Cristina (Argentina), 69, 72
Ferraro, Geraldine (US), 117
fertility rate, 269
Finland, 318, 322
fixed work schedules, 324
foreign policy, 179
framing, 69, 159
Fujimori, Keiko (Peru), 72

Gandhi, Indira (India), 6
gender, 253-58, 294-95, 300-1
gender balance law, Iowa (HF243), 87-88, 90; and applicant selection, 91;

attitudes towards 91, 94, 97-99, 102; and balance boards, 95-97; compliance with law, 93; conservative board members, 99-100; constituent representation, 91; critics of, 89, 92, 104-5; and economic boards, 95; enforcement mechanism, lack thereof, 90, 94; interpretation of, 91; monitoring mechanism, lack thereof, 90; non-conservative board members, 99-100; and non-economic boards, 95; and non-gender balanced appointments, 90; positive effects of, 88, 91-92; proponents of, 89, 92; in municipal politics, 87-90; quota appointment versus merit appointment, 103; rationale for law, 91; and recruitment of mothers, 95, 105-6; and recruitment of women, 88, 95, 104; rural challenges, 92, 94; sitting board members as gatekeepers, 89-91, 94, 101; and skewed female boards, 95-97; and skewed male boards, 95-97; and women's organizations, impact of, 103-4

gender-conditional effects, 206-7, 210-14

gender differences, 125-28

gender equality, 293, 314, 318, 320, 326-27; and political representation, 314; and policy, 326

gender gap, 139, 207, 226, 238, 330; and childcare, 139, 207; at constituency level, 227, 238; and household labour, 139, 207-9; and paid work, 207, 209

gender inequality, 251; and amelioration approach, 251

gender neutrality, 248, 251, 294-96

gender of politicians, 12, 40, 92, 95; and agenda setting, 92; and displays of family, 12, 40; and personal characteristics, 95; and political attitudes, 95

gender quotas, 9, 68-69, 315

gender role ideology, 248-54, 256-60, 262; attitudes toward, 248-49, 253-54, 259

gender roles, 112, 226, 314; and conservative natural derivation, 112; and feminist social construction, 112

gender stereotypes, 191-92, 207-8, 218

gendered norms, 9, 25, 65, 69, 76-78, 81, 191-92; of caretaking, 9, 25, 65, 78; and policy making, 69, 78, 81; and societal expectations, 76-77

gendered policy, 74, 77; abortion, 74; child support, 77; childcare, 77; children's rights, 74; contraception, 74; divorce, 77; domestic violence, 74; family, 77; inheritance, 77; marital property, 77; parental rights, 77; sexual harassment in the workplace, 74; social issues, 74; and work, 77

General Social Survey, 270; Canadian, 207; US, 203

Gillard, Julia (Australia), 3, 6

Gillon, Karen (Scotland), 58

Glover, Shelly (Canada), 145

government intervention, 255-58

gun control, 111-12, 178, 182

Hassainia, Sana (Canada), 52, 57-58

healthcare, 320

Healy, Kerry (US), 123-24

Hodge, Margaret (UK), 48

Hoffman, Gabriella (US), 121-22

household labour, 7, 75-76, 79, 228, 269-70, 278-79, 314

housing support, 320

Iceland, 322

identities, 15, 190; professional, 190; public and private, 190

ideology, 216-28; centrist, 216-17; left-wing, 216-17; right-wing, 216-17, 220; and socialization, 215, 217

image management, 138

income level, 300, 302-3

Independent Women's Forum, 111, 118

Index

intergenerational justice, 288-89
Interparliamentary Union, 315, 334
Iowa, 87, 89-90; and HF243, 90
Israel, 291

Jamieson, Kathleen Hall, 157
Jowell, Tessa (UK), 48

Korea, 322, 325

labels, awareness of, 297, 303-5
Latin America, 9, 64-68
Left's War on Women, 113
leisure time, 270
liberal attitudes, 249, 256-58
Liberal Party of Canada, 143-45
liberal effects, 205, 208-9, 212-21
local boards, 87; appointments to, 90; and civic engagement, 105; and civic training, 92, 104; and inclusion, 105; and leadership opportunities, 92; and recruitment, 90; and volunteerism, 88-89, 92-94, 105

Mackay, Fiona, 25-26, 39-40
Maddigan, Judy (Australia), 50
Madigan, Lisa (US), 3, 156, 160
Madres de Plaza de Mayo, 67, 178
male politicians, 4, 11, 37, 76; and caregiving needs, 4, 39; with children, 4, 76; without children, 4, 76; family size, 76; marital status, 76; media coverage of, 11; and paternal guilt, 37
March of the Empty Pots, 68; and change, 82; and political careers, impact on, 81; use by conservative women, 68, 111
marital conflict, 269
marital status, 27, 76, 249, 253-59, 269, 270; interaction with motherhood, 27; interaction with fatherhood, 76
marriage, definition of, 251
Marshall, Kirsty (Australia), 49, 57
Martin, Michael (UK), 48
Martinez, Richard (US), 192

Mascher, Mary (US), 91
masculine stereotypes, 6-7, 66, 71, 78, 138-40, 158-59; and branding, 140, 147; as breadwinners, 78; desirability, for political career, 6-7, 71; expertise, assumptions of, 159; of fatherhood, 140-41; of grandfatherhood, 141, 146; as normalcy, 143; and patriarchalism, 66
material self-interest, 207-9; group benefit, 207; and issue positionality, 208; personal benefit, 207; and salience, 208
maternal activism, 183, 185, 191, 193
maternal identity, 71; and age of children 182; development of, 181
maternal protest, 178-79
maternal thinking, 112
maternalism, 9, 64-68, 70, 72, 75, 80-81, 111; as cultural ideology, 64-65, 75, 80; and electoral participation, 64; and familial metaphors, 66; and gendered ideals, 72, 81; as militant mothers, 64, 72; as national caregivers, 64, 81; and political activism, 64, 68; and "republican motherhood," 66-67; as "super-madres," 64, 67, 70, 72
maternalist frames, 80, 111
maternalist politics, 182, 191; and gun control policy, 182; and gun rights policy, 182
maternity leave, 78, 320, 326
McCain, John (US), 158, 162, 166-67, 169
McKay, Joanna, 25, 28
members of Parliament (Canada), 135-48; activities external to election campaigns, 136; communication of parental status, 135-37, 142-45, 147-49; constituent communication mentions, 142, 145-48; family photographs of, 142-47; gender, 135, 141; parental status, 135-36, 141; by party affiliation 136, 139, 141-42, 144-45;

by province, 136; as strategic advantage, 135, 146, 148; as strategic disadvantage, 135, 146, 148
Merkel, Angela (Germany), 6
Mexico, 68, 73-74, 77, 79, 321-22
Million Mom March, 178, 183
minority status, 254, 258
modern welfare state, 247-48, 250-52, 293; childcare programs, 247; and division of labour, 247-48, 251; employment insurance, 247; family allowances, 247; as gendered system, 247-48; maternity benefits, 247
MOMocrats, 183, 191
MomsRising, 111, 183
Morgan, Julie, United Kingdom, 48
Mothers Against Drunk Driving, 182
motherhood, 10, 112-13, 129, 181-82, 201, 203, 207-8, 218, 227-28, 236-37, 240, 247-48, 268-70, 272, 274; as biological difference, 247; and campaign strategies, 113; and caregiving, 39, 71; and civic participation, 268-70, 272, 274; conservative constructions of, 10, 112; and employment rate, 236-37; feminist constructions of, 112; and gender roles, 113, 129; as gendered parenting, 247; marital status, 228; as motivation, 272; and political knowledge, 227-28, 240; and political participation, 268-70, 272, 274; politicization of, 181; and representation of women's interests, 113; social expectations 207-8, 218; and social welfare attitudes, 203; stages of, 181-82
motherhood eras, 184; civic motherhood, 184; politicized motherhood, 184; "republican motherhood," 184
motherhood frames, 183, 190-92; packaging of motherhood, 190
motherhood identity cuing, 14; descriptive representation, 26, 30, 32, 37, 39; and political participation, 16;

substantive representation, 39; underrepresentation, 30
motherhood media representation, 155-57; age of children, 156, 160, 172; campaign press coverage, 155-58, 161; competency, 156, 172; family photographs, 157; focus on private sphere, 155-56; privacy of children, 173; as strategic advantage, 155-56, 167-68, 172-73; as strategic disadvantage, 155, 164, 168, 172-73
motherhood movement politics, 182; affordable childcare, 182; welfare rights, 182
motherhood salience, 184-85, 190, 272
mothers, first-time, 249
mothers, lone, 317
mothers, partnered, 317
mothers, working, 228, 232, 247-50, 269; as percentage of labour force, 316-17
Mothers for a Moral America, 179
Mothers Strike for Peace, 179
Mott, Stacey (US), 116, 118
Murray, Patty (US), 155-56, 169

National Annenberg Election Survey, 161, 168-69
National Election Study, 204
Netherlands, 318
new conservative mothers, 116, 118, 127
New Democratic Party of Canada, 137, 142; and working families, 137, 142-46, 149
new media environment, 141; and political brand management, 141
New Zealand, 323, 332
Nicaragua, 68, 79
nonparents, 3-4, 202-3, 205-6, 208, 212-15, 217-18, 220, 232, 290, 293, 298-99, 302, 314, 316, 329; and choice, 3; and infertility, 4; and women, 3
non-traditional relationships, 314
North Dakota, 88-89

Index

Norway, 322
Not One More meme, 192
nurse-ins, 182

Obama, Barack (US), 158, 161-62, 166
Organisation for Economic Co-operation and Development (OECD), 315-34; birthrates, 316; lone mothers, 317; number of children, 316; partnered mothers, 317; and single-parent households, 318; and two-parent households, 318
Orloff, Ann S., 250-51

Palin, Bristol (US), 164, 166
Palin, Sarah (US), 11-12, 113, 117-18, 124, 156, 158-62, 164-73
Paraguay, 68
parent gap, 330
parental effects, 202, 206, 209, 211-17; and directional effects, 206, 210-11; as gender-conditional, 202, 206-11, 217-18, 220-21; and salience effects, 206, 208, 222
parental identity, 181-82, 190; developmental phases of, 181-82; and ideological orientation, 183; and political content, 181-83; and political motivation, 190; and professional identity 190; and other-advocacy, 182; and self-advocacy, 182
parental leave, 248, 250, 252-53, 257, 259, 260, 293, 314, 320, 325-26
parental status, 6, 88-89, 138-39, 141, 143, 145, 147-48, 168-71, 226, 229, 232, 234, 238, 240, 249, 253-58, 262, 313; age of children, 141, 145, 147-48; and candidate biographies, 138, 143; display of, 313; effects of, 316; electoral campaigns, 5, 27-28; media coverage, 156; and motivation, 90, 101-2, 105-6; and political careers, 6, 88-89, 139; and political knowledge, 15; and public opinion 168-71; representation of parents, 107

parenthood, 5, 13, 201, 206, 268-69; as adult experience, 201, 206; as gendered, 5, 335; early, 281; and issue dimensions, 15; and material self-interest, 202, 203, 206, 209, 215; and media strategies, 335; as mobilizer, 16, 298-99, 302, 304, 314; and political action, 289-90, 313; and political attitudes 202, 206-7, 211; and political careers, 335; and political engagement, 313; and political participation, 314, 317; as politicized, 13; and public opinion, 335; as role model, 289; and social integration, 271; on social media, 13; as socializing agent, 289-90, 293; socializing effects of 202, 206-7, 209
Perón, Evita (Argentina), 72
Peru, 67, 72, 79
petition signing, 273-75, 278-79, 282-85
parents, in public office, 314, 330
parents, working, 298, 300, 314, 326, 330
paternity leave, 320, 325-26; and gender equality, 325
political activism, 271-72; and women, 112-13
political activities, 227; letter writing, 227; political discussions, 227; political donations, 227; and recruitment, 231
political ambition, 139; and gender, 139
political behaviour, 229-31; and gender, 230, 231
political brand, 136-37; and elite-level participation, 136; and party brand framework, 137; and personal life, 137, 140; and media representation, 138; role of family, 137; and theories of representation, 136
political careers, 92
political consumerism, 273-75, 277-79, 282-85, 293, 298, 300-3

political engagement, 229, 231, 330; and activism, patterns of, 230; as gendered 229, 231; local effects, 229
political identity, 271
political institutions, 8-9; ethic of care, 8; mother-friendly policies, 9
political knowledge, 226; gendered context of, 226, 233, 238-39; individual context of, 227-29, 231-35, 239, 241; socio-economic context of, 226-28, 231, 233, 236
Political Parity Project, 123
political resources, 227, 240, 271; and education level, 227-228, 231, 233-37, 240; and gender gap, 227-29, 241; and local contexts, 227, 233-35, 241
political socialization, 268
politicization of personal life, 137, 140, 192
politicized collective identity, 180-81
politicized groups, 202; and internal party communications, 202
Politicized Motherhood, 179-80, 183, 190, 193; associated political meanings, 183, 185; and class, 190; images of, 179, 185; influence on collective mother identity development, 183; and Internet, 179; and political activism, 179-80; and self, 185; and race, 190
politicized mothers, 126; as political consumers, 126
politicized parental identity, 179-81, 183-85, 191, 193; as distinguished from a politicized gender identity, 181; across eras, 181; extent of identification, 181; across identity types, 181; across ideological spectrum, 181
pregnancy, 281
pre-primary education, 322-32, 326
primary caregivers, 112, 115, 125, 127, 257, 315-17; and gendered norms, 324

progressive attitudes, 330, 333-34; and men, 330; and non-parents, 330; and parents, 330; and women, 330
pro-life movement, 117, 124, 179
public opinion gaps, 201-5; cuing by media, 203, 206, 221; cuing by parties, 203, 206, 221; and gender, 201, 203-4, 206-14; and parenthood, 201, 203-4, 206-15; and policy, 333; and self-interest, 203, 206-9, 218-19, 221-22; and socialization, 203, 206-7, 215, 218-19, 221-22
public policy, 316, 320; family-friendly, 316, 320; women-friendly, 316, 320
public/private spheres, 112, 314, 335

Quebec, 232-40, 273-85
Quebec Women's Political Participation Survey, 273-85

race, 250, 254-55, 281
Race, Gender, and Support for the Welfare State Survey, 248, 252-56
religiosity, 249, 256-57, 277, 283-85
religious conservatives, 112
Republican mothers, 113; competing values, 113; and constituent mobilization, 113; media framing of, 113; as political actors, 113; and public debate, impact on, 113
Republican Party, 156, 158-60, 164
Rice, Condoleezza (US), 6
role constraints hypothesis, 271
Rouseff, Dilma (Brazil), 69, 71
rural areas, 92, 94, 234, 249

salience, 222
Sapiro, Virginia, 271
Saward, Michael, 114; and claims to be representative, 114, 127; and political actors, 114
Scandinavia, 315, 321, 324, 326, 333-34
Schlafly, Phyllis (US), 119, 125, 127-28
school funding, 182
school politics, 272

Second Amendment Sisters, 178
sex discrimination, 247; and gender norms, 259, 262
sex of children, 215-17, 221
sex of parent, 210
single-earner couple, 279
single mothers, 269, 278
single parents, 208, 218, 220, 259
Slaughter, Anne-Marie, 8, 323-24
Slovak Republic, 323
Smart Girl Politics, 116
Smith, Danielle (Alberta), 4
Smit-Kroes, Neelie (Netherlands), 140
social context, 229-30; and parental status, 232; and social networks, 230-32, 241; and workplace, 232
social isolation, 270-71
social networks, 230-32, 241, 271
social reproduction, 250-51
social welfare, 203-4, 209-13; and maternal thinking, 204; salience to parents, 204, 211; social spending on, 209-10
socialization, 206-7, 305; bidirectional, 290, 295, 300; unidirectional, 290
Solberg, Erna (Norway), 6
spousal involvement, 122-23, 125
Squires, Judith, 114; and constitutive representation of gender, 114; and public discourse, 115; and representation claims, 115
state legislators, 89; age, 89; family status, 89
state support, 320; for carers, 318, 320; for families, 320; for parents, 320, 333; for political participation, 320; for political representation, 320; and value change, 333; for women, 320, 333; for workforce participation, 320
stay-at-home motherhood, 118-19, 127; and wage gap, 118
Susan B. Anthony List, 117, 121
sustainability, 288-89, 291-96, 301, 305; energy use, 288; food, 298-300; and gender difference, 301; and household consumption, 289, 293; and shopping practices, 300-1; and values, 289-90, 292; waste reduction, 288; water use, 288
Sweden, 289, 293-94, 296, 302, 315, 322, 324
Swift, Jane (US), 11, 156, 160

Tea Party Patriots, 111, 116, 119, 121, 123
Thatcher, Margaret (UK), 6
time use, 228, 268, 270, 272; as gendered, 8, 228, and political schedules, 8-9, 28; studies of 7, 207
Toews, Vic (Canada), 141
toy brands, 297, 300; and country of origin, 297; and research by consumers, 297-98, 300
toy industry, 292; and corporate social responsibility, 292, 294-95, 297-98, 300-1
toy recalls, 297, 298
toy safety, 288, 290-92, 294-95, 297, 301, 303-4
toy scandals, 297-98, 300
toy selection, 292-94; and educational value, 292, 294-95, 297; and entertainment value, 292, 295; and motivation, 294; and safety, 292-94
toy shopping, 289, 291
toys, 288-90; consumption of, 288-93, 296-97, 302; and environmental impact, 288-89, 291-93, 295-99; and household economy, 293-95, 298, 303; production of, 288, 291, 293-94, 296, 314; regulation of, 291, 297, 300; and social equity, 288, 291, 293, 296-97, 299, 301-3; as socializing agents, 288, 296, 301, 303
toys, gendered, 291-93, 301, 303; and age of children, 292; and gender neutrality, 294-96
Trotter, Gayle (US), 111
Truppe, Susan (Canada), 145

unidirectional socialization, 290

United Kingdom, 25-45, 46-49, 54, 137, 143, 248, 252, 254-58, 260-61, 321-22, 333
UK Speaker's Conference on Parliamentary Representation, 40-41; on campaign conduct, 40; on caregiving leave, 40; on childcare vouchers, 40; on parliamentary hours, 40; omission of job sharing, 40-41
United States, 87-110, 111-131, 136-38, 143, 155-57, 202-5, 210, 212, 221, 230-31, 248-50, 252, 254-58, 260-61, 281, 321-22, 332
urban areas, 234
Uruguay, 79

values, 326-31; and attitude change, 327; and education level, 327; family values, 327-28, 332, 334; fulfillment of women, 327, 29; gender equality, 327-31; and income level, 327-28; and leadership, 327-29; parenting needs of children, 327; and workforce participation, 327; and working mothers, 327-29; and political engagement, 327-29; and political participation, 327-29
Vázquez, Josefina (Mexico), 71
volunteerism, 272-75, 277-79, 282-85; for campaigns, 281; for parties, 281
voter attitudes, 202; age of children, impact of, 160; on crime and security, 202, 204-5; on cultural issues, 202, 205-6; as female parents, 159; and headline visibility, 168-69; as male parents, 159; as nonparents, 159; on parental leave policies, 16; on social welfare, 202-4
voter behaviour, 160
voting, 273-76, 278-79, 282-85

W Stands for Women, 113
Weiss, Pat (US), 122, 124-25, 128
West Germany, 250
Western European countries, 334

Wildman, Dawn (US), 116, 121, 126
women, benefits for, 251; job security for, 251; as mothers, 252-54, 257, 260; as workers, 252-54, 257, 260
women, conservative, 10, 78-80, 114-15, 179; candidates, 117; and conservative ideology, 119; and language of choice, 119-20, 125, 128; and motherhood, 172; narratives of, 114-15; outsourcing of carework by, 79-80; personal narratives of, 114, 122-24; and professional roles, 115; role models, 119
women candidates: appearance, focus on, 157-58, 168, 171; biographical information, 162-66; children, focus on, 157, 162-63; coverage of, 157; fairness, 157-58, 160, 169, 172; family status, focus on, 157-58; gender, focus on, 158, 168-71; identification by parental status, 157, 161, 168, 171; identification of men by professional credentials, 157; identification by spousal role, 157; personality, focus on, 157; and policy issues, 158
women constituency representatives, 28, 71; age of children, 31, 32; age of representatives, 35, 37; breastfeeding, 28, 31; care work, 28, 40; core hours reform, 34; distance between work and home, 28, 30, 31, 33, 37; family size, 29; maternity leave, 28, 31, 47; out of hours networking, 28, 30, 36-37; parental status, 37-38; parliamentary timetable, 28, 30, 33, 35, 37; and political recruitment, 27, 37; relationship with children, 33-34, 37; relationship with spouse, 28, 31-34, 36-37; safety, 33; single-income, 33-34; spouses as co-parents, 12, 28, 32, 39; and supply-and-demand model, 27, 30, 38; and underrepresentation, 25, 30, 36
women in municipal politics, 87

Index

women political leaders, 65, 69-71, 81; participation barriers, 75-76
women political participants, 13, 67-69, 71-72, 77, 88, 313-16; campaign finances, 27; childcare needs, 27, 33; flexible time, access to, 27; at elite level, 313; and partisanship, 13; as party members, 77; and policies to facilitate, 315; and policy preferences, 13, 69, 73-74, 81, 105; as political activists, 68-69; as political consumers, 13; as protesters, 13, 67-68; and recruitment, 320; as role models, 315; as volunteers, 13, 88; as voters, 13, 67
women's organizations, conservative, 115, 122, 128; and childcare, 122; and family leave, 122; and incentives for private businesses, 123-24; and institutionalized childcare, 122-23; and mobilization of mothers, 122; and mobilization of women, 122; and policy debates, 78, 122; and tax cuts for businesses, 122; and role of state, 123, 128

women's parental identities, 178-79
Women's Political Participation Survey, 273-85
women's roles, 247-48, 268-69, 327; as caregivers, 182, 185; change of, 115-16, 268; education level, 269; at home, 116, 327; in politics, 122-26, 327, 330; at work, 269, 327, 330
women's suffrage, 111
workforce participation, women's, 269, 315-16; and support for, 326
workplace, women in, 112; skills, 272
work-time flexibility, 314, 320-21, 323-24; in academic jobs, 323-24; and autonomy, 323-24; and family responsibilities, 324; as gendered, 324; in public service jobs, 323-24
World Values Survey, 315, 327-29; and family, 327-28; and political engagement, 327, 329; and women, 327-28
Worthington, Byrony (UK), 49

Yelich, Lynne, Canada, 145

Printed and bound in Canada by Friesens
Set in Segoe and Warnock by Artegraphica Design Co. Ltd.
Copy editor: Dallas Harrison
Proofreader: Judith Earnshaw
Indexer: Shannon Fraser